Poetic Presence
and Illusion

Other Books by Murray Krieger

Directions for Criticism: Structuralism and Its Alternatives
    (co-editor with L. S. Dembo)
Theory of Criticism: A Tradition and Its System
The Classic Vision: The Retreat from Extremity in Modern Literature
The Play and Place of Criticism
Northrop Frye in Modern Criticism (editor)
A Window to Criticism: Shakespeare's *Sonnets* and Modern Poetics
The Tragic Vision: Variations on a Theme in Literary Interpretation
The New Apologists for Poetry
The Problems of Aesthetics (co-editor with Eliseo Vivas)

This creature fabricated

multiplies itself, but moves not;
sees itself, or sees not;
exists twice, and is not.

– Joan Krieger

Murray Krieger

Poetic Presence and Illusion

Essays in Critical History and Theory

The Johns Hopkins University Press
Baltimore and London

Copyright © 1979 by The Johns Hopkins University Press

Manufactured in the United States of America

The Johns Hopkins University Press, Baltimore, Maryland 21218
The Johns Hopkins Press Ltd., London

Library of Congress Catalog Number 79–14598

ISBN 0–8018–2199–1

Library of Congress Cataloging in Publication data will be found on the last printed page of this book.

To my brother, Leonard,
for the history we share

Contents

Preface   xi

Acknowledgments   xvii

I   Critical History   1

   1   Poetic Presence and Illusion I: Renaissance
Theory and the Duplicity of Metaphor   3

   2   Jacopo Mazzoni, Repository of Diverse Critical
Traditions or Source of a New One?   28

   3   Shakespeare and the Critic's Idolatry of the
Word   39

   4   Fiction, Nature, and Literary Kinds in Johnson's
Criticism of Shakespeare   55

   5   "Trying Experiments upon Our Sensibility":
The Art of Dogma and Doubt in
Eighteenth-Century Literature   70

   6   The Critical Legacy of Matthew Arnold; or, The
Strange Brotherhood of T. S. Eliot,
I. A. Richards, and Northrop Frye   92

   7   Reconsideration—The New Critics   108

   8   The Theoretical Contributions of Eliseo Vivas   115

   9   *The Tragic Vision* Twenty Years After   129

II   Critical Theory   137

   10   Poetic Presence and Illusion II: Formalist
Theory and the Duplicity of Metaphor   139

11 Literature vs. *Ecriture*: Constructions and
    Deconstructions in Recent Critical Theory   169
12 Literature as Illusion, as Metaphor, as Vision   188
13 Theories about Theories about *Theory of
    Criticism*   197
14 A Scorecard for the Critics   211
15 Literature, Criticism, and Decision Theory   238
16 Mediation, Language, and Vision in the
    Reading of Literature   270
17 Literary Analysis and Evaluation—and the
    Ambidextrous Critic   303

Index of Names   323

Preface

THE WORDS *metaphor* and *illusion* occur many times in the pages that
follow. Since they are perhaps my principal dramatis personae, it may
be useful to prescribe the limits I intend to place on the life I give
them. I want especially to speak here of *metaphor*, since that term
parades around these days in a common guise quite different from—
though not necessarily any more authentic than—the one in which I
place it. For me metaphor is seen not merely as the naive or primitive
half of a dichotomy it shares with metonymy—as the impulse toward
linguistic identity in opposition to linguistic difference—though it has
been the habit to view it this way at least since Jakobson. Although
surely it is a figure intended to produce the illusion of verbal identity,
I want to use it as a figure that works its momentary trick with a full
awareness of the differential nature of language which precedes and
coexists with it. It works toward verbal magic only by allowing its self-
dissolution in the same act. In this duplicitous act metaphor includes
metonymy, comes after it, and thereby transforms itself into irony. It
has, in effect, become a metonymic metaphor, if I may use a phrase I
have introduced elsewhere.[1] It is, then, this sense of *metaphor*, together with its basis in illusion, which constitutes my claim to the
poem's use of identity to create our sense of its presence. My special
notion of *illusion*, obviously indebted to Gombrich's, will emerge in
the lines that follow.

[1] The phrase appears as a central theoretical notion in *Theory of Criticism: A
Tradition and Its System* (Baltimore: Johns Hopkins University Press, 1976), pp.
166n., 195–99. But it was implied earlier in passages in *The Play and Place of
Criticism* (Baltimore: Johns Hopkins Press, 1967), pp. 55–56, and in *The Classic
Vision: The Retreat from Extremity in Modern Literature* (Baltimore: Johns
Hopkins Press, 1971), pp. 28–32, 365–67.

I was tempted to call this volume "Identity and Difference," except that the title I have chosen had certain advantages for me, including the fact that it was not a title already used by Heidegger. For many of these essays, like much of my recent work, deal with my notion of poetry as metaphor, and with metaphor as the paradoxical figure that forces an illusionary identity of terms and concepts which yet—outside the momentary aesthetic illusion—remain differentiated. So the theme of identity and difference, or—more accurately—of identity *in* difference, of difference *as* identity *as* difference, may well seem to bring most of these essays together. Still, my coupling of poetic presence and poetic illusion is another way of describing the same relationship between poetry as metaphor and the reader's sense of both reality and the poem's reality. For the poem is present before its reader—like the drama before its audience—only within an illusionary context. That is, its signs are there to stimulate his capacity to create its presence as an illusion, though one he shares with other members of his culture whose illusionary mechanism has been similarly trained. So the reader's double sense of the poem as a presence and as an illusion—as an illusionary presence and as an ever-present illusion—is my central conviction that guides these essays.

But the illusion should not be taken lightly as a false substitute for "reality." It is itself a real and positive force: it is what we see and, as such, it is constitutive of our reality, even if our critical faculty *decon*stitutes that reality into being no more than illusion. But it is an illusion we can live with—and, most spiritedly, do—though now with self-knowledge, the knowledge of *its* illusionary nature and of *our* mystification. This book examines both the workings of poems in order to trace such constitutings and deconstitutings, and those literary critics in our history who have been concerned with this doubleness. For it is based on the assumption—though it is one for which it also argues—that poems are the places where this dual action most strikingly occurs, and where it remains—thanks to their potential presence—for the rest of us to operate upon.

I acknowledge that such notions as these seem derived from the post-Kantian tradition. And I am aware that, in these post-Hegelian and post-Nietzschean days, this is hardly a fashionable source. There may be no need for me to apologize since I also betray a commitment to an extra-metaphorical, existentialist reality which undoes the illusion, and such a commitment may hardly be admitted into post-Kantian precincts (and is probably even more unfashionable). Nevertheless, I concede the post-Kantian flavor of my general position, though my existentialist modifications allow it to sanction a theory of poetry as self-deconstruction (I would prefer to say—in the spirit of

Rosalie Colie—that it is a theory which sees poetry as a metaphor that "unmetaphors" itself). I have been urging this notion for many years now—well before the recent deconstructionist vogue. However I may be convicted of deriving from Kant or (even worse!) Coleridge, then, the union in metaphor of self-affirmation and self-denial may well bring me into apparent alliances with recent continental criticism in the wake of Hegel and Nietzsche. In my essay (below) on Matthew Arnold, for example, I seem curiously to have created for him a deconstructive role in the history of modern thought not altogether dissimilar to what others have created for Nietzsche. If my Arnold seems pallid by comparison, he may be the price which the Anglo-American theoretical tradition pays for its civilized denials and its consequent sanity. But the similarity in function between Arnold and Nietzsche is there, as the reader will find me suggesting in places where—despite differences between us—I make common cause with a theorist like Paul de Man in treating the willful "blindness" confessed in literature's act of "insight." All this, perhaps, is evidence of the essential oneness of the current theoretical moment, whatever the variety among the sources and resources of those contributing to it.

I ought probably to use this occasion to remind the reader of what I say explicitly more than once in the essays that follow: that I for the most part use terms like *poems* or *poetry* or *literature* interchangeably, meaning all of them to represent fiction-making, whether in verse or prose. It is, in short, what critics used to call—with less discomfort than we now feel—"*imaginative* literature" (with the implicit slur on non-poetry as *un*imaginative), though what they had in mind, as I do, is the Aristotelian notion of *poesis*. Such matters take on a special importance these days, when it takes a lonely daring to make a separatist defense of poetry, as—with certain crucial qualifications—I persist in doing below. But to dwell further here on differences between my use of literature and others' would anticipate arguments made in these essays.

The earliest of these essays was published in 1968 (shortly after the publication of *The Play and Place of Criticism*, a collection of earlier essays also published by The Johns Hopkins University Press). Though they are scattered, in their dates of composition, from 1968 until only yesterday, about half of them appeared in the last couple of years, perhaps in anticipation of this gathering of them for collective publication. They were, of course, written for a variety of occasions; and where the nature of an occasion seems to affect the tone or the content of any essay, I have described the circumstances in an initial footnote to the essay. Otherwise the details of original publication appear in the "Acknowledgments" following this Preface. Two of the essays, appearing below as chapters 5 and 9, make their first appearance in this book. And the materials for chapter 15 have been substantially reshaped.

A word about the ordering of the essays. The essays in "critical history"—part one of the volume—appear in the chronological order of their subjects;[2] the essays in "critical theory"—part two of the volume—appear in the reverse order of their composition, most recent essays first, then moving back toward the earliest essay of those included. The reason for this difference in the two parts is obvious: history would seem to demand that the temporal sequence of those being discussed be respected, while—in theoretical areas—I chose the freedom to put my current positions first, then allowing the reader to see in older writings how these positions came to take the form they do.

I see both parts of the book united by my recurrent concern with presence and illusion, with difference as identity. In accordance with this desired unity, I have written what amounts to a title essay in two sections, with one heading each of the two parts of the book. The first focuses on a historical problem, the second on a theoretical, though the two emerge from a common perspective. Each is to give shape to the essays which follow in its part of the book and yet, in their relations to one another, to fuse the two parts in their joint theoretical objective. It would be less than candid of me to deny the sometimes miscellaneous nature of these essays and, thus, the sometimes factitious nature of their cohabitation within these pages. But I am aware enough of the limits upon my own versatility to acknowledge the continual recurrence of my few principal themes within and around these essays, whether explicitly and by pronouncement or subtly, by half-conscious implication.

Most of the recent essays reflect significantly my experience as director of the School of Criticism and Theory, which I helped to found at the University of California, Irvine. It was not possible for me to become involved with so distinguished an array of senior and junior scholar-theorists as I have these last four years without my gathering a lasting influence from their overflowing brilliance. So, to my colleagues among the Senior Fellows and others who taught at the school's sessions, and to those remarkable younger scholars, both

---

[2] The only exception would be chapters 4 and 5, both of which refer to a single period, although the former is primarily concerned with a late work by Dr. Johnson while the latter deals with many earlier works (by him and others in the period) as well. But in this case it seemed to me important for the reader to have read chapter 4 before coming to the broader (and for me later) considerations of chapter 5.

postdoctoral and graduate students, I am deeply grateful for all that I learned and all that I came to worry about in the class I taught one summer and the colloquia which I directed, with my fellow teachers, during the others. The many challenging colloquium papers which I had to read and with which I had either to do battle or to make my peace before audiences keenly restive and pressing led me to new levels of awareness which undoubtedly have found their way into my more recent work.

There are many others to be thanked, I fear too many to be listed singly—organizers of lectures or symposia for which some of these pieces were originally written and editors of journals or of books in which some of them first appeared. Because of their number, I shall have to content myself with the listings in my "Acknowledgments" and the information in my initial footnotes to some of the essays. But I must single out once more the extraordinary acts of helpfulness and forbearance by Betty Terrell, my administrative assistant, through the years that gradually brought most of these essays to their final form. And, finally, I turn—as I always have—to a grateful tribute to my wife, Joan, whose thoughts have so often stimulated and helped develop what I too easily come to think of as *my* thoughts. Nothing is a greater source of delight to me, as I contemplate this book becoming a reality, than the appearance on the frontispiece of the visual symbol designed by her; for this marks in print the collaboration to which, in preface after preface, I have sought inadequately to testify. I close by suggesting that the emblem,[3] with its epigraph, contains the metaphor implicit within an aesthetic which balances poetic presence with poetic illusion. It relates the fabrication of every fiction to the model game of the Prisoner's Dilemma: the principle of doubling inherent in the game, as explored in my fifteenth essay below, creates the mirrors and their multiplied images which only the arts can project.

[3] The emblem is a free adaptation of a West African Ashanti goldweight, which is an extraordinary example of these miniature works of sculpture. Delicately formed, though only of brass, they serve solely to measure chunks of unformed gold. Yet they are shaped in human and animal images that are to carry various symbolic messages for living and dying. The rounded spiral wings supposedly symbolize regeneration while the bird's looking backward is related to the omniscience that comes with looking both ways. The coupling of the birds is in the original, although the multiplication and reversing of the double images are the graphic inventions of the designer of the emblem. Perhaps these observations will aid the reader in applying the emblem and its epigraphic riddle to the substance of this volume. (See Margaret Webster Plass, *African Miniatures: Goldweights of the Ashanti* [New York: Frederick A. Praeger, 1967].)

Acknowledgments

THE ESSAYS " 'Trying Experiments upon Our Sensibility': The Art of Dogma and Doubt in Eighteenth-Century Literature" and "*The Tragic Vision* Twenty Years After" are published here for the first time. The other essays have been previously published and are reprinted here, some slightly revised and others in original form. In one case ("Literature, Criticism, and Decision Theory") I have put together an essay from a variety of writings which I contributed to the volume collected from the 1974 Aspen Colloquium on Problems of Choice and Decision (permission to reprint having been granted by Max Black, organizer of the colloquium and editor of the volume). In all cases I offer my gratitude to those who granted permission to make use of these materials in this volume.

What follows is a list of the other essays, in the order of their appearance, together with information about their original publication and my acknowledgment of the permission-granting agency:

"Poetic Presence and Illusion I: Renaissance Theory and the Duplicity of Metaphor," *Critical Inquiry* 5 (Summer 1979); reprinted by permission of *Critical Inquiry* and The University of Chicago Press. © 1979 by The University of Chicago.

"Jacopo Mazzoni, Repository of Diverse Critical Traditions or Source of a New One?" from *Medieval Epic to the "Epic Theater" of Brecht*, ed. Rosario P. Armato and John M. Spalek (Los Angeles: University of Southern California Press, 1968); reprinted by permission of University of Southern California Press.

"Shakespeare and the Critic's Idolatry of the Word," from *Shakespeare: Aspects of Influence* (Harvard English Studies 7), ed. G. B.

Evans (Cambridge, Mass.: Harvard University Press, 1976); reprinted by permission of the President and Fellows of Harvard College.

"Fiction, Nature, and Literary Kinds in Johnson's Criticism of Shakespeare," *Eighteenth-Century Studies* 4 (Winter 1971); reprinted by permission of *Eighteenth-Century Studies*.

"The Critical Legacy of Matthew Arnold; or, The Strange Brotherhood of T. S. Eliot, I. A. Richards, and Northrop Frye," *Southern Review* 5, n.s. (Spring 1969); reprinted by permission of *Southern Review*.

"Reconsideration—The New Critics," *New Republic* (October 1976); reprinted by permission of The New Republic, Inc.

"The Theoretical Contributions of Eliseo Vivas," from *Viva Vivas! Essays in Honor of Eliseo Vivas on the Occasion of His Seventy-fifth Birthday, July 13, 1976*, ed. Henry Regnery (Indianapolis: Liberty Press, 1976); reprinted by permission of Liberty Fund, Inc.

"Poetic Presence and Illusion II: Formalist Theory and the Duplicity of Metaphor," *Boundary 2* 8 (Fall 1979); reprinted by permission of *Boundary 2*.

"Literature vs. *Ecriture*: Constructions and Deconstructions in Recent Critical Theory," *Studies in the Literary Imagination* 12 (Spring 1979); reprinted by permission of *Studies in the Literary Imagination*.

"Literature as Illusion, as Metaphor, as Vision," from *What Is Literature?*, ed. Paul Hernadi (Bloomington: Indiana University Press, 1978); reprinted by permission of Indiana University Press.

"Theories about Theories about *Theory of Criticism*," *Bulletin of the Midwest Modern Language Association* 11 (Spring 1978); reprinted by permission of the Midwest Modern Language Association.

"A Scorecard for the Critics," *Contemporary Literature* 17 (Summer 1976), reprinted as *Directions for Criticism: Structuralism and Its Alternatives*, ed. Murray Krieger and L. S. Dembo (Madison: University of Wisconsin Press, 1977); by permission of University of Wisconsin Press.

"Mediation, Language, and Vision in the Reading of Literature," from *Interpretation: Theory and Practice*, ed. Charles S. Singleton (Baltimore: Johns Hopkins Press, 1969); reprinted by permission of The Johns Hopkins University Press.

"Literary Analysis and Evaluation—and the Ambidextrous Critic," *Contemporary Literature* 9 (Summer 1968), reprinted as *Criticism: Speculative and Analytical Essays*, ed. L. S. Dembo (Madison: University of Wisconsin Press, 1968); reprinted by permission of University of Wisconsin Press.

I
Critical
History

1

Poetic Presence and Illusion I:
Renaissance Theory and the Duplicity of Metaphor

MY SUBJECT IS THE CONCEPT of poetic imagination in the Renaissance as it relates to metaphysical claims on the one hand and to a philosophy of language on the other. I mean to search for this imagination not only in a few obvious, explicit statements found in the usual theoretical documents but, more important for me, in the language, metaphysics, and implied poetics found in certain rather extraordinary poems themselves. I hope, before I am done, to alter considerably our conventional notion about what the Renaissance mind was capable of conceiving. And I hope that what those concepts themselves were capable of hiding and revealing can be useful to us as we go through our own theoretical wranglings about the relation between language and concepts and between language and things, as well as about the arbitrary nature of linguistic signs and the principles behind them of absence and presence, difference and identity. Perhaps our own semiological notions may profit from a newly discovered sophistication in the semiology of Renaissance writers.

I

The Renaissance poetic, as we derive it from the explicit statements we normally cite, is taken primarily to be a rhetorical theory that is essentially Platonic in its interest in the universal meanings behind individual words, images, or fictions. Accordingly, poetic words, images, or fictions are taken to be purely allegorical, functioning as arbitrary or at most as conventional signs: each word, image, or fiction is seen as thoroughly dispensable, indeed interchangeable with others, to be used just so long as we can get beyond it to the ultimate meaning which it presumably signifies. This rather simple—if not simplistic—semiology leaves the body of poetry as empty as modern post-Saussurean linguistics often leaves the body of language. By treating all poetic devices as transparent elements through which various universal "truths" are revealed, this rhetorical and allegorical theory converts all the poet's dispositions of words into devices of persuasion in the service of a function higher than that of poetry. Such is the way that, for example, a conservative, widely influential theorist like Scaliger clearly formulated the principle. And for as careful a commentator on Renaissance imagery as Rosemund Tuve, these are the furthest reaches of the Renaissance poetic; she argues that any more subtle a claim is merely the consequence of the modern mind trying anachronistically to sophisticate an older tradition. Her examination of explicit statements by major Renaissance writers on poetics finds reinforcements in the logic of Petrus Ramus as she extends it to a total stylistics, or even to a linguistics.[1]

It is in accordance with a reading like Tuve's that we normally view Sidney's *Apology* as a typical instance of the explicit Renaissance poetic in its post-Scaligerian vein. So we are not surprised when we find Sidney emphasizing that poetry is obliged to give us a world "better" than the world around us, the "golden" world rather than the "brazen" world in which we live. On the other hand, it is true that we also find in Sidney a serious and significant interest in fiction as a free-standing invention of an as-if world—a representing, counterfeiting, feigning, or figuring-forth (all terms he uses). This is the particular meaning he gives to *imitation*, by which he clearly means a representation in the sense of a something-created-out-there. For while, in the early crucial passage, Sidney empowered the poet to create things better than they are, he also empowered him to create things other than they are. And the *other* seems potentially in conflict with the *better* ("making things either better than nature bringeth forth, or, quite anew, forms such as never were in nature . . ."). In freeing the poet to invent "another nature," as in his freeing the poet from the world of truth and lies for the as-if world of fiction, Sidney

[1] Rosemund Tuve, *Elizabethan and Metaphysical Imagery: Renaissance Poetic and Twentieth-Century Critics* (Chicago: University of Chicago Press, 1947).

reveals, as did others of his most acute contemporaries, a desire for pure representation, although—again like his contemporaries—when it comes to the ultimate theoretical moment, he always subjects the representation to the moral demonstration. In this sense, like others, he always appears to fill the representation up in order—ultimately— to empty it out. What is presented, and present, is forced to convert itself—by deference to universals—into absence. If the emphasis is on a figuring-forth that suggests a free-standing fiction, it turns out to be no more than a "counterfeit" indeed, no more than a counterfeit fiction, the degeneration of Aristotle's fable into Aesop's fable.[2] Figuring-forth is indeed different from counterfeiting, as presenting is different from representing, a new face different from a flimsy disguise.

Nevertheless we do Sidney an injustice if we fail to note the depth of his interest in the fictional element, however strongly his Platonism finally requires him to subjugate it to the moral element. It is true that most of his examples of fictional characters turn out to be heightened or exaggerated moral exempla (better than nature provides) rather than full-bodied invented presences. But still it would take an unsympathetic or rhetorically oriented observer to ignore what I have called Sidney's desire for representation, or rather presentation. If he finally emphasizes the counterfeit over the figured-forth, the impulse toward the latter remains nonetheless.

When we look at a more subtle neo-Platonist like Mazzoni, we find much the same doubleness. His concern with the presentational aspect of poetry is with the "image" rather than—as for Sidney—with the overall fiction. But everywhere we look in his *On the Defense of the Comedy of Dante*, we find a commitment to the fully fashioned "image" or "idol" out there as both the body and the objective of poetry. Once again there is the final surrender to the universal relationships which the image ends up standing for, but Mazzoni holds on even more strongly than Sidney does to the power of the apparently free-standing presentation itself. Eventually, however, what is apparently an autonomous invention as a totally fabricated "idol" turns out to be an allegory which the state must turn to its profit. Still, to ignore the depth of his commitment to the idol itself—here as with Sidney at whatever cost to theoretical consistency—is to miss the center of what Mazzoni is trying to do.

It is not, then, that the rhetorical claims of someone like Tuve are

---

[2] Sidney himself refers to Aesop's fables, using them as examples of fictions being put to allegorical use. See *An Apology for Poetry*, in *The Great Critics*, ed. J. H. Smith and E. W. Parks (New York: W. W. Norton & Co., 1939), p. 216.

wrong, so much as that they are seriously incomplete, and in their incompleteness they sacrifice the emotional and visionary texture of the theoretical argument to its comparatively arid structure. What is needed is the enunciation of an alternative tradition of Renaissance poetics, one which can do justice to its hunger for pure presentation, a hunger that derives from a Renaissance habit of language, a metaphorical habit that required a trickier semiology which would not so easily yield up the power and the presence of the word. Probably that metaphorical habit arises out of various medieval traditions, such as those we associate with the divine-human paradox of Christianity and the inevitable metaphors of body and meaning yielded by that paradox. The duplicitous functions of language as *figura* made available to poetry a host of verbal possibilities and semiological ambiguities beyond the reach of Ramistic logic. The poetics which relegates poetry to the role of rhetoric and shallow allegory is a poetics of absence, of difference, one based on the arbitrary nature of the poem—its language, its images, its fiction—while this other poetics which I am trying to construct and which I claim to be evidenced in the best poetry of the period is one which struggles to achieve verbal identity and presence. Although it may be a poetics which seems dependent upon the Christian metaphysics that sponsors its metaphorical habit, even so—I claim—the poets can themselves introduce a skepticism which reminds us of the merely verbal nature of their invention.

These considerations lead us to another conception of language richly available to the Renaissance mind. It is the notion of word-magic, a live theory of imagination which is far less limited by distinctions among words and concepts and things. This magical notion thrives on an inter-illumination, an inter-referentiality, among words, emblems, concepts, and things—not only mutualities and identities among them but also within emblems, within words, within concepts, and within things. It represents a naive confidence in signs which, substantially filled, turn into things as well as signs. Or, to put it more precisely, signs turn reflexive and become, in effect, things themselves, things which continually overrun their bounds and change their natures. The world, thoughts about the world, and all our signs which are both about the world and are worlds themselves—all illuminate and can replace one another in the ultimate mystification of what one might call an "ontological hermeneutic." All things can be allegories of one another in one grand dance of mutuality between microcosm and macrocosm. As in the anagogic real which Frye took from Dante, or as in the sixteenth-century episteme of Foucault, all words, emblems, concepts, and things are potentially interchangeable and even identical with all others.

Yet, despite all these magical possibilities, the explicit Renaissance poetic theory seems ready to settle for the thinness of transparent allegory and the static reduction of words to an arbitrary rhetoric. On the other side, as I have indicated, theorists like Sidney and Mazzoni settle for such consequences only while keeping the more mystifying tradition alive in the very pulse of their criticism, and this still vital force emerges as an implicit poetic in the best of their poems. It is there to be picked up once the dualistic Platonic censor that governed formal Renaissance poetics was removed. It was this urge to confer weighty substance upon mere signs—what Mazzoni called "particularizations"—which created that hunger for pure presentation which rhetorical and didactic theory could not appease.

As my previous discussion should have made clear, if we are to speak strictly, what is called for is not *re*presentation so much as presentation. For the representation to be pure—as our reading of Mazzoni should remind us—is for it to be free-standing and hence an autonomous presentation. That is the distinction I was suggesting earlier between figuring-forth on the one hand and mere counterfeiting or feigning on the other. Presentation suggests that the signified itself is imported bodily into the signifier as a presence. It is the act of presenting, by which is meant the making-present of the person or god who stands outside the language or the fiction or even the allegory. And it is just this need to invoke the presence of the god with his golden world and to make him immanent within the discourse, to fill it with his presence, that characterizes the underside of Renaissance poetic instinct—one that far more adequately accounts for the fullness we find in the poetry that coexisted with its explicit theory. The alternative is to have the god transcend a discourse which, full only of deferral and deference, is itself empty.

There is, then, a need to summon the sublime presence; and the act of invocation itself—together with the presence with which it unites—dissolves the empty incapacities of the language that normally struggles on its own. The summoning creates a poetic language that undoes all that a language without presence can manage. Sidney himself suggests the poet's power of invocation in a passage in the *Apology* in which he is trying to justify a definition of poet as *Vates* or Seer by using the psalms of David as his example of a divine, prophetic poem:

> Lastly and principally, his handling his prophecy, which
> is merely poetical. For what else is the awaking his
> musical instruments? the often and free changing of
> persons? his notable *prosopopeias*, when he maketh you,
> as it were, see God coming in his majesty, his telling

of the Beasts' joyfulness and hills' leaping, but a
heavenly posey: wherein almost he showeth himself a
passionate lover of that unspeakable and everlasting
beauty to be seen by the eyes of the mind, only cleared
by faith?[3]

Now the *prosopopeia* is a form of personification, giving a voice to
that which does not speak, thereby giving presence to that which is
absent. Through this figure, Sidney argues, God enters David's poem
(we are made to "see God coming in his majesty"). It is as if this
figure is made to serve the larger objective of *enargeia*, the verbal art
of forcing us to see vividly. Through "the eyes of the mind"—an
appropriately Platonic notion—we are shown the coming of God and
his "unspeakable and everlasting beauty." Here, then, are words invoking a visible presence, though of course to "the eyes of the mind"
alone. Though God's may be only a figurative entrance through his
personified creatures, the poet makes us, "as it were," see this entrance. God is there, in his living creation, and absent no longer.

This equivocal importation of God into the poem raises serious
questions about the entire nature of Renaissance symbolism, what it
permitted and forbade. Here again there were conflicting pressures of
several sorts on how the arts were to be used to represent the sacred.
As Ernst Gombrich helpfully groups them in his valuable essay,
"*Icones Symbolicae*,"[4] some traditions would have art obliged to imitate the divine directly, seeking to be as much like it as possible, while
others explicitly proscribed any direct involvement of the sacred in
the profane arts accessible to the senses. The first tradition led to what
we might call angelic art, in which there was an effort not only to
represent the sacred but insofar as possible to reproduce it, to create a
sensible substitute for it. The second abjured such practice as a movement toward idolatry and recommended instead the practice of allegory in which signifiers of the sacred which bore no resemblance to it
and could not be mistaken for it were to be used as a language which
could give meaning despite the absence of natural signifieds of the
discourse. If the first—the way of direct representation or even presentation—is the angelic way, the second, in Gombrich's terminology,
is the "monstrous" way, the "apophatic way of mysterious monstros-
ity" (p. 152). The first tries to approach presence and the second
works on the presupposition of absence, with the choice of monsters
and beasts an expression of the utmost desire to avoid the direct

[3] Ibid., p. 194.

[4] In *Symbolic Images: Studies in the Art of the Renaissance* (London: Phaidon
Press, 1972), pp. 123–95.

representation of the sacred by finding its polar opposite. The first—as the imitation of the like—means to use natural signs while the second —as the imitation of the unlike—settles for totally arbitrary, even if conventional, signs.

And yet, even as we refine this distinction, we must remember that we are dealing with an "ontological hermeneutic" (my earlier phrase) in which everything, at any level, can be a sign of anything else, at any other level, so that in the end all differences are transcended as semiology yields to ontology. (We saw such easy equations in the doubleness of the quotation from Sidney.) But even if, as an ontological truth, this would seem to undo any difference between the two ways of imitating, with all signs equally like and unlike all others, still—at the worldly level of making presentations to an audience for whose power of subtlety the theoreticians held little respect[5]—the two traditions and their respective encouragements and proscriptions are seen to diverge.

We can see these two ways reflected in what I have said earlier about Sidney's *Apology*, in the conflict between the production of things better than nature and the production of things other than nature. His call to the poet to produce the golden world directly, for example the Cyrus more perfect than the historical Cyrus (from which a host of Cyruses could be reproduced), suggests the direct angelic mode of imitation, while the world other than nature's would allow for the exemplary fictions that culminate for Sidney in Aesop's *Fables*, as well as in comedies and tragedies. In his list of the sort of creatures created by the free poet ("Heroes, Demigods, Cyclops, Chimeras, Furies"), the heroes and demigods would appear to belong to the species in which the poet was improving upon nature by representing the golden world directly and the cyclops, chimeras, and furies would appear to be the monsters created in the poet's other or second nature. In this division we can even see the grounds for the primary opposition between the two groups of genres which Sidney deals with in justifying the moral effects of poetry upon its audience: at the top of his hierarchy of genres are the heroic poem and the lyric, both based on the direct imitation of the better worlds ("the lofty image of such worthies"), while in such lower forms as tragedy and comedy the golden lesson must be conveyed indirectly, by the implied warning within the fiction of vice or folly punished or exposed. The angelic seems to call for directly reproducing characters worthy of our emula-

[5] It is important always to remember that sixteenth-century critics usually betrayed a contemptuous attitude toward the common audience of literature. This largely accounts for the call for the use of images and of fictions as moral allegories: to make visible those ideas otherwise beyond the common reader's understanding.

tion, and the monstrous calls for inventing encoded fables whose dire meaning all can read.

But clearly what is primary in Sidney's pleading for the highest poetry is his interest in the direct representation of the best, in the creation by the poet of a world of golden presence. If there was a fear of idolatry in those paintings which sought to represent the sacred world in gold—using actual gold as a medium which dared try to contain as well as represent the highest value—verbal alchemy was obviously a method less fraught with potential sacrilege. The rhetorical tradition of *enargeia* (the disposition of words to produce sensuous vividness), which was clearly in conformity with the Platonic concentration upon the eye—and, more spiritually, the mind's eye— bestowed upon the word an important advantage over the sensible image. There can be little danger of idolatry where—as with language —the sign is not a physical entity, and—further—where the sign is thoroughly arbitrary (though conventional) rather than natural: its character as sign permits it to bear no resemblance to its signified, so that its value can be no more than semiological.

Nevertheless, language too is a mnemonic device (though hardly in the same degree as a visual sign), a barely present reminder of the absent thing itself. We have seen in my earlier discussion the conflict between the interest in the reminiscent aspect of the sign and the interest in its own bodily presence, the conflict—in short—between the sign as representation and the sign as presentation. But of course the reasonableness of the Renaissance poet never permits him[6] to forgo the mnemonic character of the sign, no matter how committed he becomes to it as its own entity. With language itself he is especially aware of its intangible, purely mental—its intelligible rather than sensible—character. Long before modern semiologists, he knew words as symbols to be less present than more obviously sensible symbols. (Perhaps this is one of the stimulants for his interest in emblems as visible companions to verse.) By their very nature, words are a sort of *prosopopeia*, dead signs that figuratively imply life, the illusion of living, speaking presence (though a representation of an absent thing) in a medium that by its nature precludes presence. Thus the verbal creation fulfills—and exceeds—the criterion for illusion which Gombrich established for the plastic arts in that it creates an appearance

[6] I am aware that poets and critics come in more than one sex and that this word ("him") does not reflect this fact. However, I see no way for my pronouns to be sufficiently inclusive without producing an undue clumsiness, since our language is traditionally incapable of bisexual reference without an awkward straining. Thus, throughout this volume, my pronouns are meant to refer to writers or readers as a genre, not as a gender.

(*as if* present) of that which is absent. Yet the verbal illusion of presence is often enough.

So the word, as itself potentially sacred in that it is intelligible rather than sensible, can create—even in its most ambitious presentations—no more than spirit's gold in contrast to the dangerously material gold of the earth available to plastic arts—only brazen gold after all. Consequently the verbal act of producing the golden world is an act of gilding that not only is harmless (in contrast to gilding in the plastic arts) but can actually be the highest manifestation of spirit. It is a curious opening to language that permits the poet to have it both ways—and you may be sure that our Renaissance poets were quick to take advantage of it.

Thus the invocation to presence—the divine presence of God or of a divine substitute in the person of the poet's beloved—can be explicitly undertaken. The invocation is an alchemical act as well in that it confers (whether by means of an act of flattery or an act of making true) a golden reality upon the object who is invoked. For the Renaissance love poet in his deprivation, it is the beloved who is invoked, and, within the domain of love's psychology which has at hand the poet's license to use a metaphorical habit reserved for the Christian mystery, it is the presence of that beloved which dissolves—absorbing into an all-encompassing presence—the incapacities of a language based on the differentiations of the brazen world.

Whence comes this need for the poet to force the word to act as the mnemonic sign that exceeds its function by producing in itself the presence to the lack of which its own emptiness normally testifies? It comes from the distance between verbal signifier and signified which makes other words normally fail to satisfy him emotionally in their mnemonic function. This yawning distance is filled only with absence, the separateness of man from God and—by extension under the aegis of love's psychology—the separateness of poet from his deified beloved.

Such distance, such absence, calls for mnemonics, for reminiscent substitutes—except that, when our signifiers present these to us in their usual way, we can see only the differences between signifiers and their intended signifieds. These differences lead to our sense of the differences among the now unsatisfying signifiers themselves. And then nothing less is required than a miraculous leap over the distance to find an identity that dissolves differences and turns empty reminders into the fullness of originals, now suddenly fully present in their representatives. Semiological relations are belied, as meaning fuses into being, as the thing said fuses into the act of saying it, of summoning it into existence by a self-confirming ritual of prayer. The sonneteer is both worshiper of the deity and creator of the beloved as deity through the everlasting flattery which is his poem. He turns the beloved into gold, *his* gold, and the poem which does it is the act of faith, of creative faith, which makes the god he adores. Thus the poem becomes the eternalizing as well as the enabling act. It is the poem as an act of love's prayer which triumphs over the differentiating words by summoning and making the god immanent within itself, though that poem seems also to be conferring a transcendently divine character upon love's deity. The god is both outside and brought within, except that it is the act which makes both the god and the poet. At his best the Renaissance poet is aware of the trickiness of his operation, of the dependence of the god upon the worshiper when it is the worshiper who has created the god.

II

Sidney's entire sonnet sequence is moved by just this supplicating invocation to Stella, a star as seen by the star-lover, an invocation for her presence to invade the present poem and to dissolve its differences into her identity by collapsing all distance between it as intended meaning and her as fulfilled being. The lamentation of Sonnet 106 issues out of the poet's failure in it to accomplish those miracles of bodily invocation which mark his success in other sonnets. His language from the start of the sonnet could not be more appropriate to my interests here.

> Oh absent presence, Stella is not here;
> False flattering Hope, that with so fair a face
> Bare me in hand, that in this orphan place,
> Stella, I say my Stella, should appear.

This fourth line has in it the incantatory ritual of summoning up the god, converting her absence into presence. And it is her direct visual appearance ("mine eyes," line 6) that is called for. Without it the physical sense of loss, of an absence that is a tearing-away, is carried in the sense of the poet's being "new maim'd" (line 13).

Many of the best of Sidney's sonnets enact the successful invasion of the poems by Stella's presence: in them the poet's struggle with the emptiness of language and of poetic conventions is transformed and resolved as her transcendent power becomes immanent. So long as the poem tries to be *about* her, its attempt to create her *meaning* must be thwarted; but once it manages to encompass her *being*, the breakthrough beyond the failures of language and poetic convention is achieved. The very first sonnet in the sequence ("Loving in truth, and fain in verse my love to show") exemplifies this progression. The poet's need to describe his love leads him to words and to poetic models which, quite amusingly, represent only his awkwardness and his frustration as he vainly tries to express himself. Finally, after he has hopelessly enmeshed himself in a disruptive succession of violent and overstated figures (only exaggerated by the hexameter lines), the quiet simplicity of the last line resolves all: " 'Fool,' said my Muse to me, 'look in thy heart and write.' " This is not just an easy call for a lover's direct emotional sincerity. More than this, the poet, despite his anti-conventional stance, is assuming here our awareness of an elaborate Petrarchan conceit: the lover installs in his heart the image of his beloved who lodges there substantially.[7] Thus (the conceit has it) if the beloved looks into the lover's eyes, she sees not a surface reflection of her own image, but, because she looks *through* his eyes as if through a window, she sees to his very heart where her image lies and, in union with him, achieves substance. The muse is thus calling the poet away from his vain battles with words and with other poems (in terms of which the beloved would herself be absent) and to the direct vision of where she is most significantly present—in his heart. As the only object of representation, or presentation, the beloved is to be the sole presence—direct, unmediated presence—that transforms the poems which follow and become the sequence addressed to her.

It is in this spirit that, in Sonnet 3 ("Let dainty wits cry on the Sisters nine"), the poet rejects the usual appeal to the muses ("the sisters nine"), thus rejecting also the kind of poems that emerge from such dependence, but only to substitute for them the simple immediacy of Stella who becomes his only muse ("no Muse but one I know"), though not as a mythical guide so much as a physical object. How does she function as muse?

> How then? Even thus: in Stella's face I read
> What love and beauty be, then all my deed
> But copying is, what in her Nature writes.

This direct copying of Stella as person is an act at once simple, magical, and metaphysical: it is to be a presenting of her as the very incarnation of the universals of love and beauty themselves, with perhaps no other way of getting at them. In Sonnet 28 too ("You that with allegory's curious frame") the poet denies any interest in an extended metaphorical intention ("allegory's curious frame") while

---

[7] See, as a couple of examples, Shakespeare's Sonnet 24 ("Mine eye hath play'd the painter and hath stell'd / Thy beauty's form in table of my heart") or Spenser's *Amoretti* 45 ("Leave lady in your glass of crystal clean").

proceeding in a straightforward way ("When I say 'Stella,' I do mean
. . .") to make claims filled with Petrarchan extravagance ("Princess of
Beauty," "reins of love") and concluding with a final extravagance
expressed as a real physical action, authenticated by the present reality of Love:

> But know that I in pure simplicity
> Breathe out the flames which burn within my heart
> Love only reading unto me this art.

Presumably we are to accept these words as literal description, no
more "allegorical" than the description of Stella as "Princess of
Beauty."[8] In her domain even the most extremely figurative blends
into the literal; all language—as hers—becomes substantive.

There is a similar rejection of the love poet's conventional methods in Sonnet 74 ("I never drank of Aganippe well"), although here
our poet, with mock-modesty, celebrates his unconventional amateur
nature. Once again he trades all the classical machinery for Stella's
immediacy. She is to be his only muse and will work differently—
which is to say physically—upon him. Having acknowledged his unfit-
ness for "Aganippe well" and the rest, and allowing his lines to reflect
the choppiness of his plain style ("But—God wot—wot not what they
mean by it"), he—though a "layman"—can turn around to confess, in
words that convey "so smooth an ease," an unexpected capacity to
write successful verse. " 'How then?' Sure, thus it is: / My lips are
sweet, inspir'd with Stella's kiss." Just this single final line, with its
simple statement that is an outrageous exaggeration, carries the entire
burden of magical transformation, which appears to have occurred in
the writing of the poem as we watch. Instead of the figurative inspiration by the muses in the metaphorical draught from Aganippe well,
he is literally inspired by the actual breath drawn in from the mouth
of Stella in the moment of their kiss: a muse of life, of flesh, makes a
poet of the lover, makes a poet only as a result of his being a lover, the
lover of a present mistress whose active presence creates the poem as
product of their loving. In this as in the other sonnets we have dis-

---

[8] The most evident irony in the poem, of course, arises from the fact that the
poet cannot say his beloved's name without being allegorical, so that he has been
allegorical from the very conception of the sonnet sequence. So, however plain-
talking he claims to be, when he says "Stella" (see line 5 of Sonnet 28), he must
mean "star" and all the Petrarchan extensions of a guiding heavenly body, as well
as the person herself. Each time he names her as an individual earthly presence, he
automatically involves all her allegorical trappings as well, thus making her very
being into his concrete universal.

cussed, we find Sidney, in the writing of the poem, turning this way
and that in his anxiety to get beyond the difficulties and even unlike-
lihoods in his situation, and we watch as he finally breaks through to
the conclusiveness of a resolution produced by Stella's presence. As a
poem which creates the fiction that the very writing of it is an act of
searching and discovery, it enacts the creation of its goddess, who in
turn converts all its elements into her own, thereby bestowing new
meanings upon them.

The same sort of divine transformation by an earthly goddess occurs in Sonnet 44 ("My words I know do well set forth my mind").
The poet searches for the answer to one of the most stereotyped of
Petrarchan questions: since the beloved clearly understands her lover's plight, why is she so unresponsive, so "unkind," when her "kind"
(the kind of her "sweet heart") is not that of the tiger, cruel enemy of
the "hart"? The answer he comes upon satisfies him by discovering her
innocence through the act of giving her godly powers. If her kindness
does not respond to his complaints, it must be that she does not hear
them as such. And she cannot hear them as complaints since her
divinity transforms everything it deals with:

That when the breath of my complaints doth touch
Those dainty doors unto the court of bliss,
The heav'nly nature of that place is such,
That once come there, the sobs of mine annoys
Are metamorphos'd straight to tunes of joys.

Here is an explicit attribution of divinity, with the "metamorphos'd"
(a powerful notion in the Renaissance) "joys" out of "annoys" a
crucial claim of godly magic that turns all to bliss, that countenances
no sorrow or imperfection. Even the alliterative pattern of lines
10–11 is to help the equation of sorrow and joy, the viewing of sorrow
as joy, under the aegis of the divine beloved, as "the *b*reath of . . .
*c*omplaints" finds their way to "the *c*ourt of *b*liss" by way of its
"dainty doors." These phonetic transfers lead us to the heavenly
metamorphosis from "annoys" to "joys." The farfetched metaphorical
claim of the lady's divine powers rests on the presence of her receptive
senses, a sensory presence that dissolves the oppositions of "annoys"
and "joys," "complaints" and "bliss," into the golden identity of her
being.

The power of the beloved's divine presence, in dissolving oppositions, can also turn words against themselves, violating the principle
of logical differentiation which gives words their usefulness to us.

Thus in Sonnet 10 ("Reason, in faith thou art well serv'd, that still") the intrusion of Stella's actual presence causes the breakdown of reason and, through reason, the very basis of language itself as a series of potential meanings maintained by keeping distinctions among them distinct. This is one of many sonnets in which words are turned against themselves and reason is inverted through the force of a love which is an unmediated response to Stella's supra-linguistic presence, a presence that undermines all linguistic principles. In Sonnet 10 reason, performing its appropriate function, has been squabbling with love in the poet, but it stops and perverts its function, using its nature to serve its antagonist, after it is struck by "downright blows" from Stella, an act that overwhelms reason's mere words ("sword of wit," "wounds of dispraise"). Ironically, that direct attack is expressed in the figurative convention of Petrarchism, although by now we must take it literally as an actual onslaught by the sudden intrusion of a present Stella:

> For soon as they strake thee with Stella's rays,
> Reason thou kneel'dst, and offeredst straight to prove
> By reason good, good reason her to love.

The inversion of the final line ("reason good, good reason") is a graphic embodiment of the inversion of reason, the undoing of its function.

Sonnet 35 is the most brilliant demonstration of how Stella's presence *in* the poem turns words against themselves, using their self-contradictions to reveal the bankruptcy of language.

> What may words say, or what may words not say,
> Where truth itself must speak like flattery?
> Within what bounds can one his liking stay,
> Where Nature doth with infinite agree?
>
> What Nestor's counsel can my flames allay,
> Since Reason's self doth blow the coal in me?
> And ah what hope, that hope should once see day,
> Where Cupid is sworn page to Chastity?
>
> Honor is honor'd, that thou dost possess
> Him as thy slave, and now long needy Fame
> Doth even grow rich, naming my Stella's name.
>
> Wit learns in thee perfection to express,
> Not thou by praise, but praise in thee is rais'd:
> It is a praise to praise, when thou art prais'd.

The sense of controlled reasonability governs a string of self-consciously unreasonable compliments. After the confession of the incapacity of words in the opening line, the verbal paradoxes ensue. Each key word denies its own meaning; each abstraction obliterates itself by being itself in a way that identifies it with its opposite. The very possibility of language has been precluded by the reason-defying perfection of Stella. Yet it is reason itself that is forced to justify the impossibility ("What Nestor's counsel can my flames allay, / Since Reason's self doth blow the coal in me?"). The infinite reach of nature deserves a desire sanctioned by reason itself. And reason, as the principle behind language, leads the rest of the major universals (truth, nature, hope, chastity, honor, fame, praise) to follow its example of redefining themselves in accordance with Stella's superior example. In a metaphysical inversion, the highest universals are outdone by a particular, the intelligible by the sensible. Thus opposition is obliterated ("Nature doth with infinite agree") and the splendid abstract goals to which humans normally aspire must instead aspire to be associated with her ("Honour is honour'd, that thou dost possess / him as thy slave," or, finally, "Not thou by praise, but praise in thee is rais'd: / It is a praise to praise, when thou art prais'd.") Again we witness the outdoing of abstractions as mere words by the present living reality of Stella as the absolute particular.

The heightening which Stella offers to fame enables Sidney to introduce what we normally might see as a commonplace pun on her married name, Rich: "long needy Fame / Doth even grow rich, naming my Stella's name." Her name has substance even if the loftiest words have none. But the substance is Stella herself. The naming act becomes the en-Rich-ing act, as the poet—or rather Stella, if we accept his fiction—has forced the nominal to take on substance. Through her a world of empty words is reconstituted. As the final personified abstraction is outdone (and undone!) by the fleshy reality of her presence, we see her unique immediacy negating language, but only by becoming its own language—the language of *this* poem—which has itself transcended the emptiness of a general language that mediates particulars and forsakes all presence. As a "self-consuming artifact" (to borrow a phrase from Stanley Fish), the poem enters the eschatological mode, using language to end language and the very possibility of using words as we normally do; in this one final self-destructive display, language at last achieves pure presentation, but only because it becomes Stella and she—as the ultimate particular, both person and model—can point only to herself.

III

Shakespeare in some not dissimilar ways dwells on the incapacities of words as evidence of the inadequacy of logic, all swept away by the unabsorbable and present fact of love. In his Sonnet 116 ("let me not to the marriage of true minds") the word *love* itself has an instability about it: *"love* is not *love* / Which *alters* when it *alteration* finds / Or bends with the *remover* to *remove.*" The inconstancy of word (love, alters, remove) is father to the constancy of deed. The present fact of love is beyond language though it is expressed in language and supervises the transformation of language in order to convert it into an adequate instrument of expression: "If this be error and upon me proved, / I never writ, nor no man ever loved."

This is hardly the only poem which Shakespeare uses both as evidence of the present fact of love and as the very repository of it, now and—through the eternalizing function of poetry—forever. In Sonnet 74 ("But be contented. When that fell arrest") the poem itself becomes the embodiment of the poet's spirit which is consecrated to the beloved. The poem is the ultimate and the lasting fact of physical presence, testifying to the always present act of love by its very being, and not just by its intended meaning. Once death carries away the poet's body, which is all that is "due" to earth, his life yet retains "some interest" in its account—his spirit. And instead of being immaterial and Platonically inaccessible, the poem becomes the literal "memorial" which "with thee shall stay." It is the way to make the spirit one with the word and give both of them a material existence always present: "The worth of that is that which it contains, / And that is this, and this with thee remains." The repetitive emphasis on the (usually trivial) demonstrative pronouns underlines the fullness of their substance. The little "this" which is this present poem turns the testimony (and testament) of the poem into a present act, a present enactment of the claim it is making. As a living memorial, the physical container of spirit, a spirit consecrated to an always active loving, the poem is forever in the process of writing itself. The device recalls the similar use of "this" in the couplet of Sonnet 18 ("Shall I compare thee to a summer's day?"), a sonnet dedicated to perpetuating the beauty of the beloved:

> Nor shall Death brag thou wand'rest in his shade
> When in eternal lines to time thou grow'st:
> So long as men can breathe or eyes can see,
> So long lives this, and this gives life to thee.

In Sonnet 65 ("Since brass, nor stone, nor earth, nor boundless sea") Shakespeare confronts more openly the rational difficulty in claiming such eternalizing powers for the love sonnet.[9] From the start of Sonnet 64 ("When I have seen by Time's fell hand defaced") he has been expanding upon the inevitability that even the strongest creations of man and nature must be destroyed by time. If the strongest have no chance of holding out, then what hope for the weakest? "How with this rage shall beauty hold a plea,/Whose action is no stronger than a flower?" The only answer would defy man's reason, since it would call upon the paradox that the weakest must be stronger than the strongest. So he calls upon the unreason of a miraculous paradox, supported, however, by the fact of the present poem which offers the proof of its unreasonable argument in the very act of its being read. What hope? "O none, unless this miracle have might, / That in black ink my love may still shine bright." The miracle—the brightness of his love in the blackness of ink—attests, of course, to the special and magical power of that black ink in creating an always present verbal embodiment of the beloved's beauty which turns that beauty into an eternal Platonic universal that takes a material form. So it is the miracle of poetry, of this poem, that is appealed to in defiance of the world's reason. As we saw in Sidney, poetry's assault upon reason is also an assault upon the way in which words, as distinction-making entities, operate. So poetry must remake language and what words are capable of performing as it remakes our notions about reason.

It is in *The Phoenix and Turtle* that Shakespeare most explicitly calls attention to the undoing of reason and language by love and by the poem as the creative container of love. Just a few lines will do for my purposes:

> So they lov'd as love in twain
> Had the essence but in one:
> Two distincts, division none:
> Number there in love was slain . . .

Or later:

---

9 The curious doubleness in Shakespeare's attempt to find presence in the poetic word is heightened for us when we note that, beginning with Sonnet 18, the poem serves a role of embodiment which is analogous to that which is to be served by the beloved's son in Sonnets 1–17. The actual physical embodiment of the beloved as he comes again and is "refigured" in his son gives way, after Sonnet 17, to the less material, spiritual embodiment in the poem. Since he has traded an actual body for a mythic body of language, the poet-lover—from this point—is challenged to find metaphors which can give substance to the fleeting word.

> Reason, in itself confounded,
> Saw division grow together,
> To themselves yet either neither
> Simple were so well compounded;
>
> That it cried, "How true a twain
> Seemeth this concordant one!
> Love hath reason, reason none,
> If what parts can so remain."

But here too the fact of unreason is attested to by the poem and by its capacity, again as memorial, to embody the paradox to which it testifies. The "this" of this poem also remains behind as the final authority and authorization: "To this urn let those repair. . . ." It is with this same insistence on the two-in-one paradox of difference-in-identity that sonnets like 36, 37, or 39 make their delicate arguments. The indebtedness to the number mysteries of Christian mythology is obvious enough, although it is Shakespeare's task to make these paradoxes stand up in the verbal manipulations of each poem rather than simply to enunciate them as a lover's act of faith. The memorial, as a material entity, must bear its evidence within its own workings. And, as I hope we have been seeing in Sidney as well as in Shakespeare, it does.

In Renaissance love poetry it is the pain of separation that usually produces the need for the miracle of unreason. Obviously the problem of discreteness-versus-fusion is also the problem of distance, the distance between entities that prevents them from growing together and maintains the absence of one from the other. The separateness of the poet from his beloved (his god) is fostered by a normal language based on difference. His need to leap distance is akin to his need to dissolve difference. This pathos of distance—between words as between a subject and his objects—has also been a major issue in structuralist and post-structuralist writing in recent years. Shakespeare concerns himself with this aspect of the paradox too in *The Phoenix and Turtle*:

> Hearts remote, yet not asunder;
> Distance, and no space was seen
> 'Twixt this turtle and his queen;
> But in them it were a wonder.

Sonnets 44 and 45, a single twenty-eight-line unit (beginning "If the dull substance of my flesh were thought"), deal precisely with the "injurious distance" which intrudes between the poet and his beloved and with the poet's attempt to create such "a wonder." The opposition between flesh and spirit (thought), within an analysis based on the four elements as they operate in the poet, creates both the possibility of overcoming distance and the resignation to living with it. His flesh, as "dull substance," is weighed down by the material elements of earth and water of which it is composed; it is subject to the rational laws of physical reality which acknowledge distance between him and the absent object of his love. But if earth and water are the dead elements within him, his air and fire (thought and desire), as "quicker elements," "present-absent with swift motion slide." These latter two go and come in an instant, denying distance as a physical fact which does not relate to them. The poet can hold to their overcoming space, in the paradox of presence-absence, without giving up the common-sense acceptance of the earthly separation (and, by extension, the death) that remains unalterably there, outside his metaphors.

The poet retains this awareness that his metaphors are only illusionary identities in many of the best of these poems. The affirmation of two-in-one identity required by the poet-lover, who must have his beloved as his Christ as part of the illusion which love's psychology needs in order to flourish, is not the same as the affirmation of the Christian mystery: the beloved, after all, is not literally meant to be part of the typological structure. There is sacrilege enough in these poems without his persisting in any such exaggeration. The poet may be using the materials of Christian mystification, but he frequently demystifies them as he applies them to love's deity.

Still, there are several sonnets in which Shakespeare treats his beloved in typological terms, as a culmination of other "figural" individuals who dissolve their discreteness in his consummate identity. There is even a suggestion of eschatology in the function of the beloved as the summation of history, and its ending. Always, of course, this occurs within the poet's psychological history: for him it *is* history's ending in that this moment, as his ultimate present, is where history has led him and left him. Sonnet 106 ("When in the chronicle of wasted time") is quite explicitly eschatological in its claim that all the praiseworthy personages described in "the chronicle of wasted time" (time that has now been used up, all spent) function as a "prefiguring" of the beloved. All the details of individual descriptions ("Of hand, of foot, of lip, of eye, of brow") are actually attempts to describe their single, later fulfillment. The empirical differentiations of history's words fuse into the beloved's present identity, an identity earned even in the sensuous surface of the poet's words where the alliterative pattern blends "praises" into "prophecies" into "prefiguring." The praises of the many and varied long absent thus become the prefiguration of the one who is their ultimate presence.

Sonnet 53 ("What is your substance, whereof are you made") gives us an example of an even more extravagant claim that the beloved outdoes history's and nature's best examples, as well as sums them up in himself, although this poem does less to earn the claim in its own language. The poem makes its assertions without becoming their present occasion itself. The eschatological suggestion is there, together with the collapsing of all individual differences into one archetypal identity: "Since everyone hath, every one, one shade, / And you, but one, can every shadow lend." The beloved, then, is the only one who is pure substance, lending shadows to all the other ones. Yet from Adonis to Helen, from spring to fall, the friend appears "in every blessed shape we know."

In Sonnet 31 ("Thy bosom is endeared with all hearts"), as a sequel to Sonnet 30 ("When to the sessions of sweet silent thought"), there is a similar conversion of past individuals into a present consummation of them in the ultimate person, although here the poet is explicitly speaking only of his own emotional history rather than of all human history, such as is suggested in Sonnet 106. All the friends the poet has mourned still live in the heart of the present beloved. The poet has thought of them as gone ("supposed dead," "thought buried") but wrongly thought so since "buried Love doth live" in the beloved, who is their consummate memorial. The beloved therefore has collected all the affections individually bestowed earlier. In his sublime singleness he stands atop the poet's history of affections as the ultimate figure: "Their images I loved I view in thee, / And thou—all they—hast all the all of me." The accumulation of *alls* speaks eloquently of the finality of this moment. But the extent to which these extravagantly inclusive claims are restricted to the poet's enraptured vision of his beloved (rather than being absolute, pseudo-theological claims) is made clear in the subjective qualifications of the penultimate line: "Their images I loved I view in thee."

Sonnets 113–114 (beginning "Since I left you, mine eye is in my mind"), one of the most exciting two-sonnet units in the sequence, play in a sophisticated and self-conscious way with this very matter of illusion—with the relation between what the unreasoning eye of love sees and what is there to be seen—and with the opposition between the ontological and the psychological status of the miracle that converts lowly differences into the heights of identity. The two sonnets are a brilliant mingling of mystification and demystification. Because the poet's love is in control of his seeing, every item in the variegated

world which he sees—no matter how high or low—he sees as if part of
the beloved ("it ["mine eye"] shapes them to your feature"). Thus, in
a manner that reminds me of what I have said about *Astrophel and
Stella* 44 ("My words I know do well set forth my mind"), the beloved
causes his eye to create "every bad a perfect best." The beloved this
time is seen as an epistemological consummation, with all the world
apparently transformed into him: it is "alchemy" in which an en-
tranced poet-lover creates spirit's gold. The poet is aware that this
reading of differentiated experience under the aegis of a single identity is an illusion ("My most true mind thus maketh mine eye un-
true"), but it is a miraculous reading demanded by fidelity's view of
its world. Still the poet is ready to confront the alternatives which his
mystifying and demystifying impulses present: is his mind being
shown a falsely heightened world or has the world been truly turned
golden through love's alchemy (a question worthy of being asked of
poetry in the tradition of Sidney's *Apology*)? Is the apparent miracle a
psychological illusion or is it, like true alchemy, a miracle indeed?
The poet at once chooses the first, the skeptical alternative: " 'tis
flattery in my seeing, / And my great mind most kingly drinks it up"
("kingly" because "crown'd" with the beloved). But, we are told in a
strange final twist, the eye, which has prepared the poisoned cup of
flattery ("the monarch's plague"), loves so much what it has prepared
that it begins to drink it, thereby making itself its own victim first. It
really believes the heightened vision of reality it is creating. In this
case the king has been served more sincerely than we might expect
from the flatterers around him.[10]

The "I" of the poet has been reduced to his "eye": he is both king
and courtier, the flattered and the flatterer, as there is in his two roles
a mutuality of deception and sincerity. The self-skepticism of the
poem has preserved both its vision and its sense of the incompleteness
of that vision. The vision of a motley world remade and perfected
through the advent of a single person is one the lover needs and
cherishes; his eye is so newly empowered that it no longer sees any
truth but its own. It is, in effect, the flattering dream of sublime

---

[10] We may remember that, in Sonnet 33 as well, flattery, similarly related to a king
("sovereign eye"), is transformed into heavenly alchemy—at least until the reality
of clouds catches up with it.

> Full many a glorious morning have I seen
> Flatter the mountain tops with sovereign eye,
> Kissing with golden face the meadows green,
> Gilding pale streams with heavenly alchemy . . .

It is true that Shakespeare is speaking here of the sun, but it is not difficult to move
from sun either to king or to god.

possession in spite of worldly differences like the one which moves the poet in Sonnet 87 ("Farewell! thou art too dear for my possessing"). In the concluding couplet of that poem, which again yokes kingship and flattery, the poet acknowledges that reality ("matter") may wash the dream away: "Thus have I had thee as a dream doth flatter— / In sleep a king, but waking no such matter." The dream of union yields to the reality of distance.

The illusionary nature of the miracle could not be more explicitly, if more sadly, conceded. Not that the miracle is to be rejected, but its miraculous power is seen as one with its worldly impossibility. The poetic gesture as love's gesture may transform the world's ways and its language, but without undoing them. In its consummations it wins its eschatological victories for the poet-lover, though its reality-bound antagonists—wielding difference, distance, and death—are hardly dissolved. What we have seen is a celebration of word-magic, the magic that claims to produce a substantive presence in the word. If we are asked to believe in such magic, it is with the tentativeness and skepticism which even a poet-magician like Prospero acknowledges at the close of *The Tempest*.

Or I can put the matter in Shakespeare's language by using Sonnets 114, 87, and 33 to draw a composite of the mutual relations between king and subject, alchemy and flattery, dream and reality. (It might well be reinforced by some of Shakespeare's history plays—for example, in speeches by Richard II and young Prince Hal—and given additional meaning in light of the golden world of Sidney's *Apology*.) Love's flattery produces the illusion of love's alchemy, the visionary dream of a reality fit for a king and reflecting his "sovereign eye." Again as a king, the poet-lover must endure and even indulge this flattery, the illusion of the golden world, treating it as an alchemical transformation. His reality has been put to sleep to give him the kingly dream which, while thus charmed, he believes real ("In sleep a king"). Then, as poet-king and sun-king, he in turn gives the golden world to us in his work. He now flatters the world for us, and it emerges as poetic alchemy ("Flatter . . . with sovereign eye, Gilding . . . with heavenly alchemy"). But this illusionary magic makes him a god as well, as the king is a god, the reigning sun of his world, emerging from clouds to make it golden, conferring gold upon it with his look. As in Sonnet 114, his poem becomes a self-inflating song of praise of the golden beloved and—through the beloved—of the golden world. So the lover, as a poet, becomes surrogate king and god, creating the golden world as his poem, if only under the momentary illusion of aesthetics that is authorized by the prior illusion conferred by love. And flattery, posing as alchemy and momentarily believed as such, becomes at once a theory of metaphor, of love, of state, of cosmos —all deriving from the lover's skeptical version of a theological semiotics. The arbitrary act of flattery, though restricted to the illusionary realm of appearance, is, through the beholder's complicity, treated as if it were a substantive act of alchemy. But this semiotics of flattery is, primarily, a poetics, one that combines indulgence and skepticism and does so with a self-consciousness for which our more condescending notions of Renaissance linguistic awareness (like Foucault's) cannot provide. Reconsidering Sidney's *Apology* in this light, dare I suggest that poetry's golden world—an acknowledged flattery treated like alchemy—makes momentary kings of us all?

IV

This has not, I hope, been a merely historical investigation of the metaphysics and the theory of language which can account for what happens in these Renaissance poems, so that we can sympathetically reproduce their meanings. More than this, I mean to find in the poems a method by which each confronts the emptiness of words as signifiers—their distance from their signifieds—and, having thus confronted that emptiness and that distance, converts itself into an invocation of presence that becomes itself a verbal presence. Beyond observing the conflict in Renaissance theorists between representation and presentation in language, I have tried to demonstrate Renaissance poets balancing their sense of the emptiness of words with their use of a verbal analogy to the divine miracle in order to fill those words with substance. But this analogy is accompanied by a demystifying awareness of its merely verbal and illusionary nature. The theological or metaphysical is reduced to the poetic and—for all the claims of identity—the difference between the beloved and the divine is carried along as the underside of the highest metaphorical flights to identity. Language is but language after all, though for the poet-lover it must often be enough even if he knows its limits. This sophisticated view of language is one we may well borrow as we seek to account for all that the best poetry—their poetry—can do.[11]

11 I am not speaking of all Renaissance poets, of course, or of all the poetry of any of them. At some moments all of them (and some of them, alas, at all moments) seem too ready to embrace uncritically and literally a poetic claim to the substantive fullness of word-magic. I mean only to call attention to those most provocative moments in the best of them when they require their highest poetic flights to refrain—often self-consciously—from metaphysical projection.

Theirs is a view of language more modern than we normally allow to Renaissance writers, much of it deriving from their brilliant good sense as poets: they can accept words as insubstantial entities existing on their own, not to be confounded with their signifieds (though Foucault reserves this awareness for a later period), and they can accept the differential character of language (not unlike structuralists' claims in recent years). But, on the other side, as poets, they must—out of their skepticism—create a willful illusion of verbal substance, and, out of their acceptance of the linguistic principle of difference, they must force those words to turn duplicitous in satisfying the poetic need for an identity, however metaphorical, that dissolves oppositions. Yet, as poets rather than priests, they create their justification through the internal manipulation of a language forced to violate its own limited nature instead of relying on any external authorization by faith. For example, there may be a psychological faith—an illusion of the poet-lover—required to transfer the figural metaphor from Christ to the beloved, but there is no more of an ontological claim than this. The poet as both king and flatterer, at once put into action and deceived by his flattering instrument, has a constancy of faith that even converts the inconstancy of that instrument.

In Sonnet 105, which prepares the way for the eschatological ful-fillment of Sonnet 106 ("When in the chronicle of wasted time"), Shakespeare established his absolute commitment to unity, to the dis-solution of discreteness, to a constancy which is sustained only by the three-in-one god of love.[12]

> Let not my love be called idolatry,
> Nor my beloved as an idol show,
> Since all alike my songs and praises be
> To one, of one, still such, and ever so.
> Kind is my love today, tomorrow kind,
> Still constant in a wondrous excellence:
> Therefore my verse, to constancy confined,
> One thing expressing, leaves out difference.
> "Fair, kind, and true," is all my argument,
> "Fair, kind, and true," varying to other words;
> And in this change is my invention spent:
> Three themes in one, which wondrous scope affords.
> Fair, kind, and true have often lived alone,
> Which three till now never kept seat in one.

---

[12] I am grateful to my student, Joseph Church, who first showed me the special relevance of Sonnet 105 to my subject.

The poet's ritual formula ("To one, of one, still such, and ever so") testifies to his lover's oath of union.[13] As if addressing himself to structuralism, Shakespeare acknowledges the usual variety of differentiated words, which he here turns away from ("Therefore my verse, to constancy confined, / One thing expressing, leaves out difference"). This variety is collapsed into the *won*drous oneness of the poem's union with its object. But its final line acknowledges that, aside from the present poetic trinitarian occasion, difference still rules:

> Fair, kind, and true have often lived alone,
> Which three till now never kept seat in one.

---

[13] Appropriately ritualistic too is his yoking three times the three adjectives, "Fair, kind, and true."

2

Jacopo Mazzoni,
Repository of Diverse Critical Traditions
or Source of a New One?

To the student of Renaissance critical theory, Sir Philip Sidney, whose *Apology for Poetry* has become so revered a text for English scholars, must be viewed as a largely unoriginal—if marvelously graceful—compiler of commonplaces drawn from a long line of six-teenth-century Italians. Even where Sidney appears to be making claims for a premature romantic daring in a Shelleyan call to imag-ination—the free ranging of the poet "within the zodiac of his own wit"—the skeptic can tone down the temerity of these claims by re-ducing their implications to what the context of the essay permits. He can manage this reduction especially if he defines that context in the language permitted Sidney by his obvious borrowings from the tradi-tion from Plato to—shall we say—the conservative Scaliger. Despite the enormous attractions to the modern mind of passages in the *Apol-ogy*, I believe it is Sidney's failure to construct an original philosophi-cal framework for these passages that allows them in the main to be reduced, by betrayals in the surrounding context, to their less exciting —if more consistent—sources.

It was precisely the search for a radically original philosophic mind that led me to Jacopo Mazzoni. Primarily devoted, as technical philosopher, to synthesizing the systems of Plato and Aristotle, he was if anything too theoretical rather than not theoretical enough. The Dante quarrel never seems to have been more than a subsidiary interest of his, even according to his editor Tuccio, although goodness knows he ended by writing voluminously enough about it. His first-hand, profoundly systematic concern with earlier philosophers allowed Mazzoni a freedom from the limited terms of earlier Italian critics although he was clearly aware as well of the issues they endlessly circled. After all, his work, as an answer to detractors of Dante, does reflect and respond to local and contemporary issues. Thus, while we find him echoing—or quarreling with—most of what preceded him for half a century in the crowded critical arena in Italy, he can bring a theoretical freshness of approach that allows him to make unique contributions. It is therefore unfortunate that Mazzoni has been so neglected by our critical historians, has been far less often distinguished from the army of Italian theorists than have less worthy predecessors and contemporaries. It is especially ironic that Mazzoni, whom I intend to defend as a source and not merely a repository of critical tradition, should have had so slight an influence on theorists and historians of theory, while, for example, Sir Philip Sidney, whom I suggested as perhaps more a repository than a source, has had so general, so pervasive, and so profound an influence on so many.

The fact that Mazzoni came along so late in the century to add his voice to all those that had been going round and round the same tired problems that plagued Renaissance poetics very likely diminished the seriousness with which subsequent theorists and historians of theory considered him. (Sidney, just as late or later, could be felt as a new, fresh English voice rather than just another, tired Italian one.) The prolix, overly technical, scholastic nature of Mazzoni's defense of Dante's *Divine Comedy* (1587, 1688) also has precluded any extensive influence. Indeed, until Professor Allan H. Gilbert's translations of generous excerpts in his anthology, *Literary Criticism: Plato to Dryden* (1940),[1] and Professor Baxter Hathaway's treatment of him as a central figure in his recent fine volume, *The Age of Criticism: The Late Renaissance in Italy* (1962),[2] Mazzoni was hardly singled out among his fellows, if we are to judge from our contemporary historians from Croce to Spingarn to Weinberg.

His work seems to me clearly to require his being singled out. In part he was pressed to his special formulations by the fact that he

---

[1] My quotations from Mazzoni are taken from Allan H. Gilbert's pioneer translations (New York: American Book Co., 1940). Page numbers after the quotations refer to this volume.

[2] Ithaca, N. Y.: Cornell University Press, 1962.

addressed himself to the defense of Dante's great work, which, like defenses of Ariosto's epic romance, necessarily led Renaissance theorists into heterodox areas. The fact that Mazzoni's antagonist, Bulgarini, charged that Dante's comedy, as a vision or dream, could have no proper object of imitation seemed to provide special openings for the direction in which Mazzoni intended to move. It led him back to the ancients, to the Platonic and Aristotelian versions of that confusing term *imitation*, and forward to a systematic undertaking that made his more than the casual and ad hoc liberalism of critics like Cinthio, who were also in the service of the modern writer and the modern genres.

As so often in the history of theory, it is *imitation* that is at the center of Mazzoni's thinking, but a special blend of Platonic and Aristotelian senses of the term. Since imitation is for Mazzoni the end as well as the source of poetry, it is for him indeed the center, his circular system rotating around it. By allowing imitation to be the objective of poetry as well as its starting point, Mazzoni is surely courting heterodoxy, although he shrewdly deserts it, if only in part, before he is through. The Horatian dual doctrine of the useful and the sweet, which leads to the dual injunction that poetry teach and delight, transformed Aristotelian mimetic theory in the Renaissance (thanks also to Platonic intrusions) to the didactic orthodoxy of delightful teaching—delight, that is, in order to teach. Where we find a discordant voice, like Castelvetro's, it is raised for the exclusive cultivation of the alternative of delight at the expense of the teaching. Only Mazzoni seems to urge—as not even Aristotle himself would— imitation for its own sake, for the sake—that is—of the representation or the particularization, the image or the idol, itself, and for neither teaching nor delight. We shall see that even he makes a partial retraction later, although the force of his initial claim is never wholly withdrawn.

How, with so central a place given to imitation, can Mazzoni address himself to Bulgarini's assault upon Dante's visionary substitute for an external object of imitation? At once we must turn to his peculiar working of the term. In the double distinction he draws between the narrative and dramatic and between the icastic and fantastic and in the four possible combinations among them that follow (dramatic-fantastic, narrative-fantastic, dramatic-icastic, narrative-icastic), we see him invoking Aristotelian imitation although he combines it with two different senses of Platonic imitation. The distinction between icastic and fantastic rests on the relation of the poem to its object of imitation, either an object in the external world (icastic) or an imaginative picture "made by the caprice of the artist" (fantastic) (p. 360). But the other distinction, between narrative and dramatic, rests on the relation of the author to the speaking voice in his poem. Is he speaking in his own voice or is he, as in drama, "imitating" (which is to say, speaking in) the voices of his characters? This is a second of the Platonic meanings of imitation, but for Plato an important one which he used to damn the "imitative tribe" of poets. These cross-distinctions, then, would find dramatic poems doubly imitative, since there is not only the image that exists in all poetry but also the impersonation (or secondary image) of the actor, a representation of the representation. We should see clearly the Platonic derivation of these mirrors behind mirrors. But the fantastic, clearly the sort of idol Mazzoni prefers, breaks the chain of simple reflections by allowing an alternative to the representation of existing objects in the work. And since Plato was clearly contemptuous of the aping habit of poetry, its dependence on the inferior phenomenal world, it is not inappropriate for Mazzoni to prefer the fantastic to the more literally mimetic icastic (though it reverses Plato's express preferences in the *Sophist*); and it is surely useful to him in defending the *Commedia* against the literalistic mimetic demands of Bulgarini.

Mazzoni's working with his two definitions of *imitation*, at once alternative and reinforcing, allows him to look upon the Dantean epic as at once a species of inventive (as opposed to literal) imitation and a species of narrative (as opposed to dramatic) imitation; that is, at once a fellow-species of drama in opposition to history and a fellow species of history in opposition to drama. In the first case, like Aristotle, Mazzoni would claim that it is the making power of the *poesis* that, regardless of genre, allows poetry to range beyond nature and the casualty of history. It is this inventiveness that leads him, through most of his lengthy treatise, to treasure the fantastic far above the icastic—indeed, to see the icastic poet, bound as he is by nature and history, as hard put to convert his materials, via the fabulous, into poetry. But his second view of imitation, as image-making, is one which prompts him to allow the historian himself to be poet even as he is historian, the icastic to be made the equal of the fantastic. While there surely are special requirements which the historian, the would-be icastic poet, must meet to qualify as poet, the point is that it seems no longer to be the making of the Aristotelian fable that is required. Of course, since the defense of Dante does not touch the drama— indeed, in the Renaissance was often felt to be self-consciously aggressive against the drama—Mazzoni can the more easily ally poetry to history via the common device of narration. But out of this confounding of mimetic traditions, Mazzoni draws special possibilities for distinguishing in a profitable way his sense of the fable from Aristotle's, his sense of the credible from Aristotle's sense of the probable. The similarities of language must not be permitted to fool us, to deprive us of the awareness of Mazzoni's originality.

The differentia of poetry for Mazzoni must be its attachment to the credible, its involvement with the particularized image or idol, whether icastic or fantastic in its origins. The poet is distinguished from the historian or physicist not, as with Aristotle, because he deals with his own construct, his causally inevitable plot, or, as Renaissance theorists would echo, because he deals with the world as it ought to be instead of the world as it is. Rather, for Mazzoni he is distinguished because he deals only with the sensible, the perceptible image, instead of the merely intelligible concept. As regards the distinction between icastic and fantastic, nothing could be more irrelevant than whether his object of imitation is true or false. All that matters in the immediacy of its particularity is that it be credible or verisimilar—to uşe the tired Renaissance term that Mazzoni applies only with a rare rigor and precision. The poem is believable because its particularizations, its images, make it like truth, like the sensible world as we know it. This likeness to truth, its verisimilitude, is what is required to have us credit it. Its actual truth or falsity is no issue, provided the particularized illusion is sustained and hence sustains our belief. How close we are to Coleridge's "willing suspension of disbelief." We have left far behind the Aristotelian notion of probability, that refers only to the logical and temporal relations among the several portions of the plot. We have moved to the immediacy, the felt-ness, with which the poet has urged the particularity of the special case he is displaying. If Herodotus were to do this, indeed if Empedocles himself were to do it, then they would be admitted to the realm of poets by Mazzoni, even as he acknowledges that Aristotle would have to exclude them so long as they excluded a constructed fable. The poet is a poet for Mazzoni to the extent that he makes us see, that he represents with sensible images, that he creates idols. To borrow the language of Henry James, which reflects a similar perspective, the poet's task is to render experience for us in its immediacy, to render it and not merely to tell us about it. It is the presentational aesthetic that Mazzoni is pressing toward. No wonder we find him recapitulating with approval the imagist doctrine, *ut pictura poesis*, as it appears in his theoretical tradition.

Now we can see how crucially different Mazzoni's sense of the fabulous is from Aristotle's. Aristotle's refers to the architecture of fable as plot; Mazzoni's refers to our vision of fable as particularized idol, refers to perceptible immediacy in the single, particularized, realized, special case. This leads Mazzoni to add another requirement to his definition of poetry as the "credible." Rhetoric also, he tells us, deals with the credible. But while rhetoric deals with the credible *as credible* in order to persuade us, poetry deals with the credible *as marvelous* in order to give us a sense of wonder. So the poet, without sacrificing truth-likeness (the verisimilar), must join the credible to the marvelous, must—in effect—make the marvelous credible. Here is another foreshadowing of Coleridgean doctrine concerning disbelief and its relation to the commonplace and the fanciful. It is this more than it is an echo of Aristotle's apparently similar call for the union of surprise and probability, since again Aristotle's rests solely on plot relationships. According to Mazzoni, the poet is to enlarge our consciousness, the domain of the credible. He is to make us believe in the possibility of that which, before reading his poem, we would not think credible: the wonder Mazzoni would have the poet seek arises "when the hearers accept what they did not believe could happen" (p. 388). We now better understand why Mazzoni usually celebrates the fantastic poet, though we must allow (more than Mazzoni does) for the fact that the icastic poet, if he would be more than rhetorician by attaching the credible to the marvelous, confronts the more severe challenge.

But the poet who can thus stretch belief and the believable can be a dangerous influence. If he can create pictures by caprice and convert almost any materials into what we find believable, if he can force upon us an objective world of particularized, perceptible images whose felt reality we cannot help but credit, then indeed he has power over us. And we should be too aware of Mazzoni's Platonism not to expect him to be concerned about this power, however dedicated he may want to be to poetry's autonomous power as pure representation for its own sake. So it is that Mazzoni, in the spirit of Plato, sees poetry as a form of "sophistic," even as he sees Plato's attack on the poets within the framework of his broader attack on the sophists. And, given Mazzoni's emphasis on particularization, the total exploitation of the individual case, we should not be surprised to find him somewhat disturbed by the chances for questionable moral consequences to proceed from the poet's indulgence in casuistry. After all, he has been requiring of poetry only that it be credible in its representation of a marvelous idol, even though—from Plato's point of view—that very credibility is the ground of its threat to us. For us to credit poetry means that we are persuaded of the authenticity of this image, the extent to which we find it believable in representation, representation for its own sake. If Mazzoni had not made imitation the end of poetry as well as its source, we would have had to ask what we were believing in by believing in the poem, what the import of the object of that imitation was, what reality we were committing ourselves to, and what the consequences of such a belief would be. Instead, in this theory so profoundly heterodox to Renaissance notions, we are to believe in the image for its own sake within its own system. It is this requirement which would make Empedocles or Herodotus or any would-be icastic poet, were he to follow Mazzoni's prescription, indeed a poet but no longer a physicist or historian. For the power and wonder of his work, depending on his resolving the credible-marvelous in the particularized image, would in no way depend upon the truth of its references to its external object. Its value would reside, not in the object of imitation but in the imitation itself, not in the object but in the objective correlative, seen as self-sustaining. The Platonist must worry about so freely ranging a poetic power particularizing at will without guidance from any moral direction, and must see in it the casuistic temptations attributed to sophistry. And so Mazzoni does worry, although he must resist following Plato so far as to allow this worry to inhibit the circular freedom of his definition of poetry.

Characterizing poetry "as a division of the rational or sophistic faculty," then, Mazzoni has invoked Plato's perspective and cannot altogether escape the moral consequences of the poet's freely imaged cases. His lengthy and confusing discussion leads to distinctions among three kinds of sophistic as the ancients from Plato to Philostratus applied them to poetry: the icastic, which in its affiliations with truth is morally acceptable, and two kinds of fantastic, only one of which will pass the Platonic censor. The icastic sort, "which does not propound feigned names and acts, but true names and real events, of which it discourses according to the law of justice," is still poetry and a form of sophistic "because though indeed it treated of true things for the sake of justice, it still dealt with them in a credible way, and therefore sometimes abandoned the truth when it looked on the false as more credible or as a more effective instrument in persuading men as was desired" (p. 370). So, obedient to the poetic law of the credible image, this form of sophistic is yet morally innocent. Of the two sorts of fantastic sophistic, the morally acceptable is that "which, though indeed it propounds to the intellect things that are feigned, yet does not disorder the will, but rather in every way and wholly attempts to make it conformable with the just" (p. 360). The morally unacceptable sort is "that which disorders the intellect by representing false things of the gods and the heroes, and which disorders the will with the variety of its imitation and by immoderately increasing our affections" (p. 369). Mazzoni clearly means here to restrict Plato's attack on the sophists, and, by extension, on poetry, to only one of these three varieties, allowing the others to be harmless. Indeed,

Mazzoni's defense of the properly controlled sort of fantastic poetry goes so far as to claim, in a far more recognizable and traditional Renaissance critical spirit, that fantastic poetry "regulated by the proper laws is part of this ancient sophistic, since it also propounds feigned things to our intellect in order to regulate the appetite, and many times contains beneath the husk of the fiction the truth of many noble conceptions" (p. 370).

But, Plato aside, what "proper laws" of regulation can Mazzoni be speaking of, if he has been seriously putting forth a notion of poetry as true only to its own laws, true to what Mazzoni terms the laws of the poetic image? Once he has, in his defensive stance, introduced the sophistic aspect of poetry, and has had to establish good as well as evil forms of sophistic, the Plato in Mazzoni has given his argument a moral turn that has irrevocably diverted it from the aesthetic purism that has seemed to launch his theory.

When a philosopher is in trouble, he invents a distinction. Mazzoni's device is to draw a distinction between poetry and poetics, the first being "the art that forms and constructs the image" and the second, imposed from the outside, the art that "rules over and uses the image" (p. 367). So poetry is the art itself, sovereign and autonomous; poetics is the imposition by the state of a moral and political interest that may if necessary subdue the art to that interest. Indeed he suggests that Aristotle's *Poetics* is really the ninth book of the *Politics*. If the civil faculty, the state in its political aspect, governs the behavior of its citizens, it is to do so both when they are active and when they are at rest. Politics must govern both activity and the cessation of activity or recreation. And poetics is the art of governing the citizens in their cessation from activity, their pastimes. Thus, however true it may be that poetry exists only to body forth its idol, without hedonistic, cognitive, or moral concerns, it does carry as an inevitable by-product—what Aristotle calls an "accident" joined to its operation —the delight or pleasure of recreation. (". . . as Aristotle has said in the tenth book of the *Ethics*, pleasure is an accident naturally joined to some operations, and among the others it is without doubt very appropriate to imitation, since it is in such a way joined with it that no sort of imitation can be found that does not also give delight and pleasure"—p. 377.) Since poetry has such accidental effects, it becomes subject to the rule of the civil faculty in its proper control over recreation in order to ascertain that only that recreation be allowed which cannot endanger the actions of the body politic, only that delight be allowed which conforms with the good.

But we must not confuse accident with substance. In its own true nature, poetry still is seen as self-enclosed by the image that constitutes it, self-enclosed in body and in end. But its accidental effect of pleasure brings it into the political arena where political responsibilities are imposed upon it, though in violation of its nature. Mazzoni has not relented in his original definition of poetry as irresponsibly devoted to its image:

> the imitative arts are different from the others that are not imitative through this alone, that the object of the imitative arts is not good for any other use than to represent alone. But the object of the other arts, that are not imitative, is good for some other use, either profitable or pleasant. Then if the object of poetry has as its end either the useful or the pleasant, of necessity it would be good for something else than merely to represent, and in this mode poetry would not be an imitative art. (p. 376)

What Mazzoni gives us is a then unheard-of pluralism of perspectives and of modes, out of which emerge three coordinate definitions of poetry: first, in its own terms, as pure imitation for its own sake; secondly, from the standpoint of recreation, as an imitation created in order to delight; thirdly, from the standpoint of the civil faculty in control of recreation, as an imitation created in order to delight profitably. Surely in this pluralism we have a clear statement of what was so much later to be called the distinction between the intrinsic and the extrinsic functions of poetry. However far Mazzoni has gone to accommodate previous Renaissance discussions about the Horatian *dulce* and/or *utile*, he will not give up his claims to the sanctity of poetry's own nature, even if he will not exile himself from Plato's Republic by fighting against necessary violations of that nature by outside considerations. Among those desperate theorists in our history who have tried to reconcile aesthetic with moral demands, there have been few nobler attempts to have one's cake while eating it, to overcome and transcend a rigid tradition while subscribing to it. Mazzoni's three separate but equal definitions, springing from a pluralistic and modal synthesis that makes the answers you get dependent upon the questions you ask, are really not separate and—at least from the perspective of the literary man—surely not equal. Though he seems to have turned heterodoxy into orthodoxy, Mazzoni had really not given anything away; he retains a heterodoxy that can absorb orthodoxy without changing its own nature.

Let me confess that Mazzoni's effort to master and blend Plato and Aristotle, Horatian instrumentalism, and his own unique aestheticism often is less resolved than my presentation has suggested. He perhaps ended more by wrestling with problems than by overcoming them. My point is that the problems he wrestled with were not those usually recognized by his fellows and predecessors, and that the theoretical level at which the wrestling took place was a very advanced one indeed. Nevertheless, we must not forget that the apparent inconsistencies in his moral distinctions among kinds of sophistic are not convincingly done away with. The rejection of the subversive sort of fantastic sophistic, together with his embrace of that proper sort which can "regulate the appetite," which "many times contains beneath the husk of the fiction the truth of many noble conceptions," such gestures make us wonder about the firmness with which he can hold onto the irrelevance of truth or falsity, of good or evil, in that credible-marvelous idol created by the poet's "caprice." It brings us back to the Scaligerian notion of the poet's imitating the truth by fiction—the notion that serves also to reduce to itself some of the most exciting moments in Sidney. We must worry about the autonomy of that particularized idol, whose freedom from the universal Mazzoni has elsewhere done so much to establish.

Here is the heart of the difficulty, here in the relation of the particular to the universal. The Renaissance theorist normally allows particularity only insofar as it reflects its universal, to which it leads us. What is so original about Mazzoni is his defense of the particularization itself as self-justified. When he insists that the particularization "is not good for any other use than to represent alone," when he guards it in its wayward credibility from the "profitable or pleasant" as well as from the true or false, he is urging a self-sufficiency that would keep it irreducible, beyond the moral-cognitive assimilation to the universal that the Platonist requires.[3] But when, on the other hand, he speaks in Scaligerian fashion of the "truth of many noble conceptions" "beneath the husk of the fiction," we rightly see the allegorist, whose fable is Aesop's rather than Aristotle's, whose interest in perceptible images rests wholly upon the intelligible concepts which they illuminate. Perhaps the burden of Mazzoni's tradition could permit no greater sustaining of his radical, almost nominalist,

---

[3] At the same time I must confess that my emphasis has probably been too strong on one side, perhaps led astray by some of Mazzoni's daring phrases. We must not forget that, for all his defense of a self-justified particularization, in Mazzoni's dualism every particularization must, by definition, belong to a universal, every sensible object must reflect an intelligible one. So, however great the importance granted the particular and the sensible, however autonomous they appear to be in his argument, his metaphysic has from the outset invoked, by implication, the universal and the intelligible. Our more recent interest in a particularity which does not come trailing clouds of metaphysical glory may lead us to overemphasize the modernity of Mazzoni's claims. And yet, despite these qualifications, I would still urge our awareness of Mazzoni's primary commitment to image, to a presentational aesthetic that, whatever his Platonic retreats, still makes him a remarkable theorist, one we almost could not believe emerged in the Renaissance.

suggestions. When, in a momentary retreat, we find him justifying the poet's use of images by citing the ignorance and gullibility of the masses to whom the poet speaks, we are back in a familiar Renaissance country, filled with sugar-coated pills intended for dull patients, though it is not the country through which we have expected so singular a leader as Mazzoni to conduct us.

> Hence the poet treats of such matters in a credible fashion, that is, he teaches them by means of comparisons and similitudes taken from things obvious to the sense, and the common people, knowing that in such things the truth exists in the fashion presented by the poet, therefore, easily believe poetry is also true in intelligible things. (p. 366)

But we should expect no more of him; indeed, in view of what was given to him, he has given us far more than we dared expect. He tried—at moments successfully—to transcend an imposing list of oppositions deeply embedded in the history of literary theory: imitation versus expression, Platonic versus Aristotelian systems, truth versus falsity as related to poetry, the icastic versus the fantastic, the credible versus the marvelous, pleasure versus utility and both of these versus the self-sufficiency of art. I began with an opposition of my own when my title asked whether Mazzoni was a repository of diverse critical traditions or the source of a new one. Scholarly habit should have at once assured us of what Mazzoni's exciting and daring uncertainties have by now revealed: that I had to end by affirming both alternatives, both repository and source. But what true and comprehensive repository of tradition could ever end by doing less than becoming more—the source of its successors?

3

Shakespeare and
the Critic's Idolatry of the Word

EVEN IN A VOLUME centering on Shakespeare's influence, where exaggerated claims are part of the ritual, it may appear excessive to suggest that he be treated as a shaping force in modern literary criticism. Yet this is the suggestion I shall make and try to justify here.[1] Of course, I shall speak only for one variety of modern critical theory and practice, one with which I associate myself and which I therefore cannot help but see as a dominant variety: it attributes marvelous (I shall later say "miraculous") powers to poetry and centers these powers in its dislocations of normal language. Critics of this sort accord Shakespeare his special and unchallenged place as first without peers in the poet's pantheon by virtue of his capacity for the manipulation of language. Other poets—all substantially lesser poets—are to be subjected to the same measuring instruments, as the verbal analysis found

This essay takes the shape it does largely because it was written to be included in the volume of Harvard English Studies entitled *Shakespeare: Aspects of Influence.* I was asked to treat the influence Shakespeare's work has had on criticism in our time.

[1] I must at once confess that I have already written a book organized around this suggestion, as can be seen from the two rather oddly conjoined parts of its subtitle: *A Window to Criticism: Shakespeare's* Sonnets *and Modern Poetics* (Princeton: Princeton University Press, 1964).

uniquely appropriate to Shakespeare is extended into a general critical method. For these critics Shakespeare functions as a sacred book, the enabling text for their commitment to the special magic of poetic discourse. Thus, in its most recent version, bardolatry is collapsed into wordolatry.

This is hardly the first time that Shakespeare's works have served as models that are seen to justify a critical movement. Indeed, the history of criticism in English seems again and again to reveal Shakespeare as the supervising spirit of its several major moments. One might claim that the abiding liberalism of the English critical tradition was largely the consequence of Shakespeare's having been the special gift to English critics, the greatest writer given into the charge of any critics. Certainly a succession of critics credited their need to resist dogma to their need to include Shakespeare as chief among those for whom their theories had to account. For here was a writer obviously at odds with many of the conventions critics had too often invented to guide them—and, *ex post facto*, to guide the writer they treated, lest he be subject to the critics' wrath. So the critics could not retain an uncritical allegiance to those conventional "rules" and to Shakespeare too. Surely by at least the late seventeenth century—say, with Dryden—it had become clear that critical practice had to find a shape that reflected in some measure the stubborn and uncooperative fact of Shakespeare's lasting presence among us. Since that time, I would suggest, the best English criticism has continually yielded under his incomparable pressure.

One might argue that we cannot know whether, as I have indicated, it was Shakespeare whose presence breathed a special liberal spirit into the English critical tradition that had to accommodate him, or whether he himself was a product of that same liberal spirit, which we can see at work, for example, much earlier in the grand independence of Chaucer. In other words, we can ask—uncertain of ever finding a satisfactory answer—whether Dryden confronted his French antagonists with a tolerance for dramatic and poetic flexibility because he had to respond sensitively to Shakespeare or whether Dryden and Shakespeare were both moved in that freer direction we associate with English literature and criticism by a similar characteristic deep in the English literary consciousness. Is it, then, that Shakespeare is responsible for the openly empirical bent of English criticism or that he has been shaped by that English bent himself, and Dryden and others later shaped with him, though he serves as so excellent an excuse or precedent for them?

Very likely it does not finally matter which of the two is the case, so long as we note that, in "An Essay of Dramatic Poesy," for example,

Dryden resists the extremes of French neoclassical dogma in the name of moderate liberality and that he uses the example of Shakespeare as the special justification for the more open attitude appropriate to the English critic. Dryden, of course, hardly goes all the way, confessing that he must temper his love for the imperfect Shakespeare with his unsurpassed admiration for the "correct" Ben Jonson; but he has set the pattern which later critics can expand as they follow it. The gap between Shakespeare and his more correct rivals widens as later neo-classical critics seek to balance artful regularity with the sublimity of original genius and use Shakespeare to authorize their heterodoxy. As the Renaissance-Enlightenment pseudo-Aristotle gives way to Longinus, the critic justifies the change by waving Shakespeare's works before him as he goes. Addison treats Shakespeare as one of "these great natural geniuses," "nobly wild and extravagant"; Pope sees him as the archetypal "original," producing, "Nature herself" rather than mere "copies of her"; and Dr. Johnson extends this notion of Shakespeare as "the poet of nature" to the point where he justifies the confluence of the genres and the explosion of the unities by making "an appeal . . . from criticism to nature," in the interest of opening poetry from the rigidity of convention to the variety of life.[2]

The polarization between Shakespeare and the rule-bound alternative increases as we move through the eighteenth century. Thus, in comparisons between the two, the balance between Shakespeare and Jonson is gradually shifted until all the weight seems on Shakespeare's side. Early in the century Addison is anxious to defend the restrained genius "formed . . . by rules" as a kind separate but equal, in comparison to the natural genius. In his Preface, Pope seems disturbed even by the suggestion of polarity in Dryden's opposition between the poet of wit and the poet of correctness, between his love for Shakespeare and his admiration of Jonson. So Pope denies that there need be a mutually exclusive relation between the two: he prefers to find neither of the two to be without wit on the one side or without art and learning on the other, while his regret over Shakespeare's flaws leaves the neoclassical canon unthreatened.[3] But it is just this mutually exclusive opposition which Edward Young insists upon, in order to praise Shakespeare as the unlearned original and to denigrate Jonson

2 See Addison's *Spectator* no. 160 and Pope's and Johnson's Prefaces to Shakespeare. My later reference to Young is to "Conjectures on Original Composition."

3 It is also true that, in allowing Shakespeare his own bailiwick, he is not without condescension. Though it sounds generous to decline to judge Shakespeare "by Aristotle's rules" ("like trying a man by the laws of one country, who acted under those of another"), Pope is keeping his own legalistic country secure and un-challenged—and superior to the popular realm (of actors and audiences) granted to Shakespeare.

as the imitative slave of his learning. By the time we get to Johnson's Preface, the either/or becomes absolute; and, by referring to the outrageous comparison by Voltaire, Johnson allows the Addison of *Cato* to take the place usually reserved for Ben Jonson as the learned author who is dwarfed by Shakespeare's genius, thus making the disjunction the more obvious.

By now we have come a long way toward the exaltation of Shakespeare for those characteristics most at odds with the neoclassical ideal. That other country to which Pope consigned him is surely cut off from the safe neoclassical domain securely held under what Pope saw as the laws of Aristotle. It often seemed to have no laws, this wilderness produced by genius—no country for old men, or sane ones either. The youthful Edmund Burke only emphasized the irrationalist nature of this alternative to trim aesthetic propriety when he tried to institutionalize the dualism that distinguished the awesome sublime from the merely beautiful, the unclear vastness from the lucidity of finitude. In his treatise he exaggerated the association of the sublime with the limitless—and hence with our sense of mystery. This association is one we have observed to be growing since Dryden first began putting Shakespeare beyond rational criticism. The eighteenth-century notion of Shakespeare as *lusus naturae*, outside the natural order and thus beyond natural law, accentuates his inaccessibility to the critic's normal measuring instruments. The unmatched and often unexplained (or even confessedly inexplicable) depths of response to him by such critics would seem to be testimony supporting the magical character of his work and, by extrapolation, of all the work of Pegasus-poets who, with "brave disorder," "snatch a grace beyond the reach of art," though such graces are "nameless" and teachable by "no methods."[4] This *je-ne-sais-quoi* mysticism pervades the exemptions accorded Shakespeare's work and, through the accompanying cult of original genius, prepares the way for the idolatry that not only makes him our one exceptional poet but enshrines him as the prototypical poet, the Platonic idea of the poet on whom all other poets must try—however in vain—to pattern themselves, with romantic critics using their instincts to judge them accordingly.[5]

If the critic uses Shakespeare to represent the intrusion of "disorder" into the natural order, and a disorder worthy of the highest praise as furnishing the deepest insight, then he seems to be positing an unaccountable mystery at the heart of the universe, which poets

[4] Pope, *An Essay on Criticism*, lines 141–55.

[5] May I remind the reader that what I mean to offer here is not a thumbnail sketch of directions in the history of Shakespearean criticism so much as the history of Shakespeare's influence on the shape taken by general poetics itself?

like Shakespeare alone can touch. But no matter how "brave," the disorder introduces an element of chaos which imperils any unmodified rational hypothesis that would account for the real or the literary universe.[6] It is this utter polarity, fully developed by the late eighteenth century, between chaos and order or the sublime and the beautiful or the instinctive and the learned—oppositions in nature as in art—that organic theorists like A. W. Schlegel and his adapter-translator Coleridge tried to bridge, to the advantage of Shakespeare.

Their work on Shakespeare—with results they made applicable to poetry and drama generally—was intended in large part to claim, in Coleridge's words, "Shakespeare's Judgment equal to His Genius." What was being denied was that original genius precludes judgment, and vice versa. Quite the contrary: it is in the brilliant display of form-making judgment that genius is to manifest itself. As the argument runs, the neoclassical critic had to associate genius with wild irregularity because his definitions of order and judgment were narrowly circumscribed by mechanical, inflexible, externally imposed rules inherited from earlier poetic practice. Either the poet conformed or he was wild and—unless rescued by genius as in the rare case of Shakespeare—to be rejected. But the disjunctive is overwhelmed if, as with Shakespeare, a more subtle notion of form joined originality to a newly created order. "Are the plays of Shakespeare works of rude and uncultivated genius, in which the splendor of the parts compensates, if aught can compensate, for the barbarous shapelessness and irregularity of the whole?—Or is the form equally admirable with the matter, and the judgment of the great poet, not less deserving our wonder than his genius?" This passage, from Coleridge's "Shakespeare, a Poet Generally" (from the portion headed "Shakespeare's Judgment equal to His Genius"), goes on to claim that Shakespeare's greatness is as much the result of his differences from the ancients as of those elements he shares with them. For while the similarities can arise out of "servile imitation," a "lifeless mechanism," his "free and rival originality" is evidence "of living power."

This is the contrast that leads to the distinction between mechanical and organic form which Coleridge draws in the well-known passage that is little more than a translation from Schlegel. Mechanical form, the indifferent imposition of a universal formula on whatever the materials at hand, is apparently what Coleridge sees as the only kind of form the neoclassical critic could recognize. If Shakespeare did not display form of that kind, then he was put down as being wildly

---

[6] See my essay on just this consequence in Johnson's work: "Fiction, Nature, and Literary Kinds in Johnson's Criticism of Shakespeare," printed as chapter 4, below.

formless. Coleridge is arguing that Shakespeare has a far more profound kind of form, however unrecognized earlier, a form that
"shapes, as it develops, itself from within; and the fulness of its
development is one and the same with the perfection of its outward
form. Such as the life is, such is the form." So Shakespeare is to be seen
as reshaping whatever materials have been given him from outside
until they are forced to grow into the very entity they are forming in
the act of becoming it. Such is the organic interrelationship he creates
between part and whole. And of course the organic doctrine carries
with it a mystique of its own in its attack upon the rationalistic
notion of order as a mechanistic one.

This notion—the transformation of generic, borrowed materials,
by way of a creativity that is at work in both a unique act and a
unique product—marks that variety of recent criticism which draws
much of its spirit from Coleridge. But since this criticism begins in our
time as the so-called New Criticism, it tends to be language-centered,
so that it usually limits the borrowed elements, whose transformation
it must trace, to verbal ones. It is the manipulation of words, their
conversion from the empty and transparent signs they are for most of
us (and were for the poet when he picked them up) into the dense
opacity of symbol, that for this criticism enables Shakespeare to work
his magic. Later modifications by such critics, still being pressed by
Shakespeare, will extend verbal insights (by then seen as inadequate)
back into the realms of genre and dramatic structure, though they will
not deny that the word retains its primary function in their analysis
however it grows into elements with which it has dynamic relations of
conflict and resolution.

It is surely ironic that Shakespeare enters the New-Critical dialogue not only as a minor figure but as anything but a model poet.
Indeed, if any one poet was the model for the shape of verbal criticism
from T. S. Eliot to John Crowe Ransom, Allen Tate, and Cleanth
Brooks, he would be Donne and not Shakespeare. This undisputed
fact of poetic influence on modern theory would appear to make the
opening paragraph of this essay, and my major claim in it, untenable.
Certainly, when Ransom wrote his regrettable essay, "Shakespeare at
Sonnets," his readers would hardly have predicted that—almost four
decades later—one could claim (as I am claiming here) that Shakespeare was both source and model for a verbal criticism further down
the line in the same critical tradition.[7] Since he was using the metaphysical strategy as the universal strategy for poets and had selected

[7] *The World's Body* (New York: Charles Scribner's Sons, 1938), pp. 270–303.

Donne as the exemplary practitioner of that strategy, it was not difficult for Ransom, measuring Shakespeare by this single gauge, to find him failing precisely where Donne succeeded.

Ransom defined the metaphysical strategy as the rigorous logical extension of the selected conceit, carried out by the poet who had "the courage of [his] metaphors." The critic's verbal analysis, then, was to concentrate on the ways in which words carried forward this lean line of metaphorical development. Firmly committed to the antiromanticism that moved the early New Criticism, Ransom was careful to encourage clarity, logic, and denotation in language as an alternative to romantic vagueness, the willingness to indulge connotation and its blurred effects. His devotion to logicality in poetry led him to distrust even New Critics like Empson or Brooks whose cultivation of verbal ambiguity and irony in poetry would make them less inimical to some romantic practices. But, more certainly, it led Ransom to underrate seriously—and to misapprehend—the strategy of Shakespeare's language, forced as he was by his theory to see Shakespeare as trying to do poorly what Donne was to do so well. He observed correctly that Shakespeare did not pursue the single line of logical development which we find in the typical extension of the metaphysical conceit, that in Shakespeare there are detours and false starts and multiple paths and surprises. But, of course, if the logical line is weak, the words which—from Ransom's point of view—seem to weaken it may be doing so in order to create a heretofore hidden strength in themselves.[8] So the critic's problem is to determine and account for what it is that Shakespeare is doing, and doing inimitably well.

In an essay responding to Ransom's, Arthur Mizener undertook just this task, thus setting in motion a verbal analysis of Shakespeare's sonnets that focused on a strategy different from the metaphysical and yet brilliantly effective.[9] After Mizener's essay, instead of this criticism shaping Shakespeare, it would come to be shaped by him. It no longer had to reduce Shakespeare to its method; rather it could claim a method which, derived from his works themselves, not only could account for them but—using them as its supreme examples—could account for many other works as well. This was still to indulge in

[8] One might well argue that this latter possibility is more in accord with the Coleridgean notion of organic development within the poem, while Ransom's view of the metaphysical strategy, limited as it is to the logical argument within the conceit, would appear to Coleridge as a rather mechanical, universal, externally applied criterion, one which did not submit the poem wholly to the control of the developing elements themselves.

[9] "The Structure of Figurative Language in Shakespeare's *Sonnets*," *Southern Review* 5 (1940): 730–47.

methodological imperialism (the application of a method beyond its native grounds, the works that originally nourished it), but Shakespeare was now claimed as its author and beneficiary.

Mizener argues that, just as Ransom charged, Shakespeare's language in a sonnet is not totally responsive to the narrow demands of an extended conceit, but that its seeming waywardness has a method of its own. Using as his example Sonnet 124 ("If my dear love were but the child of state"), he shows the many levels on which the poem's key words operate, from private to public life and the great world, and from the merely political to the cosmic realm. He finds this broad range of simultaneous meanings spreading from the first line, with that endlessly polysemous word *state*. Its echoes in subsequent words and phrases which also have multiple possibilities persuade him that the reader is to press ahead on all levels, eliminating none of the meanings, indeed rather exploiting all of them at once. Unlike the logical delineations of the metaphysical conceit whose effect may amaze us with its farfetched lucidity but whose lucidity domesticates that amazement, the effect here is one of "soft focus," each of the meanings crowding in with the others without being sufficiently developed to prevent us from holding the others simultaneously with it. Mizener's phrase "soft focus" emphasizes a lack of developed precision in the individual images—almost, indeed, as if they formed a group of simultaneous associations. His own description suggests as much: the meanings in the sonnet are "very like the pattern of the mind when it contemplates, with full attention but for no immediately practical purpose, an object in nature." The pattern "is built for all the kinds of relations known to the mind," so that the figurative language "approaches, in its own verbal terms, the richness, the density, the logical incompleteness of the mind."

My own feeling is that, while many of Mizener's observations about words and lines are striking and important because they force us to reorient ourselves as we address the language of the sonnets, he reveals the weakness which Ransom would expect of Shakespeare and his defenders: that of resorting to romantic vagueness as the characteristic of Shakespeare's strategy which makes it worth justifying. Mizener's notion of "soft focus" seeks to justify Shakespeare's use of companion elements which, if presented clearly, might be mutually incompatible; it is thus a defense of imprecision that suggests the blurred diction of the romantic who could not totally make up his mind about what he meant. What rather is the case and what, indeed, we see, despite Mizener, to be the case even in his most striking observations, is that in Shakespeare the effect of an extravagant structure of puns is anything but imprecise.

I have written a much later essay which also takes off from Ransom's and from the dichotomy between the metaphysical and the Shakespearean strategy of wit.[10] In that essay, although many of my observations may seem similar in intention to Mizener's, I use them to support a claim to a precision of multiple meaning through Shakespeare's remarkable choice of just the word to contain that multiplicity. Although I see his strategy as an alternative to the metaphysical, I would not concede any more wit to the metaphysical than to his. The issue between them, I argue, is whether the wit is apparent, like the metaphysical, or whether it is hidden behind a disguise of innocence, as often in Shakespeare, where—as Ransom charges—little more than random association seems to prevail. But, in contrast to Mizener, I insist that Shakespeare's poems neither should be nor are like the incompleteness and randomness of the contemplating mind, though they may initially fool us with the illusion of such a resemblance. So I see "the innocent insinuations of wit" resulting from devices like "association as dialectic" and "pun as argument." All that seems no more than casual turns out, through the expanding possibilities of the right word or phrase, to have been inevitable.

Mizener may have freed this critical tradition for a verbal criticism modeled on Shakespeare and having its source in him, but just as Coleridge had rescued Shakespeare from the charge of formlessness by redefining form, it was now necessary to redefine precision and artfulness in order to find their sources outside the obvious precision and artfulness of metaphysical wit. The focus must be seen as sharp rather than "soft," even as a word's meanings multiply. In dealing with Sonnet 64 ("When I have seen by Time's fell hand defaced"), I treated that same polysemous word *state* (in the key unifying phrase, "interchange of state," line 9), but in a way that emphasized that sharpness:

> As if to prove the claim that the human political state is a microcosmic reflection of the universal state under time, the antagonists of the second quatrain, the ocean and the shore, are rendered totally in human terms, as they act in accordance with political motives. . . . All the realms of "state" have been identified and reduced to the extreme consequences of its narrowest meaning, that of human politics. The word "state," despite its range of meanings, from narrow to broad, from politics to the general condition of being (or rather of becoming), is shown to be a single reductive

10 "The Innocent Insinuations of Wit: The Strategy of Language in Shakespeare's *Sonnets," The Play and Place of Criticism* (Baltimore: Johns Hopkins Press, 1967), pp. 19–36.

entity that can contain and unite them all even within its narrowest confines. For these confines can be extended unlimitedly without losing their more precise limitations.[11]

This view sees the word as sending forth several diverse meanings (and yet not so diverse after all) and yet as collapsing them into itself as their single containing element. It is a view which was first stated systematically for these critics in Sigurd Burckhardt's essay, "The Poet as Fool and Priest," an essay which uses a Shakespearean sonnet as the source and the model of its theory. Burckhardt describes this containing and unifying element in the word as its "corporeality." The mere sensuous existence of the word, this constellation of sounds and meanings, allows it to take on a substance in which these elements are fused. The word can be forced by the poet to contain within itself a world of elements otherwise incompatible with each other. Hence, Burckhardt argues, verbal ambiguity is at the heart of poetic possibility not because a word can have many meanings (as Empson would have it), but because "many meanings can have *one word.*" "Ambiguity, then, becomes a test case for the poet; insofar as he can vanquish it—not by splitting the word, but by fusing its meanings— he has succeeded in making language into a true medium."[12] That is to say, it is made a medium like the physical realities of the plastic arts instead of the transparent, referential sign, without substance, which words are until the poet goes to work on them. The pun is the ideal example of how he forces the word to take on "corporeality," then, in that it is a single identity which, through a phonetic coincidence, overwhelms other discrete entities and, by enfolding them within itself, makes them an inevitable part of one another. The casual etymological accidents that produce a pun are forced by the poet to take on the teleological pattern of necessity—surface takes on substance—but only *in* this word. Other phonetic and metaphorical

---

[11] Ibid., pp. 25–26. Or see my comments on "state" as it functions in Sonnet 124 (in contrast to Mizener's) in *A Window to Criticism,* p. 141. It is an earlier statement, but made in the same spirit: "The word 'state' permits us to join the narrowest political notions in the poem to the broadest sense of worldly life as the politic enterprise: state as majesty and as political entity, state as rank or status, state as condition of being. . . . In effect, Shakespeare is demonstrating the sweep of the world's semantic history. He proves the justness of his political metaphor by allowing his language to establish the essential oneness of the several political levels of living. Once again the metaphor is earned totally by moving from similarity to substantive identity: the human condition *is* the political condition."

[12] "The Poet as Fool and Priest," *ELH* 23 (1956): 279–98; reprinted in *Shakespearean Meanings* (Princeton: Princeton University Press, 1968), pp. 22–46. The quotations appear in the book on pp. 32 and 33.

elements of words are shown by Burckhardt to take on similarly substantive, corporeal functions, in defiance of the way language is supposed to function normally. No wonder the poem is untranslatable into other words than itself.

For Burckhardt, corporeality obviously serves as another term for incarnation, the making of the word into flesh, in this case the sensory medium becoming physical container of otherwise incompatible worlds, unifying them because the word is a unit and they are *in it*. The overwhelming of discrete entities by way of verbal aggrandizement is a violation of verbal property and propriety, a subversion of the way language is to work. As such, and as the word made flesh, this principle of verbal teleology is the aesthetic equivalent of "miracle," though one licensed by what Shakespeare's strategy of language has revealed to us. In *A Window to Criticism* I freely call this operation of words "miraculous," borrowing the notion—ironically—from Ransom, who was hardly intending to refer to Shakespeare when he used "miraculism" to describe the remarkable workings of the metaphysical conceit.[13] He was trying to describe the way in which words as sensory and metaphorical elements overcome the limitations of words as concepts by achieving an identity in the poem that transforms the differential nature of words and concepts. And, as we have seen with other claims of Ransom, what was intended as favorable description of the metaphysicals (even if to the detriment of Shakespeare) was extended by others to Shakespeare, who was then shown to be preeminently deserving of the characterization. When George Steiner (whom one would think of as a critic of a very different sort) sought, in a quadricentennial essay, to account for Shakespeare's special magic, he had to point —in much the same spirit and even a similar language—to Shakespeare's power to create one "obvious miracle" after another.[14] "More than any other human intellect of which we have adequate record, Shakespeare used language in a condition of total possibility. . . . To Shakespeare, more than to any other poet, the individual word was a nucleus surrounded by a field of complex energies." He goes on to speak of how "a word will shade, by pun or suggestion of sound, into an area of new definitions," or to speak of words that "derive their power to rouse and control our attention from the fact that Shakespeare has made explicit the buried strength of their etymologies."

These critics, with their several ways of claiming a secular miracle —a metaphorical equivalent of the religious one—in Shakespeare's

13 "Poetry: A Note in Ontology," *The World's Body*, pp. 139–40.

14 "Why, Man, He Doth Bestride the Narrow World like a Colossus," *New York Times Book Review*, April 19, 1964, pp. 4–6, 43.

handling of his language, are making more explicit the tendency we have noted, in its varying degrees, since Dryden to resort to irrational-ist and magical terminology in dealing with Shakespeare's hold on us. They assume normal habits of semantics and logic to operate in our language, and (Ransom to the contrary notwithstanding) see Shake-speare as forcing upon language an illogic that opens for us, and yet controls, an untold pattern of semantic possibilities. Echoing earlier critics, modern critics since Mizener see Shakespeare as projecting a verbal power that makes mystics of us all. Rather than demythologiz-ing this idolatry of the Shakespearean word, they have reified it into a general critical system—a rare and daring enough undertaking in these demythologizing days.

But we must see this resort to miracle in its recent forms as a significantly qualified one. I qualified it earlier by speaking of "the aesthetic equivalent of miracle," by which I meant that it was con-fined to appearance only—as an illusion. Thus the claim to miracle is accompanied by considerable skepticism about the power of any language—even Shakespeare's—to be more than illusively substantive. His magic arises from his power to impose this illusion upon us while his words are doing their work, but of course such magic confesses its own limitations by accepting the aesthetic context within which it assumes those powers. Shakespeare himself, even while he displays his verbal mastery, uses that mastery to express his doubts about the ultimate power of words. His language everywhere reveals its aware-ness of the incapacity of words to contain their objects—its awareness of their emptiness. Yet, as Shakespeare maneuvers them, words find their unique power in the web they weave in awareness of this inca-pacity. They play violently and arrogantly with the normal workings of language, achieving a structure of their own that defies the lack to which they testify. Thus does verbal power derive from self-conscious verbal skepticism.

It is obvious, from my comments on recent word-centered criticism, that the sonnets have played a central role in its development. Whether in Mizener's, in Burckhardt's, or in my own work, these poems permitted a concentration on purely verbal and figurative mat-ters without the additional and complicating variables introduced in his dramatic poetry.[15] When Burckhardt moved to the plays in the balance of *Shakespearean Meanings*, he did so largely by way of the

[15] According this central role to the sonnets and to the words in them may seem especially revolutionary when we think of how commonplace it was for eighteenth-century critics to reject Shakespeare's language, finding unique value in him despite what they saw as either precious or clumsy, especially in the sonnets.

theoretical lessons learned in that key early essay which was enmeshed in his analysis of Sonnet 116 ("Let me not to the marriage of true minds"). Indeed, earlier New-Critical analysis of the plays had already established the practice of reading them more as poems than as dramas for the theater, so that once the words and figures were sufficiently probed, the problems of dramatic as well as poetic meanings were resolved. The procedures were similar to those we have been observing, more in keeping with the permissive attitude of Mizener than the no-nonsense attitude of Ransom. Thus the treatment of *Macbeth* by Cleanth Brooks, like the treatment of *1 Henry IV* by Brooks and Robert Heilman, is essentially that of a lengthy poem powered by Shakespearean verbal and metaphorical wit, with the dramatic elements falling into place within the poetic structure.[16] Indeed, as Brooks is establishing his method at the outset of *The Well Wrought Urn*, he calls upon his reading of *The Phoenix and Turtle* to support a commitment to a use of language that, paradoxically, proclaims the destruction of reason in order to affirm the uniqueness of its own order. These are the claims—as this is the primacy of lyric over dramatic, of lyric as absorbing the dramatic—which we have observed in his recent fellow-critics.

So this theory, tailor-made for poetry, was also—as theory so often had been—tailor-made for Shakespeare, though in this case for the Shakespeare of the poems or of the poetry in the plays, if not the plays as poems. The theory is committed to the power of verbal structure that undermines the capacity of words in order to create the possibility of its own equivocal existence. Hence, in the work of most of these writers we find an accompanying critical theme, similar to what we have just seen Brooks claim, about the subversion of reason by the poem—as by love—so that the poem, like love, can create its own more-than-logical order. Such an accompanying theme would seem inevitable, given the nature of the theory. It is the metapoetic theme: that each poem must finally turn out to have been about the possibility of its own verbal creation. In effect, then, each poem is an implicit work of poetics as well as whatever else it explicitly may be. Such a development, we should note, is consistent with the historical claim with which I began: that, rather than being a history of Shakespearean criticism, the last three centuries of English criticism have been a series of literary theories developed in large part in response to

16 In Cleanth Brooks, *The Well Wrought Urn* (New York: Reynal & Hitchcock, 1947) and Cleanth Brooks and Robert B. Heilman, eds., *Understanding Drama* (New York: Henry Holt, 1945).

Shakespearean texts which have been seen as licensing certain theoretical directions. So his poems, dramatic and otherwise, have long been permitted to function in the realm of poetics.

The metapoetic theme has permitted recent critics to adapt the principles of word-centered analysis to other centers of critical interest that are less reductive and more respectful of the other-than-verbal elements in the plays. I see no more promising example of such expansion of critical focus than in the work of the Renaissance comparatist, Rosalie Colie, who in the years preceding her death had turned increasingly to Shakespeare and had permitted her methods to be increasingly influenced by what she found in him and in those who have treated him in ways I have been describing here.[17] She modified the study of his language with the study of the genres and *topoi* of the Renaissance and the earlier periods that influenced their evolution. What made this study excitingly productive—and unique—was the way she showed the literary work to be the product of the mixing and mastering of these genres and *topoi*, showed it in the act of producing itself as a transformation of its informing elements, becoming at once a repository and a consummation of the literary past that nourished it. The problem of understanding the work becomes a reflection of the problem of the work finding itself in its elements, making itself out of those elements. Here is the metapoetic theme once more, though it is now functioning to trace the poet's remaking of the commonplace elements of genre and *topos* and not just his remaking of the commonplace words which have occupied our other critics.

We should note also the criticism of James Calderwood as one which moves beyond purely verbal elements to dramatic ones, turning metapoetry into metadrama in order to preserve Shakespeare's theatrical along with his poetic brilliance.[18] Calderwood puts the word

---

[17] In her encyclopedic work on Renaissance paradox, *Paradoxia Epidemica* (Princeton: Princeton University Press, 1966), she found in Shakespeare's work the moving force for several of her chapters (esp. chaps. 7, 12, and 15), and her concern with paradox naturally led her to mix verbal matters with ideational ones. Besides several other later essays on Shakespeare, the final work she saw through to completion was the lengthy study *Shakespeare's Living Art* (Princeton: Princeton University Press, 1974). In addition there was the series of lectures, assembled for publication posthumously—*The Resources of Kind: Genre-Theory in the Renaissance*, ed. Barbara Lewalski (Berkeley and Los Angeles: University of California Press, 1973)—in which she culminates her argument by using as model her special favorite, *King Lear*, to which she refers as "an ultimate."

[18] *Shakespearean Metadrama: The Argument of the Play in* Titus Andronicus, Love's Labour's Lost, Romeo and Juliet, A Midsummer Night's Dream, *and* Richard II (Minneapolis: University of Minnesota Press, 1971). He presses this method further in *Metadrama in Shakespeare's Henriad*: Richard II *to* Henry V (Berkeley and Los Angeles: University of California Press, 1979).

as spoken onstage into a dynamic relation to the action onstage, seeing the two as both partners and antagonists through which the Shakespearean drama works to solve the problem of its reality. We may feel the presence of Burckhardt's method at the starting point of Calderwood's work, but he has advanced the method by incorporating nonverbal elements as he makes the metapoem into drama. With recent work like Colie's and Calderwood's, we have the right to look for continuing developments in this line of criticism as, making use of its word-centered heritage, it yet escapes the limitations from which a devotion to the lyrics can suffer when applied to drama.[19]

Still, whatever we may say in defense of the continuing energies being displayed by this kind of criticism or in defense of its broadening directions, we must admit it to be partial and unbalanced—like all criticism. But any criticism so dominated by the experiencing of Shakespeare—and by the need to rationalize that incomparable experience—is perhaps fated to be especially unbalanced. We have noted that Burckhardt's "The Poet as Fool and Priest" found its way into a volume on Shakespeare's plays, and that my own recent contribution to modern poetics is joined to, and grows out of, my study of Shakespeare's sonnets. There seems to be a hidden assumption in such critical works that a theory of poetry must begin by being adequate to Shakespeare, if it is to be adequate at all. I have been suggesting some such assumption as haunting the long, unbalanced succession of the best English critics since Dryden, with George Steiner's tribute to Shakespeare's verbal power perhaps the epigraph to this historical consensus.

This is to make Shakespeare the test of a literary theory, to define and measure poetry by its most splendid and incomparable examples —as was sometimes regretted, alas, when the measuring instruments were applied to lesser poets. But so be it. I began this essay, after all, by calling it a study of bardolatry in its most recent form. So how can Shakespeare not be treated as the model poet? And it should do more good than harm: in an anti-verbal day Shakespearean criticism of this sort can give the embattled humanist new courage. I said earlier that idolatry must be either demythologized or reified into a critical system, and that the new bardolaters had done the latter. When we hear all around us of the need to "decenter" discourse, the need to decenter the word's sense of the world, it is heartening to be instructed in

19 This promise of further development is justified by other recent work in this line. See, just as a single example, Marjorie B. Garber, *Dream in Shakespeare: From Metaphor to Metamorphosis* (New Haven: Yale University Press, 1974). The subtitle alone would delight most of the critics I have been treating.

finding Shakespeare's capacious verbal center as the center of order. Perhaps recent demythologizing critics have suffered from not having Shakespeare to influence *their* theory. When we hear such critics speak of the absence and the emptiness of language, surely the claim that the word can be made utterly present—a claim supported by a poet whose works everywhere invite reverence for the potentiality locked in language—must constitute one of the few healthy signs for the future of criticism.

4

Fiction, Nature, and Literary Kinds
in Johnson's Criticism of Shakespeare

THE DEDICATED eighteenth-century scholar must be very wary of those (like me, I confess) who peer back into his period with a sensibility tuned to, or formed by, all that comes from the other side of the Kantian revolution. And so the eighteenth-century scholar normally *is*, with a proper sense of his professionalism and of his territorial rights. He must warn the interloper, who may be anxious to reinterpret major figures or documents, of the dangerous likelihood that the post-Kantian mind may assimilate pre-Kantian attitudes only by transforming and distorting them. Yet, despite such dangers and the warnings that accompany them, I shall proceed to exercise just such freedom—though I hope not altogether carelessly—on some critical notions of Samuel Johnson, in the hope that there are corresponding advantages for the period specialist to have this outsider's view, despite its occasional perversions, thrust upon him. I should like to study closely certain of Johnson's pronouncements with the (almost unscholarly) naiveté of open encounter, even as I admit that such readings are affected by the alien perspective of their source.

This paper was originally delivered at the Eighteenth-Century Studies Conference of the University of California, held 31 October–1 November 1969, at the Clark Library.

Let us examine three of Dr. Johnson's central claims, all made in his "Preface to Shakespeare" (1765), together with the several, sometimes rather strangely instructive ways they tend to disagree with one another. First, the early axiom: "Nothing can please many, and please long, but just representations of general nature."[1] Here is an august contention of more than a century and a half, the "just representations" echoing the French seventeenth century, as reflected in the conservative half of Dryden's "Essay of Dramatic Poesy," and the entire notion accounting for "the great style" called for by Johnson's friend, Sir Joshua Reynolds, in his *Discourses*.

We can note in the statement that curious juxtaposition of the rationalist's assumptions of a general nature with the empiricist's concern with audience reaction (the notion of pleasing many and pleasing long). Thus, although there is no questioning of the dogmatic belief in the objective existence of discoverable universals, there is also the insistence that the sanction for these universals comes, not from a priori deductions from the nature of things, but from the combined judgments of individual experiences.[2] The justification of the neoclassical canon arises, then, "not from any credulous confidence in the superior wisdom of past ages, or gloomy persuasion of the degeneracy of mankind," but from a Hume-like confidence in the collective observations of common sense. Indeed, like the David Hume with whom he would least like to be associated, Johnson trusted that the differences among enough idiosyncratic judgments of assorted kinds (many and long: enough judgments spread over enough time) would resolve themselves, for a distanced observer, into universal wisdom, however empirically derived. Given sufficient subjects sufficiently varied, their many partial perspectives would cancel one another out, unpeeling the layers of idiosyncrasy until the core of their common humanity stood revealed as their common-sense judgment. This explains why the century is "the term commonly fixed as the test of literary merit. Whatever advantages [the poet] might once derive from personal allusions, local customs, or temporary opinions, have for many years been lost." And Shakespeare, unable to rely on "effects of favour and competition," "his friendships and his enmities," on factions or on the indulgence of vanity or gratification of malignity,

---

[1] "Preface to Shakespeare," in Johnson, *Selected Prose and Poetry*, ed. Bertrand H. Bronson (New York: Rinehart & Co., 1952), p. 241. Other citations from this volume follow quotations in the text.

[2] At least, for Johnson, this holds for judgments of works "of which the excellence is not absolute and definite, but gradual and comparative; to works not raised upon principles demonstrative and scientific, but appealing wholly to observation and experience" (p. 239).

can appeal only to the audience's "desire of pleasure" and can win their praise "only as pleasure is obtained; yet, thus unassisted by interest or passion, [his works] have past through variations of taste and changes of manners, and, as they devolved from one generation to another, have received new honours at every transmission."

In the mirror-universe of universals, like recognizes like, so that the universal subject reflects the universal object. The general nature outside us, then, is the natural object of the general human nature in us which responds to it. And, as is true even of so rigorous an empiricist as Hume, there is for Johnson no questioning of the rationalist assumption that is smuggled in, the assumption that there surely *is*, beneath the infinite variety of individuated nature and of the individual human responses to it, a general nature and a general core of human nature. As the particulars of nature can be shed to reveal the underlying universal that sustains them, so our particular responses can shed what is partial about them to reveal the response of a common humanity. It is this response, of course, that the critic, as disinterested observer, is to achieve; and that, with the aid of more than a century of varied responses, he is with older writers enabled to achieve. He is, in effect, to check his idiosyncrasies together with his overcoat when he enters the museum of literature, thus attaining the view of common humanity, although with recent writers this is more difficult since we do not yet have enough variety of responses for the necessary canceling out of partialities to have occurred. The empirical consequences of the School of Taste, then, have made themselves felt even though they serve only to bolster the governing claims of rationalistic universalism, whose objective status is not shaken. The advent of epistemology has not, after all, chased the dogmatic certainty of metaphysics from the scene. But such certainty now must depend upon experiential verification if we are to feel convinced. So a good deal *has* been given away, even if the kind of art justified by our responses is the same as that dogmatically insisted upon from the nature of things.

But whatever their sanction, whether from without or within, whether objective or commonly subjective, the universals themselves continue to be affirmed, continue to be sought after as both the metaphysical and the aesthetic object of art. Thus Johnson's often cited praise of Shakespeare as "the poet of nature," with nature at once defined in universal terms. Instead of characters "modified by the customs of particular places" or "by the peculiarities of studies or professions" or "by the accidents of transient fashions or temporary opinions," Shakespeare's "are the genuine progeny of common humanity, such as the world will always supply, and observation will always find." Not particularities, peculiarities, or accidents, but the universality of common humanity. Instead of the individual, Shakespeare gives us the species.

Such characters "act and speak by the influence of those general passions and principles by which all minds are agitated, and the whole system of life is continued in motion." This notion of the poet providing a "system of life" in accordance with general principles would seem to require him to provide us with a tight, rationally justifiable series of causal relationships between motive and action. Hence Johnson can claim favorably, a bit later in the essay, that "Shakespeare always makes nature predominant over accident." He excuses Shakespeare's carelessness with "distinctions superinduced and adventitious" ("His story requires Romans or Kings, but he thinks only on men") by giving the poet the right to overlook "the causal distinction of country and condition." The poet, then, in service of the universal system, rather than the particular aberration, is to neglect the *casual* for the *causal*. (And I mean to dwell on this strangely anagrammatic and contradictory pair of words.)

It is just two brief paragraphs later that Johnson, defending Shakespeare's mingling of tragic and comic as true to life, refers to our common experience (hence nature?) as a "chaos of mingled purposes and casualties." And it is just this chaos of casualties which he praises Shakespeare, his poet of nature, for imitating. But how radically the notion of nature as his object of imitation has shifted! Now the causal has been forsaken for the casual. Far from being overlooked, the casual is, however maddening, to be cherished as all there is. Here, then, is Johnson's second claim which I wish to consider—especially in its apparent contradiction of the first.

True, Johnson is now addressing a different issue; but the implied consequences of his argument here reverberate harshly against his earlier claims about universals. Johnson's claim here is that the dramatic categories of tragedy and comedy are arbitrary and hence artificial impositions upon the undifferentiated materials of life which the poet must imitate. Shakespeare's only obligation was to these materials, so that it is dully conventional of us to complain of his failure to pursue bookish distinctions among genres. But Johnson carries his argument with more vigor and extremity than is required, and its theoretical consequences—provided we take them seriously—will persist to haunt his more orthodox claims.

He speaks of the world Shakespeare was imitating as "the real state of sublunary nature," a disorderly, purposeless mass of particulars which are surely resistant to the neat, man-made, critic-made categories of tragedy and comedy. Johnson may strike us almost like an anti-Frye critic of today speaking of "sublunary" experiential realities, in opposition to universal lunar inventions, as the proper subject of poetry. However it may be up there in the supernal world or the world of human invention—the lunar sphere—down here we must put up with

> the real state of sublunary nature, which partakes of good and evil, joy and sorrow, mingled with endless variety of proportion and innumerable modes of combination; and expressing the course of the world, in which the loss of one is the gain of another; in which, at the same time, the reveller is hasting to his wine, and the mourner burying his friend; in which the malignity of one is sometimes defeated by the frolick of another; and many mischiefs and many benefits are done and hindered without design. (p. 245)

Precisely—without design.[3] What else could we expect of a world described as a "chaos of mingled purposes and casualties"? No wonder, then, that Johnson speaks of "endless variety." In this mood he continually calls for endless variety or diversity, apparently forgetting about the unity which is the central quality of the causally controlled system he called for earlier. A world "without design," a chaos in which all is casual, is obviously resistant to any attempt to impose a causal system which must rest on universal models of possible relations among its seeming particulars (only *seeming* particulars because in such a system there are no true particulars insisting on their particularity). But in the chaos of casualties, without design, there can be only the resistant particulars, the "endless variety" and "innumerable modes" precluding the gathering together of particulars into universals that could constitute a system. The poet who before was praised for overlooking the casual for the essential is now praised for cultivating the casual since there is no essential.

We can now consider in a rather changed light Johnson's earlier pleasure with Shakespeare's naturalness, a naturalness so great "that it seems scarcely to claim the merit of fiction" (p. 242). Indeed, there would seem to be a greater merit in Shakespeare's resistance to fiction, in the directness of his mingling with the unfictional stuff of experience. The word "merit" is applied to fiction almost ironically, the "merit of fiction" turning out to be merely meretricious. Fiction is

---

3 Robert C. Elliott has properly pointed out that my argument seems to require that "without design" refers to cosmic purposelessness when the context of Johnson's passage limits the phrase to the betrayals of private human intention. In defense I would claim only that Johnson's usage—trapped as it is in a passage that emphasizes chaos and the casual—can be seen to treat the futility of human purpose as a microcosmic reflection of the gap between cause and effect that precludes order in our entire "sublunary nature."

thus mere artifice mediating unnecessarily between the poet and reality. Indeed, Johnson can treat fiction with downright contempt. Witness his pronouncement in "Milton," where he complains of the unnaturalness and hence the insincerity of Milton's lament in *Lycidas* as demonstrated by his dependence on mythological allusions: "Where there is leisure for fiction there is little grief." For Johnson, mythology is a likely dress for fiction, and his antagonism to the stereotyped artificialities of the one is key to his rejection of the other. We can recall his preference for Dryden's "Alexander's Feast" over Pope's attempt at an "Ode for St. Cecilia's Day" largely on the ground that the one is derived from history and the other from mythology: "history will always take stronger hold of the attention than fable."[4] This is to say, better fact than fiction as the subject of poetry. And this too is pretty much what he does say when he expresses his pleasure over the subject of "Eloisa to Abelard" because the story is drawn from "undisputed history" (and "The heart naturally loves truth").[5]

The basic error, the one he attributes to Milton, is bookishness, the seeing of nature—in the words he quotes from Dryden—"through the spectacles of books." This is why, for Johnson, Milton's "images and descriptions of the scenes and operations of Nature do not seem to be always copied from original form, nor to have the freshness, raciness, and energy of immediate observation."[6] And it is why Shakespeare is so ideally the poet of nature. Refusing to allow "the books of one age [to] gain such authority, as to stand in the place of nature to another . . . Shakespeare, whether life or nature be his subject, shews plainly, that he has seen with his own eyes" (p. 266). This echoes Johnson's earlier claim that Shakespeare "caught his ideas from the living world, and exhibited only what he saw before him" (p. 243).[7] Here is a preview of the spirit of Wordsworth, and of his words that

---

[4] In "The Life of Pope," *Selected Prose and Poetry*, p. 389.

[5] Ibid., p. 395.

[6] In "Milton," *Selected Prose and Poetry*, p. 460.

[7] Yet I must confess that Pope himself earlier makes a similar point, and makes it similarly, in *his* "Preface to Shakespeare" (1725):

> His *characters* are so much Nature herself, that 'tis a sort of injury to call them by so distant a name as copies of her. Those of other poets have a constant resemblance, which shows that they received them from one another, and were but multipliers of the same image; each picture like a mock-rainbow is but the reflection of a reflection. But every single character in Shakespeare is as much an individual, as those in life itself. . . .

How Shakespeare forces his critic to discover his liberality!

speak of keeping his eye on the object. It is a similar response to a similar rejection of artifice as mediator.[8]

In Johnson it can become a rejection of the neatness of universalizing systems too. His famous comparison between the small proprieties of Addison's *Cato* and the magnificent monstrosities of Shakespeare ("Addison speaks the language of poets, and Shakespeare, of men") leads him to denigrate, in *Cato*, the "splendid exhibition of artificial and fictitious manners" (another contemptuous treatment of the sense of fiction). The metaphor by which his comparison proceeds is positively Gothic and reminds us of Johnson's young friend Edmund Burke on the sublime.

> The work of a correct and regular writer is a garden accurately formed and diligently planted, varied with shades, and scented with flowers; the composition of Shakespeare is a forest, in which oaks extend their branches, and pines tower in the air, interspersed sometimes with weeds and brambles, and sometimes giving shelter to myrtles and to roses; filling the eye with awful pomp, and gratifying the mind with endless diversity. Other poets display cabinets of precious rarities, minutely finished, wrought into shape, and polished into brightness. Shakespeare opens a mine which contains gold and diamonds in unexhaustible plenty, though clouded by incrustations, debased by impurities, and mingled with a mass of meaner minerals. (p. 261)

Although the sense of the passage is common in the century and some of the language is reminiscent of a critic as early as Addison himself,[9] we have seen enough of the theoretical context in Johnson out of which this passage emerges to be persuaded of its profoundly nominalistic tendencies. In its heterodoxy the passage rejects the sense of universal order, emphasizing—along with the "endless diversity" of Shakespeare's forest—the equal role and equal necessity of the weeds

8 Perhaps even more obviously Wordsworthian is Johnson's praise for Shakespeare's language, which "is pursued with so much ease and simplicity" that it seems "to have been gleaned by diligent selection out of common conversation and common occurrences." This is consistent with Johnson's later (also Wordsworthian) definition of an ideal style in a nation's language as that which is "to be sought in the common intercourse of life, among those who speak only to be understood, without ambition of elegance." On these grounds and others, Johnson's criticism of Milton as artificial and bookish seems preparatory to Wordsworth's criticism of Thomas Gray.

9 See *Spectator* 160: "The genius in both these classes of authors may be equally great, but shows itself after a different manner. In the first it is like a rich soil in a happy climate, that produces a whole wilderness of noble plants rising in a thousand beautiful landscapes without any certain order or regularity. In the other it is the same rich soil under the same happy climate, that has been laid out in walks and parterres, and cut into shape and beauty by the skill of the gardener."

and brambles with the myrtles and roses, of the impurities and meaner minerals with the gold and diamonds. Here is the metaphorical equivalent of the "chaos of mingled purposes and casualties" in which "many mischiefs and many benefits are done and hindered without design." It is the revelation of such uncontrolled diversity which the limiting conventions of fiction—all that which is of art, artificial—are designed to inhibit. And Johnson's occasional addiction to a radical naturalism leads him to reject such inhibitions of history's unrestrained dedication to the casual.

Just about all definitions of poetry since Aristotle had rested on a distinction between poetry and history (as empirical reality), between the "ought" and the "is" or "was," the causal and the casual; yet Johnson at times blandly takes on history's casual truths as the poet's. That he is running afoul of the Aristotelian tradition of poetry-as-making as well as the neo-Platonic tradition of the poetic fable as mask for the true and the good seems not to disturb Johnson in these passages—perhaps because he is so firmly committed to just such notions in his own more orthodox passages elsewhere. For the Platonist, of course, experiential reality (Sir Philip Sidney's "brazen" world) is just not good enough—which is why the poet creates the fable, the fiction (to return to that key word), that invokes the "golden" world. This is consistent with the formula of the conservative Scaliger that calls upon the poet "to imitate the Truth by fiction." This is Truth with a capital "T" and to serve it is the highest function poetry can hope for. But history's truth (or rather lower-case truths, endlessly multiplied and related) are a far lesser sort, though they seem to be all that concern Johnson in these passages.

Yet when Johnson complains about Shakespeare's failure to write with a moral purpose because he is "so much more careful to please than to instruct," he seems to be complaining precisely about what he has been praising Shakespeare for doing. For the moral order he now wishes to see operating in the plays could operate only if the casual, disorderly realities were forsaken for a rational, universal system of possible relations. Fact would have to be forsaken for a fiction in the service of the higher Truth. Nevertheless Johnson, apparently reverting to the universalism we found in him at the start, charges that Shakespeare "makes no just distribution of good or evil, nor is always careful to shew in the virtuous a disapprobation of the wicked; he carries his persons indifferently through right and wrong, and at the close dismisses them without further care, and leaves their examples to operate by chance" (p. 249). How different a sort of universe and how different a function for poetry this call for poetic justice assumes, if we recall his description of "the real state of sublunary nature" of only a few pages back. Johnson can say here, rather stiffly, "It is always a writer's duty to make the world better, and justice is a virtue independent on time or place," and with these words returns us to the confident universalism we just saw him challenging so profoundly. But in his "Milton" Johnson gives his own powerful answer to the moralism of this passage, an answer far more in keeping with the tone we have been developing in the "Preface." "Dryden, petulantly and indecently, denies the heroism of Adam because he was overcome; but there is no reason why the hero should not be unfortunate except established practice, since success and virtue do not go necessarily together" ("Milton," p. 458). "Except established practice": here poetic justice is reduced from the imperious demands of the moral universal to the conventions, the fictions, of earlier books which threaten to take the place of nature. Success and virtue not going together is here claimed to be the way of the experiential world which the poet may well imitate, and with no obligation—it would follow—to make a "just distribution of good or evil" such as Johnson demanded of Shakespeare.[10]

The reduction of moral universal to fictional convention returns us to what is theoretically crucial about Johnson's defense of Shakespeare's violation of the purity of genres, his collapsing of tragedy and comedy. Actual human experience is out there in all its chaotic, casual contingency, beckoning the poet to follow it without mediation; and the conventions of art threaten, by their arbitrary habit of dividing and limiting, to inhibit the poet from capturing the endless variety or diversity of life. Yet the only justification for the genres appears to be limited capacities of narrower poetic sensibilities to pursue more than one sort of experience.

> Out of this chaos of mingled purposes and casualties the ancient poets, according to the laws which custom had prescribed, selected some the crimes of men, and some their absurdities; some the momentous vicissitudes of life, and some the lighter occurrences; some the terrours of distress, and some the gayeties of prosperity. Thus rose the two modes of imitation, known by the names of *tragedy* and *comedy* . . . considered as so little allied, that I do not recollect among the *Greeks* or *Romans* a single writer who attempted both. (p. 245)

---

[10] Johnson again takes the more moralistic position, rejecting the mixed virtues and vices of real experience for their pure forms, in his earlier treatment of fiction in *Rambler* No. 4. I discuss that work and relate it to the "Preface to Shakespeare" in the next essay in this volume.

How arbitrary it all seems, and how nominal. We have "the names of *tragedy* and *comedy*," suggesting entities of no substance. The laws governing genres are prescribed by no more than custom, custom developed to suit the convenience of insufficiently ambitious writers. It is therefore clear that, if a Shakespeare violates such customs and writes "contrary to the rules of criticism," we must choose him rather than the rules since "there is always an appeal open from criticism to nature." And, we have seen, Shakespeare has more of nature in his work than criticism would normally allow. We are a long way here from Pope's dogmatic confidence about the rules: "The rules of old discover'd, not devis'd, / Are Nature still, but Nature methodiz'd." For we have moved from the objective, the metaphysically sanctioned, to the nominally conventional.

This is the heart of the difference between what lies behind the first of Johnson's claims and the second. The generalizing insisted on by the first, whatever its deceptive basis in a pseudo-empiricism, postulates universal structures as objective realities; the second posits an irreducible chaos of errant particulars, upon which all attempts at classification become arbitrary and deluding superimpositions. Is the lunar transcendentally real and the sublunary a delusion? Or is the sublunary all we can know, with the lunar an unreachable fiction, at least for the poet in his proper function? What is at stake is both a metaphysic and an aesthetic, both a definition of nature and a definition of the function of art. Since the mimetic workings of poetry are not in question, the issue must concern the nature of that reality which is the object of imitation. Which is to say that the issue is metaphysical. Either there is an objective structure or there is not; the role of particulars, as well as the existence of universals, must follow accordingly. Consequently, the poet must either bypass the peculiar properties of the particular in order to imitate its universality or he must dwell on its peculiarities since there is no going beyond them. We all know about Johnson's properly neoclassical impatience with numbering the streaks on the tulip, but we must remember also his praise of Shakespeare as "an exact surveyor of the inanimate world; his descriptions have always some peculiarities, gathered by contemplating things as they really exist" (p. 266). Again the preview of Wordsworth's injunction about keeping the eye on the object.[11]

It would of course be foolish to press the Johnson of these (almost post-Kantian?) naturalistic claims too strongly. I have pushed him as

[11] For the eye and the object in Wordsworth, see the well-known essay by Frederick A. Pottle, "The Eye and the Object in the Poetry of Wordsworth," in *Wordsworth: Centenary Studies Presented at Cornell and Princeton Universities*, ed. Gilbert T. Dunklin (Princeton: Princeton University Press, 1951), pp. 23–42.

hard as I have only because the other, safer one has been so much more commonly with us. The fact that he can so blithely utter an eighteenth-century commonplace right after a suspiciously revolutionary suggestion indicates how secure he remained in his orthodoxy —so secure that he could not see how profoundly some of his own subterranean tendencies threatened it. We have seen him juxtapose contrary, if not contradictory, meanings and tones to words like "fiction" or the "casual"; or follow his momentarily radical empiricism with his steadfast didacticism. Notice how easily he moves as he argues (pp. 245–46): ". . . there is always an appeal open from criticism to nature." Then, without pause, "The end of writing is to instruct; the end of poetry is to instruct by pleasing" (p. 245). He can then shift his argument from the nature of things to the nature of the audience. The "mingled drama" can instruct as much as the pure genre and it can please more by appealing to the audience's love of variety ("all pleasure consists in variety"—a strong statement for a stalwart representative of a tradition almost wholly focused on unity). Yet Johnson can properly insist on justifying the combining of tragic with comic elements by asking only that they "cooperate in the general system by unavoidable concatenation." Has he already forgotten that the major initial thrust of his argument for mixing genres rested on a denial of any general system, rested rather on the need for poetry to reproduce the sublunary state that is without design?[12]

The ins and outs and inbetweens of these varied and undulating moments in Johnson could occupy us much longer, but with little additional profit, I believe. What I have been finding in his criticism, as I find it in his poetry and in his life, is a fundamental allegiance—a willed commitment—to those dogmatic beliefs whose universalism and objectivity gave such comfort, such assurances of order and sanity, to his predecessors and contemporaries; this allegiance together with a fearful suspicion of alien forces, inhospitable to the anthropomorphic tendencies of human reason and incapable of being absorbed by them. These forces are defiant of order and make us anxious about whether the general structure in which we have reposed our confidence really belongs to the universe or to our own fictional needs to shape a universe out of our wishful thinking. Clearly it is the Johnson of affirmation who is dominant, who barely acknowledges the existence of doubt. But the other, half unadmitted, shows his hand (or his

---

12 Of course, it is always tempting for one to argue that Johnson only suggests the *appearance* of experiential chaos, beyond which the general system securely rests. But I wonder if this way out, though faithful to Johnson's usual attitude, really does justice to the revolutionary implications of some of the statements—however out of tone with the main drift—which I have examined here.

sleight-of-hand), though damaging the consistency of the discourse. He is the one, of course, who has interested me as the alien intruder upon his period; and he is the one who so clearly foreshadows what lies just ahead in metaphysics and literary theory.

The all-or-none polarity in some of these contradictory impulses is reflected in the theoretical extremes that see the poem either as partaking wholly of the order of art, of total system, or as forsaking all system for a living reality seen as "without design." In the first case nature (like the poem imitating it) is made into the order of the artful; in the second the poem (as art escaping from its own nature) is made into the disorder of "sublunary nature," nature in its raw, un-neoclassical, anaesthetic naturalness. If the first sees poetry exclusively as artful unity (with little concern about the breadth and resistance of materials unified), the second sees art exclusively as unartful variety (with little concern about art's need to create some perceptible system after all). Although, clearly, Johnson is so steeped in the tradition of unity that he is in little danger of being captured by the consequences of his more extravagant statements that appear to call for unmitigated variety, those statements seem to stand—in their antagonism to art and to the restrictions of conventional fictionality—as blatant examples of what has been called the fallacy of imitative form.

But there is that in Johnson's "Preface" which mediates with brilliance and, once more, with prophetic light between the implied extremes of aesthetics and anti-aesthetics. This is the third area of claims with which, by way of epilogue, I mean to close. They occur in the well-known defense of Shakespeare's neglect of the unities. Again the arguments themselves were by this time standard, one crucial argument coming as early as Sidney; but their theoretical significance, especially as they reflect on the others that have busied us here, is of great concern in Johnson.

Johnson's defense of Shakespeare, which involves his attack on the unities of time and place, finds him insisting both on the distinction between art and immediate reality and on their profound and intimate relationship. It was the case, after all, that the rationale for such unities as Castelvetro and, after him, the French proposed rested on a confounding of art and life, through a strange commingling of the physical circumstances of the audience in the theater and the fictional time and place represented on the stage. Since the audience has not moved and since very little time has elapsed during their stay in the theater, they will not find credible any gaps of time or shifts of place on the stage. The time-and-place circumstances in the play should come as close as possible to reproducing those of its audience. Thus the theater of delusion must rest, theoretically, on our capacity to confound the play with reality, our reality—which is to say it must rest on our *in*capacity for fiction and its *il*lusion. And this attitude sounds not altogether dissimilar to what we have seen of Johnson in his second, anti-aesthetic disposition. At the same time it must be granted that, whatever their theoretical foundation, these unities demanded the sort of artificial contrivances that seemed most annoying to Johnson's realistic temper. And it was perhaps on these grounds that Johnson found himself forced to oppose them. When Johnson opposes these unities, then, it is not surprising that we find him turning on himself, moving to a defense of illusion, and, with it, of fiction and its artful accompaniments.

When Sidney denied the charge that the poet was a liar, he did it by arguing for the illusionary or fictional aspect of poetry as a feigning or a "figuring forth." In thus detaching the poet from fact ("for the Poet, he nothing affirms, and therefore never lyeth"), Sidney uses the make-believe of fictional place on the stage to make his point: "What child is there, that coming to a Play, and seeing *Thebes* written in great Letters upon an old door, doth believe that it is *Thebes*?"[13] Here is the basis for Johnson's famous, but similar, attack on the theater of delusion, "that place cannot change itself . . . that what was *Thebes* can never be *Persepolis*".

> The objection arising from the impossibility of passing the first hour at *Alexandria*, and the next at *Rome*, supposes, that when the play opens the spectator really imagines himself at *Alexandria*, and believes that his walk to the theatre has been a voyage to *Egypt*, and that he lives in the days of *Antony* and *Cleopatra*. Surely he that imagines this, may imagine more. (p. 254)

The argument for the theater of conscious illusion clearly rests on the argument for its fictitiousness. And on this matter we again find Johnson turning himself around (pp. 255–56): "The delight of tragedy proceeds from our *consciousness of fiction* [my italics]; if we thought murders and treasons real, they would please no more." Like Sidney, Johnson emphasizes the hypothetical, iffy nature of drama: it is not "that the evils before us are real evils, but that they are evils to which we ourselves may be exposed." It is not what we feel, but what we would feel *if* we "were to do or suffer what is there feigned to be suffered or to be done." "It is credited with all the credit due to a drama . . . a just picture of a real original." But credited only so far. For, always self-conscious of our role as spectators, we know "that the stage is only a stage, and that the players are only players." The

---

13 *An Apology for Poetry*, in *The Great Critics*, ed. J. Smith and E. W. Parks (New York: W. W. Norton & Co., 1939), p. 216.

fiction does not quite tease us out of thought, not ever, "from the first act to the last." We should not violate the spirit of the frame by expecting to be shaded by trees or cooled by fountains represented in a painting, Johnson warns, much in the spirit of one who would ask that we not rush onstage to rescue Desdemona toward the close of *Othello*.

All this is, clearly, Johnson's consciousness of "our consciousness of fiction," such as we have not seen in him earlier. The poem may be—nay, must be—*like* reality, but the imitation is not to be confounded with its object; nor is the mimetic process, as the making of art, to be underestimated. Thus it is that, in this mood, Johnson, while willing to forgo the unities of time and place, insists on the unity of action. Nothing else may be "essential to the fable," but this unity is. When the other unities are further condemned because, "by circumscribing the extent of the drama, [they] lessen its variety" (a familiar argument drawn from the Johnson of several pages back), he conveniently ignores the fact that even the unity of action is a circumscribing and limiting affair. Some inhibiting of unlimited variety, after all, is what unity is all about. This concession to the unity of action marks the advance of these claims of Johnson over the second we considered.

Elsewhere too he reverts to his realistic framework as he persists in having Shakespeare's unity of action an especially free and even various one. Johnson acknowledges Shakespeare's failure to have

> an intrigue regularly perplexed and regularly unravelled; he does not endeavour to hide his design only to discover it, for this is seldom the order of real events, and *Shakespeare* is the poet of nature: But his plan has commonly what *Aristotle* requires, a beginning, a middle, and an end; one event is concatenated with another, and the conclusion follows by easy consequence. (p. 253)

But is this, we might ask, "the order of real events"? Should not Shakespeare, as the poet of nature, be exempted even from such mild impositions upon the variety with which he pursued the infinitely various order of real events? Still, Johnson has by now advanced beyond the applicability of these damaging questions. He can conclude his acknowledgment of Shakespeare's meager unity: ". . . the general system makes gradual advances, and the end of the play is the end of expectation."

So we are back to a "general system" after all. But it is no longer, in this context, the general system with which we began. Johnson may not have been able to rest in the unrestricted variety implied by the realism of his most anti-bookish, anti-systematic moments, but neither is his only alternative an externally imposed general system. It is now the system created by the poet as his fictional unity of the endless variety found in "the real state of sublunary nature," a unity freed of all artifice but that required to be "a just picture of a real original." If the first claims of Johnson we considered, all-universalizing as they were, seemed exclusively dedicated to an existentially blind unity; if the second, in their particularization, seemed anarchically dedicated to variety; these third seem to point ahead to the organicist's call for unity in variety, for a *discordia concors*.

It was in this spirit, I believe, that Johnson earlier spoke of what so moved him about the strangely realistic genius of Shakespeare: "*Shakespeare* approximates the remote, and familiarizes the wonderful" (pp. 243–44). In this spirit too, in his "Cowley," Johnson improves upon Pope's definition of wit, rather considering it as that "which is at once natural and new, that which though not obvious is, upon its first production, acknowledged to be just . . . that, which he that never found it, wonders how he missed. . . ."[14] In such passages, the later English poet-critic whom Johnson reminds me of is not Wordsworth, but Coleridge, who, in the *Biographia Literaria* (chap. XIV), described Wordsworth's imaginative task and his own in their plan for the *Lyrical Ballads* in much the same way: "the two cardinal points of poetry," from which the description develops, are "the power of exciting the sympathy of the reader by a faithful adherence to the truth of nature, and the power of giving the interest of novelty by the modifying colors of imagination." Are we so far from Johnson? "Approximates the remote, and familiarizes the wonderful"; the natural and the new; the "just picture" and the "real original"; fiction and the endless diversity. More than theoretical inconsistency, there is in Johnson a rich, many-directioned mind standing at a critical crossroad. Not quite fulfillment, nor yet quite prophecy, but somehow something of both.

If nature's universal structure has become questionable in the heavy drag of "the real state of sublunary nature," man need not surrender to the imitation of experiential chaos. Through an organizing act of mind, man can impose his own system, thus opening the prospect of unity in variety. Here lies the romantic imagination and with it Coleridge. But if Coleridge looked as I have here, he may have found how much of his path had been cleared by a few casual master strokes by that arch-neoclassicist himself, Samuel Johnson. Here indeed is the fulfillment of my initial warning and prophecy of these, my post-Kantian distortions.

14 In "Cowley," *Selected Prose and Poetry*, p. 470.

5

"Trying Experiments upon Our Sensibility":
The Art of Dogma and Doubt
in Eighteenth-Century Literature

THE QUOTED PHRASE in my title is from Dr. Johnson's review, in 1757, of Soame Jenyns's *A Free Inquiry into the Nature and Origin of Evil.* It may be unfair to me to begin with this as my example of his relation to his period's rationalism, as it was unfair of him to use that *Inquiry* as *his* example of what that rationalism was. Indeed, it may be surprising to find me treating Johnson as something approaching an empiricist, if not an existentialist, who rejects those abstract speculations which do not touch the man of flesh and bones; but the human insistence on the primacy of our experience, such as we frequently find in his work, clearly moves in this direction. In the passage from which the quotation was taken, Johnson is referring—with restrained irony—to those inhuman licenses which indifferent superhuman powers presumably exercise (with "merry malice") in maintaining the disinterested operation of the great chain of being. What Johnson is with some impatience commenting upon is, of

The nature of this essay is influenced by the fact that it was originally written for delivery at the 1979–80 Clark Library series with the general title, "Augustan Myths and Modern Readers."

course, the rationalist's habit of postulating—as an a priori necessity —a series of outlandish, and morally outrageous, entities, utterly at odds with our experience, only because the rationalist stands in need of stipulating a primal cause, even though that cause has at best an arbitrary relation to the effect it is to account for.

> That a set of beings unseen and unheard, are hovering
> about us, trying experiments upon our sensibility, putting
> us in agonies to see our limbs quiver, torturing us to
> madness, that they may laugh at our vagaries, sometimes
> obstructing the bile, that they may see how a man looks
> when he is yellow; sometimes breaking a traveller's bones
> to try how he will get home: sometimes wasting a man to a
> skeleton, and sometimes killing him fat for the greater
> elegance of his hide.[1]

Johnson is decrying the ontologist's confidence in the "unseen and unheard," a confidence sustained even when it makes an absurdity and a mockery of man's earthly sorrows. For Johnson's concern is not so much to find the causes of such sorrows (since his faith assures him the causes cannot be removed and the sorrows are an inevitable part of our mortal burden), as to find the means of enduring them. As a morbid empiricist, he accepts the human experience which history and learning assure him is our common lot, and he rejects the rationalistic attempt to deprive us of the dignity of suffering by seeking to account for its causes through an elegant cosmology, "unseen and unheard," which reduces us to "puppets" in the grand scheme.

Among the foulest tricks of those invented beings who are to exercise indifferent control over the scale of being is their sport of leading on a foolish mortal too stuffed with pride, filling him with "idle notions" until he becomes just such an extravagant philosophical author dedicated to writing of such elegant metaphysical matters "for the sake of some invisible order of beings, for surely they are of no use to any of the corporeal inhabitants of the world." For these latter, ourselves, subject solely to human experience and the pain associated with it, can look at such bloated ontological claims only with the

---

[1] In Johnson, *Selected Prose and Poetry*, ed. Bertrand H. Bronson (New York: Rinehart & Co., 1952), p. 206. Johnson earlier notes sardonically the reasoning by which Jenyns establishes the role of these superhuman beings (italics are his): "He imagines that as we have not only animals for food, but choose some for our diversion, the same privilege may be allowed to some beings above us, *who may deceive, torment, or destroy us for the ends only of their own pleasure or utility.* This he again finds impossible to be conceived, *but that impossibility lessens not the probability of the conjecture, which by analogy is so strongly confirmed*" (p. 204).

"doubt and uncertainty" with which Johnson admitted himself to be filled from the beginning of his review. As we note Johnson's turning of the cosmological absurdity upon the authors who sponsor such a metaphysic—his suggestion that the most infuriating of the inhuman sports of these callous gods is to foster such inflated authors as these— we understand that his assault is not upon such amoral universal rulers, but upon the would-be philosophers who, out of a failure of sympathy for man's suffering, would willfully invent this "set of beings unseen and unheard." The problem for the man who lives and reads—who reads in order to help himself learn the endurance he needs if he is to keep living—is not that supernal beings are "trying experiments upon our sensibility," but that lowly—all too lowly— authors are. Johnson thus seems well launched on a deconstruction of his period's most "constructed" metaphysic.

One might argue that the entire enterprise of rationalistic phi- losophy is one such wild experiment and that our best eighteenth- century writers at once indulge it and test it upon their sensibilities, that the best literature of the period reveals a struggle between the extravagance of commitment which permits an evasive invention cut out of whole cloth and the "doubt and uncertainty" felt by the inner being in reaction against such flighty fictions. Because many in the period were impelled, for their sanity's sake, to avoid—at all costs— being alienated from an increasingly hostile sense of exteriority, they found themselves receptive to rational inventions which promised an order behind the disorder, an order, at once sublime and humanly maddening, which gave abstract reasons even if it could not provide immediate comfort.

For Johnson such an invention had to be another one—indeed one of the most flagrant—of those fictions which he frequently recorded himself as despising. He would have to see it as an invention more imaginative than rational, since for him reason was invariably tied to the warmly common truths of human experience. It is thus likely that Johnson's negative response to the invented abstractions which con- trol the rationalistic projection of the great chain of being is just another version of his general distrust of fictions which is revealed throughout his literary criticism. It is of course not at all the case that Johnson is opposing this extreme rationalism as a self-conscious em- piricist: he is hardly an ally of David Hume. It is rather that he has a profound and homely commitment to man's living reality, and writes in defense of human experience and man's right to an emotional integrity which Johnson sees threatened by the extravagance of imaginative invention ("Where there is leisure for fiction there is little grief"[2]).

The fictional extravagance which is implicit in the controlling elements of the rationalistic cosmos may well be reflected in the airy creatures whom Pope added, many years before Soame Jenyns's treatise, to *The Rape of the Lock*. Their hierarchical sense of levels—with each in its place—and their inflated, if absurd, self-importance as those who would bring about or prevent the actions of earthlings—these suggest the supernal beings attributed by Johnson to the world of Soame Jenyns's *Inquiry*. If it should surprise us that Johnson, for all his usual objections to farfetched fictions, should speak with pleasure of Pope's addition of these creatures, we should perhaps remind ourselves that Johnson's shrewdness may well have observed that Pope's lighthearted and half-bemused treatment of them was a fore-runner of his own impatience with creatures implicitly projected by metaphysical extravagance. What is perhaps more surprising is the fact that Pope's ironic indulgence of them, with the skepticism implied by it, did not prevent him—a couple of decades later in *An Essay on Man*, Epistle One—from postulating, rather uncritically, a world which shares much with that set forth by Soame Jenyns. (Indeed, Johnson associates Pope's doctrine with Jenyns's.) If Pope reveals a doubleness in his own allegiances in these poems and gives us no sign that he sees a metaphorical relationship between the two of them such as I mean to suggest, Johnson is more consistent in his "Life of Pope" in his unfavorable reaction to the doctrine of *An Essay on Man*, treating "the poet's Leibnitian reasoning" little better than he does Jenyns's. In rejecting Pope's metaphysical construction, he only reenforces his readiness to enjoy the whimsy of Pope's apparent deconstruction of several decades before in *The Rape of the Lock*.

In light of my suggestion of these relations, I find myself wondering whether we might not find in *The Rape of the Lock* an early hint of the maddening indifference to human suffering of those superhuman creatures who try their experiments upon us in sublime indifference. I am referring here not to the inefficient sylphs so much as to those unfeeling beings who are given a quasi-divine function and exercise it in no more sensitive a way than do those invented by Jenyns:

> The hungry Judges soon the sentence sign,
> And wretches hang that jurymen may dine. (3.21–22)

---

2 The sentence is from Johnson's too well-known attack on *Lycidas* in his "Life of Milton."

This frightful world which Pope momentarily presents as an alternative to the "toyshop" world of his poem may well suggest the comparative innocence of the inconsequential angelic creatures of his airy invention next to the cruel indifference of worldly judges who control the fate of others. In the Jenyns review, Johnson's was an implied attack on social inequity and on the careless doom passed on helpless mankind by those acting as its doomsayers who passed on to higher beings the responsibility for their actions. The attack may well be extended from Jenyns's supernatural beings—and those who act in their name—past the good-humored sylphs to those who casually dispense injustice in our world. Pope's juxtaposition of the judges and jurymen to the mock-doomsayers—like Belinda, about to decide the "doom" of two knights at Ombre—and his turning in relief back to his "toyshop" world, from real doom-dealings to make-believe ones, suggest a rejection close to Johnson's.

And yet, of course, it is not that I wish to claim Johnson altogether for the skeptical and heterodox attitude toward eighteenth-century dogmatics. There is, in the main, too much and too profound a fidelity in him toward the rational precepts common to his period for me to argue against the usual placement of him as one of its high priests, both in literary criticism and in philosophical attachment. His attack on particularity for the sake of the general and his moralistic objectives for poetry hardly require discussion for us to acknowledge them and the principal place they occupy in his thought. But it is those errant moments in which he speaks for "the real state of sublunary nature," however destructive it may be of our neat moral generalizations, or in which his impatience with literary fictions leads him to the defense of the poet's acute observation of here-and-now experience, which make him a unique spokesman in a period which boasted so many common ones.[3] Indeed, it is Johnson's extraordinary capacity to

[3] I discuss this aspect of his thought in "Fiction, Nature, and Literary Kinds in Johnson's Criticism of Shakespeare," the preceding essay in this volume. In the current essay I am trying to collect my claims about eighteenth-century literature and ideas which have been scattered in a number of essays and to put them forward within the terms of a single general insight which can hold them all. I shall, directly or indirectly, be alluding to these essays in the course of my argument, and the reader is referred to them for fuller discussions of what may be only lightly touched upon here where I have, in my ambition, so much more ground to cover. Besides the essay already mentioned, the others are "The 'Frail China Jar' and the Rude Hand of Chaos," *The Play and Place of Criticism* (Baltimore: Johns Hopkins Press, 1967), pp. 53–68; "'Eloisa to Abelard': The Escape from Body or the Embrace of Body," "The Cosmetic Cosmos of 'The Rape of the Lock,'" "Samuel Johnson: The 'Extensive View' of Mankind and the Cost of Acceptance," "The Human Inadequacy of Gulliver, Strephon, and Walter Shandy—and the Barnyard Alternative," *The Classic Vision: The Retreat from Extremity in Modern Literature* (Baltimore: Johns Hopkins Press, 1971), pp. 83–103, 105–24, 125–45, and 255–85, respectively.

contain the alien elements of his historical moment—the defense of the period's most ambitious generalized constructions together with the common-sense demystification of them—that gives him his special place as his culture's most broadly representative spokesman.

I have shown elsewhere that in Johnson's "Preface to Shakespeare" the responsibility to the realities of ungeneralizable particulars (the "chaos of mingled purposes and casualties") and the responsibility to moral universal manage to coexist, even at a cost to theoretical consistency.[4] Somewhat earlier, in his *Rambler* No. 4, Johnson mixed these notions even more ambiguously, if (apparently) more conclusively.[5] The essay begins by defending contemporary fiction for the reality of its portrayal of "accidents that daily happen in the world," for its "accurate observation of the living world" (a favorite phrase of his which we find repeated in the "Preface to Shakespeare"). By contrast, he treats with contempt the fiction of "the last age," governed (as he sees it) by a "wild strain of imagination" which encourages the author to "let loose his invention," filling his work with "incredibilities," but "without knowledge of nature, or acquaintance with life." These are the extravagances of a too literary (or too fictional) fancy which Johnson everywhere scorns, preferring as he does works which—as he says in his "Preface to Shakespeare"—in their fidelity to "common occurrences," seem "scarcely to claim the merit of fiction."

But the advantage he grants to literally mimetic writings soon fosters a correlative difficulty: their very realism creates in their audience a credibility which leads to moral influence, and the similarity of fictional actions to real ones permits the first to set examples for the second. These potential moral consequences give those works a responsibility which more extravagantly "literary" works could not—with their "incredibilities"—worry about. Consequently, the contemporary writer must make his realities compatible with what is morally uplifting. He must keep good and evil separated, however mixed they may appear to most of us to be in the world, and be certain that only the good is commended for emulation. So to the writer's obligation to reflect actual experience instead of fanciful invention is added his obligation to give the reader a morally improved version of that experiential reality. But Johnson refuses to acknowl-

---

4 See preceding note.

5 In writing my previous essay on Johnson's criticism I did not want his earlier discussion of fiction to intrude upon the problems I was there treating in his "Preface to Shakespeare" because in the *Rambler* essay he confounds issues which he treats separately, if not altogether consistently, in the later work. But I must turn to that earlier essay on fiction here and examine it against the background of what I have found in the later one.

edge that what the writer gives us is better than reality (instead of being a faithful imitation of reality itself). For Johnson will not permit the work to be an unreal fiction, even a moral fiction.

This may have been for some time the standard argument of didactic theorists (that the fiction is a morally better world than the real world); but Johnson, in his dedication to commonplace experience (as the appropriate object of imitation) was reluctant to make such an argument his own. He shifts the emphasis of the writer's obligation from the true over the false to the good over the evil. But he is not ready to suggest that the good is not also the true. It is the writer's task to select the moral elements of real experience and make them alone available to his impressionable audience. If many of that audience, like most of us, see good and evil as inevitably mixed in experience, it is because we are not being sufficiently selective. The writer must do better. If, in his commitment to "sublunary nature," he describes the world "promiscuously, [Johnson] cannot see of what use it can be to read the account; or why it may not be as safe to turn the eye immediately upon mankind, as upon a mirror which shows all that presents itself without discrimination."6 In other words, if art does not improve upon raw experience, who needs it? Of raw, amoral experience we have enough. Johnson appears less secure in his rigid moralism in the later Shakespeare essay, since apparently Shakespeare has taught him—with whatever misgivings—to revere an art devoted to revealing experience in all its amoral complexity.

So we watch Johnson straddling, in a curiously ambivalent way, the question of how fiction is to be related to reality and to morality. He began by seeing fictional writings of "the present generation" as preferable to those of "the last age" in their commitment to immediate experiential reality, apart from the wild inventions (or previously invented stereotypes) of a too literary imagination. But then, worried about the undiscriminating character of such a commitment and the greater moral risk to the audience of a realistic portrayal, he warns the current writer to modify his realism with a moral selectivity calculated to educate his reader. But in this moral world, as a selection from real experience, still a true representation or only a moral fiction? Clearly, Johnson must not, at least in this essay, permit himself the skeptic's luxury of seeing the actual world of experience as hopelessly mixed in its moral values, so that the author gives us, not the real world, but a moral transformation of it. For this argument would leave Johnson with the earlier didactic theorists in a simple Platonism which would indeed see the literary work as amoral fiction—from the standpoint of

6 *The Rambler*, No. 4 (March 31, 1750), *Selected Prose and Poetry*, p. 63.

our worldly experience—no matter how ultimately, metaphysically true it might turn out to be. And Johnson's own distrust of invisible metaphysical abstractions—as we have seen in the Soame Jenyns review—kept him closer to "sublunary nature" than that. So he had to manage somehow to affirm that the exclusively moral representations were indeed reality, even if selectively so. He had to confront his own sometime feeling—urged brilliantly years later in the passage from the "Preface to Shakespeare" concerned with the "chaos of mingled purposes and casualties"—that in reality all our values and crossed hopes are inextricably confounded and that great art often reproduces this mixture. He had to confront it and, in the *Rambler* essay, to reject it in favor of art's moral purpose which was yet to remain true to experience. But in the Shakespeare essay too, we must remember, he could scold Shakespeare for moral indifference after praising his truthful adherence to our morally indifferent world.

Johnson wants art true, but he wants it good; and he is more certain at some moments than others that the good is true. To say the good is not true is to make it a fiction, and to that extent objectionable for Johnson. But to say it is true is to run the risk of making abstract metaphysical claims which our experience cannot sustain—again objectionable to him. Johnson is only enunciating again—though in his way and at times with an honesty that threatens his consistency—that age-old dilemma which vainly seeks to make the mimetic compatible with the didactic. In order to effect a tidy closure in this essay, Johnson simply asserts the selective truth of the separate dominion of "the most perfect idea of virtue," condemning the "fatal error all those will contribute, who confound the colors of right and wrong, and instead of helping to settle their boundaries, mix them with *so much art*, that no common mind is able to disunite them" (p. 64, my italics). The art of telling the whole, mixed truth is an enemy to any didactic function: it is, for Johnson, akin to "the art of murdering without pain." Yet the charge of just "so much art" is what Johnson was later to level at Shakespeare in the Preface that so mixed the aesthetic and the ethical, confounding art's ambiguous obligations to reality and to morality.

Does the writer's art consist in his extracting the good from the mingled mass of experience or in his portraying that mingled character in its richness and fullness? If the *Rambler* essay insists on the first alternative, Shakespeare persuades Johnson to yield, grudgingly, to the second. Let me note two passages, one from each essay, in which a single metaphor is used to represent these opposed alternatives. From *Rambler* No. 4:

> The chief advantage which these [moral] fictions have
> over real life is, that their authors are at liberty,
> though not to invent, yet to select objects, and to
> cull from the mass of mankind, those individuals upon
> which the attention ought most to be employed; as a
> diamond, though it cannot be made, may be polished by
> art, and placed in such a situation, as to display that
> luster which before was buried among common stones. (pp. 62–63)

But in the passage from the "Preface," Shakespeare's advantage over other writers (in this case it was Addison who served as Johnson's example of such another writer) was found in his resisting the polishing art and his keeping the "common stones" with the diamond: "Other poets display cabinets of precious rarities, minutely finished, wrought into shape, and polished unto brightness. *Shakespeare* opens a mine which contains gold and diamonds in unexhaustible plenty, though clouded by incrustations, debased by impurities, and mingled with a mass of meaner minerals." The mingling of diamonds with meaner minerals echoes the "mingled purposes and casualties" of the "chaos" which is the "real state of sublunary nature." Here once more we see Johnson drawn to the two apparently incompatible concepts of art, the moral and the wholly revelatory, and to the two versions of reality which each presumably claims.

I can return this discussion to my larger interest by pointing out that what is at issue is Johnson's category of fiction, of which he was usually suspicious. Can he with consistency claim that there is available for the artist an unmixed element of the good while he also claims that all is casual and chaotic in our experience with its "mingled purposes"? Can he, in other words, find access to the universals he needs while he wants to restrict the artist to our particulars? Or should not the concept of the good as a universal (even if derived from selected experiences) be seen by Johnson as just the sort of conventional and mythological fiction (however morally tinged) which he rejects in writers who evade immediate reality?

The word *fiction* is itself ambiguous in Johnson. Primarily, in the *Rambler* essay on the subject, fiction is the literary genre of prose narrative, what Johnson equates with the "comedy of romance." Though as an imitation it is distinguished from real life (and in its older, extravagant forms Johnson points out it was a fanciful escape from all reality), it now "must arise from general converse, and accurate observation of the living world." Yet defined by him as an aesthetic alternative to historical reality, fiction retains an Aristotelian character. Thus a fiction faithfully imitative of particular experience is, in effect, a genre in flight from its own nature; but Johnson's distrust of invention leads him so to conceive it. As the years pass, fiction's unreal nature, as an irresponsibly arbitrary alternative to what actually happens, seems to take over Johnson's sense of the word and turns it derogatory, as he comes to see fiction as literary (that is, unreal and conventional) extravagance. He can thus use it to condemn the mythological allusions in *Lycidas*: "Where there is leisure for fiction there is little grief." This sense of the word *fiction*—as pertaining to the artificial, the unreal, the arbitrary—also governs its use in much of the "Preface to Shakespeare" and helps account for the ambivalence of Johnson's attitude toward Shakespeare's fidelity to "the real state of sublunary nature."

The doubleness we have been witnessing in Johnson reflects the conflict in him between a hardheaded commitment to everyday reality which seeks to demystify all that would provide a fictional substitute for it and an orthodox commitment to the universal moral commonplaces of his period. He did not relish the metaphysical assumptions implied by such moralism and preferred not to confront them; but he was—despite occasional and exciting resistance—too much a man of his period to yield so completely to an amorally mixed reality as to give up his moral impulse, however it led him to opposed claims which could be seen as undermining one another. Anxious to see experience without borrowing "the spectacles of books" and thus anxious to avoid the fiction-making he sees going on around him, he still indulges the Platonic myth of moral universals which requires such fictions (though he seeks to find such universals in experience). But then, at other moments, the skeptical and openly empirical mood returns—fitfully and inconclusively—as he himself falls victim to the seductions of experience in its wholeness and to the poets whom he sees as making it available to us.

In this doubleness of fidelity and skepticism, as he relates his own complexities of attitude to the simpler orthodoxies around him, Johnson is again representative of the most exciting writers of his age. The historian of ideas, dealing with this period, is often tempted to keep its ideological affiliations simple, though at the expense of not being able to respond to writers like Johnson in all the density of their cross-commitments. Perhaps no period has been treated so reductively by those who seek to characterize its philosophical nature. In my own commentary on the period in the past, I find myself yielding to simplifications as I summarize its rationalistic flavor, making it too one-dimensional in order to furnish my favored writers the reductive norms against which their complex deviations may be measured. Thus, for example, I have expanded upon the naive philosophical realism of Epistle One of Pope's *Essay on Man*, making it representative of an existentially blind eighteenth-century rationalism, and then concentrated upon those moments in which Pope reveals his distrust of such dogmatics and introduces his subjective uncertainties. I thus set Pope against his more orthodox self as Johnson set himself against the rationalism reflected in Soame Jenyns. Strategically, then, it is less important for me to deal with an altogether minority voice, like Vico's, than with those who, primarily part of the majority chorus, yet betray an ambivalence such as I have been suggesting.

So my strategy has been to claim to find in the period a widely accepted myth and, in the period's best minds, the deconstructors of that myth (often in spite of—or along with—some lingering allegiance to it). But my candor about that strategy leads me to ask whether the myth was constituted by their belief (which they occasionally distrust) or whether I (and others) have created the myth of their belief in order to simplify that belief into an orthodoxy and to introduce as complications some opposed beliefs, though these are equally period-bound and perhaps as commonly felt. In other words, perhaps the complications of belief are themselves part of the period's commonplaces, which sustain a much less parochial system of beliefs than we are giving them credit for. We must remember, for example, that empiricism is as much an enlightenment movement as is its antagonist, rationalism. Every would-be historian of ideas must face up to the possibility (if not the likelihood) that he has reduced the central ideas of the period to what suits the convenience of his neat discursive model, enjoying an arrogant confidence in his ability to break through those ideas to the felt human reality of the private existent in that far-off time. This danger of ideological simplification is greater in dealing with the eighteenth century than with rival periods because of the general conviction held by many intellectual historians about its monolithic nature.

I must, then, recognize the prospect that the monomyth of the eighteenth century, which its more sensitive minds could not *only* accept, but also undermine, is a myth we have imposed upon it. It is undoubtedly the case that Johnson found in Soame Jenyns such a simplism to be undone, but then it was he who chose Jenyns, who surely *was* a straw man, as others who were fitter to debate Johnson were not. Johnson's complaint against Jenyns would seem to be that his position fails to account for the common human experience of his time; in other words, that a common-sense philosophy, based on what every man lives through and feels, would have to reject such empty rationalistic abstractions precisely because they do not touch the experienced reality that surrounds each of Johnson's contemporaries. So the simplism is not a failure of eighteenth-century sensibilities, but a failure of those philosophers who are out of touch with those sensibilities and try to work outrageous cerebral experiments upon them.

Pope's *Essay on Man*, we can now note, seeks to use the epistles after the first to modify that epistle, which seeks utterly to reduce our confusing reality to the clarity of a perfect, if unresponsive, art world ("All Nature is but Art, unknown to thee"). What follows casts back intimations about the vanity of that confident human projection of cosmos which fills the first epistle. In the earliest lines of the second epistle there is an abrupt shift to the fragile human perspective against which the confident projection of Epistle One can no longer stand so confidently. Indeed, in light of those magnificent lines, very little confidence in human knowledge can be left standing. So I may well have jumped too quickly in charging Pope, as I have elsewhere, with reducing a metaphysic to an aesthetic, draining the world of human need so that it may satisfy our formal demands for totalization. Thus, if we sense the full impact of the total *Essay*—Johnson to the contrary notwithstanding—it should support our awareness that Pope has more in common with Johnson than with Jenyns.

From this perspective, which requires the critic to be critical of himself and to see his literary subjects as no more naive than himself, the inner complexities and the doubleness they yield are themselves commonplaces of the period, although they are most visibly present in the self-conscious work of its best writers. It is not that these writers are exceptional in their feelings—indeed it is their value to us that they are representative—but that through the controls of their complex verbal expression we catch hold of what is commonly felt and ready to be expressed in the minds of their contemporaries, if not yet expressed at all or not widely expressed. It is in this sense that a period's leading writers become its spokesmen. The subtleties and the divided allegiance we find in what they speak trace the otherwise unexpressed sensibilities of their fellows, though these sensibilities are there, and in a state of delicacy which asks them not to be trifled or experimented with by an inhumanly thin ideology.

If Pope himself, even in the *Essay on Man*, shows the need to go beyond the abstractions which that *Essay* sets forth, how much more distrust of such abstractions we must expect from Johnson. In Johnson's poetry too, though filled with the language of generalities which we have learned to expect in mid-century style, we find a primary concern with the private human ills which either give those generalities life or deny their applicability.[7] If the *Essay on Man*, perhaps in spite of itself, seems to point to the vanity of metaphysical hubris, Johnson's "Vanity of Human Wishes," of course, points to a broad range of pride and ambition which are invariably frustrated in a world crowded by throngs of particular breakdowns. The more the poem concentrates, in language and argument, on its large and pompous hopes, the more they are brought down by earthly realities. All that is left, in turning away from the grandly universal wishes, is the small, private prayer—for forbearance as we accept the doomed single life. We are now ready for the modest "narrow round" of Dr. Levet. The rest is fiction.

Many years before, in the earlier days of this period, Jonathan Swift, in his utterly different way, showed a similar distrust for grandiose, universal projects and for the overestimation of the human capacity for reason which stimulated them, while—by contrast—he found minimal salvation in the miserable routine details of the unelevated round of daily life. Swift's contempt for self-inflated projector-rationalists is of course evident in many places. Especially prominent in Book Three of *Gulliver's Travels*, it is echoed in his impatience with the absurd extremes of misanthropy in Gulliver in his last stages as a would-be Houyhnhnm, who makes unreasonable demands—in the name of reason—on those around him as he, in his own mind the only extant rational man, retreats to the stable. Even Swift's excursions into scatology end in disdain for those who, like Strephon in "The Lady's Dressing Room," react squeamishly to the facts of man's biological reality and must reject man's painful—and almost noble if ultimately futile—effort to mend this reality by art, all because they cannot, without the hatred produced by disappointment, relinquish their fiction about man's divine nature, not unrelated to the fiction about man's purely rational nature.[8] We must not ignore the extent to which Swift is himself devoted to man's reasonable aspect, but—like Johnson after him—he must distrust it when it is taken in abstraction from the mixed (and mixed-up) reality of the human existent to whom he is primarily devoted.

There can in this period be a doubleness—what I have elsewhere

[7] I refer the reader to my "Samuel Johnson: The 'Extensive View' of Mankind and the Cost of Acceptance" (see note 3, above), in which I discuss "The Vanity of Human Wishes" and "On the Death of Mr. Robert Levet." At one point (p. 133) I relate this discussion to the claims I make about his "Preface to Shakespeare."

[8] See my essay referred to in note 3, above. In it I try to bring *Gulliver's Travels*, "A Description of the Morning," "The Lady's Dressing Room," and "A Beautiful Young Nymph Going to Bed" within the terms of this general claim.

in a treatment of Pope termed his "systematic duplicity"[9]—in the very meanings thrown out by its words. (Johnson's word *fiction* was less systematically double.) Yet this is a possibility that should surprise us in view of our usual impression of his period's rational doctrine of language as a system of discrete meanings which refer to a system of discrete entities. One can observe that the neoclassical semiotic, at its purest (as it was in Pope), insists on sharp and clean separations among all its categories of language and concept. It is as if its language is to echo the many distinct metaphysical levels which *An Essay on Man* so carefully sets apart from one another. Those limited but self-justified links in the chain of being are seen as being equally sustaining to the whole, so that, while they are mutually reflective structures, they are at all costs to resist blending into one another, giving up their own place to merge into a higher one. Cosmic indifference produces a structuralism which assures each separated level that it is functionally indispensable and analogous, in its principle of composition, to all the other levels. Egalitarian analogy among separate fixed entities, in spite of vast differences in their hierarchic positions, ends by controlling both metaphysic and poetic. Elements of language are to have the same discrete character as our concepts of reality, thereby keeping words from being confused with their concepts or with one another. Thus Addison can praise "true wit" as the "resemblance of ideas," can condemn "false wit" as the "resemblance of words" only, and can condescend to "mixt wit," which is partly one and partly the other. (These definitions occur only shortly after Pope's own discussions of "wit"—just as clean in their delineations— in *An Essay on Criticism.*)

This sort of "wit" is far removed from the all-absorbing neo-Platonic wit of the Renaissance, which served another metaphysic and sanctioned another semiotic: the Renaissance word was allowed to become a metaphor possessing an unlimited power of aggrandizement.[10] This power of verbal identity, achieved through an ever-

---

[9] In *The Classic Vision*, pp. 103, 105.

[10] One can perceive the metaphysic and, by implication, the semiotic behind the two doctrines of wit—let's say the "erected wit" of Sidney and the "true wit" of Pope or Addison—by comparing any number of poems of the two periods. The differences cannot be more immediately apparent than they are in the comparison between two essays on man, Pope's poem of that name and George Herbert's "Man." Both clearly project a hierarchy of levels of being, but while each of Pope's levels is insulated from the others in its autonomous function of simply being what it is, all of Herbert's are moving upward to empty themselves into man even as man moves toward God. Thus Herbert's man is consummately inclusive ("For man is ev'rything, / And more . . . / He is in little all the sphere"). All things rush toward him to become him, and the very words similarly turn into one another, turn into him, as he strives to collapse the distance, verbal and spiritual, between him and God. In

enlarging union among words and concepts (words *becoming* concepts) surrenders, in the neoclassical semiotic, to the neatly analytic faculty which differentiates between words and concepts and— since words are to be no more than transparent substitutes for concepts—which differentiates between words. The poets sponsored by these opposed assumptions about language and the world of thought (and the world itself, finally) differ from one another as Shakespeare or Donne differs from Pope. Indeed, one might argue that the apparent differences in the two metaphysics, the Renaissance and the neoclassical, can be reduced to the differences in the two semiologies which then loftily disguise themselves as metaphysics. Their reflection in the two poetics is immediate and profound.

The brilliance of the wit of Pope as a poet is displayed in his manipulation of lines and couplets to search out every delicate shading in the distinctions between the words and the syntactical forms he plays against one another. At his most characteristic, the rhetorical devices he employs to divide his couplet and to divide each line within the couplet create a four-part structure of parallel and contrast which exaggerates the cutting-edge of his wit, producing an always more closely shaved verbal precision. The rhetorical-syntactical fabric of his couplet magnifies the differential aspect of his period's reasonable semiotic. Yet so keenly does Pope press those devices which implement neoclassical wit that his wit is forced to exceed what it was created to perform. At its most acute, Pope's working wit overruns the careful boundaries he imposes upon wit in theory. And the bounds of his period's rigid metaphysic may be overrun as well. We are returned to his "systematic duplicity," which arises out of the concentrated and dynamic equilibrium he achieves within the poetic line through the resources which rhetorical and poetic devices provide for the syntactical perfection of the heroic couplet.

In Pope, chiasmus, zeugma, and metonymy, for example, seem to stress their minor half as strongly as their dominant half, thereby exceeding their function of one-sided satiric comparison. This impression is created in large part by Pope's reversal of the literal and the figurative halves of his tropes: the literal or the materially immediate use of language occurs in the trivial half of the comparison, and the merely figurative, immaterial use of language occurs in the half which

---

Pope, of course, the discreteness and the gaps remain, a multiple stasis instead of a monistic impulse. And the words of his wit are fashioned accordingly.

For a fuller discussion of the Renaissance semiotic, see the opening essay of this volume, "Poetic Presence and Illusion I: Renaissance Theory and the Duplicity of Metaphor." I see that essay and this one as contributing to a partial history of poetics considered as a consequence of the poets' semiological consciousness.

really carries the argument. It is as if the tenor and the vehicle have been reversed. The consequence is that we are lured verbally into wanting to follow the wrong half, in bestowing importance upon it and, thus, in crossing the two halves in a way that rights the balance between them. And the balanced duplicity is sustained, the intrinsic importance in the argument (and in the dominant world of the poem) of one half being matched by the careful literalness of the applicability of the words in the other half.

Let me cite just one of many possible examples of each of these devices. First, chiasmus:

If on a Pillory, or near a Throne,
He gain his Prince's ear, or lose his own.

("Arbuthnot," lines 366–67)

Pope has been explaining his identical scorn for every "knave," whether successful or not, whether in the great world or in the common world ("A knave's a knave, to me, in every state"). This final couplet collapses—and *equates*—all the possibilities. The perfect parallelism of the two lines, reinforced by the identically placed alliterative nouns ("Pillory," "Prince's"), is obviously jarred by the reversal in the second line. The gaining of the prince's ear occurs near the throne, and it is on a pillory that one may lose his ear. So the elements have criss-crossed. Yet the deceptive alliteration suggests the parallel order that relates prince's ear to the pillory and the loss of the ear to the throne—the reverse of the obviously intended meaning. Further, the culprit's losing of his ear is literal, while he can, of course, gain his ultimate goal, the ear of his prince, only figuratively. The prince and the pillory, high life and low life, success and failure, the figurative and the literal, all are at once joined and interchanged.

Second, zeugma: "Or stain her honour, or her new brocade" (*The Rape of the Lock*, 2.107). The yoking of the two objects, one important and intangible and one trivial and material, by the one verb is a yet more tightened version of the same tropological intention. There may not be any reversal here, as there was in chiasmus, but the single controlling verb, functioning doubly—figuratively for its crucial object ("honour") and literally for its trivial one ("brocade") which is presumably included only for the sake of satiric comparison—creates a similar effect of confounding the hierarchy of its worlds. The poem as a whole concentrates on just this question of what really counts, the visible ornament or the underlying (if often opposite) virtue. The sylph who speaks the line, a sympathetic observer-supervisor of Belinda's worlds, recognizes in this and other zeugmas (for example, "Or lose her heart, or necklace, at a ball," 2.109) that in this world honor is seen exclusively in its material guise, as if it *was* a brocade. Yet, as the poem also reveals, it somehow remains honor too, so that the stain never stops being figurative as well as literal. The zeugma truly works because it does not reduce one to the other but continues to the end to work both ways.

Finally, metonymy—and here I cite again a passage whose singular brilliance has prompted my comments elsewhere:[11]

> On shining Altars of *Japan* they raise
> The silver Lamp; the fiery Spirits blaze.
> From silver Spouts the grateful Liquors glide,
> While *China*'s Earth receives the smoking Tide.
>
> > (*The Rape of the Lock*, 3.107–10)

These lines explicitly refer—though in inflated terms—to the ceremony of the heating and pouring of coffee but most of the words in the second of these couplets have secondary meanings which reach beyond this refined world of ritual to remind us of the biological world its refinement excludes. Once we recognize the crucial pun in "*China*'s Earth"—that in its ceramic frailty it is only the artful reduction of the continent itself and the flesh of its people—we are ready to see a new doubleness in "spouts," "grateful Liquors," and "the smoking Tide" that is received by "*China*'s Earth." For the elegant coffee cup, earth of China, is but an aesthetic and symbolic substitute for the real thing, and yet, through double meaning, reminds us of it. Like the "hungry wretches," such a moment acknowledges by indirection the unrefined world out there from which the poem represents a metonymic escape. The poem both excludes that world and allows its language *almost* (but only almost) to become it. To call the cup "China," though it is so unrepresentative of the realities of its continent, is a figurative indulgence indeed. Yet it is the persistence of such figurative reductions which dominates the poem. That the poem itself seeks to be only a frail metonymy, an escapist reduction of the biologically real world, is what its double meanings never let us forget, so that it ends by becoming more.

Such are the simultaneous expansions and contractions of the world of Pope's poems which are won by the tight manipulations of verbal, rhetorical, and poetic devices. We can enlarge upon the impulse behind these examples—especially in a writer like Pope—and arrive at what I have termed the systematic duplicity which marks the

---

[11] For a fuller discussion of these lines, see chapter 10, below.

mock-heroic habit. The very idea of the mock-heroic, combining the free indulgence of an entire framework of fictions with parody of them, seems built on the total exploitation of duplicity. Thus Pope's mock-epics quite appropriately give rise to an entire system of duplicity which sustains his most acute verbal devices.[12] Behind the mock-epic is the assumption that the poet's materials do not merit heroic treatment and yet reveal themselves in a strange way—at once ludicrous and peculiarly elevated—from that perspective.

But behind this assumption there is for Pope a yet deeper assumption: that, as Virgil is the epic model for the mock-heroic Pope, so Augustan Rome is the heroic model for the mock-heroic England. In other words, Pope's own times are beneath heroic stature and cannot have heroic treatment applied to them except as a parody of more properly heroic times. Still, the Augustan comparison—a fiction which the period deeply felt—does hold, and it enhances the period's sense of itself. At the same time, the Augustan myth, generously indulged, is countered by the anti-myth of mock Augustanism; and the strategy of the mock-heroic rests upon the mock-Augustan basis that authenticates it—or rather unauthenticates Augustanism. So mock-Augustanism, the demythification of the period's controlling fiction, can be viewed as the basis for its most brilliantly representative poetic device, the mock-heroic: the duplicity of the one leads to the duplicity of the other. One might say, accordingly, that Pope's "Epistle to Augustus" (an "imitation" of "The First Epistle of the Second Book of Horace") is a poem of mockery cutting yet a lower layer than the mock-epics and in effect authorizing them. The relation Pope forces between George and Augustus is similar in its ambiguity to the relations between his mock-heroic characters and actions and those of their epic models. Indeed, they all may constitute a subgroup of that most two-faced of eighteenth-century genres, the "imitation"—the mock-epics no less than that special "imitation" of Horace, the "Epistle to Augustus."

As I have suggested, the Augustan myth supports a number of other fictions, and I have tried to trace some of them in this essay. In Pope I have pointed to the airy perfections of artful fabrications both to be adored as if they constituted the universe itself, and to be returned to the flesh-and-blood reality of which they are but an empty, rarefied abstraction. In Swift I have pointed to the setting forth of reason and of the human capacity for artifice as if these

---

12 Because I realize that I do not touch on the *Dunciad* in this essay, I refer the reader to "The 'Frail China Jar' and the Rude Hand of Chaos" (see note 3, above), in which I treat this mock-epic in conjunction with *The Rape of the Lock*.

constituted our substantial reality, sadly undercut by our potential for the depravity and bodily filth lurking beneath. As we move beyond the Augustan moment and its Horatian Pope to Johnson, a less rabid Juvenal of neoclassical decadence, we find a more self-conscious confrontation of the problem of fiction itself as it masks a reality in which he clearly believes. Yet he at times pledges his faith to a moral fiction at whatever cost to that reality. If each of these writers can be seen as undermining one of his period's fictions, each yet puts forth his own, though from time to time self-critically—at least, if we read him as I have been suggesting.

In previous essays on these writers I have more than once worried about the distortions my readings may produce in them because of my own post-Kantian perspective.[13] The question really concerns the extent of their (and their period's) uncritical pre-Kantian dogmatism. I raised this question earlier, but I hope that—at this stage in my argument—my claims about their innate capacity to indulge in a critical perspective are more convincing. It may be (and I hope it is the case) that I have in other places overstated the case for my post-Kantian intrusions in my desire to be methodologically candid. Perhaps what I claimed to see in the work was there to be found, though in my self-consciousness I had to warn about the likely distortions which—self-advertised post-Kantians or not—we all share from our position in history. When the late W. K. Wimsatt and I argued this matter in print and in private some years ago,[14] his charge was that I had to read the eighteenth century like a post-Kantian existentialist. It was answered by mine that he had to read the eighteenth century as a committed philosophical Realist, but that he was no less likely to distort its meaning. Both of us were shaping it to our philosophical categories, with no claim to a privileged position of historical sympathy being granted to the Realist. Given the complexity of what feelings and ideas were historically available to these writers, and given the doubleness which stares at us from their writings, I think we only perpetuate fictions which they were themselves capable of seeing beyond, when we limit their allegiances too one-sidedly.

This area of argument focuses upon the subject of this lecture series, "Augustan Myths and Modern Readers," a title which itself suggests the deconstructive enterprise. Are the myths theirs or ours? dare we undo them on our own or can we claim to find them already

13 See especially the opening and the closing of my essay on Johnson's "Preface to Shakespeare," the preceding essay in this volume.

14 I can, alas, share only the printed materials: see them collected in "Platonism, Manichaeism, and the Resolution of Tension: A Dialogue," *The Play and Place of Criticism*, pp. 195–218.

undone on *their* own? Is it, then, we who, from the other side of the Kantian revolution, have de-ontologized the fictions of the period or is it that its writers, with only a sporadic commitment to these fictions, began the demythification process themselves? My preference in answering these questions is by now clear. Whether it is supported by my findings or by the reader's own readings under a guidance I have tried to make persuasive, I must leave to others to decide.

But I do believe that, before he finished with his quarrels with other critics, with Shakespeare, and with himself about the relations between Shakespeare's fictions and reality, Johnson turned once more on his materials and created a new train of argument—one I find consonant with my own. In defending Shakespeare's violation of the unities of time and place, Johnson turns from the previous polarity which occupied him—the claims of conventional, "bookish" fictions and of the varieties of actual experience—to give special license to a third category: the category of dramatic illusion. Between the generic man-made fiction and raw reality he now interposes the stage reality— a feigning—the illusion in which we self-consciously believe *as* illusion. Because of "our consciousness of fiction," the play "is credited with all the credit due to a drama . . . a just picture of a real original." Johnson has revolutionized his concept of fiction—and his attitude toward it. Here, well before Kant's writings, we find a theory of fiction as a self-critical object to which we attend *as if* it were real, but without any commitment to belief outside the realm of illusion. This sophisticated argument for our capacity at once to believe and not to believe—to be guided by fictions even as we know them as such— seems to open us to epistemological possibilities beyond what we might expect of the period. Rather it looks forward to Kant and beyond. Indeed, may it not be that the duplicitous capacity we have been witnessing in these writers both for belief and for skepticism anticipates the movement to come, thus leaving to Kant only the technical expression in philosophical terms of attitudes and ideas which, in less systematic form, our poets, as forerunners, have already made available?

However uncomfortable Laurence Sterne's work may have made Johnson, his *Tristram Shandy* is a superb projection of this notion of illusion. The realities Sterne creates for all his characters are illusionary realities. In each case a reality is constituted through language as a character's exclusive vision, his metaphorical vision: his "hobby-horsical" reality. Yet Sterne, with considerable subtlety, provides also an extra-metaphorical reality of pure facticity, of clock-time and with it the biological facts of birth and death. This ineluctable reality threatens to undo all the others, though in the end they are somehow left intact and capable of being cherished still.[15] There can be no more profound example, in the two centuries since Kant, of the simultaneous pursuit of the metaphoring and "unmetaphoring" impulses.

But this is almost to move beyond our period; so let me retreat a final time to an earlier representative. Even Pope, I have suggested, has this deconstructive impulse, despite his openly proclaimed and sustained fealty to the reigning orthodoxies. Once we look for it, we can find it not only in more likely works like the mock-epics and the "imitations" (both finally being seen as forms of "imitations" more broadly defined), but even—if far less perceptibly and only momentarily—in as unexpected a place as the *Essay on Man*. Let him be my final spokesman here, as Johnson was my first. In my earlier examples of his various technical devices, there was an obvious—in that it is a celebrated—example of zeugma which I would have used, had I not wanted to keep my examples clustered in their satirical intent. In speaking of what seems, from the human perspective, to be divine indifference, Pope describes the "equal eye" of God as seeing

> Atoms or systems into ruin hurled,
> And now a bubble burst, and now a world.   (I.89–90)

Does not this claim to unmitigated cosmic egalitarianism—whatever the painful cries uttered by man's pride—justify the yoking power of the zeugma to equate these apparently opposed subjects by the leveling power of their shared predicates? And what is yoked is the trivial and the cosmic, the literal and the figurative. How easily the largest abstraction contrived by man, the entire structure which sustains his sanity, can burst, like the bubble it is. Have we arrived at a metapoetic point in the poem, when Pope confronts the fragile nature of his own ambitious construct, momentarily turning the poem on itself? To reduce the world to the bubble, or to inflate the bubble to the world, is already to destroy it as an ontological reality; it is to acknowledge it as a fiction, a human "system" hurled like atoms into ruin.

It is no wonder, then, that Pope can follow the utterly absolute ontological affirmation of cosmos which closes the first epistle with the tragically skeptical human perspective which opens the second. After seven magnificent and almost confessional couplets on the state of man, the final one says it all:

> Sole judge of Truth, in endless Error hurled:
> The glory, jest, and riddle of the world!   (2.17–18)

---

[15] I expand on these points in my essay on *Tristram Shandy* (see note 3, above).

The "glory" is our heroic fiction, the "jest" its mock-heroic anti-fiction; and the residual reality which we can know of ourselves? nothing but "riddle," though we will seek to solve it with the illusions we construct, to be in their turn deconstructed by the doubts produced by the consciousness of our "endless Error." And the poem, itself a riddle, can now proceed to do the best it can as a human creation, suspended, like man's "middle nature," between glory and jest.

6

The Critical Legacy of Matthew Arnold; or, The Strange Brotherhood of T. S. Eliot, I. A. Richards, and Northrop Frye

THE HISTORIAN OF contemporary literary theory can clearly trace influential notions of Matthew Arnold in the critical writings of a variety of twentieth-century theorists who might seem, otherwise, to have little in common. They can be seen as strongly at work in a T. S. Eliot, whose attitude to Arnold is consistently antagonistic, as in those like I. A. Richards or Northrop Frye, who themselves at times suggest their sympathetic allegiance to Arnold. Indeed, the haunting suggestion of Arnoldian doctrine may be the more significant as it appears, unasked and unwanted, in the work of an alien mind that cannot rid itself of the influence. And Eliot, surely, could not get the reviled Arnold off his back.

We can note once more the strange fact of the occasional similarity between the positivistic early Richards and the orthodox Eliot who is repelled by the notion that poetry (or anything else!) can take the place of religion. But we may be able to account for such unexpected theoretical brotherhood by marking the significance of their joint Arnoldian legacy. Eliot's apparent colleagueship with a natural ideological enemy like Richards, especially in the matter of "poetry and beliefs," was clearly a source of discomfort, or at least embarrassment, to him. We have only to look at the lengthy, half-apologetic Note he appended to his Dante essay. If Eliot would feel little comfort in an assertion of momentary brotherhood with Richards, he would feel less in being even more intimately related—as a child—to the theories of that alien humanist, Matthew Arnold. Yet Eliot's incongruous, if momentary, kinship with Richards should point us toward their common parent, Arnold, to find a major source of the direction—if not the temperament—of his critical notions.

I

Arnold may be seen as ultimately (or, rather, originally) responsible, not only for Eliot's (as well as Richards's) ideas on poetry and beliefs, but also for such other central doctrines in Eliot as the objective correlative and the unity of sensibility. Indeed, if we account for the Arnoldian basis of these, we have accounted for about all the distinctly Eliotic notions. The odd thing is that at least three different —sometimes almost incompatible—stages in Arnold's critical writings are represented in these influences. There is, first, the Arnold of the 1853 Preface, whose Aristotelianism is used to explain the exclusion of "Empedocles on Etna." There is also the Arnold of the 1864 "The Function of Criticism at the Present Time," whose historical concern with the source of ideas—the enabling factor of poetry—leads him to belittle the Romantics. There is, finally, the Arnold of the 1880 "The Study of Poetry," whose devotion to poetry's moving power—its power to unify our sensibilities—leads him to make it the substitute for "what now passes with us for religion and philosophy."

It seems clear enough that roots of Eliot's objective correlative can be traced to Arnold's 1853 Preface. We recall Eliot's infamous complaint against Hamlet as suffering from "the buffoonery of an emotion which can find no outlet in action." But we must recall also that this complaint is all too reminiscent of Arnold's rejection of his "Empedocles" because it is a representation of a situation "in which the suffering finds no vent in action." Arnold goes on, in language suggestive of the language Eliot is to apply to Hamlet: such situations are those "in which a continuous state of mental distress is prolonged, unrelieved by incident, hope, or resistance; in which there is everything to be endured, nothing to be done." Obviously, what the Aristotelian Arnold here requires to head off such "morbid," "monotonous," and hence "painful" rather than "tragic" representations is an objective structure of action (Eliot's "chain of events"?) which can justify externally (become the objective equivalent of?) the otherwise unvented subjective expression.

Partly in debt to Arnold for his objective correlative, Eliot seems also to carry on Arnold's unfortunate separation between "ideas" (or, even worse, the creation of ideas) and the creative act of the poet. The opening paragraphs of Arnold's "The Function of Criticism at the Present Time" offer a sharp distinction between the functions of criticism and of poetry-making, one based on an equally sharp distinction between the materials of each. And both distinctions seem founded on a pessimistic determinism borrowed from the historicist tradition extended through Taine and Sainte-Beuve. It may well be argued that Arnold is invoking these distinctions—and arguing for the primacy, indeed the greater creativity, of the critical rather than the creative—in order to justify, to himself as well as to others, his own decision to turn his career from poetry to criticism. For surely there seems to be in this distinction an implied criticism of his own poetry which his critics have shared. In any age insufficiently stocked with mature ideas, the poet finds himself burdened with the need to create, as well as to combine, ideas; puts on himself the role of critic as well as the role of poet; and in part fails at both. Thus Arnold implicitly apologizes for the excessively bare, prosaic, ideational nature of his verse, as he signals his turn to criticism.

It is the critic's responsibility, then, to create the ideas which must be made available to the poet. These the poet can only combine: they are his received materials, but their creation is not under his control *qua* poet. The critic's task is "analysis and discovery," the poet's is only "synthesis and exposition." So, in historicist and determinist fashion, "two powers must concur, the power of the man and the power of the moment, and the man is not enough without the moment; the creative power has, for its exercise, appointed elements, and those elements are not in its own control." In an age not supplied by ideas, an age for which criticism has not paved the way, the poet—rather than being insufficient as poet—should sacrifice himself to the poets of the future by turning critic and creating the needed materials that can turn a non-poetic age into a pre-poetic age, into at least a forerunner of a poetic age. It is in this sense that I earlier suggested that perhaps the "critical power," as the only inventor of ideas, is more creative than the "creative power" for Arnold, so that his forgoing of the creative for the critical in his own career may not be such a "sacrifice" after all. He must not fail the future, he argues in an indirect self-defense, as the Romantics failed him.

The poet can create only poems, not ideas. Arnold is this explicit about precluding the poet from the genesis of ideas, thus making him dependent on previous ideas "current at the time, not merely accessible at the time." This separation of the poet from ideas must lead to a distinction between the poem as made and the beliefs it incorporates; it is this distinction that turns up everywhere in the work of Eliot that grows out of his concern with the objective correlative. The prohibition of ideas for the poet surely throws a pall over his possible creativity, even as it unleashes the creativity of the critic (again a seeming act of self-serving at this stage in Arnold's career). And it remains to affect Eliot's restriction of the poet as well.

Thus it is that Eliot is able to praise his idol, Dante, despite (or because of) the fact that "when [he] has expressed successfully a philosophy we find that it is a philosophy which is already in existence, not one of his own invention. . . ." He and Lucretius "both drew their material from the work of philosophers who were not poets." How closely this resembles Arnold's assignment of their respective functions to the critic (critical power) and the poet (creative power). And when Eliot, by contrast, laments the unavoidable failure of Blake, we see the unhappy consequence of a single figure trying to encompass both powers in his poetry:

> What his genius required, and what it sadly lacked, was a framework of accepted and traditional ideas which would have prevented him from indulging in a philosophy of his own, and concentrated his attention upon the problems of the poet. . . . The concentration resulting from a framework of mythology and theology and philosophy is one of the reasons why Dante is a classic, and Blake only a poet of genius. The fault is perhaps not with Blake himself, but with the environment which failed to provide what such a poet needed; perhaps the circumstances compelled him to fabricate, perhaps the poet required the philosopher and mythologist. . . .[1]

Do we sense here an echo of Arnold's implied judgment of himself as poet? Now we understand why, in his Dante essay, Eliot speaks glowingly of "the advantage of a coherent traditional system of dogma and morals like the Catholic."

Of course, these statements are also the consequences of Eliot's well-known traditionalism—if, that is, they are not rather the source of it. Eliot's famous criterion for beliefs, that they be "coherent, mature, and founded on the facts of experience," is his way of saying that they must be the consequence of one of the great traditional systems of belief, since their staying power is the proof of their serving the requirements of coherence, maturity, and adequacy to experience. Otherwise Eliot could not see how they would be likely candidates for

1 Eliot, "William Blake," *Selected Essays*, new ed. (New York: Harcourt, Brace and Co., 1950), pp. 297–80.

the allegiance of a substantial following of people for many years. (Shades of Dr. Johnson's dictum that "nothing can please many, and please long, but just representations of general nature.") Clearly it is on this conservative basis that Eliot can distrust the more esoteric sets of beliefs and the sort of poetry stemming from them, as he moves to his lamentation for such as Blake. While it may be that Eliot's traditionalism causes him to deny the poet a role in creating new beliefs, it may also be the other way around: that so puristic a conception of the poet's role must lead the poet to search out the comforts—with the freedom they allow for his intellectual irresponsibility—of a fully formed and easily borrowed tradition. In either case the fact remains that Eliot as traditionalist is quite at home with the Arnoldian separation of ideas and poetry and that Eliot's objective correlative comes to depend on this separation.

The poet, we are told, is only to show us how it feels to hold certain beliefs rather than to present the beliefs themselves. Thus Dante, assuming that we are instructed in the beliefs presented by St. Thomas Aquinas (which Dante borrows for his own), gives us the emotional equivalent of those beliefs. But the poet also gives us "words for [our] feelings";[2] that is, he gives us, not the feelings themselves (which, according to the impersonal doctrine of the objective correlative, must be kept out of the poem), but the objective or verbal equivalents for those feelings. So to take these equivalences to the second power, as Eliot does, we may say that the poet is to give us the verbal equivalent of the emotional equivalent of the beliefs he borrows from his intellectual environment. In thus eliminating the ideological responsibility of the poet in this Arnoldian manner, Eliot enables himself to utter such strange judgments as his claim (which, despite its initial impression upon us, he meant as unqualified praise) that Henry James had a mind too fine ever to be violated by an idea. He is rarely any more liberal in what he allows or denies the poet than in the following passage:

> I believe that for a poet to be also a philosopher he would have to be virtually two men; I cannot think of any example of this thorough schizophrenia, nor can I see anything to be gained by it: the work is better performed inside two skulls than one. Coleridge is the apparent example, but I believe that he was only able to exercise the one activity at the expense of the other. A poet may borrow a philosophy or he may do without one. It is when he

[2] "The Social Function of Poetry," in *Critiques and Essays in Criticism*, ed. R. W. Stallman (New York: Ronald Press Co., 1949), p. 113.

philosophizes upon his own *poetic* insight that he is apt to go wrong.[3]

But if the poet must keep his beliefs separate from his poetry, he still is to preserve behind both beliefs and poetry the psychic unity that enables him to work one within the confines of the other. Here we have that other central Eliotic doctrine of the unity (in opposition to the dissociation) of sensibility. One might predict that so sharp a separation between poetry and belief in the poetic function would be seen to flow from a dissociated rather than a unified sensibility. Yet Eliot insists on having it the other way round: apparently the mark of the poet of unified sensibility is his capacity to feel his beliefs with an emotional immediacy that frees him from the self-consciously intellectual need to conceptualize them (although, as we have seen, the Arnoldian inheritance suggests that we cannot be sure whether this unity is found in the poet's capacity to contain his belief or in the belief's capacity to contain its poet). In either case, what counts is the poet's sense of being so at home in his world of beliefs, so comfortable in them and so secure in their unchallenged sway, that he is free to poetize without intruding them self-consciously, argumentatively, from the outside. For they are inside, inside him, informing the emotional complex that seeks verbal objectification as the unimposed-upon poem, the poem that guarantees the unified sensibility behind it.

Eliot's notion of the unified sensibility is clearly indebted to Arnold's nostalgic admiration for the unity in the Middle Ages of the senses of conduct, beauty, and knowledge. It is the splitting up of these senses, and the rivalry among them—now with their separate ends and methods—that mark the divisiveness of the modern world. (This is Arnold's equivalent for Eliot's dissociation of sensibility.) It is this desire for unity, for the enfolding of the practical within the coordinate Kantian virtues of the true and the beautiful, that is the basis for Arnold's call for disinterestedness (also Kantian). Hence the Arnoldian insistence on the separation, in our intellectual life, of the sphere of ideas from the sphere of practice. The overpowering need is to keep our ideas free of the personal intrusions of interest and desire. It is these ideas, after all, which are to feed that ripe critical moment that can sustain the poet's creativity. This disinterestedness that preserves the purity of the world of ideas leads, in the domain of criticism, to Arnold's attack on the "personal estimate," surely a forerunner of Eliot's doctrine of impersonality, the notion that poetry is "an escape from emotion" rather than "a turning loose of emotion,"

---

3 *The Use of Poetry and the Use of Criticism* (Cambridge, Mass.: Harvard University Press, 1933), p. 90.

that in the poem there must be an absolute separation of "the man who suffers and the mind which creates." The submerging of the poet's personality in his poem, like the submerging of his beliefs in their emotional equivalents and the submerging of his emotion in its objective equivalent, is permitted by the unity of his sensibility and that in turn by the unity of his culture, external or internal. These are the ways he can absorb ideas and contain them in his work, disinterestedly in order to objectify them, rather than to be taken up by them in a manner that would sacrifice his status as poet.

This impersonal union of elements in poetry that properly flows from the properly fused sensibility—backed by a properly fused culture—may be a Goethean ideal that Eliot adapts from Arnold. But it seems to be allied—if not confounded—with the psychological unity he derives from the Coleridgean imagination. Thus, in speaking of Marvell's union of levity and seriousness, of the self-consciousness of wit and the devotion of imagination, Eliot can invoke the all-inclusive claims of Coleridge's now famous "elucidation of Imagination" (the capital "I," which doesn't appear elsewhere when Eliot uses the word in this essay, is significant).

> This power . . . reveals itself in the balance or reconcilement of opposite or discordant qualities: of sameness, with difference; of the general, with the concrete; the idea with the image; the individual with the representative; the sense of novelty and freshness with old and familiar objects: a more than usual state of emotion with more than usual order; judgment ever awake and steady self-possession with enthusiasm profound or vehement. . . .[4]

This passage, with much else in Coleridge, came also to influence I. A. Richards, and, through either or both of these masters of Cleanth Brooks, came to exert its force on an entire school of criticism. It may be at points such as this that such divergent influences as the Coleridgean and the Arnoldian are crucially joined, perhaps in ways not unlike the joining in our own day of the even more divergent influences from Eliot and Richards. Be this as it may, the fusion of ideology in the poetic complex must be seen—thanks to the poet's unified sensibility sanctioned by Arnold or thanks to the poet's organic imagination sanctioned by Coleridge—as a victory over ideology, a disinterested freedom from it. The freedom from the self-conscious creation of ideas, like the freedom from the practical service performed on

---

[4] This well-known description from chapter 14 of *Biographia Literaria* is quoted by Eliot in "Andrew Marvell," *Selected Essays*, new ed., pp. 256–57.

behalf of ideas, is a freedom to play with them, the sort of play that Schiller, as Kantian aesthetician, used as the defining quality of art.

II

The freeing of the poet from responsibility for ideas, freeing him for the unity of his poem as impersonal object, is seen—from the perspective of Arnold's influence on Eliot—as developing from the dependence of the poet's sensibility on the unity of the culture he inherits. Poetic unity is thus grounded in psychic unity. It is here that we see the point of union between Eliot and the early Richards as the common heirs of Arnold. It is true that we find the early work of Richards marked by a far narrower selection out of the broad range of Arnold's concepts, so that we perhaps feel that work to be far less in the Arnoldian spirit, even a distortion of that spirit in its excessive concentration and in the partiality of that concentration. If, unlike Eliot, Richards adapts only one or two of Arnold's points of emphasis, he attaches himself to them with an intensity that almost persuades us (but, in the end, only almost) that these may after all be the very center, the reduction of, Arnold's varied plenty. The reduction is created out of that notion of psychic unity that Arnold wistfully attributed to the outworn faith of the Middle Ages. This created or discovered center of Arnold, what Richards believes to be Arnold's indispensable definition of the capacities and limitations of modern culture, and poetry as its spokesman, is found behind the selection which Richards quoted for his epigraph to *Science and Poetry*:

> The future of poetry is immense, because in poetry, where it is worthy of its high destinies, our race, as time goes on, will find an ever surer and surer stay. There is not a creed which is not shaken, not an accredited dogma which is not shown to be questionable, not a received tradition which does not threaten to dissolve. Our religion has materialized itself in the fact, in the supposed fact; it has attached its emotion to the fact, and now the fact is failing it. But for poetry the idea is everything. . . .[5]

Richards could have added the last two sentences of this paragraph in Arnold, sentences which foreshadow the mood of George Santayana: "Poetry attaches its emotion to the idea; the idea *is* the fact. The strongest part of our religion today is its unconscious poetry." And, in

5 This and later quotations from "The Study of Poetry" are from its opening paragraphs.

the same spirit, he could have added words from the next paragraph in that essay, "The Study of Poetry":

> Without poetry, our science will appear incomplete; and most of what now passes with us for religion and philosophy will be replaced by poetry. . . . our religion, parading evidences such as those on which the popular mind relies now; our philosophy, pluming itself on its reasonings about causation and finite and infinite being; what are they but the shadows and dreams and false shows of knowledge? The day will come when we shall wonder at ourselves for having trusted to them, for having taken them seriously; and the more we perceive their hollowness, the more we shall prize "the breath and finer spirit of knowledge" offered to us by poetry.

What is central here is the conviction (1) that religion has lost its influence on modern man because of its dependence on supposed facts that turned out to be error and (2) that poetry, so long as it does not depend on facts that have a claim to truth, can take on the role of the now defunct religion. Clearly, poetry must be kept clear of the claim to truth if it is to be spared the fate of religion.

It is the development of modern science, with the revolutions it has forced upon our sense of man's place in the universe, that for Arnold has destroyed the possibility of faith. Arnold sees medieval faith, with its cornerstone in the Church, as providing enormous psychological advantages. Primarily, it is the psychic unity allowed by the hegemony of the Church which related our senses for knowledge, conduct, and beauty to one another as they met in the transcendently controlling domain of theology. Each sense moved only in accord with the others, with a watchful eye keeping it from straying too far on its own, in response to its own objectives. The autonomy of the free pursuit of knowledge awaited the grand breakup of disciplines that marked the Renaissance. The explosion of inductive knowledge, with each science unleashed to create its own methods for authenticating its own discoveries, responsible to no authority or inhibition beyond its own orbit, led to fantastically impressive results, but at an enormous cost. For what was being exploded was not just the previous unity of "supposed" knowledge, but the psychic unity required for human emotional satisfaction. Lost, then, were the great psychic advantages of the unity of our senses of knowledge, conduct, and beauty. This is to say that the Middle Ages—to the extent that it created a theocratic unity of arts and sciences—had the advantage of being everything but right. Just as a positivist like Thomas Henry Huxley would, Arnold concedes that the supposed knowledge that was humanly comfortable, warm, and wishfully complete and rounded, turned out to be utterly false, disproved by the empirical criteria of sciences whose only authority is from contingent experience below, not from dogmatic necessity above.

Once exposed to the convincing verifiability of the knowledge of modern science, for all of the psychic comforts it precludes, man is no longer able to will his return to those wrongly supposed facts—source of his prior faith—which sustained the psychic unity needed by man to sustain *him*. However discomfited by the new facts that coldly put him in his cosmic place, man will not deny them or their consequences as they affect his psychic security. So Arnold is one with the positivists in conceding to laboratory-controlled science the sole access to truth. But he will not concede, as did the Huxleys, that the human psyche can live without the satisfactions, now foregone, that the now out-moded supposed facts had afforded. If then, the need is constant and the supply is cut off, some substitute way of supplying that need must be found. Poetry is to be that way.

The special usefulness of poetry to perform this function stems from its power to unify our sensibilities without founding this power on supposed fact. Psychological power founded on supposed fact will founder as the supposed fact crumbles under the impact of proven counter-fact. Poetry must then be prevented, by the very nature of its assumptions and the modesty of its presumption, from exposing itself to the fact of science. We remember that for Arnold it was religion which "materialized itself in the . . . supposed fact . . . attached its emotion to the fact and now the fact is failing it." Hence religion becomes "but the shadows and dreams and false shows of knowledge." We must retain the psychic efficacy of religion without involving the commitment to those supposed facts that can undermine that efficacy. Or, put from the other side, from the positivist's viewpoint, we must not permit the advance of an independently empirical science to be slowed by the intrusions of the comforting warmth of human needs and the wishful thinking it sponsors. From either side the answer is poetry, an art which would have to be invented if it did not already exist, which now can come into its own to substitute for religion. Let it perform the psychological function, which science with its new facts is obliged to ignore, but let it leave all claims to knowledge to science, lest it enter into the impossible competition which will explode it as that competition exploded its predecessor. Indeed, we are almost brought to wonder why, in those earlier days when religion could do its job unchallenged, poetry ever did exist!

Viewed from the perspective of Richards's positivism, Arnold's concessions to Huxley seem to have been this substantial. Still, as humanist, he unremittingly defends poetry's power to minister to human needs—as he unremittingly defends the unchanged nature of those needs despite the changed world produced by science. As his disciple, who read the underlying concession and defense in Arnold's words, Richards may well see himself as spinning *Science and Poetry* out of the quotation which is its epigraph. From this he derives the central separation of poetry from all questions of knowledge, the separation which Richards sees as the freeing of poetry to perform its therapeutic psychological task, created by the heartless but necessary "neutralization of nature." Science marches ruthlessly on, annexing ever more territory in the land of "what is," having long abandoned the proper province of poetry, with its pastoral tending of the nonsensical land of "what ought to be." The latter, however, must not be taken seriously beyond the psychological occasion for which it is invented. For that occasion requires that poetry produce, not the singularity of commitment, but the balance of forces that permits an equilibrium, with its consequence of paralysis that prevents cognitive or practical decisiveness. This equilibrium is again a consistent outgrowth of Arnold's adaptation of Kantian disinterestedness.

So long as poetry makes no cognitive claims, it cannot be denied. (Shades of Sir Philip Sidney's claim that the poet "nothing affirms, and therefore never lyeth.") Its future as "an ever surer and surer stay" for man is assured, whatever the aggrandizement of cold scientific certainty. Indeed, the greater science's successes, the more we will need the soothing, unchallenging, unchallengeable, "emotive" accompaniments of poetry. Richards's invention of the distinction between emotive and referential (or between pseudo-statement and certified statement) as an absolute dichotomy is inevitable. It is true, of course, that the nineteenth-century Arnold, trapped in an older language, still reverts to archaic phrases like "poetic truth," suggesting to the less committed of us some uncertainty in him about taking the consequences of his occasional insights as agnostic humanist (distinguished from the religious humanist on the one side and the agnostic positivist on the other). He is, we must remember, father to Irving Babbitt as well. After all, he does admit that, if poetry does not attach its emotion to the fact, as religion does, it does attach its emotion to the "idea," which must still strike us as an intellectual commodity. But Richards, systematizing the more radical of Arnold's suggestions by rushing to take their consequences, must see such reversions as momentary lapses that may blunt the keen thrust of his pioneer daring without diverting us from its direction.[6]

6 I will shortly, with the help of Frye, propose a way to make these terms, *idea* and *poetic truth*, less retrograde than I now suggest they are.

Though propelled this time by another motive and from another part of Arnold's forest, we find ourselves very close to where Eliot had earlier brought us in consequence of *his* response to Arnold. With Eliot too, poetry was to find its function by turning aside from any direct responsibility for world views or systems of belief. In restricting himself to verbal equivalents of emotional equivalents, Eliot's poet was—not altogether unlike Richards's—to steer clear of the question of intellectual assent. He was to allow his poem to perform its therapeutic task unencumbered by our agreement or disagreement with his beliefs, since these beliefs were not to offer themselves separately from our judgment of them *as* beliefs. No wonder the orthodox Eliot felt embarrassed enough with his obvious similarity to the radically positivistic Richards for him to append the apologetic Note to his Dante essay, with its *ad hoc* struggle to mark off some differences between them.

III

It is, however, in his Arnoldian awareness of the distinction between a determined, if neutralized, nature and the willful, emotive act of man needed to save his humanity, that the early Richards anticipates Northrop Frye. It may seem that we are trying to tame Frye if we temper the influence of Blake on his work with that of Arnold, but his own expressions of such a debt encourage us to do so. For the starting point for Frye is his distinction between the order of nature and the order of words, the first being the world of science and the second the world of language, the imposition of human forms. As we see that Frye's nature is an objectively determined order while his language is an order determined only by the free act of imagination, so we see in his distinction both the reflection of Kant's opposition between the realms of nature and of freedom and the operation of the Kantian categories. With the absolute break between subject and object, there is the total differentiation between that world out there that goes its indifferent way without regard to how we would have it and the world created—as Frye would say—in response to human desire, in accordance with our imagination and the creatures with which it chooses to people its world. Thus we can define the world of nature and the world of human freedom, or, more precisely, nature given the scientific forms of objective necessity and nature transformed by the requirements of human imagination. It is the opposition allegorized by Goethe in his Faust who, shut out from the indifferent world that exists before man and outside man, must create his human world—in competition with it and beyond it—out of his own subjectivity that wills how man must have what he chooses to live in, his own humanly responsive world. This opposition also furnishes the answer, made in the shadow of Kant and Goethe, that Schiller's sentimental poet provides for the lost naiveté of the simple poet, his defunct ancestor.

All of which, from the point of view of Richards, may seem to be only an inflated way to speak of the emotive, and to authorize it by thus elevating it. To the still existing human needs which, for Arnold as for Richards, prolong the role of poetry in its pseudo-religious obsolescence, Frye adds the mythography of Blake which authenticates —all but metaphysically—the land of heart's desire. But still the central distinction in Frye between the worlds of nature and freedom, of science and language, for all the heavenly glories of the free word, can be seen to grow out of the lineage that moves from Kant, Goethe, and Schiller to its positivist reduction that, suggested in Arnold, we have seen realized in Richards. The transformation of nature by human creativity is, after all, what is being allegorized at the end of Faust's career in Part II when he literally remakes nature's waste in accordance with the orders of his human will. He reclaims land from the sea for the human purposes of its social future.

It is this concentration upon man's remaking of science's nature in his own image, upon his continuing act of symbolic construction, that enables Frye to speak interchangeably about imaginative literature and other, non-fictional modes of discourse since, whatever the differences among them, they are equally to be thought of as forms of imaginative projection. Of course, Arnold had more systematically treated all the major forms of human expression as coordinate, if not finally identical. We think of the several kinds of endeavor which Arnold asks to be concerned with "the best that has been thought and said in the world," and we recall the application of this criterion at various times to what he calls "poetry," what he calls "literature," what he calls "criticism," and, most broadly, what he calls "culture." Frye himself acknowledges the inclusive supremacy of Arnold's term, although in this regard he clearly separates himself from Richards and Eliot, who, however Arnoldian in most respects, cherish the role of poetry more exclusively. Frye's breadth in this matter is explicit: "But it seems clear that Arnold was on solid ground when he made 'culture,' a total imaginative vision of life with literature at its center, the regulating and normalizing element in social life, the human source, at least, of spiritual authority."[7] This concession to culture, which is in effect the stretching of poetry to include the very process of imagi-

7 *The Well-Tempered Critic* (Bloomington: Indiana University Press, 1963), p. 154.

native vision, can clearly be seen to have its philosophical sources in the tradition we have traced back through Goethe and Schiller to Kant.

The basis for Arnold's broad conception of human creativity, what Frye thinks of as its democratic appeal, is found in Arnold's special employment of that word *idea*. It is, though Frye himself may not credit the word, Arnold's ubiquitous *idea* that makes Arnold—for Frye as for others—the humanist *par excellence* who readies man to live, imaginatively and self-sufficiently, in a ruthlessly objectified world that lacks all awareness of subjects. Thus the question of the *objective* reality of God can be bypassed as humanistically irrelevant. It is now in a more profound sense that we return, through Frye's perspective, to Arnold's claim that "poetry attaches its emotion to the idea," rather than to the failing fact, as did religion. Further, the troublesome and seemingly retrograde notion of "poetic truth" may now be seen to fall more consistently into place with Arnold's other claims.

The ideas which his culture must furnish the poet clearly are the ideas to which he must attach emotion—much in the manner of Eliot's poet in his search for an objective correlative. But we now understand the sense of *idea* as a human creation, not to describe the state of nature (the proper business of science), but to create the conditions under which man wills to live in that nature. The idea, in the tradition which Arnold as middleman may have passed from Goethe to Richards and Frye, dares make no claim to objective truth, no religious or metaphysical claim.[8] Otherwise it risks obliteration by those self abnegating, dehumanized disciplines dedicated only to indifferent fact. But those ideas, unfit for attachment to fact, are fit for attachment to emotion. If not true of nature, they can be true of man in his imaginative freedom. Without risking the chance of being false to

[8] Were I writing this essay today, I would have emphasized the extent to which Arnold's distrust of metaphysics is in accord with the spirit of deconstruction which has been attributed to other nineteenth-century figures, like Marx and Nietzche, and has made them spiritual fathers to recent criticism in the continental manner. It is true that Arnold's faith in scientific fact goes well beyond theirs and that his commitment to poetry as an emotive substitute for metaphysics suggests a formalistic humanism which they could not share. But his call for a discourse free of metaphysics and subject only to man's will to create on his own in an empty universe—this is a call which echoes other calls we hear from his contemporaries. And these others are credited by my contemporaries in ways that deprive the milder Englishman of his influence among those making our current critical theory. I speak here for Arnold since his version of deconstruction preserves a major role for poetry, as the versions of the others do not. I would have liked, in other words, to add a number of my more widely read fellow-critics to Eliot, Richards, and Frye as unlikely brothers in their common inheritance from Arnold. Thus, despite yawning differences, links emerge between adjacent periods, in this case the modern and the postmodern.

nature, the idea can become a human truth, a "poetic truth." All ideas, by their very constitutive power, become poetic ideas, poetic truths. Thus the ideas which the poet must have to do his work, the ideas for which Arnold must sacrifice himself as poet so that he may create them as critic, are those which man must invent for himself to live with in the faithless age. Better for Arnold to contribute to the invention of such ideas than to lament poetically, but without new ideas, for the loss of faith—which is to say, the loss of bogus ideas, naively in hopeless competition with science. Here Arnold most anticipates Frye, if it isn't rather that Frye forces us to reinterpret Arnold. In either case, Arnold can be seen as authorizing the Frye who has man imagine the forms that shape his world in response to human desire, thus creating his culture that has its own authenticity, in distinction from that objectively authenticated world of nature, bound by its ineluctable processes. That culture is our dream. But we are doomed to be creatures of the night, the time of dreams, so that it becomes our truth, the truth of our poetry. And all our ideas are in that sense poetic.

IV

We began by noting something close to an inconsistency in Eliot and Richards as in Arnold: They assert, on the one hand, the need for a separation between ideas and poetry and, on the other hand, the need for a fusion and unity in the poet's work (as well as, for Eliot and Arnold at least, in his sensibility and his culture). Frye seems to resolve this difficulty, for Arnold as well as for himself, by overcoming the extra-poetic character of ideas. Of course, he can accomplish this, as we have seen, only by broadening poetry until it encompasses ideas, although Frye might prefer another, less Arnoldian term for *ideas*. Still, as the shaping of nature to human ends, ideas become poetry, become coextensive with poetry. The cost to poetry in this broadened sense is that it now is no longer limited to poems. It characterizes, not uniquely fashioned works with their specially manipulated medium, but all symbolic projections of human vision. It is a price which Eliot and Richards, whatever their other difficulties, need not pay. By elevating poetry to vision itself, Frye may seem to have freed it from the earthly burden of mere discourse. We have more than once noted the sense in which Arnold himself seemed anxious to free ideas, on which poetry and its "truth" depended, from the drag of material nature with its alien, inhuman laws. Frye has pursued this liberation of the human dream more extremely. The stubborn, intransigent reality that goes its way in indifference to us must be abandoned by imagination for the forms of human desire, the world as we choose to have it, as we must have it if we are to preserve our humanity. The dream of imagination must dismiss everything in nature that objectively *is* for a mythic transformation into its sense of the ought-to-be.

It may be that the extravagance of Frye's theory, in its most distinctive form, most consistently fulfills the promise implied by Arnold's criticism, with a theoretical courage beyond what was possible for the late nineteenth-century mind. But it must leave out that extra-poetic, perhaps inhuman reality—the ineradicable something-out-there in experience and language, whatever its downward pull—to which Eliot and Richards in their different ways paid homage by allowing it to disrupt the unity of their theories. That they too are children of Arnold is probably evidence that the world outside both man and his shapings of it, operating in its own maddening way, is one which Arnold also, for better or worse, could never altogether relinquish.

7

Reconsideration—The New Critics

IT WAS WHEN I read J. Hillis Miller's survey of last year's books in literary criticism (in the November 29, 1975, issue of the *New Republic*) that I realized it was time to consider again, in such new light as he throws, the contributions of the New Criticism—as represented, say, by John Crowe Ransom in *The World's Body* (1938) and *The New Criticism* (1941), by Allen Tate in *On the Limits of Poetry* (1948) and *The Forlorn Demon* (1953), and by Cleanth Brooks in *The Well Wrought Urn* (1947). I have been told that my book, *The New Apologists for Poetry* (1956), helped bury the New Critics twenty years ago; if so, Miller's essay prompts me to try to exhume them. For I had hoped that post–New-Critical movements, while sophisticating their epistemology and resisting their mystifications, would build upon their insights. But Miller's essay reminds us how thoroughly all vestiges of that old New Criticism have been swept away by the new wave of our newer criticism, dominated by recent continental influences. As he shows us, recent critical fashions in the academy have sprung forth from assumptions that altogether preclude those of the New Criticism, thereby denying us their methods of literary analysis and the considerable fruits which such methods could bear. If our

This essay was written for the *New Republic*'s series of reconsiderations in 1976.

newer new criticisms go as Miller sees them going, then all continuity with earlier criticism in our century is severed, and we must unsay some rich decades of critical sayings. So I thought it worth looking again at what was being recanted and measuring the cost of that recantation.

What seems, from Miller's alien perspective, most central and unifying in the varied writers we (sometimes unfairly) have lumped together as New Critics is their insistence on the linguistic presence of (and *in*) the poem. Because they attribute to each poem the power to generate its verbal form, they see poems as entities uniquely privileged to struggle with and overcome the (otherwise) universal character of language, which, for them as for the structuralists, tends to degenerate into empty signs. This claim to the victory of verbal presence in poems—and, through it, the refounding of meaning in words—is the common conclusion of Ransom's licensing of a self-generating poetic ontology (in "Poetry: A Note in Ontology," the key essay in *The World's Body*, and "Wanted: An Ontological Critic," the all-resolving final chapter of *The New Criticism*), of Tate's notions—at once hybrid and synthetic—of "tension" and "proximate incarnations" (in "Tension in Poetry" from *On the Limits of Poetry* and "The Symbolic Imagination" from *The Forlorn Demon*), and of Brooks's paradoxical justification of poetic irony (throughout *The Well Wrought Urn*).

I have suggested what may sound surprising: that these New Critics hold certain notions about the workings of language in common with the structuralists, who represent a dominating force in that continentally influenced criticism championed by Miller. But I also suggested, as a qualification to this agreement, that critics like Ransom, Tate, and Brooks argue for the emptiness of verbal signifiers only while insisting upon exempting poetry from such general linguistic incapacities, building the very function of poetry upon this exemption. That is to say, they see the poem as generating a verbal form which reveals itself in its power to fill its signifiers with meanings—those very signifiers which, in their habitual use, have previously lost all meaning. Despite this crucial qualification, it remains important for us to see the similarities between the New-Critical and the structuralist conception of normal language behavior.

One may see I. A. Richards functioning for these New-Critical claims much as Ferdinand de Saussure functioned for structuralism, with each providing a rudimentary linguistic analysis which becomes the basis for the criticism that followed. The New Critics derive from Richards's dualistic opposition between sign and thing in his argument for the referentiality of science and the non-referentiality of poetry, much as the structuralist needs Saussure's opposition between signifier and signified to define discourse as the manifold dispositions of empty signifiers. The difference, of course, is that New Critics, anti-positivists all, tended to be less faithful to Richards's dichotomy than structuralists have proved to be to Saussure's. The New-Critical contribution consists in their struggle to convert Richards's linguistic reductionism into a theory that can account for the newly embodied world they find in poems, even if it is but a world of words. For *these* words are full, and their fullness is one with their meaning, though a meaning founded (and found) only in their form. Ransom, for example, freely grants the arbitrariness of language in its sensory dimension as sound—grants it as freely as any structuralist would—but he sees the poem as parading that arbitrariness with a self-consciousness that makes it the necessary precondition for the poem's presence—as well as for the presence and fullness of its meaning.

Here, then, is the parting of the ways between the New Criticism and the structuralism with which it seems to share a common view about the general workings of language. Though both may agree that there is an absence of proper signifieds in language generally, the New Critic insists on allowing for the presence in poems of a discourse that generates and fills itself with its own signifieds. As aesthetic elitists, they see the debased democracy of *écriture* being forced to yield the privilege that each true poem earns for itself as a closed verbal system. If humanists these days view the world of words as one emptied of meaning just as the world itself has been emptied of God, these humanists see that world as being forced to sustain—though it is belied by—a word now made flesh by man as poet, who creates a verbal identity within a linguistic system of ineluctable differences. It is their holding open this opportunity to create a verbal presence that has left them vulnerable to the monolithic positivism of spirit that has succeeded them.

I press this comparison between the New Criticism and structuralism because of the extent to which—as Miller reminds us in his survey —all academic criticism that "counts" today (which is to say, all criticism that is currently fashionable in the academy) is continentally derived, the dominant continental modes being assumed to be structuralist and post-structuralist. Indeed, in the Miller essay itself it seems enough to dismiss the sensitive study of George Herbert by Helen Vendler (the first book Miller mentions) by praising her as "the most distinguished contemporary practitioner of the New Critical tradition of 'close reading.'" Since such an attachment means that she is likely to be "implicitly hostile to continental criticism or indifferent to it" (and is "mostly innocent, whether innocently or not, of any continental tinge"), it is clearly time, after the single sentence mentioning the book, for Miller to move past it toward what he sees as theoretically more consequential (which is to say, theoretically more fashionable) works, which he can treat at his leisure. About the Herbert volume we are left with the implication: splendid work, though quaint.

What accounts for the current domination of the critical scene by the continental ideas we associate with the terms *structuralism* and *post-structuralism* is their antagonism to verbal and poetic presence, which is the very heart of New-Critical doctrine. Wary of presence as a mythical delusion, they succumb to metaphysical emptiness and would have it sanction a verbal emptiness that not even poetic powers can replenish. Seeing all our books authorized by the original Book authored by God, the structuralist finds the belief in the word to die with the death of our belief in the Creator whose Word gave all words meaning: when God evacuates our world, meaning evacuates our language. All worldly signifieds follow the Transcendental Signified out of our realm, the empty shell of Word and words. Such are the existentialist assumptions behind the structuralist negations, the latter being the semiotic consequences of "the disappearance of God" (to borrow the title of one of Miller's books).

The work of Paul de Man, to whose importance Miller testifies in his essay, continually emphasizes the desperate inability of our language, since the early Romantics, to leap the void that separates the word from its would-be references in the world. This hopeless distance between signifier and signified is a reflection of the chasm between the interiority of the human subject and the deadly indifference of the object out there on its own. But, de Man to the contrary notwithstanding, the New Critic can claim that a dualistic thematic like his, for all it denies to language and for all the existential failures it visits upon the poet as human subject, need not preclude the poem from creating a monistic verbal structure that contains such denials within its expressive unity. On the other hand, for de Man, and for the structuralist and phenomenological view he in part inherits, man's existential failure to remake a now alien nature must be echoed by the failure of his poem to remake its language—again a linguistic analysis that masks the theorist's existential anguish. So for him the possibility of poetic union in the created symbol dissolves into the dualism of a hopeless allegory. Poetic absence, with God's overwhelms us.

No less than de Man, the New Critic had inherited the shambles left by the collapse of faith in the signified and—consequently—the signifier. But, unlike de Man, the New Critic claimed the unique capacity of the poem to fill itself as a new-born signifier that recreated the fully signifying power of language again and again. And, retrograde as I may appear, I too am concerned about the loss of the filled and centered word, so that I must recall again the virtues that have now been demythologized, and lament the small gains given us in return for all we have given up.

It must be conceded that the New Critics habitually reified their poetic experiences into an absolute, if mythic, object. What we may see today as a fictional claim about the poem's integral self they uncritically asserted with epistemological naiveté. But their lesson for us today is their unquestioning willingness, consistent with their (and our) critical tradition, to treat the poem as a creative centering of words. It is true also that, in echoing the humanist's insistence on man's obligation to re-fill word and world with meaning—*his* meaning as a lower-case, still creative, creature—the New Critic may be seen, especially from the Structuralist perspective, as falling victim to his own mythologizing powers, which will not face up to the emptiness of his universe. Of course, a critic's defense of the power of the poet, as fiction-maker, to fill his world of words can be made without his turning it into a metaphysical defense of the world's fullness. Must such a critic be charged with invoking the myth of metaphysical presence if he claims no more than a constructed verbal presence?

If belief in the poet's power to find embodiment in the word is a myth, it has been, for the critical tradition in the West from its beginnings, the necessary fiction that has permitted more than two millennia of our greatest poems to speak to us. Few critical schools in our history have done more than the New Critics did to give them voice. Thanks in large part to these critics—but before them as well— the poems have been *there*, speaking as they do, as if there is a presence in them. They make their own case for presence, and it is out of no mere nostalgia that we continue to value it in them. For presence is present tense, and while we live we must not allow ourselves to be reasoned out of it.

It may well be that the post-structuralist mood is the most appropriate one to account for the revolutionary art produced in our culture these last decades: an anti-aesthetic for an anti-art. The philosophical assault on man's symbols may both mirror and justify what man has been of late doing with them—or refusing to do with them. It would hardly be a flattering comment to suggest that, if post-structuralism turns out to be a theoretical partner of recent activities in the arts, they deserve one another. And I trust it is more than just a reactionary comment to suggest that the recent wars on metaphysics and art alike have hardly produced in the arts worthy successors to the tradition they would destroy. In reconsidering the New Criticism here, I mean to stimulate us to reconsider at the same time the brilliant and extensive artistic repertoire which it was created to serve. These works in our tradition still stand, demanding the traditional aesthetic to account for them. It was this aesthetic of which the New Criticism represented a climactically productive moment.

I have made more of a school than is perhaps warranted by the several writers whom Miller treats jointly and favorably. Miller admits considerable differences among them, although he goes on to claim their common importance in light of the attention they pay to directions in continental theory, whether sympathetically or not. Certainly the exclusively extended treatment he accords Jacques Derrida, Paul de Man, Geoffrey Hartman, and Harold Bloom may suggest the embarrassing fact that the only school represented by these critics is Yale University. Yet there is what I have called a post-structuralist mood, if not a unified doctrine, in the work of these critics, and it is a mood that is now attracting academic critics throughout the country. That we should find a tentative alliance built on a mood, a temperamental rather than an ideological affinity, attests to the existential rather than the linguistic or methodological motive behind their varied writings.

Even Bloom's recent books can be viewed as making common cause with the others, unlikely as that may at first seem. Bloom licenses the critic to use the present critical occasion to undo and replace the primacy of the historically prior piece of writing (as its author had sought to use his poetic occasion to displace *his* precursor). Any potential presence of the poem that confronts the critic is thus dispersed into what Derrida would term "traces" of the burdensome past, now exploded by the present critic's self-gratifying ego. So the critic, indulging his narcissistic moment as the latest in a sequence of such moments indulged by the poets whom he deceives us into believing to be his subjects, tries to win his competition with his predecessor-poet, substituting his presence for that of the poem which, thus transformed, recedes as an unrecognizable point of origin. The critic supplants his precursor-father, remaking his work into his own. This self-conscious usurpation by the critic of the primary role of the literary work is another version of the post-structuralist's reduction of that work to the common domain of *écriture*, which equalizes all discourse and de-privileges the poem, denying its pretense to presence.

It would seem to be this radical reorientation of the role of the critic and the role of the poem as it spins out of our general discursive habits that characterizes the continental mood which Miller, probably accurately, sees as currently most influential. And it is in light of this tendency that the New Critics seem obsolete with their traditional sense of the poem as the critic's object. As we are reminded by Miller of the place of Yale in history's vengeful conspiracy to "de-center" the poem, we may muse ironically about the fact that Yale was not too long ago the equally well-armed bastion of another all-dominating movement—the New Criticism now so severely declared outmoded, one fashion undone by another. Let me compound the irony: if Bloom's theory, so different from and yet finally in tune with some continental theorizing, legitimizes and indeed issues a summons to literary patricide, it is appropriate, after all, that his generation of Yale critics make this place for themselves by annihilating the preceding generation of Yale critics—and with an intensity and exclusiveness equal to theirs. In its consequences for our culture, however, the act is a negative one, an enactment of the murder of the past which modern society through its art has generally been practicing. The New Criticism reminds us that we can de-center past objects and can undo their presence only by obliterating all entities, ours among them. The murder of our fathers leads not to the assertion, but to the denial, of ourselves.

8
The Theoretical Contributions
of Eliseo Vivas

THERE IS SOME embarrassment attendant upon contributing to an occasion of this sort. The essays which are assembled—and this essay in particular—are justified by the honor they pay to a man who has had a long and distinguished career as scholar and teacher. And yet the appeal they are to hold for the potential reader (especially as a publisher might view it) is dependent upon the distinction of those whose essays are being assembled: due testimony of the rightfulness of the distinction being claimed for the honoree, that these would come together to acknowledge their debt to him. Hence the writers are in the awkward position of having to justify themselves in order to justify the presumed object of the occasion they are together creating. And there is a presumptuous ambiguity about who is being honored: the present writers or the absent personage whose work was to have inspired their dedication.

To avoid this embarrassing ambiguity and the unjust presumption behind it, it is important that the work of the honored scholar-teacher be seen as influential and as worthy of being influential without being

This essay was written for a volume published to celebrate Eliseo Vivas's seventy-fifth birthday.

115

treated as if in competition with those it has influenced: as if its splendid historical role must be proved by proving the excellence of its followers. For the work, at least in this case, is—self-evidently—its own best testimony. Yet it is difficult to speak of this work, if one sees himself as having inherited it, without seeing it from his own vantage point, seeing it—that is—as it has helped to shape his own vision and, hence, his own work. And this is to run the risk of creating an impertinent competition among the objects of praise and defense in the essay; in short, to create a potential conflict of interest that can only damage the occasion and distort the appropriate object of study. Yet one must try to let modesty do its work.

Few can claim a greater right than I can to bear testimony on the present occasion, in view of the extent to which my work has been shaped by the writings and the teaching of Eliseo Vivas, in and out of the classroom, before and after I went to school to him. And, feeling with him so completely the student with the teacher, I should be in a convenient position to keep first things first, and myself second. Since I have just written yet another preface to a book in which I acknowledge my indebtedness to him, I should be especially and gratefully aware of his influence and, thus, should welcome the opportunity to discuss his contributions to developments in theory these last several decades.[1] And I do welcome it.

Given this personal entree into what follows, however, the reader should be alerted to the likelihood that, even in my case, what I claim to see as his contributions will be colored by my sense of what I have needed most indispensably to make use of in my own theoretical work. Though I shall try to look dispassionately at the state of theory and the extent to which it was Eliseo Vivas who worked to constitute it, I, as a former student forcefully shaped by his teacher, cannot help but have *my* Eliseo Vivas strongly influence my judgment about his shaping force upon theory itself. And the aspects of his theorizing which will most concern me may well not be those which history (or perhaps he himself) would properly think his most distinctive gifts to his philosophic beneficiaries, though they are what has most characterized his work for me. It is precisely these fears about the distortions produced by my subjective angle of vision and the special investment I have in it which have led me to those distrustful words about *Festschriften* with which I began.

As I see them, the contributions to theory of Eliseo Vivas must be

[1] I speak mainly of literary theory and aesthetics, although some of what I say may well apply to his work in ethics and value theory generally. Though I cannot claim the competence to make these connections myself, his contributions in these areas would certainly seem equally deserving of an assessment on this occasion.

traced through a lengthy and continually productive career, one controlled by a developing, finally unified philosophic vision, however varied the problems to be solved and the solutions found. But it is worth distinguishing the successive phases of his career, since it is in the development itself that I believe the unity, as a complex, dynamic entity, can be best discovered and described. The deepest and most obvious division found in his work is that between what we can crudely term his early naturalistic phase and his more mature, self-consciously metaphysical phase, which is militantly anti-naturalistic. Perhaps more important for the theorist, however, is the fact that these phases are reflected in the changing theoretical problems on which he concentrated as well as, more obviously, in the differing sorts of solutions he proposed to them. So we must also begin by seeing separately the two major areas of his distinctive contributions: on the one hand, those emerging out of the essays of the late thirties and early forties which throw a new light on the nature of aesthetic experience and, on the other hand, those found in the books and essays after the middle forties, which reconstitute first our notions of creativity and values, and then our sense of the role played by art in shaping culture.

Yet his career gives us reason to resist polarizing these phases, though his earlier philosophic commitments seem opposed to the later and though the aesthetic issues on which he concentrates show a correspondent shift. For, whatever the turnings in his development as philosopher and theorist, Vivas did not reject the gains of his early theorizing (however he may have rejected the philosophic substructure on which they were based) even as he added his later transformations in metaphysics and aesthetics. Yet I do not mean to suggest that he merely piled newer notions onto incompatible ones in an eclectic accumulation. To the contrary, he remained always wary of systematic requirements: he might make his system complex, even apparently paradoxical, but never internally inconsistent, if he could help it. So the merging of his early doctrine of aesthetic experience, seemingly a byproduct of Deweyan naturalism, into an anti-naturalistic and metaphysical theory of objective value and original creativity (with their anthropological yield for society) is a praiseworthy example of philosophic growth and not merely of ideological alternations.

Let me trace these phases more closely, relating them to each other and assessing their roles in the unfolding aesthetic of Eliseo Vivas. Very likely it was his early attachment to the Deweyan tradition which disposed him to do his most exciting work on our peculiar response to art. Given the centering of value on the experientially dominated interests of man, it was the more consistent—with Vivas as with Dewey—that the heart of our theorizing about art should be man's experiencing of it. But though in conformity with instrumentalist value theory and the objective relativism which generated it, Vivas's aesthetic breaks with the concern for expression and emotion to the extent that these were the defining features of aesthetic experience for Deweyan and near-Deweyan theory. His early critique of expressionist and emotionalist theories, together with his development of his own theory of "rapt, intransitive attention" as a more adequate substitute for them, is his first, and remains a continuing, major contribution to aesthetics.[2]

As I have suggested, Vivas originally saw no need to break with Deweyan naturalism to develop this theory as (he thought) a more adequate extension of naturalism into the domain of aesthetic experience, which, for the instrumentalist, was the dominant moment in the "aesthetic transaction." The very notion of the "trans-action," so central to his argument, suggests the relational basis of his claims about the subject's response to the stimulating object, a comfortable notion for the instrumentalist. But he uses this relational basis, we shall see, to move from the experiencing subject to an object that possesses certain normative properties. These features in the object lead in turn to the doctrine of the phenomenal objectivity of aesthetic value, and although he argues even later that this doctrine can be held by naturalists and non-naturalists alike, it is clear that the doctrine is held the more comfortably by the philosopher who would ground phenomenal objectivity in what the non-naturalistic Vivas would later term ontic objectivity. So the "new naturalism" he first worked for, a broadening of naturalism that would accommodate his (still naturalistic) theory of aesthetic experience, had to give way. As he joined to his concern with value a concern with a theory of mind commensurate with his notion of creativity, his naturalism had to give way to a metaphysical conception that began with ontic substructures as philosophical realities which came to be reflected onto the phenomenal level, thanks in large part to the artist and the experience of rapt intransitive attention which his object has been organized to force upon us.

But let us observe more closely this aesthetic experience which his

2 See especially "Four Notes on I. A. Richards' Aesthetic Theory," *Philosophical Review* 44 (1935), "A Definition of the Aesthetic Experience," *Journal of Philosophy* 34 (1937), "A Note on the Emotion in Mr. Dewey's Theory of Art," *Philosophical Review* 47 (1938), "A Natural History of the Aesthetic Transaction," in *Naturalism and the Human Spirit*, ed. Yervant H. Krikorian (New York: Columbia University Press, 1944), and "The Objective Correlative of T. S. Eliot," *American Bookman* 1 (1944). For a much later refinement of this argument, see "Animadversions on Imitation and Expression," *The Artistic Transaction and Essays on Theory of Literature* (Columbus: Ohio State University Press, 1963).

naturalism may have led him into, but which by its own implications ended by leading him out of naturalism. The advantage for Vivas of defining the experience as intransitive attention is that, in contrast to subjective notions like emotion and expression, it directs us to the object as the seat of the power that traps our attention. His definition has the further advantage of inviting an experience which is unique to its object rather than, as with emotion or expression or even pleasure, being assimilated to a broad human response, which is capable of being aroused by many sorts of objects, aesthetic or not. For the attention, as rapt and intransitive, is induced and controlled by the special features of the object which prevent our escape from it to the world of more general or stereotyped responses. Hence it is a response, *sui generis*, to this object that keeps our attention rapt and, as intransitive, riveted on itself. Of course, the object should then be seen by the critic as displaying features capable of enforcing this attention upon it.

It is important to note in passing that Vivas makes these claims about the object modestly and with qualification. He continually professes his awareness that the aesthetic experience, as defined by him, is a psychological phenomenon, a datum that will occur when it occurs, regardless of any consensus we can reach about the aesthetic quality of the stimulating object—indeed, regardless of whether the object is even intended to serve such an experience. If, then, it can be any object and if no one can predict when the experience will occur for any subject, how can we use the experience to make the normative claim which I have suggested is the main advantage of defining the experience this way? Here Vivas would remind us of the relational basis of his notion of the "transaction": that the object functions as the object in what is conceived as an aesthetic experience only because it so functions and is so conceived as it interacts with the subject of the experience. (We see again at this point the advantage for Vivas of his emerging out of the Deweyan tradition. But this notion does not commit him to naturalism, as he later came to discover. Even the ontologist must leave phenomena to the phenomenal world, relating subject and object in a mutual dependence that is implicit in the meaning of *phenomenon*.)

But this relational basis can support an objective claim of value if we seek an experience of an object that can be shared by many subjects rather than be found, idiosyncratically, in one subject. Granted that an experience which might satisfy Vivas's definition as aesthetic can result, for a single subject, from a confrontation with any object, we can still try to decide whether the ground for the aesthetic character of the experience is in the features of the object or in the projective powers of the subject. If we come to expect the experience to be aesthetic as we move from subject to subject before the same object, it must be because we are attributing the control of the experience—and the largest share of the responsibility for it—to the features of the object. We are claiming, in effect, that a knowing and submissive subject—accustomed to aesthetic transactions—*ought* to be led into an aesthetic experience by this object. Further, the lapses or deficiencies are in the subject if he fails so to respond. If we do not find such characteristics in the object, on the other hand, then we are likely to claim that it is the subject who is responsible for any claimed aesthetic experience, so that we would not expect it to be repeated with another subject. The experience would be seen as more idiosyncratic than appropriate as a response to this object with the features we are specifying for it. By this manner of proceeding, the experience, in the case of a particular object of the first sort, becomes normative after all—or at least the aesthetic response becomes normative since the object is seen as soliciting it. In short, we are making an affirmative claim of aesthetic value for the object. So the Vivas argument runs, as he uses a relational theory of aesthetic experience to get to an objective theory of value.

It is, of course, the characterization of aesthetic experience as intransitive attention that enables him to manage this movement. If the subject, in such an experience, is required to be contained by the object, searching out all the possible interrelations among its elements playing on its surface and in its depths but being held by it from searching beyond, then his experience—so long as one maintains that it is a response appropriate to this object—must point to the features of the object that enforce and sustain that containment. The object invites attention and, keeping it intransitive, holds that attention upon itself terminally, presenting its world as the subject's total world for the course of the experience, without leading to the commonplace world beyond that comes before and after—though it is this world to which its symbols seem, in a non-aesthetic context, to point. This leads Vivas to emphasize that its meanings, during the experience, are "immanent" and "reflexive" rather than, as with objects functioning in non-aesthetic experiences, "referential." Representation becomes presentation, as signs that normally point the subject to the world are forced by the pressures of his attention to become mutually sustaining with meanings that become self-sufficient. A work thus would be seen to be other than aesthetic (in the experience toward which it seeks to lead its subject) to the extent that its meanings are referentially directed, moving the subject's attention outside instead of constantly renewing the internal relations that trap him within.

As Vivas licenses him, the critic thus sees as the psychological "factors of advantage" (by which is meant factors of containment and control) for our intransitive attention those aesthetic features of the object as an entrapping structure. Antique criteria like unity come to be newly justified, and more recent New-Critical criteria like irony or paradox or ambiguity—complexity in general—are theoretically earned in a philosophical context that has us looking for characteristics whose equivocal nature blocks our tendency to escape with a single referential meaning. It is the potential completeness of aesthetic system growing out of his concept of the aesthetic experience that led Vivas to be looked upon, *ex post facto* and not altogether accurately, as the aesthetician of the New Criticism. For these promising but hardly philosophically minded critics needed one, and the tendency of Vivas's work was corroborative of many of their findings. Certainly it is the case that, in the light of his work, the New Criticism, whatever its inconsistencies and divagations among its varied practitioners, was accorded a more understanding and useful role in the history of modern aesthetics.

Throughout his career, despite the disruption in his philosophical allegiance, Vivas has held to essentially the same notion of aesthetic experience. In the early and brief, but justly influential, "A Definition of the Aesthetic Experience," he acknowledged that a lengthier treatment was required. He provided this fuller statement in "A Natural History of the Aesthetic Transaction," written as early as 1939 though the Krikorian volume which contained it appeared only in 1944. The commitment to naturalism is the more evident as the presentation becomes the more detailed in the longer essay. Ironically, by the time the volume appeared Vivas had undergone serious doubts about the philosophical underpinnings that were the more apparent in that essay.[3] It was not until two decades later that he wrote the final and most complete version, this time in accord with the metaphysic he had adopted.[4] And it was a full statement indeed, one that incorporated his total mature aesthetic. Yet it remains essentially compatible with his earliest statement.

As I have suggested earlier, the role of the object in the aesthetic experience leads Vivas toward an objective theory of value insofar as that value is "anchored" in the perceptible features of the object. Values, as axiological or tertiary qualities, may well be intuitive

[3] For this reason it was the less revealing "Definition," rather than the fuller essay, that he preferred to reprint in *The Problems of Aesthetics* (1953) and *Creation and Discovery* (1955).

[4] "The Artistic Transaction," *The Artistic Transaction and Essays on Theory of Literature*, pp. 3–93.

affairs which cannot be reduced to perceptible or secondary qualities of the object; yet, in the case of an object whose features can be shown to lead the subject toward the aesthetic experience by controlling his attention and rendering it intransitive, we can claim its aesthetic values to be "anchored" in those features.[5] This commitment to phenomenal objectivity, a claim which he has always conceded is possible for the naturalist as well as the value realist to make, led him nonetheless to an awareness of the incapacity of even the "new naturalism" to account for the metaphysical basis of such values. His growing attachment to ontic objectivity had stimulated his attack on naturalistic value theory in ethics before "The Objective Basis of Criticism" extended it to aesthetics.[6] And, whatever the common elements in his naturalistic and anti-naturalistic phases, his new philosophical position would have to be reflected in the shift in the areas to be emphasized in his aesthetics.

His conviction about the inadequacy of naturalism led to (if it did not result from) his championing of a theory of mind and its creativity which suggested metaphysical consequences—and origins. If his theory of value was realistic, his theory of mind was idealistic; but both seemed to him equally to require a non-naturalistic metaphysic.[7] Nor is there any inconsistency, although there is a dynamic tension, between these two theories (of value and of mind) as he builds his aesthetic on the apparently paradoxical relations between them.

Far from being inconsistent, it is rather clear that his definition of aesthetic experience as intransitive attention would assume the radical creativity of the artist. This entails the claim, in accord with Coleridge's definition of "imagination," that the artist brings to his product a creative addition, the result of a spontaneity of mind that gives forth a synthesis beyond the materials that it has taken in. If the artist is author of the object whose features have a structure that holds us intransitively in its unity, then that integral complex of immanent and reflexive meanings which has transformed his would-be referential materials can have its source only in his creative act. Not that the

[5] "The Objective Basis of Criticism," *Western Review* 12 (1948).

[6] "Animadversions on Naturalistic Ethics," *Ethics* 56 (1946). This essay, which officially indicated his change of philosophical allegiance, was an early version of what grew into the opening section of *The Moral Life and the Ethical Life* (Chicago: University of Chicago Press, 1950). It is unfortunate that the strength and vigor of his attack kept some readers from appreciating the force of his positive argument in the balance of that book.

[7] "Two Notes on the New Naturalism," *Sewanee Review* 56 (1948). A portion of this essay appeared in *Creation and Discovery* with the appropriate title "Naturalism and Creativity."

artist's spontaneity is a literal one that creates *ex nihilo*, like the God of Genesis; but the changes he works upon the materials given him lend to his emergent object an apparent newness, for the rapt aesthetic observer, that makes it appear to be the product of a human genesis. In effect, it is, as Coleridge would have it, the lesser genesis, finite imitation of "the infinite I AM." And Vivas sees this doctrine of creativity, so dependent upon the aesthetic realm for its most dramatic demonstration, as one for which no naturalistic theory of mind can account. For the doctrine requires an idealistic claim, while the naturalist cannot finally move beyond the materialistic and behavioral. This inadequacy in accounting for creativity joins with an inadequacy in accounting for objective values to summon the philosopher to a less reductive position—or at least these inadequacies so summoned *this* philosopher.

But it should be seen from what I have just said that it is not altogether accurate to speak of Vivas's description of the creative process as representing an unqualifiedly idealistic theory of mind. For his insistence on the finitude of human creation as less than God's infinite creation, *ex nihilo*, arises from his concern with those materials given the artist from outside. To cite the artist's finitude is to remind us that he can create only mediately rather than immediately —in short, that he is dependent upon a medium. Vivas is drawing back from making the idealist's gnostic claim (of unmediated creativity) for the artist. The fact that his theory spins out of an aesthetic experience defined as intransitive attention requires that the artist work in a manipulable but sharable symbolic medium, one with properties that can be shaped into an objective structure which can perform its captivating function when confronted by the observer. It is this medium that he shares with his contemporaries and with all earlier artists. Thus the mind of the artist, for all its creative capacity, is dependent upon the sensory realities of his objective and traditional medium to express itself. And that expression is the result of the give and take between what the creative mind demands and what the limitations of the medium will allow, although that give-and-take may result in breakthroughs by an artist who has forced a new plasticity upon the medium. Not that he has exceeded the limitations, but that they have been reconceived so that they seem to be working for him. Thus, even where Vivas most approximates idealism, he brings in the real as ineluctably there, a formative element to be reckoned with in whatever is to be created.

In effect, Vivas is saying that what the artist is in one sense creating he is another sense discovering in the flexible potentialities of his medium. This paradoxical notion—that creation and discovery are equally just, and simultaneously present, descriptions of the relation between the artist's product and his reality—persists throughout Vivas's complex system of aesthetics. It explains his impatience with the partiality of unqualified idealism or expressionism on the one hand and of traditional theories of imitation on the other. The artist must be seen as creating beyond his materials, the biographical materials of his experience and the traditional materials left him by the history of his art; but he must also be seen as discovering what his product is becoming only as he works it out in the objective form it must finally assume. It is not a prior mental creation which he then translates into the form we finally see; it is a creation only as it is discovered in the making, the making in those materials that fix it for us.

Yet we have seen that what is created is a great deal indeed, and—once created—it is an indispensable gift for us all. Perhaps the greatest contribution made by Vivas's work after the middle forties was his analysis of the nature of the gift which the artistic creation makes to its culture. According to this analysis, through its symbolic structure the work of art gives its culture the perceptual norms that create an elementary order for the inchoate flow which is "the primary data of experience" which we all undergo. Vivas claims to find four "ideal" modes of experience, of which we have seen only his crucial examination of the aesthetic (as intransitive attention).[8] Unlike the other three—the religious, the moral, and the cognitive—only the aesthetic has this peculiarly intimate relationship to "the primary data of experience." Indeed, it is likely that the other modes, rather than dealing with the primary data directly, deal with the symbolic forms provided largely by the aesthetic mode. So it is the aesthetic mode that puts the world at our disposal for us to act upon it in the other modes, the various transitive modes.[9]

[8] The reader should have been reminded, in my earlier discussion, that what Vivas has been defining as the aesthetic experience must not be expected to occur in its pure form in our actual experiences, which in fact are various mixtures of the four modes he defines. The experiences we have, whatever their composite natures, contain elements which can be extracted for a definition of what an ideal aesthetic experience would be. And, as we have seen, we can move from there to the kind of object whose structure would appear to predispose its subject to such an experience. But Vivas does not confuse ideal with actual mixed experiences; nor does he claim any superiority for the ideal experience, though it is philosophically useful for him to deal with it.

[9] There have been several key essays since the early 1950s in which Vivas treats the relation of the aesthetic mode to the "primary data" and to the other modes. Chief among these is "The Object of the Poem," *Creation and Discovery: Essays in Criticism and Aesthetics* (New York: Noonday, 1955), in my opinion the single most important essay in aesthetics he has given us. At least two other essays in *Creation and Discovery* are especially useful: "Literature and Knowledge" and "What Is a Poem?" The "Appendix—The Constitutive Symbol," in *D. H. Lawrence: The Failure*

Vivas clarifies his argument for the role of art in culture by distinguishing, first, the moment *before* the poem when the "meanings and values" which are to become "the object of the poem" "*sub*sist" in the culture, secondly, the moment *of* the poem when those "meanings and values," as the "object," "*in*sist" in the poem, and, finally, those many moments *after* the poem has organized them for our symbolic perception when they become "*ex*istent" in the culture, thanks to the poem.[10] Meanings and values are only subsistent when they are potentially within a culture, unrecognized and unnamed, awaiting the creative act that will bring them to active entity-hood. The poet fulfills his role of organizing and presenting the primary data of experience, identifying them by giving them symbolic form, when he creates an insistent order for these meanings and values, the order which is his poem. Since they have had no proper existence outside the poem, prior to the poem, they can be referred to *through* the poem only by the "insistence" they achieve *in* the language of the poem. Having thus achieved a full identity, these meanings and values can enter the language and the discursive life of the culture by being ripped out of their insistent context in the poem and being generalized to apply to other contexts, having been thinned for referential use. It is how the language of our meanings and values grows, though it becomes, as we use it, a debased and inaccurate language which refers to its object *through* but not *in* its words. Vivas sees culture as standing in continual need of the poet to enlarge as well as to refresh its language, although its need for his gifts forces it to use them badly. The poet indeed plays a major anthropological role as maker of culture by making his poem "Thus to the extent that the poet succeeds in revealing meanings and values which are actually involved in an emergent sense of the social process, he becomes the creator of culture and the meanings and values thus revealed become constitutive of culture."

---

and Triumph of Art (Evanston, Ill.: Northwestern University Press, 1960) supplements these essays by applying a series of useful distinctions among kinds of symbols, and "The Artistic Transaction" (1963) adds a later refinement by determining the relation between all the modes of experience and "the basic symbolic activity." In the earlier of these writings the aesthetic usually appears to be prior to the other three and the basis for them, though there are moments when the aesthetic rather seems coordinate with the others. Vivas attempts to resolve this problem, substantively as well as terminologically, in "The Artistic Transaction," where he introduces the notion of "the basic symbolic activity" (in some ways similar to, but not identical with, the aesthetic) as prior to all four of the modes, now viewed coordinately.

10 For the discussion in the balance of this paragraph, see *Creation and Discovery*, pp. 137–41.

Here indeed is a statement of the poet's privilege and priority. Yet
in reaching these heights Vivas still can be seen to have traced a path
leading back to his original definition of aesthetic experience. What
he has now done is to demonstrate how the enclosure of that experience is transformed, when we turn from the object to the world beyond and to the other modes of experience, so that what served for its
own sake now serves our total humanity. Meanings have to be "immanent and reflexive" when they are *in*sistent since they are organizing primary data which do not yet exist discursively in order to be
pointed to. But meanings that are immanent and reflexive during the
course of the aesthetic experience in its intransitivity can become
transitive and referential once they enter the language of the culture
by allowing us to point to objects through them. This change can
occur only after the aesthetic mode of experience has given way to the
service of the other modes.

Here, then, is a second view of the artist's creativity, though the
two views are clearly wedded in Vivas's theory: as the artist created a
unique structure to contain and control our response as intransitive,
so he creates what comes out of that structure to stay with us after that
response—the symbolic identities which form the constellation of
meanings and values that constitute our culture. The artist's aesthetic
creation is matched with his anthropological. But the anthropological
creativity of the artist is as much qualified by the notion of discovery
as was his aesthetic. We observed Vivas modifying the incipient idealism of the notion that the poet was radically creative by treating him as
dependent upon the objective medium, co-conspirator with him in the
expressive act. The poet's role as creator of culture by way of its
meanings and values is even more circumscribed by external reality.

To begin with, we have seen that the meanings and values which
the poet forces into "insistence" within his object are hardly arbitrary
ones; rather they are those which are historically potential within his
culture, awaiting the conferring of identity. They are, in other words,
awaiting his discovery of them, although we do not know they have
been waiting there until he has discovered them for us. In this obvious
sense his act of creation is indeed—or had better be—an act of discovery. He may seem free to create as he will and persuade us by the vigor
of his invention to accept his creation as what we were ready to
discover (with his help). But there is, outside him, a reality that is
ready to clip his wings if he flies in the face of it.

More than this realistic limitation is imposed by Vivas. When, in
their pre-poetic state, the meanings and values are termed "subsistent," it is clear that he means the word literally, in its technical
philosophical sense. Not only are the meanings and values potentially

within the culture, beginning to stir and helping to move the culture, though as yet without name or recognition; but they also, as subsistent objects, have "status in being" or "ontic status." Since they "are actually to some extent at least operative in the culture prior to their discovery by the poet," they *are* before we have phenomenal awareness that they are: just the essence of "subsistence." What the poet discovers, what he brings to our phenomenal awareness, appears to be a creation, except that it is a revelation of an ontological structure. "Insofar as the objects of poetry subsist prior to their revelation, they have the same status, for ontology, as is enjoyed by the operative invariant relations in nature—the 'forces' and 'powers' and the actualizing potencies which subsist as the structures of the physical world and which the scientist 'discovers' and formulates as his 'laws.' "[11]

Here is philosophical realism indeed, although Vivas never permits it to undo his commitment to what, at the phenomenal level, he defends as significant and radical creativity. In emphasizing the aspect of discovery which paradoxically accompanies what the artist uniquely brings to our awareness, he seems to have moved beyond Kant and Croce, and more strikingly, even beyond Cassirer, but only after having absorbed his lessons from them fully. Though challenging the philosophic temper of our times by calling himself an "axiological realist," Vivas would rather court paradox than do less than justice to the creative capacities of mind as it interacts with matter to produce its utter originals. The object may itself function only at the phenomenal level, but by making visible the meanings and values it brings to that level, it has transformed them from the ontological seat where they were found. Thus the conjunction in his theory of creation and discovery echoes on the one hand the unlikely conjunction of the phenomenal and the ontological and on the other the equally unlikely conjunction of idealism and realism. But, Vivas would claim, his need for more adequate descriptions of the aesthetic experience, of aesthetic value, and of the role of art in creating our cultural vision has led him to his theoretical claims; and, as a dedicated empiricist (as he defines this term), he must follow. As he follows, in the complexity of his struggle he may indeed have moved beyond Kant, Croce, and Cassirer in the precision of his claims for art's symbolic workings on us and on our culture.

It is Vivas's most remarkable trait as a philosopher that he tests his

11 Ibid., p. 139. "But," lest he lose all that his aesthetic has gained for us, Vivas hastens to add, "we must not forget the all-important difference between the objects expressed through the scientific hypothesis and the objects revealed through and in poetry."

problems and himself so relentlessly.[12] If his observations of those problems warrant it, paradox does not frighten him, though inconsistency does, as he tries to resolve the paradox without reducing any part of it in a way that would cheat experience. So he worries those problems continually and never lets them stop worrying him. When naturalism would no longer serve, he had the metaphysical courage to turn to axiological realism if there was where his answers were to be found, though he also had the empirical courage to retain the experiential basis of his theory and the creative claims for the poet consistent with it. He thus has worked to preserve the freedom of the poet, justifying the best of the experimental tradition in poetry, but binding that poet to his traditional medium and his culture's history by way of the fixed objective structure he has made. Though not himself one of the poets of his theory, Vivas has been his own example of the gifted mind that need not imitate or fall prey to the expressed idols of its culture, the mind that insists on its moral and aesthetic freedom to struggle with its materials in order to create beyond them. But he is exemplary of his philosophy also in denying himself pure creativity, the license to spin out any wishful theory; for he has also the conviction that this theory must be put into the service of solutions and underlying truths that—found or unfound—are surely there, there to be hunted.

---

[12] He has been equally relentless in testing his contemporaries, producing many polemical studies, "animadversions" that took courage but were hardly calculated to give comfort within a fraternal order. Much of his best work is found in these searching studies—I think of the essays on Jordan or Wheelwright or Leavis or Morris or Wimsatt just offhand—and, though sometimes harsh and unsparing, they have never seemed to me to be personal or petty. His eye and pen are dedicated to the problem at hand, and philosophy is not to him a game for sensitive egos.

9
The Tragic Vision
Twenty Years After

IT IS NOW JUST twenty years since the *Kenyon Review* published my essay, "Tragedy and the Tragic Vision," which two years later became the crucial opening chapter of my book *The Tragic Vision*, and then had its life renewed in several subsequent anthologies. I think it is useful—at least for me—to look with hindsight at the full significance, together with the limits, of what I was doing then, and at the way in which it turned out to relate to developments in criticism since that time.

What stands out was my attempt then to carve out a place for the dark, underground, private vision we think of as tragic outside the soothing, containing form of tragedy; in other words, to create a thematic genre—characterized even to the end more by tension then by resolution—which expresses the rebelliousness and disbelief of a protestant anti-ethic such as has dominated our great and most moving fictions since the early nineteenth century. In other words, the secession of the radically subjective tragic vision from the ultimate

This paper was written to be delivered at the 1978 Convention of the Modern Language Association, in a Special Session entitled "The Tragic Vision Revisited." In places the paper reflects the fact that it was addressed to an occasion in which theatrical performance in the drama was to be emphasized.

radiant fullness of tragedy as a transcendent literary form was seen as
a reflection of the Kierkegaardian secession of the individual, as absolute particular, from the claims of the ethical universal. And a
number of our most distinguished modernist works were then viewed
(the more clearly, I hope) within the perspective permitted by this
generic model.

What we were left with was not simply a new thematic claim to a
form created in the teeth of unyielding tensions rather than a form
riding the crest of resolution, but also a historical claim that such a
form was representative of our existential plight. So the studies in the
book were to trace the tug-of-war between the character's (that is, the
represented "tragic existent's") pull toward chaos and the literary
work's pull toward a transcending and containing order, especially
since the work is no longer a properly licensed tragedy (properly
licensed, that is, by a society with transcending universals sufficiently
authorized to make them stick) and since all ethical universals have
come to be seen as fraudulent impositions sponsored by social complacency. The work, in other words, tries to exercise formal containment of its materials in order to permit them to be apprehended by
our form-receiving categories of sense and mind, though those
materials—let loose in the now uncontained protagonist—seem in
their chaotic nature to be committed to tearing apart all forms,
including that of this very work. There is in such a work a constantly
self-undoing crisis, an ongoing conflict within an aesthetic (that is, a
sensuously perceived) whole which seeks to define itself by its power to
contain thematic elements even as they threaten its permanent frac-
ture.

So the work, supervising the tension between ethical universals it
cannot believe in and the demoniacal particularity it cannot permit
to wander unleashed, constantly is both repairing and undoing itself,
both a seamless unity and coming apart at the seams. It alternately
and simultaneously both maintains and subverts its authenticity as
vision and as the object of a single act of our attention seeking to hold
itself together. But what the work of the tragic vision undermines
most of all is the attempt of our aesthetic habit to see it as tragedy
itself in its wholeness. As a consequence, it is denied—or rather denies
to itself—the overarching formal reassurances, indeed the absolution,
which the cosmic security of tragedy used to provide for *its* materials,
forever giving itself the last word as it gathers them up, however
shattered we thought they were, lying about the stage.

In retrospect, it now seems to me that, by my defining the literature of the tragic vision as that which demolished the metaphysical
substructure on which the cosmic assurance of tragedy rested, I was

anticipating the deconstructionist critical temperament which was soon to follow. We have seen the transcendent security provided by the cosmic form, which masquerades as the aesthetic form of tragedy, now reduced to the psychological dimensions of the character who dismantles that form. It is a reduction of ontological absolutes to society's shabby universals sanctioned only by its crassest motives of self-preservation and, in the protagonist himself, a reduction from hero to outcast madman, wallowing in self-aggrandizement. As I viewed his disruptive actions—and the vision that flowed from them— what was deconstructed was both the ontological and the aesthetic, both the structure of the world and the structure of the work. I sought to rehearse a reality sponsored by the disbelief which emerges from the Nietzschean temper and gives rise to a literature of the thematic underworld; and legions of Nietzschean disbelievers have come along since then, echoing this literature, but with sharpened deconstructionist tendencies, invariably "finding" just those tendencies in the objects of their discourse. And these objects, whether they are newly created ones or representations of older ones, take on a self-consciousness, a self-deconstruction, which forces them to find themselves at odds with themselves, repeopling their self-disrupted worlds as they go along.

The Tragic Vision, then, was an extreme statement about the radical transformations which tragic materials had undergone in the modern world; and I balanced the reckless embrace of extremity a decade later in *The Classic Vision*, a "retreat from extremity," although the latter is not our concern here. What does remain methodologically interesting to me now—although I'm not sure how conscious I was of it or how formative a notion it was if I *was* conscious of it—is the extent to which I depended on the role of the narrator's voice to establish distance from the tragic existent's and to try at once to carry the tension and to relieve it. The voice was usually one of sanity, yet of absolute interest in the protagonist stopping just short of obsession or even identity with him; but most of all the voice betrayed the tension generated by the collision between sanity and commitment to a mad surrogate. The paradoxical combination of ethical distance and existential empathy in the narrator's relation to the protagonist sustained the strained balance between the level of vision and the level of existence. I now suspect that I was less than fully aware of these separations as I notice that only in the new preface to the two-volume paperback reprint, *Visions of Extremity in Modern Literature* (1973), did I explicitly seek to retract the ambiguity in my use of the phrase *tragic visionary* in the earlier volume in order to distinguish the tragic-existent protagonist from the tragic-visionary narrator.

I am consequently able to see now the probable reason for my

dealing exclusively with the novel in *The Tragic Vision,* that is, for
my insistence that the tragic vision required the giving up not only of
tragedy as a form but also of drama as a genre. And it had, I think,
nothing to do with the questionable commonplace that successful
dramatic tragedy is a thing long ago departed from us. What I sought
in prose fiction must have been the extra dimension created by the
narrator's dialogistic voice, the dimension of a reflexive self-consciousness which permitted the novel to display a breakdown of the brilliantly and objectively controlled form of old tragedy. But of the novel
of the tragic vision, one could say, here was a work willfully out of
control and kept that way by a narrator conscious of his role and of
the finally irreconcilable conflict between him and his materials—
most of all, between him and his mad creature, or creature-as-surro-
gate. Here is our narrator-companion, a voice unfit for tragedy in that
he is less than tragedy would allow, telling us about *his* companion,
an agent unfit for tragedy in that he is more than tragedy would allow
to be untamed by its transcendent (and dramatic) form. And it must
have been my instinctive judgment that this narrative voice, which
was our existential alternative, but also—and more importantly—our
visionary absolute (if nothingness can achieve absolute status), was
not simply a newer, novelistic version of the dramatic Chorus; rather
that in its role as fictive creator it was a deconstructionist God, who
saw chaos and said—not that it was good—but that it *was* and that he
could *tell* it, find a word for it, without making it into order.

I now believe that I was very likely wrong to exclude drama from
the tragic vision just as I excluded the healing aspects of tragedy from
it. But even as I utter this judgment, I suspect that it may well be the
product of what has happened to the theater—or, to be more accurate
and more modest, what has happened to my sense of the theater—
since my original conception of the tragic vision. My guess now is that
I saw the novel then as a potential deconstruction of the drama—just
the sort needed to reduce tragedy to tragic vision. This is to say that I
singled out for value those recent manifestations in the novel which
self-consciously played upon the reflexivity that is built into its narrative point of view: the ruminations of Ishmael confronted by his
Ahab, of Marlow confronted by his Kurtz or his Lord Jim, of Zeit-
blom confronted by his Leverkühn, to name a few. And in these auto-
dialogues-without-resolution I thought I found the unending tension
which was to replace catharsis as the dominant moving power in a
literature—and in a world—too late for tragedy.

But I am now aware of developments, in our time, in the writing
for the theater and in the production (as well as the criticism) of older
as well as newer plays (which, in effect, turn them all into newer

plays), developments which use the peculiar devices available to drama in order to emphasize the self-conscious reflexivity which has always been locked in its form. Writers, critics, and directors have been breaking through the long-sustained veil of objective dramatic presentation, a veil naively held before would-be writers and would-be readers of what was presumably written within the terms of such strictures. I now understand that it was naive of me unconsciously to have accepted such a notion of drama as a prerequisite for the construction of tragedy, so that my deconstruction of tragedy into tragic vision called for an implied deconstruction of drama into novel. For what I now see clearly is that the drama, more than any other genre, has self-consciousness and reflexivity built into its very presentational nature. There it stands before us—with its actor-impersonators and their make-believe pseudo-actions, its masks and masquerades—the very stuff of mutually complicitous illusion, as commentators since Dr. Johnson have been constantly reminding us and as playwrights from the dawn of dramatic works in the West have been saying to those of us who would try to read them that way. For any play which would exploit its *merely* mimetic character and for any producer who would approach his theater with an insistence on such exploitation, the drama—as a would-be imitation of *reality*—is swallowed up into its radical of presentation, its reality deconstructed, if not altogether dissolved.

So it may well be that, as the novel developed into a self-consciously aesthetic form, it learned to manipulate its narrative nature—that which differentiated it from drama—as a way of getting beyond drama and giving itself a special role in the development of self-consciousness in the nineteenth century, hardly a strong period for the drama, which was for the most part still stuck in archaic conceptions about itself. The novel had shown, in those moments when it restricted itself to the objective presentation of dialogue with stage directions, that it could try to catch up to the naive conception of drama; but in its more developed moments (at least those which critics like me look for and find to be more developed) the novel showed it could move beyond such a conception by freeing itself to break its apparent form, to fragment it into reflections produced by an endless set of mirrors. In its turn the drama, once it rejected a naive conception of itself, could move forward toward where the novel had gone, and even beyond, because the full consciousness of the ambiguous realities represented by the drama creates such mirrorizing effects as the primary element of its aesthetic definition. The self-conscious construction of drama *as* drama is a deconstructive act. In increasing numbers playwrights, directors, and critics have been telling us so.

It may well be that what even I have at last learned can be traced, not to this mythical historical race and rivalry which I have suggested between the novel and the drama—with one catching up with and passing the other, only to be caught up with and passed in turn—but to the crucial recent influence upon our awareness of what the film is capable of, with both the drama and the novel racing to keep up with the many new dimensions which, thanks to the film, they can now envision and which, they instinctively know, can be envisioned by their audiences as well. The film lies between the two and is accessible to both: it apparently shares its radical of presentation with the drama as a physical, living representation before its audience (a natural rather than an arbitrary sign, an eighteenth-century aesthetician would say), but it can explode time and space and image with a freedom that the novel can share in kind although it cannot approach it in degree. And the recent theater has frequently tried to borrow for itself this breakaway power of the film, though it has had to struggle with its own traditional nature to do so. Surely, as we look at developments in both fiction and the theater from our vantage point today, we must see the self-conscious indulgence in multiple realities through eyes which have watched such indulgence reach the extravagant degree it has in the recent history of film.

Whatever the cause, it is surely the case that the deconstructive impulse now maintains itself at a highly self-conscious level both in the dramas written in the last several decades and in the older dramas produced as new ones during that period. And any notion of a reduced tragic vision, built as mine was on the dismantling of the total form which was tragedy, would have to include within its range the fruits of both the recent revolution in playwriting and the equally revolutionary concepts governing every facet of recent dramatic production. I will leave to the many among us who can speak with authority of such recent developments in the theater the expert discussion of examples of plays and productions; and I will be prepared to change my mind if such examples do not substantiate my impression. For as of now I am convinced that these revolutions thoroughly reconstitute our dramatic canon, both which plays we include and how we newly construct (and deconstruct) even the most venerable of our automatic inclusions.

Our new perception may well lead us to worry about whether, so far—at least—as we can conceive, there is left standing anything so transcendently full in its unquestioned construction as we had thought tragedy to be, or whether all has dwindled into the tortuous reflections and re-reflections of the tragic vision. Behind the promise of healing which the illusionary veil of tragedy seemed to offer, the raw edges of the tragic vision lie waiting to break through, once our self-consciousness—sponsored by the reflexivity of the presentation—is roused. Or is it that the tragic by this point so overlaps the ironic vision that the two in effect become the same? With full tragedy now beyond the reach of our vision—even in the case of those venerable old, but now remote, plays that went by that name—perhaps the adjective *tragic* is itself no longer deserved and should wither away, as the state does in the mythical version of communism. The total indulgence of reflexivity and self-consciousness, the collapsing of literature and all our literary realities by way of that absurdity we call "life," these must lead us to the threshold of the ironic and the absurd. It may indeed be history's irony for the tragic vision, having reduced tragedy to itself, now itself to be reduced to no more than the ironic, although—in the light of the world around us—it will have to be enough.

II
Critical
Theory

10

Poetic Presence and Illusion II: Formalist Theory and the Duplicity of Metaphor

I MIGHT WELL start by addressing the "crisis in formalism," except that it appears quaintly archaic today to speak of formalism as being in crisis, probably because formalism has now for some time been seen as a movement no longer vital, that is, as a movement for which no new usefulness could be found within a theoretical context which had outgrown it. The death of formalism, assumed now for some time, has been followed by what most would feel to be the collapse of the many efforts to see it through any "crisis" invented in hopes of reviving it.

Yet let me be unfashionable enough to suggest that the assault on formalism (or at least on some versions of formalism) was launched on partly false grounds, so that the victory over it was announced over a misrepresented antagonist, an elusive enemy which had already slipped out of the grasp of the post-formalist terms that claimed to

This essay was originally delivered in April 1978 at the *Boundary 2* conference, "A Symposium on the Problems of Reading in Contemporary American Criticism," in the section entitled "The Question of Formalism: From Aesthetic Distance to Difference." I wish to thank the Rockefeller Foundation for providing the Humanities Fellowship during the tenure of which much of this essay was written.

have vanquished it. We should thus examine the nature of the formalism which was under attack, the nature of the crisis caused by the attack, and the grounds of the attack, in order to discover the extent to which formalism may claim to have evaded its destruction, surviving in newer guises even as its demise was being taken for granted.

The impatience with formalism, which led to those counter movements which supplanted it, rested upon a very narrow definition that, in effect, equated formalism with aestheticism as a doctrine which would cut the art object off from the world while treating only its craftsmanlike quality as an artifact. This narrow definition of formalism may have accounted for much of the doctrine of Russian formalism[1] as well as for the neo-Aristotelianism of the University of Chicago critics. The narrow definition would also account for some of the more mechanical practices of many of those parading under the banner of the New Criticism. But we would need a broader definition of formalism—one more concerned with the relations between the forms of art and the forms of personal or cultural vision—to account for some of the more daring philosophical possibilities that could be seen as extensions of the New Criticism. The formalism which most post–New-Critical movements have destroyed is the narrow formalism, which isolated the work of art as a fixed ontological entity, an object, and went analytically to work upon it as upon Eliot's "patient etherised upon a table." Aside from the obvious unrealities involved in thus cutting off the art object from its creator, its audience, and its culture, this formalism—especially when translated into a literary criticism which deals with verbal sequences—seemed to require the assumption of an extremely naive epistemology, one which rests upon the mystification that posits the poem out there as a thing, and a self-sufficient thing at that, related to no other things. Such a reification, made in the face of the sequential nature of language and experience, would have to neglect the treatment of poetry as a product of man and his discourse.

But a formalism more broadly defined need not restrict itself to the conception of the poem as a static and isolated object. What I began by calling the crisis in formalism, then, I see as its need to redefine itself in this broad way, so that it can earn its right theoretically to open outward, as it frequently has opened at its best, and thus ride clear of the charges lodged against its more narrowly conceived shadow-theory. At its broadest, formalism must recognize (and has

[1] It is ironic that certain basic tenets of Russian formalism, which I treat here as too narrow a formalism to withstand the usual attacks against it, returned to become a bulwark of structuralism, which is one of the major anti–New Critical movements designed to supplant its formalistic insufficiencies.

recognized) the several elements in the aesthetic transaction to which the word *form* may be applied. There is the imaginative form as it is seen, grasped, and (it is to be hoped) projected by the mind of the poet; there is the verbal form, at once diachronic and synchronic, that is seen, grasped, and projected in the course of the reader's experience; and there is the form that becomes one of the shapes which culture creates for its society to grasp its sense of itself. A shrewd formalism would try to account for and bring all these together. It would concern itself with that fixed spatial configuration of words on paper, but without ontologizing it into a static idol which would freeze into itself the humanly and empirically vibrant forms, whether phenomenological, psychological, or anthropological.

To the extent that formalisms have not worried about their epistemological mystifications and have indulged in uncritical objectification, they have not been shrewd. But as soon as we take into consideration that broader array of forms with which the formalist should concern himself, we come closer to that original sense of form bequeathed to us by its Kantian heritage, a sense of form which ties it at once to our vision of the world. This would make nonsense of those anti-formalist claims that denigrate the study of form by seeking to empty form out, excluding all worldly relations from it. If, on the contrary, we look at form as the primal agency of human functioning, we see in it the phenomenological categories for our coherent apprehension of the world's "given." It is what gives us the shapes of our world, the creation of the worldly stage and its objects within which we move, which we seek to manipulate though they often appear to manipulate us. Form in this sense is primal vision and, far from escaping reality for empty shows, it becomes the power that constitutes all the "reality" which we feel and know. A formalism deriving from such a fundamental notion of form—precisely the notion of form which philosophers have left with us for two centuries—must be phenomenological as well as anthropological from its very outset. If it is aboriginally aesthetic too, it is aesthetic in the sense of that word first given it by the philosophers who, deriving the term from *aesthesis*, meant by it no more than immediate sense perception. It is this immediacy of our perception of the objects which people our world, rather than the distanced observation of the techniques and patterned symmetries of art for their own sakes, upon which formalism, as a proper aesthetic, should concentrate. There would thus be in it neither vapidity nor unworldly dilettantism.

If we see the object within phenomenological terms, it is de-ontologized into an "intentional object" (though that should be enough for us); and this would permit the co-presence of all the kinds of forms I have been delineating—all under the aegis of illusions fostered by the particular intentionality which is functioning. In the spirit of Roman Ingarden, we can claim at once that the author as poet intended a form as his object, that the attending reader yet intends a form as his object, and that the moving verbal structure appears (though differently to each of them) to have intended its own form as an object and, as a formal object, appears to intend itself as an enclosed vision of the objects of a world, the world now having become its own world. The broad formalist hopes to find that these projected teleologies, though deriving from potentially conflicting perspectives, may be seen as converging. These several intentional objects draw their character from what our human and cultural (and aesthetic) habits of creating and perceiving forms expect them to become—nay, insist on their becoming—whether under the pressures of their being created or their being perceived. The poet does his work by using the habitual resources of language and the conventions of language considered as a medium for art both to encourage and to reinforce those perceptual habits. The reader tries to be responsive to the "objective form" as an external stimulus with its own intentionalities, though his own habits, needs, and past commerce with the arts and their media (as well as his commerce with the world) lead to intentionalities of his own, whether or not he tries (vainly or not) to subject them to normative considerations.

Out of such intentional objects, discrete or overlapping, emerge the illusionary worlds of poet, reader, and the objects each intends to project or find. The illusion is what, as Ernst Gombrich has taught us, becomes our reality, what the world for now is seen as having become, either for the artist seeking to complete, in his medium, what seems to want to be completed that way, or for the reader seeking to confirm a pattern which he imposes in order to make the world he finds, or feels he should find in the object. And when the literary work works well, there is a congruence among these worlds, which encourages the satisfying mystification that it is *the* world of *the* object; and at an uncritical—an un-self-conscious—phenomenological level, it may even be so. Far from being static, spatially contained objects, however, these are worlds in motion, reflecting the diachronic character of verbal sequence and experiential flow.

These illusionary worlds, as our imaged realities, may also appear to be satisfying simulacra of "the world" outside, though that world has now been reduced not only to the bounds of our intentional perception but also to the capacities of language to enclose within itself what would seem to open it outward (except for those moments when it is viewed from within what we intend as an aesthetic act).

Nor is the world any longer cognizable except by way of such illusionary reductions, or what Gombrich terms "substitutes,"[2] even if the substitutes are our only free-standing prototypes. The illusion is all; it is the seer's imaged reality, since there is no independently available reality against which the image can be seen as distorted or false, as a *de*lusion. Whatever hangover awareness we may skeptically retain of the fact that our aesthetic indulgence (in both the original and abridged sense of "aesthetic") is a "fiction," we yet permit the fictional to become the lens through which reality comes to us as reality. Thus we become provisionally persuaded of the presence of the poem as our present world, whatever the lingering suspicion we have about it as an intended presence only, as a mere substitute behind which is a real reality which would make it vanish as no more than a delusive appearance.

Within our qualified sense of its presence, then, the poem remains as a reduction of the world to the dimensions of humanly imposed form, a human metaphor that is supposed to "stand for" extra-human reality except that, by way of the illusion which is as much of reality as we intend, the metaphor is the formal expression of all that reality has become, has been compacted into. Since there is no universal archetype for it to reflect, it is a microcosm without a macrocosm behind it. That is, we cannot speak of a structured ontological totality out there (or macrocosm) since what lies behind our experiential "given" does not come to us bearing a form which would make it a cosmos until a human form is imposed upon it, at which time it becomes but another reduction, another metaphor, another microcosm. Using the old-fashioned meaning of "metonym" considered as a figure of speech, we could say that it functions metonymically—except that, as in the case of metaphor itself, we cannot firmly say or point to the larger term (or entity) behind the miniature image to which it has supposedly been reduced in order to serve our perceptual habits.

The poem, then, is a signifier which must carry its authenticity within itself since no external signified is accessible to us. But the

2 I think especially of Gombrich's "Meditations on a Hobby Horse or the Roots of Artistic Form," *Meditations on a Hobby Horse and other Essays on the Theory of Art* (London: Phaidon Press, 1963), pp. 1–11. The most immediate argument for the claim that the "substitute" becomes the free-standing, indispensable "reality" (since the world is uncognizable outside it) may be at once grasped in the well-known Alain cartoon in *The New Yorker* with which Gombrich opens his *Art and Illusion* (London: Phaidon Press, 1960). In it, you will recall, the ancient Egyptian drawing class, rendered as conventionally drawn male figures seen only in Egyptian paintings, is trying to reproduce with mimetic precision the female model, a profiled figure which is the "woman" as represented in Egyptian paintings. There is, in other words, no pre-artistic or extra-artistic real world of either artists or models for us (or them) to perceive.

nature of aesthetic intentionality, both for poet and for reader or audience within our culture, is such that close study of the signifier discloses its constantly enlarging capacity to be its own signified and to provide an ever-increasing sense of its semiological richness. Among the arts this is most spectacularly true of poetry, in which the nature of the medium is such that words can both exploit their meanings exhaustively and remake them utterly. But the presentational aspect of drama makes it perhaps the most spectacular of the genres of poetry in its power to make us aware of persons, happenings, and real consequences on the one hand, and of characters (or even mere actors), stage action, and curtained endings on the other. The poem's trick of being at once self-authenticating and self-abnegating enables it to proclaim an identity between itself as metaphor and its reality, a collapsing of the binary oppositions between signifier and signified, and yet enables it at the same time to undercut its pretensions by reasserting its distance from an excluded "real world." It is this acknowledged distance which seems to make the difference between signifier and signified impossible to bridge, since the signifier can find its formal nature only in the irreparable absence of the signified.

My last remarks depend upon an alliance between the terms *distance* and *difference* which is commonplace in the language of post-structuralist critical theory. I point this out to dwell for a moment on the fact that the title for our group in this symposium, "From Aesthetic Distance to Difference," assumes some degree of opposition between the terms by suggesting that formalism has had to put up with history's demand that it move from one to the other. The notion of aesthetic distance or detachment has had a major place in that variety of formalist theory which developed in the wake of the formulations of Kant with their stress upon disinterestedness. The phrase itself can be traced back to the work of Edward Bullough and his influential pioneering essay on "psychical distance."[3] Clearly this doctrine refers exclusively to the relationship between the art object and its audience and, as a spatial metaphor, rests on the assumption of a fixed and insulated object whose separateness from its audience and their interests is the prerequisite for their aesthetic response to it. It is just a newer version of the classical view that insists, with epistemolgical naiveté, upon the objective status of that object out there which establishes itself by its distinctness from its viewers as subjects. The post-Kantian formalist asserts this view as the classical alternative to the nineteenth-century doctrine of empathy, a romantic view which calls

[3] "Psychical Distance as a Factor in Art and an Aesthetic Principle," *British Journal of Psychology* 5 (1912): 87–98.

for the overrunning of all bounds. The doctrine of empathy would obliterate all distance between subject and object and, instead, would require the subject to fuse with the object, to feel himself into it. Aesthetic distance, on the other hand, seeks to reestablish the coolness needed for an aesthetic judgment of the object as a finite, made thing; it rejects as irresponsible enthusiasm the emotional subjectification of what it prefers to see as out there, apart from us.

With this disposition, aesthetic distance functions as an indispensable accompaniment to formalist critical theory, and it has contributed to the theoretical failures of formalism by its isolating of the object in space—even so temporal and fleeting an object as a poem. But if distance, as a spatializing metaphor, is a term we associate with formalism, it has also—though in a different sense—become associated with recent continental theorizing. For if formalist "distance" refers to space between audience and object, structuralist "distance" refers to space between signifier and signified, or between signifiers within a semiotic system. And this latter "distance" is essentially a synonym for the structuralist principle of "difference," representing the spatial gap, the hiatus, between differentiated elements. It has led post-structuralists to dwell upon the lack of presence in language, to the emptiness of the spaces marked by distance, now used as a spatial metaphor for the gap established by the structuralist principle of difference. This sense of the word would collapse the dichotomy between distance and difference which seems to exist within the formalist perspective (like that which provided the title for our group here).

Despite the implications of that title, however, one might argue that even the formalist devotion to aesthetic distance implies difference (instead of differing from difference) in that it indicates the extent of the difference between subject and object. But this should not suggest any closing of distance between formalist and structuralist perspectives, since the formalist object—however distanced and differentiated from all subjects—is at one with itself, achieving a present, undifferentiated identity (unlike the structuralist object). This internally unified fulfillment is observable to the formalist observer who, seeing the object as a distanced "other," responds to it disinterestedly as to a single, centered presence. He resists empathic involvement which would dissolve the distance and difference between his self and his object, for he would rather have a unity in the object which demands an exclusion of the self than, as in empathy, a unity of self-in-object (or object-in-self, for the two would be interchangeable). If this self-effacing formalist would freeze the object for analysis, the self-assertive alternative position loses it altogether in a romantic blur.

Of course, I must argue against the attempt to pit aesthetic distance against empathy in view of what I have said earlier about the capacity of a broader formalism to merge, within a phenomenological doctrine of intentionality, all the kinds of form which the narrow formalism would separate from one another with its naive epistemology. The narrow formalist performed this separation in order to eliminate what he saw as the form imposed by the author and the form imposed by the reader so that he might concentrate upon his metaphysical reification of the form of the "object itself" which was to be totally in control of the form "received" by the reader. Of course, this controlled stimulus provided the reader by the object is one that a critical epistemology beyond the narrow formalist's reveals has actually been projected by the reader's self. The circuitous route by which readers provide stimulating forms to which they then respond as if to a stimulating object—and the role that external stimulus, internally recast and cast outward again, properly plays—these become issues which only a phenomenology can resolve, though it must be resolution by overlap and merger rather than by exclusion. And the respective claims of detachment and self-involvement, of aesthetic distance and empathy, must be joined in ways the narrow formalist prevents himself from understanding. In the relation between the subject and object of experience, one must account for identity as well as difference (that is, aesthetic distance), just as—earlier—I argued for identity as well as difference when, looking within the verbal artifact, I spoke of the relation between signifier and signified.

This is only to observe that the peculiar nature of the intentional object as aesthetic—whatever else it is—is surely duplicitous. This observation is confirmed wherever in it we look. Most obviously we find such duplicity in the peculiar status-in-being of fictional characters and actions, in the justifications we can make of them simultaneously as mimetic and as real. There is, perhaps, a more subtle doubleness within the single claim that they are illusionary, because when we take them seriously as illusion, we encompass both the mimetic and the real, the mimetic *as* real. As a dramatic performance unravels before us, this claim is both superficially and profoundly demonstrated in the paradoxical nature of the "stage reality" (to use an oxymoron which bears the paradox on its face). And the drama wants us to be alive to this doubleness, so that, with its use of its conventions, it is not loath to remind us of it, to have us look at it both ways—at the world of people and at the stage on which actors pose as the not-quite people we term characters: all the world's a stage and a stage is all the world. For whichever way we look, we look *as if* it was the world we were looking at. Thus illusion becomes self-conscious, thanks often to the devices of fictional self-reference. Even the most "realistic" of works use such conventions because, rather than trying to "take us in" (that is, to delude us), they prefer to show us how close they have come to doing so, how marvelously verisimilar their illusion is: one cannot appreciate the verisimilar without being aware that it is not the thing itself.[4] One might thus argue that no work is more illusionary than the most literally mimetic one.

Fictional characters and actions portrayed in narrative writing may not have quite so immediate a claim as drama does upon our illusionary capacities, but surely there is something equally duplicitous about their status-in-being. The illusionary reality of Tom Jones in Fielding's "history" of him is something Fielding is at great pains to leave us in no doubt about, and yet his make-believe status at every moment persuades us to yield to the as-if and follow his fortunes in a way appropriate to a true history, provided we retain an awareness of its mimetic basis. Thus poetry insists upon its ambiguous relation to reality-unreality in less literally mimetic modes of presentation than that of dramatic performance. A similar ambiguity is aroused by the confessional disclosures of the first-person persona in lyric poem or pseudo-autobiographical narrative, as we both indulge the responses to true autobiography or confession and, in mimetic awareness, withhold them for responses to the as-if-ness in the unfolding lines and pages.

Granted that the non-dramatic genres, existing only on paper or as voices which our eyes persuade us to hear, cannot afford us the blatant ambiguity of mimetic presence which the stage does; still our habits of reading and verbal imagination, and the intentionality fostered by them, create sufficient illusionary opportunities for duplicitous apprehension. Gombrich would quickly (too quickly, perhaps) grant that the visual arts, especially when representational, have an immediacy of illusionary possibilities which is denied to the non-dramatic verbal arts. (And even in the case of performed drama it is the other-than-verbal aspect, the spectacle of illusionary persons [or rather personae] acting, which is immediately illusionary, and not the words they speak [however these may imitate the act of speaking by real persons].) There is the obvious fact that words are intelligible rather than sensible—arbitrary rather than natural signs, as aestheticians used to

---

4 I take these arguments up at greater length in *Theory of Criticism: A Tradition and Its System* (Baltimore: Johns Hopkins University Press, 1976), chap. 6 and the opening pages of chap. 7 (esp. pp. 182–83).

say—so that we must be aware that, in contrast to representational painting for example, there is no visible presence of any concept within them. Consequently, illusion in the purely verbal arts must come as a result of a strenuous, self-conscious effort, sturdily sustained by conventions which induce illusionary intentionalities among us if we attend to them.

Perhaps nothing in poetry is a more obvious illustration of this conventional effort than the age-old aural devices which focus attention upon the sensory character of words. Meter and rhyme, for example, call attention to the arbitrary element within the verbal medium which is capable of poetic manipulation without regard to meaning—a play among signifiers considered as absolutely empty of signifieds, in effect a play among the phonetic sequences themselves. Such exploitation of language as a sensory medium forces upon us an awareness of artifice, of conventionality, that allows us to return to the poem the illusionary character of which it seems to be deprived when we consider it strictly as intelligible discourse. For this concentration upon its sound (or rather its imagined sound, since we may be only reading silently) confers upon it the illusion of a physical presence, perhaps analogous to the sense of presence in the plastic arts or in dramatic performance. If this fixed sequence of words thus appears to take on body which makes it sensible as well as intelligible, then it may well be taken by us as a fully present entity, seen apart from the general system of language out of which it flows. Or so, at least, aesthetic intentionality, encouraged by the poet's manifestly self-conscious labors, permits us to say.

Further, this body of verbal presence can be seen as creating its own system of meanings with which it fills itself when we find arbitrary phonetic coincidences (like the pun, for example) being converted into substantive necessity. In the shrewdly extended pun, the accident of similar sound in differing words or meanings is forced to yield an identity of substance between them. We are to countenance their union because the two—though at variance with one another—have found a corporeal oneness growing out of the playful accident with which the pun was introduced. As I have demonstrated elsewhere, Shakespeare's sonnets are filled with brilliant examples of such verbal manipulation. What begins in the poem as an arbitrary system of sounds, arising out of an "aesthetic surface" which we normally expect to find only in sensible media but which convention has permitted us to find in verse, appears to develop into an utterly new system of meanings such as only this verbal system (with *its* compound of sound and meaning structures) can sustain as it creates it for our learned response. It is in this sense that I would argue for our viewing the poem as a *micro-langue*, a *parole* that has developed into its own language system by apparently setting up its own operational rules to govern how meanings are generated.[5] Though obviously the poem is but a *parole*, a speech act made in accordance with what the *langue*, as the general system of discourse, permits, it rises as a *parole* to become its own *langue* with its own set of licenses—within the intentionality of aesthetic experience and through the recognizable devices which encourage us to find a bodily presence in it.

Thus we have the illusion of its self-sufficient discontinuity with other discourse while our skeptical awareness of it as just another *parole*, continuous with the general system of discourse, remains to demystify that illusion. But we shall never read it in accordance with the intentionality we accord a poem unless we grant it this capacity to entrance us. This defense of a unique *parole* that creates its own *langue* is another form of my earlier plea for the reading that permitted signifiers to fill themselves with the signifieds they create. There is in poetry the need to overwhelm, under conditions of aesthetic intentionality, the binary oppositions (signifier-signified, *langue-parole*) constructed by modern semiologists to govern all language-functioning. But I ask that the exception for poetic discourse (along with the claim itself that there is anything like a poetic discourse) be entertained only *pour l'occasion* and under the prodding of what we habitually think we ought to find in poems, without our surrendering to its magic our stubborn common-sense view of language.

But even this provisional invocation of presence in poems, tied as it has been so far to their aural character, may seem to belie their character as writing and thus to ask for the sort of complaint lodged, for example, by Derrida against Saussure. The issue arises when we question whether we are considering the word as spoken (*parole*) or as written (*écriture*). The claim to verbal presence, a pious assumption in need of being demystified, is said to arise only because we think of the word as spoken and a spoken word implies a speaker, actively present and participating in a speech act. Thus a deconstructive critic can argue that the recognition of writing rather than speech as the major literary expression of our culture justifies his argument for verbal absence (by way of difference) over verbal presence (by way of identity). As *parole* requires the voice of a speaking presence, so *écriture* requires only the impersonal blank page filled with empty traces, arbitrary marks which lead away from themselves to testify to their

---

5 See ibid., pp. 188, 227–28 for a developed version of this argument.

unsubstantiality, to the field of utter absence in which they float. So the deconstructionist can use the transfer from *parole* to *écriture*, the removal of the word from the mouth to the page, as his argument to remove the myth of presence from discourse. My own use of the aural features of poetry, of the discovery and exploitation of the sensory features of the verbal medium, was meant to sponsor at least the illusion of presence, so that I must concern myself with this shift in emphasis from speech to writing and face whatever consequences it may pose to a poetics of presence. For I must concern myself with what happens to my manipulation of the *langue-parole* opposition when it is systems and samples of *écriture* we have to deal with.

To begin with, there is at least as much of a basis for a claim to presence in writing as in speaking. The history of theory has produced at least as many mystifications in behalf of the one as of the other. We can easily reverse the argument summarized in my preceding paragraph to find writing as an inevitable stimulant for claims to presence, with speech as the antidote prescribed on behalf of absence. If we concentrate on the word itself rather than on its source, the products of the speaking voice seem anything but present: a sequence of fleeting sounds, gone in the air as they arrive, without even a momentary presence as they fly off on the wings of Zeno's paradox. Literature as voice and speech is a total surrender to the un-present domain of time. From this perspective it was the invention of the book, the cherished and highly ornamented thing of lines and pages and weight, which created a physical and spatial fix with which to catch the vanishing phonemes in order to make all of the literary work co-present, from beginning to end. It gave an enormous boost to a critic's formalist impulses and led him to ape critics of the spatial arts, the very arts used visually to enhance the written literary work and one's sense of its spatiality, its presence, with the attractive ornaments they provided. Hence the sacred Book and the interpretive industry provided by its sacralization.[6]

It is of course this industry applied to secular writings rendered equally sacred, which has come down even to the narrow formalists about whom I have worried in this essay. Indeed the tradition of mystification in this history of the Book and the theories of literary presence to which it gave rise has been a frequent subject for deconstructionist commentary. So, despite the fact that the speaker and his voice are absent in *écriture*, and despite the reduction of writing to marks on the page with their "differantial" motions, the written

[6] For my own discussion of this history, see ibid., pp. 146–48.

word provides a something-in-hand and a staying presence which gives "heft" to a temporal art. It encourages that reification of the literary object as object about which I earlier joined many others in complaining. Next to these claims to presence, one could argue, the implied presence of speaker and voice in *parole* is not very impressive, especially if our concern is with the word itself rather than its human source. For, whatever the sensuous presence of the spoken language, the dissipation of sound in air hardly encourages a secure feeling about it. Further, the speaker, however we may sense him when we hear his spoken word, is not *in* his word, cannot *become* his word, since only God *is* his created Word, converting that Word into substance, the ontological being of true presence. And his presence reveals itself to man only in writing, as the Word is transcribed into the sacred Book.

Let us agree, then, that the human need to reify our temporal encounters is reflected even more in our dealing with language in written form than it is in our dealing with language as spoken. Yet, beyond the mystifications created by this need, a sobering inspection of oral language sees (or rather hears) it fade away as it is spoken, and a sobering inspection of the written page sees the blankness of absent signifieds which the empty verbal signs finally cannot hide. Both the presence of the person in speech and the presence of the book in writing, however appealing in the human needs they satisfy, can be undone in a flash of anti-metaphysical skepticism which withholds belief in the God-in-the-voice or in the sacred, staying authority of the book. What I have said earlier about the poem as intentional *micro-langue*, however, bestows upon it the power, under the conditions of aesthetic illusion, to create a presence in the verbal sequence that does cut it off from the absences inherent in the nature of language generally. The signifier, which is seen as struggling against its nature to create the signified it contains, seems to have forced its god into itself and thus to have become fully substantiated. It is this fullness which creates the illusion of a self-sufficiency that justifies our treating the *parole* as its own *langue*.

I find this creative transformation to be impressed upon us as much by written as by aural effects, although my earlier argument for presence seemed to depend on phonetic coincidences arising out of the sensory properties of the verbal medium. Nor do we, in the act of reading, sort out what responses are owed to *parole* and what to *écriture*. The fact is that in reading poems (and I am discounting here the response to the oral performance of poems) our illusionary habits of response have taught us to *read* sounds. As much as it requires the illusion that its signified images are seen, the poem also requires the illusion that it is being heard as it carries forward—for those of us who know about it—its long-standing inherited aural character. Although puns, for example, often rest upon our aural recollection, they may also arise simply out of orthographic (and etymological) identities which never need go beyond the eye. Surely the reading of literature for the learned participant is a complex mélange of visual and quietly aural activities and sensory memories, making what is read a sample of *écriture* with significant intrusions from the realm of *parole*. And both the elements of writing which is read and silent voice which is heard have their invisible and unheard universal structures behind them giving form to each, *langue* for the *parole* and *écriture* (as a general system) for the lines and pages before us. As I claimed earlier that in poems there were verbal manipulations which imposed an illusion of presence, thereby converting the *parole* into a *micro-langue,* so I would similarly see the piece of writing converted as we watched into a unique system of *écriture,* obedient to ad hoc rules created for the occasion. In both cases violence appears to be done to general systems with new rewards emerging out of such discursive subversion.

I am suggesting that one of the extraordinary impositions which poetry appears to work upon normal discursive systems is its creating the sense of being at once *parole* and *écriture,* borrowing from the character of each as it creates itself as a unique system. It is as if each of these aspects uses its opposition to the other to argue for its own presence, so that this double and paradoxical nature aids the creation of a complex micro-system out of what might seem to be the mutual blockage of a speaking system and a writing system which are each exclusive in their grounds for establishing presence and absence. The multiple devices in poems for turning verbal sequences in upon themselves vastly extend the powers of the medium to stir the feeling of presence when they can call upon the intertwined benefits of *parole* and *écriture* for mutual reinforcement. There comes to be the conviction of an always present speaker who is forcing language to become his-always-present-word, despite its tendency to be no more than fleeting sound; and the conviction arises in part because of the staying power provided by the play of written words, with their (apparently) fixed lines and stanzas permanently present before us on the page which takes its place in a book, a miniature analogue to the Book of books, repository of the eternal creative Word. The mutual benefits of poem as speech and poem as writing help create the micro-system that evades the normal limitations of *paroles* and *écritures,* which fail equally to convince the wary reader of any presence in them.[7] Moved by these effects, one might thus define the poem as being (among other things) the interanimation of language both as speech and as writing, a single present micro-system out of the two impulses stimulated in the reader. The illusionary nature of his response is both double and ambiguous. As it has language turning upon itself in several ways, it exploits rather extraordinarily the special character of language as a medium at once visual and auditory, intelligible and sensible.

Our aesthetic intentionality that would see the poem as a mode of discourse in which the signifier has swallowed its signified and the *parole* its *langue*—as well as the poet's intentionality to create a verbal structure which can be so viewed—probably derives from human need as well as habit. The need to cultivate at least an illusionary sense of presence in language may well express our cultural nostalgia over the myths of presence which earlier ages could uncritically maintain but which growing skepticism has been draining away. Any attempted renewal of a claim to verbal presence would now have to be earned in the teeth of a wariness bred by the successes of two centuries of critical philosophy.

The history of our culture's sense of its language, with the gradual emptying of its signifiers, seems not unlike the layman's sense of the history of money as repositories of value and as a medium of exchange. Let us indulge the analogy for a moment. An obvious observation about the minting of coins in the modern developed nation is that there is an enormous difference between the value the coin signifies and the value of the metal it contains, indeed that the first, as an arbitrary signifier, is utterly irrelevant to the second. Let us assume, in this mythological history of money, that coin-making begins —long before the sanctions of the modern government—by creating objects of intrinsic value, say the solid gold piece. That is to say, coins contain materials of value; they *are* what they are worth. This would really be an extension of the bartering system, in which the intrinsically valuable coin serves as a general item of a certain quantifiable measure which can be exchanged for other more specific items one desires. But its value is *in* it: the value it signifies is limited to the value of the signified it contains.

[7] These are the failures which Derrida reminds us of. On the matter of speech versus writing as it concerns the need to demystify any notion of presence, I find it unnecessary to choose between Saussure and Derrida. For in neither of them is there a theoretical concession to the illusion of language as a medium of art which can authenticate our response as a response to verbal presence. (I must at once acknowledge, however, the brillance with which Derrida indulges this very capacity of language in his own writing.)

Once governments begin to guarantee the exchange value of the coins they sponsor, then, to the extent that people have confidence in the government's capacity to make good that guarantee, a difference can develop—a larger and larger difference as governments and their stability grow—between what the coin intrinsically is and the value it signifies. From this point the phrase, "what it is worth," as directed toward the coin, becomes increasingly ambiguous. The coin is of course moving in the direction of becoming a purely semiological object which arbitrarily (though bindingly) signifies a value without having to contain it. The coin "has" value only in the most figurative sense, since there is no presence of value in it. The nation's monetary system, then, moves toward functioning like a language system. Still, however, the coin may nostalgically carry some small value in the metals within it. And in order to heighten the illusion of the now-absent intrinsic worth, it continues to be decorated, in some cases quite elaborately. The face of the sovereign may usually be reproduced on it as a symbol and a mnemonic warrant of its worth.

As inflationary pressures permit the coin to buy less and less, thus suffering a reduction in the value it signifies, the government must take care to reduce the value of the metal it still contains. The least valuable denomination of any currency, when it is a coin, always must avoid the embarrassment of containing more value than it signifies, as when a copper penny was discovered to have more than a penny's worth of copper in it. Here is too much signified for the signifier: the true presence of value is a danger to the entire semiological system and must be reduced at once. So the response to such inflationary pressure is to eliminate the lowest denominations, starting the monetary system further up the line, or to make even the lowest denominations an exclusively paper currency. Of course, paper currency would already have been long since introduced for higher denominations as a silent acknowledgment that the monetary system had been reduced to a purely arbitrary status. (It is a constant irony that coins are usually reserved for the lowest denominations, while the higher denominations are paper currency, which can have no slightest pretension toward intrinsic value. It is the frequency of exchange of lower denominations which argues for the use of metal—an argument which concedes utterly that the value of the tender itself is unrelated to the value it is to signify.) Nevertheless, it is the case that, even with the total elimination of intrinsic value, nostalgia coupled with national pride continues the practice of artful decoration and the use of the sovereign's face, even on the paper currency. And an advanced industrial nation can learn to make synthetic metals cheaply enough to retain coins in their lowest denominations in the interest of nostalgia and durability. But at this late stage there has been for some time little point in disguising the arbitrariness of the signifier and its utter dependence upon convention backed by the confidence of those who partake of it. However artful the decorations, there is no longer any illusion of value in the material product itself.[8]

The history of book-making is enough like the history of coin-making for me to have used it as my example here—except that there was an obvious advantage in my being able to point to the agreed-upon degrees of value, whether in signifiers or signifieds, in monetary systems. But books also have an early career, which extends for a long time (and still is not altogether finished), during which their intrinsic value as a manufactured and ornamental product seems meant to serve as a material guarantee of the discourse within—a present, sensible accompaniment to the intelligible verbal code which was to have been the reason for the book's being there. More extremely, the book's existence as material art object may make its verbal contents irrelevant. But the original ornamented books—bibles and other religious works—wished to prove to frail humankind the divine presence within the book by marrying the sensible and the intelligible arts, an allegory of the marriage of flesh and spirit, which thereby guaranteed the appeal of the message by the richness of its embodiment. But, as with the actual gold we find as a material in some religious paintings, man's most precious goods—used symbolically—can physically create a present god even in the immaterialities of language. I hardly need remind anyone of the always growing deterioration of the material book, the increasingly unadorned, naked display of the words themselves—for as little time as their pages and bindings will permit them to last. To the loss of the myth of presence *in* words has thus been added the loss of any pretense at an allegorical making of the material book itself as a presence.

Whether in coin-making or book-making, always there was the impulse to preserve the immediacy of sign systems as a potential form of magic by trying to get the god inside the signs. And invariably the movement in history has been to become more and more conscious of the absence of any god and the emptiness of discourse. Aesthetic in-

8 I am reminded here of the Ashanti goldweights (one of which served Joan Krieger as the model on which she fashioned the emblem on the frontispiece of this book). They are magnificent miniature sculptures, and, though fabricated only in brass, they are used as measures of the gold dust and nuggets which were the culture's only medium of exchange. However handsome, they are still only base signifiers of value, of value contained elsewhere, in the unshaped bits and pieces of a gold metal which does have a worth intrinsic to its substance. Thus, unlike the gold, the brass goldweights have a well-wrought worthlessness that contributes to the phantom nature of those artifacts and the images they embody.

tentionality, as I have been treating it, seems committed to creating an experience, and a stimulating object as its ground, which permits us again to feel the god within. That is, it wants to pack literary coins once again with gold, to feel in signifiers the signifieds that transform them from arbitrary to indispensable. If the rich materiality of the external book has for some time been denied to writing, the poet's task is to regain presence by turning the poem itself into an object— though an illusionary object.[9] Through an extraordinary manipulation of the words themselves, he seems to turn them into a newly filled system of signifiers which no longer drives us away from them in search of extra-verbal substance.

Still, the artificial nature of the poet's instrument and the fictional nature of his appeal clearly limit the magic of our experience to the realm of self-conscious illusion. But these become the terms which govern the way we want to see the poem and its world. The poem thus provides categories for our immediate aesthetic apprehension of our reality, if I may return to a theme with which I began. It helps constitute our aboriginal ways of perceiving and knowing, leading us to our primitive vision of a world of identities before our common sense reintroduces the logic of difference. The illusion is of fullness, and we take it seriously, though we are self-consciously aware of it as illusion and do not mystify ourselves by projecting it outward into an ontology. So we are in the untenable position of having at once to believe and to look skeptically at that belief; we have to subject ourselves to an illusion which we allow to become the phenomenological bounds of our consciousness, and yet we must summon the hardheaded critique which sees only an illusion, a figment.

I have been justifying a theory which talks out of both sides of its mouth in order to encompass identity and difference, as I earlier tried to find a broad intentionality which could speak about formal intentionalities that did not exclude one another. But my purpose is not simply to seek a friendly eclecticism that would embrace antagonistic positions or to make the more respectable claim to synthesis (and isn't synthesis what eclecticism often becomes when friendly hands take over the description from unfriendly ones?). Indeed, the relations between the opposed claims which I develop, as I seek to affirm both of them, are not meant to be mutually supportive; they are rather meant to be polar, though in a duplicitous way that permits polarity to become transformed to identity, but without being any less polar. By

---

[9] The climax of this movement occurs in the modernist's "ekphrastic" impulse (seen most clearly in poems from the Symbolists to Wallace Stevens) to get the object inside the poem via the concrete image which forces the poem to shape itself into its object of imitation.

polarity I mean only the extreme form of difference, the logical consequences of the mutual exclusion between differential elements which
turn them into binary oppositions. As mutually dependent as they are
mutually exclusive, they undergo their will-o'-the-wisp transformations, leaving us unable to take our eye off either of them without
losing the other.

As centrally poetic, metaphor furnishes the exemplary model for
this complexity.[10] As we pursue each of the two poles of the poetic
metaphor, we engage just the duplicity which I have been trying to
describe. Our common-sense reading habits tell us to assume the distinctness between the two elements of the metaphor, one present and
one absent, except that we also persuade ourselves to see only with
metaphorical eyes and reduce all to presence.

What I suppose I am claiming is that our poetic habits (for both
writing and reading poetry) encourage a paradoxical logic (or illogic)
of metaphor. It requires us to entertain, in the operation of language
and metaphor, or language *as* metaphor, the self-contradictions which
allow us to view identity and polarity as I have suggested. In contrast
to what discursive logic can recognize—the moment of opposition
succeeded by the moment of compromise and reconciliation—in poetic metaphor the poles are to be seen as at once opposite, reversible,
identical. These multiple views, mutually contradictory and yet
simultaneously sustained, are permitted by the special character of
fictional illusion, with its strangely duplicitous appearances and "realities." On the one hand, we perceive the tenor of the metaphor as
collapsed wholly into the dimensions of the vehicle. That is, we see
through the vehicle exclusively, reducing the world to it, finding it
meaning-laden: we find it utterly identical with its meanings, or
rather find its meanings in *it* as a fully embodied metaphor. All this
we see though, on the other hand, we are also aware that the vehicle is
not its meanings, is utterly separate from them, is *only* a metaphor for
them, an empty verbal substitute. We remain conscious of the
common-sense view of language, resigned to the unbridgeable principle of difference on which it is based, and yet we permit the poem to
seduce us into a magical view of language as creator and container,
creator of what it contains, collapsing all (whatever its differential

10 I could speak of metaphor in the broad sense, in the way I spoke of it earlier as
the reductive form, *multum in parvo*, through which we envision the intentional
world of this poem. This is what I have in a number of other places referred to as a
work's "master metaphor" (see esp. *Theory of Criticism*, pp. 194–204). But this
discussion may be the more easily followed if we think of metaphor also as the
narrow rhetorical device, composed of tenor and vehicle and trying to lose the first
in the second.

variety) into an identity within itself. Because we do not lose our consciousness that the language of the poem is still only language and thus differential (mere empty words with absent signifieds), we indulge the miraculous powers of the poem only as we remind ourselves that miracles cannot earn their name unless they cannot occur. Differences can be reduced to identity, via metaphor, only if concepts, as things (or their signifiers), lose their self-identity (which distinguishes them from all others) by becoming one another, overrunning their bounds in defiance of the rules of property (and propriety). Metaphor becomes all-inclusive in the world it compacts within its identities and yet, in its consciousness of its artifice, it excludes itself, as mere illusion, from reality's flesh and blood. The illusionary basis of our commitment to the metaphorical fiction limits it to being an as-if commitment, complete in the magical verbal vision it provides, yet incomplete, even resistant, in that it allows us a skeptical retreat to the logic of difference.

I have elsewhere used a single quatrain from Pope's *The Rape of the Lock* as an extraordinarily spectacular example of this metaphorical duplicity—both by examining the language of the passage and, more broadly, by seeing in it a key to the master metaphor which is the constitutive principle of the poem.[11] I quote this passage and my commentary because I doubt that I can do as well in as little space to demonstrate this view of metaphor and of poem as metaphor.

> Pope forms his poem out of the tension between the sylph-protected, drawing-room evasions of time-ridden reality and the persistent biological promptings themselves. In several passages [he juxtaposes] the fragile China jar both to actual chastity and to his chaste and bloodless "toyshop" world. . . . But one of these passages takes this common metaphor of China and forces it at once to sustain the entire weight of both the delicate art world and the teeming continent itself.

> On shining Altars of *Japan* they raise
> The silver Lamp; the fiery Spirits blaze.
> From silver Spouts the grateful Liquors glide,
> While *China*'s Earth receives the smoking Tide.   (3.107–10)

> Here is the utterly empty coffee ceremony rendered in a mock-heroic euphemism that seems unintentionally to bring in what this ceremonial world must exclude—the heaped, fleshly realities of birth and death. These are excluded as the decorative crockery

---

11 *Theory of Criticism*, pp. 165–66, 196–97. See also my discussion of metonymy in this passage in chapter 5 above.

from China excludes that peopled place itself: the refinement of the earthen rejects earth. We see "grateful Liquors," heated by "fiery Spirits," gliding from "silver Spouts"—a "smoking Tide" received by "China's Earth." Here is a ceramic charade of coitus, an artful imitation of history's brute facts that is also a metonymy that evades them. For it is an imitation that the poet's characters must take for all the reality there is, although the poet has shown us he knows better. . . .

[I emphasize] the doubleness of the relationship between the aesthetic reduction and the resistant reality beyond: "China's Earth" . . . is the polished refinement of art—like that of the poem and of Belinda's toyshop world. Though it is, in other words, the aesthetic reduction of China, the phrase itself carries in it the meaning of China's flesh, the endlessly peopled earth of that crowded land, but only to exclude it. As purified emblem, the earthenware is the metonym for the earth, a refined representative of it, and yet, of course, not at all like it: its artfulness excludes flesh, its precise manufacture excludes the numberless consequences of the chanciness of nature. Just so the other double meanings ("fiery Spirits," "smoking Tide") suppress what they suggest: the pouring of hot liquid from silver spouts in the coffee rite excludes as its language, seeming to include, reminds us to associate it with —other "grateful Liquors" pouring from other spouts, filling China's earth as these fill another sort of China's earth. Much of this sort of doubleness—an exclusion whose language seems to spread its meanings to encompass what it, more narrowly, is seen as rejecting—occurs in other rites and games and mock battles throughout the poem, always reminding us what this purified world must neglect, as a prerequisite to its existence. The words seem bent on revealing the limitations of the world they describe, in their doubleness defining it by exclusion as well as inclusion. To return to the China example, we can say that, in reducing one kind of China's earth to another, the poem creates its emblematic metonymy (China for China, earth for earth) as its central metaphor (art for nature), while the fullness of its language denies the existential validity of the reduction. The metaphor, like the world of the poem, is brilliant, with a wrought surface ever admirable, but it is also reminding us constantly that, however satisfying its limited vision, it is not the world.

This example demonstrates that, within this uniquely sustained system, the very closing-in of the metaphor insists, through negative implication, on opening us (if not *it*) outward to embrace (while it rejects) the world. What seems contradictory is made to hold together in this language.

The abstract relationship between the opposed elements in the poetic metaphor can be theoretically illustrated in a diagram I constructed some years ago to describe the opposed thematic extremities in post-Renaissance literature.[12] It demonstrated graphically this ambiguous give-and-take between the polarization and identification of these extremities. I now see that the applicability of the diagram is far broader than I realized, that it brought to definition certain more general tendencies which had been undercurrents in my theoretical work for many years. The diagram furnishes a model which moves beyond the thematic elements which inspired it, moves to the binary oppositions at the root of all aesthetic illusion. It accounts for their duplicitous character which forces their differential relations into identity without forgoing their polarity. As I have already suggested, these paradoxical workings of poetic metaphor—so contrary to the permissible logic of discourse—can be accounted for only by a system of relations between opposites which defies our normal sense of contradiction.

Let us imagine two diagrams: one (Fig. 1), which I think poetic metaphor rejects, represents the conventional Hegelian conception of the tension between a pair of opposites followed by their reconciliation and synthesis, and then followed by the generation of further tension and further reconciliation. First there is a line of tension connecting the opposing pair, A and $Anti$-A, which are pulling apart from one another in polar repulsion, although they are also subject to pressure at either end to get them together. Under that pressure the line bows upward, becomes more and more bowed until it snaps, the two segments of the newly broken line now forming an inverted V. Repulsion has been converted to mutual reinforcement, with the high point of reconciliation the synthesis won at the apex. This is the *New A*, which once again generates its polar opposite, with which it becomes joined in a line of tension, and the synthetic process starts again, always moving from opposition to synthesis at higher and higher levels in a continually progressive sequence which like history is essentially linear. As description of language in poetry, this model seems to me delusive in its optimism and in the neatness of its movement from antithesis to union and back again. The firmness of its entities just does not seem responsive to the slippery behavior of the elements of poetic metaphor.

[12] In *The Classic Vision: The Retreat from Extremity in Modern Literature* (Baltimore: Johns Hopkins Press 1971), pp. 24–28.

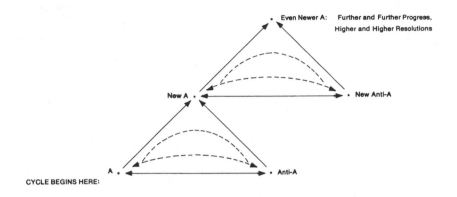

Fig. 1

Let me try an alternative diagram (Fig. 2). The action of the opposing pair, *A* and *Anti-A*, starts the same way, with the tensional line of polar antagonism between them subjected to increasing pressure that bows it ever upward until it snaps, breaking into two segments which move upward toward union with each other. But this time I shall suggest that what appears to be their meeting point proves to be only a momentary illusion of their merging, a stage which they both move *through*. The directional arrows heading each segment go through the midpoint of meeting, continuing straight on their way to reasserting their polar relationships, though in reversed positions. Having started as polarities occupying opposed positions, they have come through an illusory moment of identification to occupy positions which are equally opposed, though now opposed also to their own earlier ones. Now the line of tensional opposition is regenerated between them and the cycle begins anew: at the end of the next stage, after moving through another momentary meeting point, they will each appear to be about where they started, only to begin the cycle once more and continue to move through the stages of opposition, identity, and reversal. Which pole, then, is which? How can we place any position for either of them in this movement which defies identity and difference alike and yet embraces both? Let me confess that, as I see them, the relations between the terms "identity" and "difference" themselves—at once opposed and touching and criss-crossing—are representative of the movements I am trying to describe.

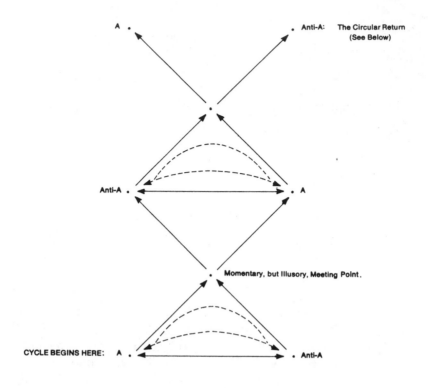

Fig. 2

In contrast to the first diagram, this one is anything but progressive. The repeated pattern of reversal and return suggests instead a circularity. Perhaps we could simplify the demonstration and make it more accurate if we shifted the diagrammatic figure to a circle (Fig. 3) and put the opposed elements, *A* and *Anti-A*, at the poles, connecting them with the diameter that serves as the line of tension between them. Here too the fixity of position and opposition would be revealed as illusory only, once we became aware of the pointlessness of the circle: always turning, it has no isolable points around the indivisible circumference. Thus no single polarity can retain the pointedness needed to define itself and the diameter it creates. Each pair of poles constitutes only one of an infinite number of possible diameters, each with poles at its opposed ends. These polar extremities, as infinite, run into one another, thereby losing all possible definition, so that they all become ultimately identifiable. The certainty of eventual return for the poles is no greater than the certainty of their being inverted.

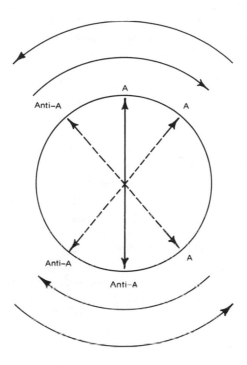

Fig. 3

Viewed from the perspective of metaphoric illogic, fixity and movement, along with identity and difference—and the very possibility of
pointed definition and entity-hood—all are illusions produced by the
discursive necessities defined by the logic founded on the principle of
difference. But of course, from a logical perspective outside the grasp
of the poetic moment, the paradoxical dissolutions prompted by
metaphor are no more than ghostly visions, even if we find them
expressive of the most immediate phenomenological responses of our
consciousness.

As I now view the vain chartings of polar relationships in these
diagrams, I see them as trying to account for all the binary oppositions
which a language-oriented theory would have to treat, if—now—only
as apparent oppositions: those between signifier and signified, vehicle
and tenor, the metaphorical and the literal, poem and reality, word as
substance and word as arbitrary marks on the page or a fleeting breath
—and, behind all of these, identity and difference themselves. The
illusionary doubleness, which I see within aesthetic intentionality as it
characterizes the literary canon within our tradition, is built into our

primitive sense of metaphor as we inherit it from earlier ages of literal belief in the magical power of words. Our belief is provisional and limited by the self-consciousness with which we address the nature of illusion.

We borrow our capacity to respond to such forms of metaphor—as the poet borrows those forms themselves—from the precedent of theological metaphors of presence. It is already the case in the Renaissance that poets take over and secularize Christian Neoplatonic paradoxes of divinity in humanity, spirit in materiality, unity in division (which is to say, identity in difference). It is the *form* of metaphor alone—with all its paradoxes—which is appropriated and our habit of metaphorical apprehension which is appealed to. The principle of transformation, of violations of verbal property, continues to be urged without any attendant substantive ontology or mystification. The demythification leaves standing the illusion created by the verbal structure, testifying to the need of our consciousness to *see* metaphorically and not just differentially. Even in a deconstructed form, then, the Neoplatonic habits of semiology persist, retaining a duplicity which limits itself to the realm of aesthetic illusion (in the original sense of that adjective). This claim turns out to be a defense of Matthew Arnold's old insistence that poetry does replace metaphysics once the latter has been demystified. In poetry as metaphor the equations do provisionally hold, but only while they are seen as self-realized absurdities incapable of being held. Perhaps the most fascinating literary works in our tradition are those which recapitulate these teasing powers of metaphor and thereby become allegories of the metaphorical process itself.

Very late in *Tristram Shandy*, in the mock-romantic section (volume IX) devoted to "The *Amours* of My Uncle Toby," the widow Wadman asks Uncle Toby a curious—but to her an almost desperate —question: "And whereabouts, dear Sir . . . did you receive this sad blow?" Given her secretly sensual concerns, she anxiously pursues the specific location of the wound received by Uncle Toby in battle in Flanders since she knows it to be in the area of the groin and worries about its possible effect on the marriage she hopes for. So, after all the delays invented through many pages and chapters and books by Sterne's ingenuity, she is ready at last for the answer. "And whereabouts, dear Sir . . . did you receive this sad blow?" Uncle Toby, remember, has promised, "You shall see the very place, Madam"— nay, more provocatively, "You shall lay your finger upon the place." And Uncle Toby is as good as his word, though at this final moment of disclosure he does not notice her "glance towards the waistband of my Uncle Toby's red plush breeches," since she expects him, as a start, to "lay his forefinger upon the place." After concluding his scale measurements, he takes her hand and lays her finger on the very place—the very place, that is, on his much treasured large map of the fortifications of the town and citadel of Namur, "the *identical* spot of ground where he was standing when the stone struck him." Sterne warned us much earlier, and repeats now, the claim that, after his lengthy study of the map, Uncle Toby "could at any time stick a pin" upon that "spot of ground." The widow's disappointment is more than matched by Uncle Toby's when he later learns the real object of her question and, shocked, breaks off his *Amours*.

Clearly, the issue between the not-quite-lovers is semiological and hermeneutic, revolving about words like "whereabouts" and "place." Whereabouts is the place where Uncle Toby received his wound? There are four "wheres" and "places" to which Uncle Toby may have been referring. Two of them would appear to be properly substantial signifieds, already ambiguous—one on the body of the man (in his groin) and one in the body of the battle (in the actual siege of the actual town of Namur in Flanders). But in Toby's mind a third "where" and "place," the point on the map, is a totally substantial signified, though of course as a map it will seem only an empty signifier to us. The final reality of the map is sufficient for Toby to take full comfort in it during those long weeks when he was first recovering from his wound. Yet of course Sterne is reminding us of the absurd confusion of signifier and signified when in two places[13] he has Toby refer to the point on the map as "the *identical* spot of ground" on which he received his wound. Further, Sterne reminds us of the absurd confusion of signifieds themselves, forcing us to remember the place on the body by insisting, in the same two passages, that Toby could stick a pin into it. But this is hardly the only time Sterne has offered us the geography of the body for the geography of physical space. For example, brother Bobby is earlier sent on a trip to the continent, we are told, because "the eldest son . . . should have free ingress, egress, and regress into foreign parts before marriage . . . for the sake of bettering his own private parts. . . ."

To compound semiological confusions, there is yet a fourth kind of place to which much time is devoted in the novel, a place that falls somewhere between signifier and signified (between the large detailed map and the town itself) in that it has elements of each: the area on the bowling-green, "a rood and a half of ground," on which Toby and Corporal Trim constructed a miniature replica of a town in Flanders

---

13 I hasten to add, two "places" *in the text*, lest I be guilty of adding yet another level of ambiguity. The passages appear, almost verbatim, in II.1 and IX.26.

in order to follow the course of the war. Here indeed is a body of reality capable of giving Toby satisfaction even beyond that of his cherished map, though it does not—as we see in that final scene with Mrs. Wadman—detract from his sense of the substantive reality of the map too. But Sterne is capable of telling us that Toby took a ride on his horse out to Dunkirk without a suggestion that there is any other Dunkirk but the one reproduced on the bowling-green. The bowling-green reality, both signifier *and* signified, is dwelled upon at such length in the novel in order to reduce all semiology to absurdity. As a body of reality, it is even connected to the human body—that part of the body functioning in procreation—when Trim removes the weights which hold up the window to use them as "field pieces" on the bowling-green and the window falls, almost emasculating the young Tristram. ("You have cut off spouts enow," Yorick says only half-metaphorically to Trim.) Here too the body of love may have to yield to the body of battle.

This reminder that the places of battle in the novel are inevitably yoked to the places in the genital area—the first working to the detriment of the second—returns us to the widow's question and Toby's response. We are surely to recall that earlier point in the novel when we were told, with Sterne's usual ambiguity, that "the wound in my uncle Toby's groin, which he received at the siege of Namur, render[ed] him unfit for the service." Nor should we overlook the site of the battle which inflicted the wound, Namur, or ought we spell it "N'amour," or even "no more"?[14] The very name "Namur," "place" of the love-denying wound, thus reinforces the prudishness Toby shares with his brother. But not with Corporal Trim, who, on the very page after Uncle Toby's version of "where" the "place" is, shows Mrs. Bridget (Mrs. Wadman's maid) that it was "here," having moved from the map to his body, putting her hand on the very place. But Corporal Trim much earlier rejected all language but the body's; and the story of his own wound and the therapeutic use of her hand upon it by the Beguine, which he recounted only shortly before as a preview of the final *amours* in the novel, indicates clearly enough the alternative reality to Toby's.

Where is the metaphor and where is reality in this discourse? Looking for reality, where can we find its "place" in this novel in which, as in the circle in my final diagram, nothing holds its "place"?

14 To reinforce the pun with "N'amour" we should remember that it was Sterne himself who gives us the word, entitling volume IX "The *Amours* of My Uncle Toby." I should like to thank my class in the School of Criticism and Theory during the summer of 1977, and Professor Stuart Peterfreund in particular, for the suggestions which enrich my discussion here.

Of the four kinds of wheres and places which Sterne provides in dealing with Toby's wound, we should remember that the one apparently literal signified—that town in Flanders, Namur itself (whose very nature is negative, if we are to believe the pun on its name)—is the only one which never appears in the novel. And of course, as far as Toby is concerned, neither does his own body exist, the "place" sought by Mrs. Wadman for which the point on the map represents "the identical spot of ground." The novel constantly turns away from such substantial signifieds as presumably real towns and real genitalia (only "presumably real" since the novel does no more than note their absence) to let us dwell among those newly substantiated signifiers— the maps and make-believe replicas which turn into linguistic realities for the hobby-horses which all the characters mount to ride off to their respective Dunkirks. Where conflicts between metaphor and reality are converted into conflicts among reified metaphors, language becomes the only enabling act: we recall Walter Shandy's auxiliaries (auxiliary verbs) marching off in order and presenting themselves to Toby, who converts them into *his* auxiliaries (soldiers) without really changing them at all. Again it is the language which is the reality, creating instantaneities of metaphor which collapse all the varied versions of reality into its own single identity of the word.

Tristram Shandy may thus be constructed around the fallacy of verbal reification—the conferring of a single substantial thinghood on empty polysemous words—as it is practiced by its several hobby-horse riders; but the novel is no mere game played among verbal ambiguities. It is rather a profound semiological instrument, tying visions of reality to a language which is potentially neutral but is never neutral: it is only present, insisting on reducing all human realities to itself while acknowledging its own empty indifference to reality. Though what we are shown are the naive epistemological errors of Sterne's characters, these are compounded into the truth of the work's totality, which plays with us and asks us to have the patience to learn to play with it. We must take these reifications seriously as illusions which constitute an entire world for each of the characters. Thus Toby lives, on hobby-horseback, in mimesis of the one act in his life which has meaning, confounding ambiguous signifiers and signifieds in all-out sacrifice to the symbolic reality of his wound, the sole isolated fact.

But our sympathy for the seriousness of the illusions of the characters is cut short: we laugh at their illusory nature, assuming that we would know better. Sterne encourages our hold-out, anti-verbal skepticism by stimulating our sense of absurdity. We watch all the hobby horses, like Gombrich's "substitutes" for reality (foremost among which is, we remember, a hobby horse), while we are probably mounted up on our own. Tristram acknowledges as much when he shows us himself mounted up on his and riding, that is, writing this book. Or is he, as he suggests in volume VII, *literally* riding as he flees through the continent, trying to escape that "arch-jockey of jockeys" who he feels is mounted up behind him and is in pursuit? But of course in this form death itself becomes just another metaphor, another hobby horse and hobby-horse rider. There are, then, no horses but hobby horses, though man is never anything but a jockey.

Sterne's many-leveled language, which would appear to be our only reality, is the one sure presence in a world where everything resists our touch and points us to a verbal map. Where signifieds and signifiers reverse and re-reverse their roles, what, besides the poet's language, is "here"? Where is the body of this reality before us and how does it relate to the body of words, if Sterne has persuaded us to grant his words body? How identical do the differences in the novel become for us who see the language create our awareness of them even as it collapses them into itself? What, then, is the book *about*? Where is its object of imitation? How can we touch the wound with which it has left us? We discover how difficult it is to answer precisely when, like Uncle Toby and the widow Wadman, we try to put our finger on the very place.

11

Literature versus *Ecriture*:
Constructions and Deconstructions
in Recent Critical Theory

I WANT TO BEGIN by surveying in a brief compass the theoretical
conflicts currently animating our academic literary criticism and to
make clear my own attitude toward them. Since I want to be brief in
my summaries, I shall have to oversimplify various critical positions in
order to place the variety of statements within each of them into
patterns that I hope are accurate, even if only generally so.

Since those days, now at least two decades back, when we could
speak confidently about the dominance of American criticism by the
so-called New Criticism, a number of contenders has arisen to claim
the place of primary influence. Whatever the differences among them,
they seem to share the role of exacting retribution upon the New
Criticism for its excesses. We associate the New Criticism with an

This essay was originally written for the Literary Theory issue of *Studies in the
Literary Imagination* (Spring 1979). Perhaps I should make explicit at the outset
my intention to limit my use of the term *literature* to "*poesis*" in the Aristotelian
sense of self-conscious fiction-making. Hence my use of the term *poetry* or even *poems*
(with no reference to verse, of course) as a synonym for it. If, then, I am defining
"literature" at its narrowest point, I am defining "poetry" at its broadest.

exclusive focus upon the isolated literary work to the neglect of its relations to its author, its audience, and the language of which it is representative. Thus New Critics overemphasized the discontinuity of the poem and the experience appropriate to it, rejecting any continuity with the experiences of its creator and its reader or its continuity with discourse in general. Each of these areas of neglect seems to have sponsored a variety of criticism which has claimed some following in these post–New-Critical days.

If their idolatrous approach to the insulated poem as something like a sacred object led some New Critics to ignore authorial consciousness and with it the act of writing, some post–New Critics turned from work to author with a vengeance, blending the work into his consciousness. Others turned instead to the passing moments of the actual and even wayward experience of the reader and dissolved the work into them. And since New Critics, in their exclusive concentration on the poem, conferred upon it a privilege which cut if off as a discrete entity from the rest of language, still other post–New Critics have tried insistently to reestablish the unbroken continuity of all our discourse, poems and non-poems, as they merge the aesthetic into the continuity of all our experience.[1]

In the later 1950s it was Northrop Frye who, with his followers, led a resurgence of interest in romanticism which sought to undercut the antagonisms of the classic dispassion that characterized the New Criticism. Then the influence of newer continental critical movements began to assert itself, first by the so-called phenomenological critics, more accurately called "critics of consciousness" after the model of the Geneva school, most often seen in this country as represented by Georges Poulet. Though there have been other, philosophically more faithful versions of phenomenological criticism after Husserl, Ingarden, and Merleau-Ponty, it was the freer, more subjectivistic variety introduced to us by Poulet that attracted the neoromantic mood already aroused by Frye. It also fed the neoromantic return to an interest in the writer and his world as his consciousness constitutes it for him. Those other critics we more accurately call phenomenological have usually preferred to concern themselves with the mental states of readers in their perceptions of literary works. Such reader-oriented

[1] I of course do not mean to suggest that these movements were primarily motivated by the desire to counter any aspect of the New–Critical orthodoxy or, in some cases, that they were even aware of the New Criticism as a movement to be countered. But I would argue that the effect of these movements, seen from this end of recent critical history, was to undo the several aspects of what we think of as New–Critical doctrine.

criticism is reflected not only in the so-called School of Konstanz but—perhaps even more influentially among younger American scholars—in the critics trying to apply speech-act theory to the work's confrontation of its reader, and especially in the "affectivist" work of Stanley Fish. But on this occasion I cannot pursue these several directions since there is one other major movement on which I want to dwell.

Only with structuralism, together with post-structuralism, also derived from continental sources, do we find a movement with the spread and attempted dominance to match the New Criticism's. Indeed, in the semiotic ambition that would synthesize all the "sciences of man," structuralism would claim a far greater hegemony. And its following among younger scholars threatens to become far more extensive, spreading as it does well beyond the precincts of literary study. Its power rests on totally new and revolutionary grounds that would destroy the basis of all traditional criticism which it would replace as it deconstructs. For, in its most forceful posture, it would do away with any distinction among the modes of discourse, indeed in its extreme form even the distinction between criticism and the poem which is its object: it would deny that criticism serves, as a secondary and derivative art, the primary art of poetry. Instead it would see them both, with all their sister disciplines, sharing—as coordinates and equals—the common realm of *écriture*. There are, of course, many different voices in the domain of structuralism and post-structuralism, and they are often raised in violent debate with one another, as we move from a Lévi-Strauss to a Lacan or a Foucault or a Derrida, or as we move through each of Barthes's new and changing pronouncements, as these debate with one another. And we must ask, with some of these writers, whether he is structuralist or not, as he protests his freedom from the movement. More generally, we must ask when post-structuralism ceases to be structuralist.

What these positions share derives from a Saussurean view of language, which, by way of its universal analysis of discourse into *langue* and *parole*, must come to the leveling of any privilege which poems have been granted. Man is seen as an identical speaker-writer in all his varied discourses, each built upon equally arbitrary signifiers, based upon a monolithic principle of differentiation. We are instructed to find the unity of all discursive disciplines in a common structure of signifiers, whatever their arbitrary signifieds may turn out to be. Thus our analysis of any of these disciplines rests on the methodological assumption that homology is all. However favorable our attitude toward interdisciplinary study may be, however intense

our search for a unifying principle for the human sciences, this procedure may well suggest too easy and undifferentiated a series of analogies (or rather homologies), especially—we should add——for a theory
expressly based on the doctrine of difference. Still, these theorists
surely represent (among other things) history's egalitarian revenge
upon the New Criticism's aristocratic worship of the poem as a privileged and hence elite object, an object as separate from all others as it
is from our normal experience. (This socio-political language is intended more than figuratively as it is used by many in the structuralist
tradition.)

In the extreme form of Barthean semiology, the literary work (as
we may obsoletely term it) flows with all others into the sea of écriture,
part of an anonymous universal and intertextual code that is a single
system. The structural sameness behind the disposition of signifiers,
though they parade their would-be signifieds before us, should remind
us that it is but a mythification for us to take those signifieds literally,
as if they and their claims represented a conceptual "reality." For,
instead of signifiers embracing their signifieds, they stand at a hopeless
distance from them, with a relationship between the two that is arbitrary at best. And, for the post-structuralist, the world of discourse
becomes as empty as the world itself. With this claim, we are reminded that the post-structuralist, if not the structuralist, impulse,
though its motives seems to be linguistic, may be seen as springing
from the metaphysical (or rather anti-metaphysical) anguish that accompanies our sense of the "disappearance of God." Verbal meanings
seem to follow God out of our experience, the one abandoning our
language as the other abandons our world. Thus in Jacques Derrida
or Paul de Man we often see linguistic terminology disguising an
existential sense of absence. It is a lingering Heideggerian impulse. If
their literary theories seem breathtakingly new, the motivating notion
of the death of God does not. (It is not difficult to understand the role
of Nietzsche as one of the major prophets of the movement.)

In such theorists both world and language come to be seen as
decentered since, in the grand marriage of Nietzsche and Saussure, the
world is reduced utterly to language, a now-empty world of language
defined as the disposition of signifiers alone. Both world and language
are seen as decentered; for any of us to claim to find a center ringed
by signifieds, concepts whose would-be meanings we reify into reality,
is for us to resort to the mythology of metaphysics, ripe for deconstruction. But if *all* language, as the common écriture, is equally doomed
to emptiness, then our long-standing convictions about poetic presence in the book and the word can be demystified and revealed as the

pious delusions they are. The study of poems becomes, for such theorists, the study of such decentering, such emptiness. The critic, thus licensed (or thus deprived), must content himself with the absence rather than the presence of meaning, with verbal deferral rather than self-assertiveness, with poems as centrifugal rather than centripetal movements. As in de Man, criticism studies the poet at a distance from himself and the world, sending forth words that acknowledge the gap, the awesome void, between themselves and their would-be objects. Linguistics, having yielded to thematics, now claims a poetics, what Joseph Riddel, in the spirit of Derrida, terms "the poetics of failure," the failure of the word. The "uncreating word" of the _Dunciad_'s apocalyptic end has come again, this time heralded and theoretically shepherded.

As I have suggested by mentioning Nietzsche, this movement may well represent an extreme extension into poetics of the mood of wan despair that has been with us for over a century. We may recall that Matthew Arnold's own concern to come to terms with the new unmetaphysical realities, while retaining a special role for poetry, led him to grant to poetry the psychological powers lost by religion along with our belief in its claims. If we share Arnold's loss of faith, we can go either of two ways: we can view poetry as a human triumph made out of our darkness, as the creation of verbal meaning in a blank universe to serve as a visionary substitute for a defunct religion; or we can—in our negation—extend our faithlessness, the blankness of our universe, to our poetry. If we choose the latter alternative, then we tend, like de Man, to reject the first, affirmative humanistic claim about poetry's unique power, seeing it as a mystification arising from our nostalgia and our metaphysical deprivation.

Stubbornly humanistic as I am, I must choose that first alternative: I want to remain responsive to the promise of the filled and centered word, a signifier replete with an inseparable signified which it has created within itself. But I am aware also that my demythologizing habit, as modern man, must make me wary of the grounds on which I dare claim verbal presence and fullness. And I am grateful for my recollection that the aesthetic domain—the domain of _aesthesis_, of _Schein_—has been, from Plato onward, acknowledged to be the world of appearance, of illusion, so that verbal power, under the conditions of the aesthetic, need not rely upon a metaphysical sanction to assert its moving presence.

I have before now in several places argued for the power of a poem to persuade us of its own verbal presence, even while its "theme" may

well have been that of separateness and absence.[2] The point I have
been trying to establish is that the existential theme of absence, of
distance, indeed of one's very failure to touch the world while being
overcome by it—however moving and universal this theme has been
in our time and earlier—need not lead to an equal absence, distance,
and failure in the created language of the poet who deals with it.
Critics used to believe that a mark of the great poet was his power to
overwhelm with his expression the gaps in the commonplace language
of the rest of us as we try to stammer out our sense of the human
predicament. It does not require us to surrender our sense of that
predicament if we claim that combinations of words can be created
which permit us to grasp it as we cannot for ourselves. Although Yvor
Winters was not one of my favorite critics, I begin to sympathize with
the impatience with which he used to invoke "the fallacy of imitative
form" to characterize the activity of the poet who deprived himself of
the capacity to transcend (and thus to transform) his materials.

It may be instructive, as an indication of how criticism has moved
from valorizing the formal overcoming of thematic distance to valorizing the formal (or rather the anti-formal) echo of it, to compare
Cleanth Brooks's invocation of romantic irony to Paul de Man's.[3] For
Brooks, as the representative New Critic, the poet employs irony as his
device to master the several separated and even opposed layers of
meaning and being—through the conflation of them within a word.
For de Man, irony is a reflection of the subject's isolated and powerless
state as he relates himself to the nature (object) from which he is
alienated. Poetry cannot for de Man succeed in escaping the fate of
language as a differentiating instrument, trapping itself within its
speaker. So in de Man irony returns the subject upon himself, thereby
guaranteeing the inefficacy of his language to touch the endlessly
differentiated world—differentiated, most of all, from himself. On the

[2] See my treatment of the poems by Ben Jonson and John Donne in *Theory of
Criticism: A Tradition and Its System* (Baltimore: Johns Hopkins University Press,
1976), pp. 234–40; of Sidney's and Shakespeare's sonnets in "Poetic Presence and
Illusion I: Renaissance Theory and the Duplicity of Metaphor" (above); and of
Tristram Shandy at the conclusion of "Poetic Presence and Illusion II: Formalist
Theory and the Duplicity of Metaphor" (also above). In each case I have tried
to demonstrate the poem's capacity, by its own verbal nature, to collapse the distance
which it acknowledges.

[3] Just about any work in Brooks's early career will serve my purpose here (with
perhaps *The Well Wrought Urn* [New York: Reynal & Hitchcock, 1947] my best
example), while the discussion of irony in de Man's influential essay, "The Rhetoric
of Temporality," in *Interpretation: Theory and Practice*, ed. Charles S. Singleton
(Baltimore: Johns Hopkins Press, 1969), pp. 173–209, furnishes the most obvious
contrast.

other hand, the irony of Brooks enables the speaker—whatever the dehumanized state of the outside world as it oppresses him—to capture it all in his word and thereby, at least aesthetically, to humanize it after all. If neither's irony alters the fallen reality, at least that of Brooks asserts man's formal power to comprehend it, whatever his existential status as forlorn subject.

Now it is true that the New Critics tended to bestow this substantive ontological role upon the word too literally, so that a later linguistic skepticism provided a needed demystification. Still, within the provisional nature of our aesthetic habit of response, is there not an illusion of verbal presence which we can find in the poems which constitute our canon? And from here can we not move to the further illusion that existential space and its gaps are collapsed into the sensible unity contained in words exploited for themselves? Would these moves not seem to preserve literature as a kind of discourse which seemed to be performing differently from its fellows?

Can we, then, propose a theory of literature that allows for literature even while taking into account the warnings about mystification which the structuralist movement has effectively used to displace its precursors?[4] I see this as the major question I must answer since, as we saw at the opening of this essay, post–New-Critical movements seem to have defined themselves by their opposition to one or another element of neglect (poet, reader, or discourse as a whole) indulged in by the New Criticism as it reified its object. Need all the gains bequeathed by this movement be washed away along with the metaphysical orthodoxy and epistemological naïveté that apparently made those gains possible?

Clearly, any defense of a separatist concept of literature must today be provisional, if not paradoxical, in that it must free itself to attend to an object in whose independent existence it cannot afford to believe. It is for this reason that I see the critic dealing with intentionalities and illusions, even though his attention to our habits of aesthetic perception and the history of artistic conventions permits him to salvage what he can of an art object—not altogether unstable —functioning within its culture and serving that culture's visionary needs. Under the literary man's pressure to do justice to the art he tends, but equally under the pressure of recent deconstructionist theory, I feel both the presence of the object and the phantom nature of that presence. In this way I hope that—if one is candid enough—it is

4 This is to use, for a moment, the language of Harold Bloom, who has been showing some signs—despite his vast difference from them in emphasis—of becoming their ally.

possible to evade a wishful reification on the one side and the dissolution of the literary experience on the other.

So, despite contrary tendencies, I mean to urge not only our recognition of the poet's verbal power for humanistic affirmation even in the face of the blankness of our common language, but also the availability of the poet's product as a special sort of stimulus for our response. Still, I must emphasize our present instinct for demystification in order to remind us of the crucial phenomenological qualification which reduces the art object from ontology to illusion. As we yield to the prodding of our aesthetic experience which would have us reify literature as an autonomous entity, we dare not forget that its illusionary role must somehow allow for its existence within the indivisible domain of *écriture*. It is thus the case that any concept of literature which recognizes its ties, before and after, to a continuum of language and experience will have to treat its status as literature most delicately if that status is to be salvaged at all.

Even a modified phenomenological defense of literature as a special mode of discourse is likely to depend upon some claim in behalf of a peculiarly literary use of language. Such a claim rests, in turn, upon an assumption that there is a "normal" use of language and that language becomes poetic through deviations from the norms of "non-poetic" language usage.[5] But the long-accepted doctrine about language norms and deviations from them has been steadily undermined in recent years. Stanley Fish's attack on "deviation theory" and its dependence on the concept of an "ordinary language" is only one—if one of the more effective—of such attacks.[6] The insistence of Hayden White that all language is tropological, that it all has a "swerve" in the direction of the peculiar figurative vision of the discourse, leaves no neutral linguistic ground for language to swerve *from*.[7] One could observe this general tendency in recent theorists who, with a neo-

[5] Such deviations do not, of course, refer to anything as superficial as "poetic diction." Rather, in the tradition of Russian and Prague School Formalism and the New Criticism, these are seen as "dislocations" or "defamiliarizations" in the semantics or syntactics of language, breaking in upon our normal responses to discourse in order to promote a special fictional or aesthetic function.

[6] Fish, "How Ordinary Is Ordinary Language?" *New Literary History* 5 (1973): 41–54, and recently, "Normal Circumstances, Literal Language, Direct Speech Acts, the Ordinary, the Everyday, the Obvious, What Goes without Saying, and Other Special Cases," *Critical Inquiry* 4 (1978): 625–44.

[7] Originally in *Metahistory: The Historical Imagination in Nineteenth-Century Europe* (Baltimore: Johns Hopkins University Press, 1973), especially "Introduction: The Poetics of History"; but more carefully and persuasively in "Introduction: Tropology, Discourse, and the Modes of Human Consciousness," *Tropics of Discourse* (Baltimore: Johns Hopkins University Press, 1978). The term *swerve* is of course borrowed from Bloom.

Kantian awareness of the constitutive nature of language and cognition, insist on seeing all language as revealing a version of reality rather than reality itself, a context-controlled shaping of verbal figures rather than a transparent show of universal meanings outside and independent of all language. So all language comes in recent theory to be seen as constitutive of its visions, creative of its fictions, in poetry and non-poetry alike. Consequently, any line between poetry and non-poetry is seen to be mythical as all discourse is similarly gathered under the blanket of *écriture*.

How, then, can I at this late date urge the deviationist claim for poetry which I need if I am to urge its separatist mode of functioning? For how—to ask the same question another way—can I still speak of "normal" discourse as a mythical background against which deviations are to occur? Perhaps my answer is summed up precisely by such an acknowledgment that the concept of normal discourse *is* mythical, though it is a necessary fiction if we are to account for the effects which the poetry in the Western canon is capable of producing in those of us who come to it with the trained habit of aesthetic response. Can recent arguments for a seamless *ecriture* altogether wipe out our common-sense awareness of the distinction between those discourses which are predicated on the assumption that they are telling us about a "reality" outside language—that they are more or less "true"—and those which are self-consciously cultivated fictions? We of course approach made-up stories about imagined people differently from discourse which claims to say things directly to us about the world; and we do so in part in deference to what we assume the writer means to do with us and to us. Yet the sophisticated claim about the similar metaphoric fictionality of all discourse would lead us to deny any such "common-sense" distinction as naive.

I would urge our "common-sense" awareness of yet a second distinction, this one between discourse which seems anxious to sacrifice itself in order to transmit extra-linguistic notions available in several possible verbal sequences or languages and discourse which seems to generate its meaning out of the very internalized play of its verbal medium, so that its meaning is untranslatably locked in "these words in this order." Recent theorists may well argue that there is no synonymity in *any* discourse,[8] thus reinforcing the antagonism against

---

[8] E. D. Hirsch, Jr., to the contrary, argues that there *is* synonymity in discourse, and —since for him literature exists within "the continuum of discourse" without a "special nature" to separate it from that continuum—synonymity can exist in poetry and non-poetry alike (*The Aims of Interpretation*, Chicago: University of Chicago Press, 1976, esp. chaps. 4 and 8). It should be noted that his argument for synonymity is one I am quite prepared to accept for all discourse in which the satisfaction of

a claim for a poetic discourse which would create its nature through its unique untranslatability; but shall we not distinguish between the grappling with language to generate meanings as special as the very words and the lazier, stereotyped thing most of us do most of the time? It is refreshing to recall that the one earlier and most universally recognized contribution of the New Criticism was its power to distinguish the originally creative use of language from the general storehouse of stock expressions which appear, in borrowed form, in discourse. To call the latter "creative," whatever the epistemological likelihoods in the mind of man as language-user, is to engage in a basic misuse of the language of creation. (I thus acknowledge my belief that, even in my desire to say something original here, I am essentially discovering—picking up as best I can to satisfy my minimal verbal requirements at each step—the langauge I am using and not, in any way that suggests what the poet does, creating it in the sense of making it new.)

I argue, then, that most trained readers of poetry feel an acute difference between discourse characterized by a self-generating play of words which maximally exploits all that is potentially in them, exploding them into its meaning, and the loosely instrumental "use" of words selected from the bag of almost equal candidates for service which our culture places at our disposal to carry—one or another of them in its minimal way—a predetermined extra-linguistic meaning. Of course, this is a matter of degree rather than of kind, so that boundary cases will have to exist and be debated about—and perhaps with almost every case a potential boundary case. Yet the theoretical distinction is a crucial and felt one for so many readers that there is likely to be considerable agreement about poetic and prosaic extremes. Between extremes of verbal manipulations tending toward and away from synonymity, and all that synonymity implies about the verbal satisfactions of maximal or minimal requirements, there may well be difficult and confusing examples of discourse which may appear to some to ask to be read one way and to others another way. And these often turn out to be the not-quite-philosophical-not-altogether-"literary" texts at the center of much recent theoretical discussion. But, far from proving the non-existence of literature as a relatively separate entity demanding unique interpretive methods,

---

minimal criteria of meaning is all that operates in the selection of words. But this very argument leaves open the place for a discourse (if it can be shown to exist) in which the maximal exploitation of the potentialities of words precludes the possibility of synonymity. And this would move us again toward separating literature from other discourse, though Hirsch would obviously have to hold back.

such texts (as they have recently been treated) may rather be seen as broadening the applicability of literary methods, thereby enlarging the peculiarly literary domain of literature to include self-consciously reflexive writers whose fictions include the illusion that they are non-fictional.

So all discourse may indeed be a metaphorically derived fiction at its source, and its language may indeed be creative of its reality. But, in the face of such epistemological concessions as I make here, I still suggest the phenomenological distinctions which the differentiated structures of our verbal experiences present to us. The self-consciously developed fictional illusion of discourse to which we respond as aesthetic creates in its turn the illusion that there is a "normal" discourse from which it deviates. (Of course, we must grant that by this time there is nothing either shocking or blameworthy in our creating—among all the fictions we create—the fiction that there *is* a "normal" discourse or that, except in poetic discourse, there is a synonymity among words.) As we contemplate and seek to define what *can* happen in that fused linguistic "corporeality" which poetic discourse sponsors the illusion of attaining, our habit of finding (or making) binary oppositions may be pressed to the invention of another class of discourse, a prosaic sort that helps us mark by opposition the magical behavior we feel we have witnessed and been partner to in poetry. And we come up on the other side with the ruthless instrumentality of a neutral, normal discourse which is self-deceived in its intention to be self-effacingly referential. The structuralist insistence that the signifier cannot have more than an arbitrary relation to its supposed signified is perhaps the strongest way of putting this claim of universal synonymity—a claim that is supposed to allow me here, for example, to grab onto any word that satisfies the minimal requirements, from moment to moment, of the field of linguistic forces developing before me. The invention of binary opposition as a structuralist principle can thus win the literary man's assent through his own need to have such a principle as one from which the uniquely monistic principle of poetic discourse can deviate, and with apparently magical results.

In behalf of this sort of literary man and his cherished response to his favored works, we have been doing little more than circling and recircling his one tautology: that a poem is a speech-act and writing-act which deviates radically from our non-poetic uses of speech and writing. It is seen as becoming a version of *parole* which has been made to deviate from others so significantly as to make it autonomous and self-regulatory such as no *parole*, by definition, can be. Thus the experienced and properly initiated reader of poetry may be encouraged by the successful poem to sense the generic language system, or *langue,* behind it as violated and distorted until what is before us is seen as a self-generating and self-responsive—in short, as a reflexive— system.[9] As this reader comes to view it, every deviation from normal usage is converted into a constitutive element of an apparently new system which can occur only this one time. The minimal functions of language, which usually satisfy us as speakers and writers are thus converted—as he watches—into maximal functions of the totally re- alized poem.

In this way the need to operate in a special way upon all that goes on in a poem forces this reader to retain the opposition between "normal" and "deviationist" models of discourse as his binary fiction. The contrary claim—that all *paroles* stand in a similar relation to their *langue* so that a poem is just another *parole* on the same level as all others—collapses the opposition, of course. If the *parole* is to the *langue* as the particular to the universal in the Platonic model, then all *paroles*—poetry among them—are equally subordinate, common subjects all. Structuralist uniformity, extending *parole* into *écriture,* here makes alliance with the claim of E. D. Hirsch in precluding—or at least demystifying in advance—the very concept of poetry as a kind of discourse.

Yet must we not resist such a denial to the extent that our pro- foundest literary experience is otherwise? In the greatest literary works, those documents which have—throughout their history with us—been treated as elite, those which, in other words, constitute the literary canon in the Western tradition, the illusion of an autono- mous, self-generating reflexivity in language persists for those trained to read them appropriately (that is, in ways appropriate to our conven- tions for reading our elite literary works). We are persuaded toward viewing such a work as a self-sufficient system because we grant to it a peculiar status as a fiction, a free-standing fiction which seems con- scious of that status, building that consciousness (which we grant it) out of the self-referential devices we claim to find in it. Skeptically aware these days of the literary man's propensities for mystification, we may be uncertain of the extent to which we have been hypnotized by it or merely self-hypnotized. Yet the sensitive and knowing reading

---

[9] It is thus that I have argued elsewhere for the paradoxical term *micro-langue* as a label for this verbal creation. See *Theory of Criticism,* p. 188: "Like all the other generic and minimal elements, the *langue* has been violated to the point that the *parole* appears to have become its own *langue,* a system of which it is the only spoken representation. In effect it becomes its own *micro-langue,* the only *langue* that speaks, the only *parole* that is its own system—the true concrete universal. Not that it is literally incompatible with the existing *langue* of which it is a *parole,* but that the *langue* cannot account for what this particular speech act has performed."

of the work which seems to do its work upon us somehow each time breaks through our wariness and our willfully irreverent inclination for demystifying our idols.

In this discussion I have been using the terms *langue* and *parole* and other references to linguistics in a metaphorical sense far broader than what is meant technically by them. To those who know my work it should be clear that the norms I speak of, or the deviations from them and the systems constituted by those deviations, are not to be thought of as exclusively verbal, though surely in many poems the words are the major element of the literary medium being manipulated into its own constitutive form and into its own self-consciousness. But as we move outward from lyric to narrative and dramatic modes, we find a number of presentational elements which serve as the manipulable medium, whether the staged presence (at once real and unreal) in drama, the point of view in narrative, or the great variety of received conventions—stylistic, formal, topological, or tropological—in all the genres. In effect, the medium is anything which the poet can convert into his performance space within his fiction, within his radical of presentation, within his language. That is, it is the space within which he performs his reflexive play, and persuades us to join him in it. We learn the internally generated rules fabricated for the occasion, and what they give rise to—within that performance space, whatever the genre—is the special sort of fiction we call literature.

Still, once we have decided—with whatever qualifications—to separate out literature from *écriture*, we must concern ourselves with the placement of a theoretical dividing line between literature and non-literature. This problem is especially troublesome if we have acknowledged the authority of those arguments which would deconstruct any separatist notion of literature. But whatever the mystifications of its more idolatrous critics, literature itself is no enemy to the deconstructive impulse. Far from it. Indeed, one might well argue that in its reflexivity and self-consciousness literature not only deconstructs itself but is the very model for our use in the deconstruction of other discourse. Modern theorists may be anxious to undercut the privilege granted literature by leveling it into common *écriture*, but what they have for the most part done is to raise *écriture* (or at least those non-literary examples of *écriture* they are dealing with) into literature. If these critics argue against the exclusiveness of poetry (that is, fictions, "imaginative literature") as the proper subject for criticism, and rather seek to include a wide range of works by essayists, philosophers, and even social scientists, they do so by treating these works as texts to which techniques appropriate to literary criticism may be applied.

Even more, their techniques of deconstruction, of "unmetaphoring" their texts, are to a great extent echoes of what poems have always been doing to themselves and teaching their critics to do to them.

It is for this reason I suggest that, instead of the concept of literature being deconstructed into *écriture*, *écriture* has been constructed into literature. As a consequence, everything has become a "text," and texts—as well as the very notion of textuality—have become as ubiquitous as writing itself, with each text now accorded the privileged mode of interpretation which used to be reserved for discourse with the apparent internal self-justification of poetry. But if the no-longer-elite object of criticism has fewer characteristics which seem to deserve this concentrated treatment, it is a boon to criticism (and a boost to critical arrogance): as deconstruction ceases to be an element in a work no longer reflexive and device-filled, it increasingly becomes a central feature of the critic's interpretive reading of it. And the text of the critic, in its deconstructive shrewdness, can now expect to outdo its object-text, whose native qualities are no longer a match for the critic's own.

Yet even in the face of this development in recent theory, we still can seek a separate phenomenological definition for the peculiar forms we call literature, those whose justification for deconstructionist treatment appears to lie within themselves. We can very well grant, with Hayden White, that all the varieties of discourse are similarly constituted by their guiding tropes.[10] We have already observed that, in theorists like White, the egalitarian principle works to claim, not that no discourse is art, but that all discourse is art. Each discourse is at its source creative: each creates its own tropological fiction; even discourse which pretends to deal "objectively" or "empirically" with its data from the outset "emplots" that data in accordance with the fiction permitted by the trope. What place, then, can there be for a "literature" which has a peculiar tropological functioning of its own?[11]

According to the tropological universalism of White, discourse (poetic or otherwise) as it comes under analysis may be seen generally as tracing similar figurative patterns. And all such examples are then

[10] For the following discussion, see the introductory chapter to *Tropics of Discourse* (note 7, above).

[11] In a recent essay ("The Epistemology of Metaphor," *Critical Inquiry* 5 [1978]: 13–30), Paul de Man shows an interest in making common cause with those like White who see figuration as a discursive necessity which, at the epistemological level, breaks down our attempts to put up barriers between poetry and philosophy as kinds of discourse.

equally literary as they present themselves for analysis by the critic of tropes. Each is seen as moving from metaphor to metonymy to synecdoche to irony, although there is some ambiguity about whether, as observed in discourse, these are analytic coordinates or (as in Vico) progressive stages. The sequence of figures surely leads from the primitive to the sophisticated, from the instinctual to the cerebral, from the naive to the self-conscious, in what seems to be a common romantic and post-romantic pattern of the fall of man, usually the fortunate fall.[12] The sequence seems to move from an immediate, prediscursive, subjective identity (metaphor) to the particularizing differentiation, as of items in a contiguous series (metonymy), to the totalizing of particulars into generalizations (synecdoche) to the self-consciously subversive reflection upon the entire process (irony). We seem here to be dealing with modalities of consciousness as much as with linguistic tropes (or is the first utterly reducible to the second?), and we seem to have a series marked by cumulative progression even though there is a temptation to valorize each stage on its own.

(This pattern of discourse is seen as a reflection of the psychic history of the individual human consciousness as well as the collective history of Western consciousness. So, besides being an instrument for understanding discursive structure, it seems to propose a way of accounting for human development, both individual and collective, and in an identical sequence which suggests the principle that phylogeny reproduces ontogeny. No wonder, if all private consciousness and public history reveal these structures, that they invade all our varied discourses equally, or at least similarly. Of course, such structural analogies may reflect our own monomyth based on a privileged plot we have invented and projected onto discourse, consciousness, and history alike. White's own radical skepticism allows us to doubt that the ubiquitous pattern [like the pattern of the fall on which it appears to be based] is seen because the tropology reflects a true state of universal structuration [of consciousness as well as language, or of consciousness because of language]; it rather allows us to suspect that the pattern is seen because of a romantic and post-romantic convention of thought of which this tropological claim is no more than a recent version. From this perspective the pattern accounts for so many poets and thinkers of the past two centuries not because we have unlocked the secret of their common discursive structures, but because

---

12 I trace the common early romantic fascination with the "fortunate fall" from innocence to experience in both man and culture in chapter 6 ("William Wordsworth and the *Felix Culpa*") of *The Classic Vision: The Retreat from Extremity in Modern Literature* (Baltimore: Johns Hopkins Press, 1971), esp. pp. 153–57.

their conventional mythologies of emplotment have invaded our own discursive habits, turning our own work into just another historically controlled example of an influential tropological habit of writing.)

In this series of the four tropes, the crucial movement—at least for getting discourse started—is from the first to the second, from metaphor to metonymy. The metaphorical world of similitudes and analogies must dissolve its unity of a universally mirrorized sameness, dissolve it into a differentiated sequence of separated entities, so that language and rational science may begin. From individual verbal boundaries, carefully demarcated and observed, words can then be marshaled into the generality of propositions, a new unity in synecdoche, but now safely arrived at through the observance of the rational law of verbal differentiation upon which the very beginning of discourse in metonymy was predicated. Beyond this would-be scientific security, nothing is left except the occasional reminder, by an ironic wisdom, that this has all been a movement only in the world of tropes, and that the clean scientific objective has been a deceptive one in that the continual urge for differentiation, in depriving language of its metaphorical moment with *its* urge for sameness, has also deprived itself of its content, has in effect emptied itself. Yet our skeptical awareness of the tropological bent which diverted the referential pretensions of the discourse reminds us of its figurative basis, so that structuralist analysis reveals it to be more literary than scientific.

It is here, in this universal model for the tropes of all discourse—the model which for all practical purposes is to turn all the varieties of discourse into literature, that we find a unique characteristic of literature as distinguished from non-literature. It rests—as we should have remembered from Jakobson—on literature's special relation to metaphor, on its need to overcome the normally differential character of language. We must note, in White's scheme (whose elements seem to be as much borrowed from Piaget as they are applied to Piaget), that prior to the differentiating action of metonymy, the metaphoric stage—with its commitment to identity—was essentially pre-linguistic. What I mean to suggest is that, if discourse normally must find its nature by making its way from identity (metaphor) to difference (metonymy), literature has the role of earning its way back to identity from the differential nature of normal discourse from which it deviates. Thus literature has the peculiar task of becoming a kind of discourse which, as discourse, can yet appear to occupy the normally non-discursive metaphorical stage.

As I conceive it, literature performs this feat, not by struggling toward an impossible return to naiveté in a romantic search for the origins of language, but by borrowing the appearance of a discourse of

identity through an ironic self-consciousness which knows the metaphorical indulgence to be an illusion. Once we think beyond the
nostalgic notion of literature as primal metaphor, like that of a Vico
or a Shelley, we recognize that literature is not an innocent: it cannot
be defined in terms of naive metaphorical identity because it has
already known metonymy, springing as it does from the ordinary uses
of language such as metonymy creates. An advantage of White's tropological model is that it permits us to see literature as an ironic discourse, transcending and transforming both metonymy and synecdoche,
though it does so in the guise of metaphor. Seen thus, literature is a
sophisticate, a beyond-metonymy, rather than a before-metonymy,
discourse.

I prefer White's enumeration of the four traditional tropes to
Jakobson's reduction to two because a binary distinction between
metaphor and metonymy restricts poetry within the former, thereby
failing to account for the post-metonymic character of poetry which
masks itself as metaphor. The romantic opposition between metaphor
and metonymy thus tends to leave poetry as pre-discursive, pre-
rational, and pre-realistic, so that it takes other complicating elements
(additional tropes) to account for poetry's metaphorical nature as post-
metonymic. To see poetry as a literal return to—or as an original
beginning in—the pre-discursive state of metaphor is to fail to do
justice to its sophisticated nature. Now it is true that the twofold
scheme furnishes a distinct place for poetry, however romantically
irrationalist it may be, while the fourfold scheme may seem to tie
poetry to other discourse as being similarly tropological. But the latter
scheme permits any distinction between poetry and other discourse to
reflect the duplicitous relation poetry has to metaphor.

Although the ironic is seen by White as the final trope for all
discourse, it is different for literature from what it is for non-literature
in that it permits literature an illusionary return to metaphor under a
show of identity that comes out of a full sense of difference as the
essential principle behind words. Non-literary discourse may well attain the reflexive air of self-consciousness which irony permits, but in
literature such a reflexive self-consciousness becomes a precise verbal
device which momentarily alters the nature of our perception of language, reopening us to a vision of verbal identity, though it requires
us to hold it as an illusion only. Consequently I object—in White as
well as Jakobson—to the use of terms like *similitude* or *analogy* to
characterize metaphor as if they were interchangeable with *identity*. It
is my point that the special character of the poetic device which
achieves the show of identity is marked by its distinction from similitude or analogy, since either of the latter two terms reminds us of the

commitment of language to difference. I recall John Crowe Ransom's important claim that the fully earned metaphor finds itself only where similarity and analogy end, where utter identity is achieved, achieved in the teeth of language's differential habits.[13] According to this view, similarity and analogy both acknowledge the wide range of differences between the two items being compared because of— perhaps—only a single common element or structure. The poet's task is precisely to move from such similarities or analogies as non-poetry affords us, to the illusionary miracle—in violation of language habits —which shows us the two as utterly become one (except that, as the poem may also remind us, our metonymic memory knows better).

We can say, then, what the peculiarly poetic illusion is: that there is in the poem the collapse of verbal difference into the receptive capacity of a corporealized word which has achieved its fullness as a spatialized entity. It is an attempt to use language to return it and us to the primal identity which metaphor alone affords. But it is an ironic attempt which acknowledges that the world of linguistic difference is not only the world from which it springs but also one that, though paradoxically, coexists even in the illusionary metaphor itself, denying the metaphor even as that metaphor affirms itself.

This duplicitous relationship between the identity and difference of originally distinct linguistic entities is like that which I have some time ago noted (or rather noted Shakespeare as noting)[14] between us and our mirror image. The image in the mirror, as our double, seems to match our reality with its own, except that, as an illusion, it is without substance and not ourselves at all. Further, I saw the magical nature of glass as permitting the unsubstantiality of the mirror image to open outward—through the mirror become window—onto a separate reality of its own. In a recent essay, Geoffrey Hartman finds a similar double that yet has its own life in the mirror—"the specular name"—and defines literature by its unique "nominating" capacity to

[13] The passage occurs in "Poetry: A Note in Ontology," *The World's Body* (New York: Charles Scribner's Sons, 1938), pp. 139–40. He finds a special "miraculism" in the poem "when the poet discovers by analogy an identity between objects which is partial, though it should be considerable, and proceeds to an identification which is complete. It is to be contrasted with the simile, which says 'as if' or 'like,' and is scrupulous to keep the identification partial." Ransom blunts my point a bit by speaking of "partial identification" when I would prefer "similarity" (with its implication that the one moment or area of likeness is surrounded by moments or areas of difference), reserving "identification" for the completeness which the poet has forced. Still, Ransom makes the point tellingly for us even now.

[14] See *A Window to Criticism: Shakespeare's* Sonnets *and Modern Poetics* (Princeton: Princeton University Press, 1964).

establish a paradoxical sense of its reality and to create a language to speak it.[15]

The mirror plays a major self-referential role in Jan van Eyck's famous wedding portrait of Arnolfini and his wife. In the painting, hanging on the far wall behind the couple being married, a mirror re-reflects the scene already being mirrored in the picture. In that second-order reflection, we can make out the artist himself seated before the couple and painting the picture we are looking at, thereby corroborating visually the statement he has written on the painting, which testifies to his witnessing of the marriage: "Johannes de eyck *fuit hic.*" There are here several orders of illusion and reality, of art and life, being collapsed into an identity for all the differences that are mutely acknowledged. They thus reveal the several kinds of paradoxical relationships I have been observing in literary language.

As with poetic metaphor, whatever reality the illusion persuades us to confer upon that double in the mirror, we must remind ourselves that the mirror never stops being an illusion even if—like van Eyck—the artist also was here, breaking through his created reality to our living reality. So too, despite his ironic reflexivity that puts us off, the poet asserts his presence and with it the presence of his poem; and he means—at least momentarily—to overwhelm our anti-metaphorical skepticism with such presence. Confronted by his fully charged literary work, for the occasion we become—for all our metaphysical disclaimers—magic-worshipers once again.

---

[15] "Psychoanalysis: The French Connection," in *Psychoanalysis and the Question of the Text: Selected Essays from the English Institute, 1976–77*, new series, no. 2 (Baltimore: Johns Hopkins University Press, 1978). Hartman derives his notion of the "specular name" from the "mirror phase" of Lacan, seeking as he does (yet while escaping differentiation) a linguistic equivalent for Lacan's pre-linguistic moment of identity in the image.

12

Literature as Illusion, as Metaphor, as Vision

Yet may I by no means my wearied mind
Draw from the deer, but as she fleeth afore
Fainting I follow. I leave off therefore,
Since in a net I seek to hold the wind.
                    Sir Thomas Wyatt, "Whoso list to hunt"

I WAS TEMPTED to use the general title of this volume as my own title here, except for my recognition of the fact that my colleagues in this undertaking might claim an equal interest in it and, like me, will have to resist. But these days there is a better reason to avoid the title "What Is Literature?" Many theorists of late would argue that it is a question-begging question in that it assumes what must be demonstrated: the existence of an entity which is widely denied existence. In other words, it assumes the existence of a discrete body of things called literature which stands out there waiting to be defined. But much of the most influential theory these days, preferring the blanket term *écriture*, would refuse to grant that discriminable groups can be justi-

Written for the volume, *What Is Literature?*, ed. Paul Hernadi (Bloomington: Indiana University Press, 1978), in which each author was briefly to define his conception of literature.

fied as having a separate status within the generic character of the act and product of writing. Consequently there can be permitted no privileged group of writings called literature. And the nominal act of creating such a group, as we critics have traditionally done, is converted into just another mythology which some recent semioticians would deconstruct. While not many years back even a Sartre could address himself to the question "What is literature?" current thinking suggests the question itself betrays a naive complacency in what it takes for granted.

So, rather than ask the question, I choose in my title to proceed aggressively to answer it, and in a way that affirms both the myth behind such a term as *literature* and literature itself functioning *as* a myth, though one sustained by us with an awareness—already demonstrated in my opening paragraph—of its deconstructibility. So I proceed from one substitute noun for "literature" to the next: in claiming the literary work[1] to be an illusion, I am acknowledging our awareness of its make-believe, as-if reality, which is not to be confounded with the factual reality to which we may tend to relate it; in claiming it to be a metaphor, I am acknowledging that in it the two differentiated entities of normal discourse (signifier and signified) are made identical—though only by poetic fiat, not by propositional equation; and in claiming it to be a vision—an author's and, through him, his culture's—I am focusing upon our seeing, as distinguished from the thing apparently seen. Each of these definitional substitutes for "literature" emphasizes our skeptical willingness to undo literature's "reality," just as the nature of this defining process is meant to emphasize our skeptical willingness to undo the reification of "literature" as a definable entity.

In the limited space suggested for this essay I can barely—too barely—move assertively from one to the next defining characteristic, leaving it to my lengthier discussions elsewhere to argue for their preferability to other possible definitions.[2] But my brevity here may

---

[1] The reader will note that I move easily—here and in the balance of this essay—from literature to the literary work and back again. The obvious assumption behind such a movement is the simple notion that literature refers to a class of works which we are lumping together for definitional purposes, so that what is found true of the single work is representative of what would be true of them all as a class. Clearly for other definers of literature (Northrop Frye is a most striking example) literature is more than this uncomplicated collective made up of sovereign individual works, but rather has its own life which transcends its individual manifestations. One of the chief values of this volume should be its revelation of such differences in assumptions about the work and the larger entity we think of as a collection of such works.

[2] Let me suggest, among other places, my *Theory of Criticism: A Tradition and Its System* (Baltimore: Johns Hopkins University Press, 1976).

suggest too much assertiveness, too great a commitment to these defining characteristics as substantive entities themselves, although I am
primarily interested in promoting the awareness of literature's illusionary nature. At each stage of my definition I mean to press our
self-conscious myth-making, not our pretension to metaphysical discoveries.

I make one additional observation about this attempt at definition, whether one sees it as propaedeutic—implying that substantive
arguments to support it may now follow—or as a conclusion of arguments made on other occasions. It is a confession of the obvious: that
the definition has normative as well as descriptive elements, so that it
opens the way, automatically as it were, to evaluation as well as mere
identification of literary works. By virtue of satisfying the definition, a
work qualifies as literature; but to qualify as literature, in accordance
with this definition, is already to be judged as successful literature. In
other words, the definition is prescriptive of how the individual piece
of writing ought to function in the human economy if we are to
accord it the honorific title of literature. If it so functions, then it
must be both literature and satisfactory as literature. The interpretive
analysis of the work thus smuggles in the evaluation as its inevitable
companion. In this sense, there is no poor literature: if a work is poor,
then it fails to qualify as literature in that it does not reveal the power
to function in this way. So it is not truly literature, but is something
else parading as literature. Obviously, any such prescriptive definition
is woefully circular, assuming beforehand the characteristics for which
it then searches and excluding whatever fails to conform. Only a total
philosophical anthropology can systematically establish such functions
and authorize such a defined and exclusive class, though the present
essay is hardly the occasion for so elaborate a construction.

Of course, this defining process, conceived in a simple, common-
sense way, presupposes that our substantive (in this case *literature*)
does exist as an enclosing form for a number of entities out there
(presumably individual pieces of "literature"). This would spring
from a pre-structuralist (if not pre-Humean) naiveté which would
assume that the existence of a signifier implied the equivalent and
prior existence of its signified. However, not only do the written works
not fall into real classes for us to name, but the works exist as individuals for us only as a result of our illusionary act of reification out
of our radically temporal experience of them. We know that it is the
reader who must construct the object out of the sequential patterns
given him. Yet he tries to be responsive, and such an attitude suggests
a controlling thing he is being responsive to. He has only his actual

experience to which he can refer, and yet out of this limited experience he must derive a normative experience and the object which that
experience would project.

Even with these experience-bound qualifications, forced upon us
by a sophisticated epistemological awareness, there is the pragmatic
need—if we are to make the definition usable—to draw the line between literature and non-literature. I suggest it be drawn, in accordance with the characteristics I am offering here, by appealing to
the phenomenological notion of intentionality. That is, there is the
special kind of experience we intend as we confront this object, and
we intend it because we intend this object as one having the discriminable features that sustain such intentionality. We must assume that
we can on occasion be disappointed, and that sometimes the object
will not be seen as sustaining what we intend it as being and doing, so
that we can escape the circularity of inevitable self-confirmation. In
such unfortunate cases it can be claimed that the object should more
appropriately be sponsoring another sort of intentionality. It stands,
in other words, outside the domain of the intentionality that produces
the requiredness of the literary work: instead, it is functioning as a
work of non-literature, of whatever sort in the particular case.

It must be granted that, in the practice of criticism, many works
(one thinks, for example, of first-person, confessional works—Rous-
seau comes at once to mind) can be viewed as functioning (and
functioning well) on either side of the line separating literature from
non-literature, although—I would hope—the far greater number
would turn out to be less ambidextrous. With the latter the placement
within the intentional category would carry with it (as I have suggested) an implied judgment about the literary value of each. And the
gray area constituted by the works more difficult to place may call
attention to the impression inevitable to the grounds of our discriminations of intentionality—phenomenological and not realistic
grounds, after all; but it does not undermine the definition so much
as it makes it necessary for us to move beyond the definition as we use
it to solve major critical problems, though each case remains open to
argument. In the humanities, after all, definitions should be beginnings only, pointing toward opportunities rather than conclusions
which would preclude further work and further uncertainty.

Given the definition as no more than a phenomenological postu-
late, it is little wonder that I see something mythic about our very
naming of the literary work as literary, and even more so about the
class of such works we term *literature*. But, as I define it, the work
functions for us as a myth that—if we watch it closely enough—knows

itself to be one. This characteristic is an inevitable accompaniment to our sense of it as a fiction, emanating from the work as an inner skepticism about itself and its peculiar status in being.

It is at this point that I see the cogency of E. H. Gombrich's work on illusion and self-reference[3] as illuminating our experience of literature as well as of the plastic arts. There is a peculiar unreality—or a strange reality peculiarly distanced from our own—about the characters and actions in literary works. As members of the audience we are not prompted to intrude ourselves into the action onstage during a dramatic performance any more than we would try to step into a painting. Further, the people out there on the stage are characters rather than real people, however much they may resemble the latter: those characters and the experiences they undergo have a repetitiveness, an inevitability (indeed an everlastingness) about them that transcends any single performance or silent reading. As Aristotle reminds us, their beginnings, middles, and ends—absolute in their relations among one another and in their capacity to begin the tale again —differ radically from our mortal and contingent beginnings, middles, and ends. This is the sense in which the work is an illusion, only an appearance of a reality that it eludes, keeping for itself a freedom from chancy contingency, a freedom to play in its special immunity from *our* kind of death. And no sophisticated reader—however caught up he may be (and he *should* be) in the action—thinks it other than illusion, or confuses it with the dimensions of his own life. In its self-referential dimension the work itself reminds us of its make-believe status.

Perhaps the characters and action in a dramatic performance, based on the actors' impersonations of the characters and their actions, furnish the clearest example of literature's illusionary nature. But, though perhaps in less obvious ways, illusion functions similarly in the non-performing literary genres: the illusion of history or biography in the epic or in some prose fiction or the illusion of journal or confession or autobiography in lyric or first-person fiction. More prominently, there is the illusion of the normal use of language in all literature, but especially in the conventional lyric, where even the sounds of words, as sensuous elements, have an illusory aspect that is freely exploited. We must, that is, feel—as it were—the sensory appearance of the words, as it joins with common and uncommon meanings to create a use of language that is anything but common.

---

[3] The obvious starting place for Gombrich (though he later goes off in many profitable directions) is *Art and Illusion: A Study in the Psychology of Pictorial Representation* (London: Phaidon Press, 1960).

Yet the illusion persists, though undercut every moment, that it is only the same old words that are being mouthed. And another dimension of reality is being evaded for an illusory world which at once takes itself seriously *as if* it were reality, and yet shows us its awareness of its make-believe nature by being conscious of its artifice. I would argue, then, that the literary work is described more accurately as a self-referential illusion of reality than (as has been suggested since Aristotle) as an imitation of reality. (I am aware that making literature an illusion, rather than an imitation, of "reality" deprives the latter term ["reality"] of precise meaning or epistemological status.)

In no aspect of the work is its own apparent awareness of its illusionary nature more strikingly revealed than in its character as metaphor. I see each work as constituting itself and its relation to reality through a master metaphor that is coextensive with its own body: that is, it seeks to reduce the muddled contingencies of normal experience to a controlled appearance under the formal rubric of its own reality. As metaphor it equates as it symbolizes, rendering the large and incomplete world out there as the small and complete representation which is the work. It is as if this reduced and perfectly coherent part could contain the unimaginable whole, without remainder. Thus the work's pretension is metonymic as well as metaphoric. Its every aspect conspires to make it a satisfying totalization which, as an apparition, gives us itself for the world. Our sense of the work's "corporeality" (to use Sigurd Burckhardt's term[4]) arises from the substance we attribute to it as its language and its events take on body that substitutes for our reality by becoming its own apparent reality. It transforms the motley materials it borrows from the world of normal discourse, having forced them to deviate from their common generic uses and converting them into elements of its own, now maximally exploited to create its reductive totality.

But if the metaphor, as the work itself, is an absolute reduction, in the security of its aesthetic completeness it also betrays from time to time an awareness that it is in the end only metaphor and not reality. Out of its word it creates its world as if it were our world, while the very perfection of its creation reminds us of all in our world which it is not. It creates its words out of our words, except that it seems to turn its signifiers into the shapes of their own signifieds, into the inevitable product of what had been an arbitrary series of relations; yet they are still but words. If there is something miraculous about a literary presentation that takes on body—about empty words filling themselves with substance and persuading us of their fullness—we

[4] *Shakespearean Meanings* (Princeton: Princeton University Press, 1968), pp. 22–46.

know it can be a miracle only if we also know it cannot happen. The world, the work, and the word seem one in the master metaphor. Or rather the world seems enfolded in the work which seems one with its word. But outside the terms of the metaphor, alas, the world is not in the work, and the word, as an illusion and an illusionary metaphor, is, like all miracles, seen from an outside view as a deception. In the fictional self-consciousness of its most metaphorical moment, the work reinforces our awareness of its duplicity. It encourages us to look at it both ways—at its best, both ways at once.

In its most developed form in our finest works, the metaphor is both complete in the reduction of everything to its terms and utterly aware of itself as an inadequate measure of the world. As Rosalie Colie describes the metaphor, in the very act of being wholly established it "unmetaphors" itself.[5] As a myth it is a totalized world, and as it demythifies itself it is not part of the world—the unpatterned workaday world—at all. Thus it is both a constructed emblem that contains the world and a deconstructed breath of air that does not begin to describe it. What it denies about itself at no moment detracts from the fullness of affirmation to which its every element contributes. Its paradoxical capacity to combine self-affirmation with self-denial—to see itself as the world and to see the world as anything but itself—is its most brilliant manifestation of its commitment to literature as illusion, illusion as that so persuasive as-if reality which seems to be all the reality there is while it reveals its merely make-believe (dare we say counterfeit, even fraudulent?) character.

If literature is illusion and that special manifestation of illusion which I have described as metaphor, it is of course also vision. But by now it should be obvious that I can see it as visionary not, as in romanticism, in any vatic or gnostic sense, but only in a sense—consistent with its inner skepticism—that would restrict the visionary to the merely illusionary. The emphasis is on a sustained seeing without any assurances about the existence of the seen. The illusion of reality which the metaphor creates for us is a reduced moment of vision, a reduced moment of a culture's vision of its reality as that vision (and hence *its* reality) is constituted for that culture by its poet. For through the metaphor is created the illusion of reality as vision. It is reality trimmed to the confines of aesthetic creativity and, through that creativity, to the confines of aesthetic apprehension and then of apprehension of the world itself as aesthetic. Through this sense of vision

[5] This is a central notion and a controlling methodological device in her brilliant study of Marvell, "*My Ecchoing Song*": *Andrew Marvell's Poetry of Criticism* (Princeton: Princeton University Press, 1970).

(even if illusory vision) we can see how even this self-deconstructing view of literature opens the aesthetic to broadly anthropological considerations. The very history of culture depends upon it.

But here again the reflexive character of illusion asserts itself, and we are reminded, even as the vision asserts itself, that the vision of the world may not after all be the world, indeed that it stands at odds with the world and is threatened with being engulfed by the world. Still, we return to the work to sustain the vision once again, frail and too delicate an emblem though it may finally prove to be, for while we renew its life we renew our own capacity for seeing.

There is one constant in this movement from illusion to metaphor to vision: it is the claim that the literary work borrows elements (words, thoughts, characters, actions) from the commonplace world and presents illusionary equivalents of them, except that these equivalents are severely transformed by the created microcosm that sustains and reshapes them. All that is minimally efficient or meaningful in "life" is maximally exploited into a total functionalism. What is arbitrary in a loose system of signifiers in which substitution seems uniformly permissible emerges in the illusionary artifacts as both indispensable and inevitable. If the structuralist has reason to emphasize the gap in normal discourse between signifier and signified, the literary work challenges his analysis as in it the signifier fills itself with signified and thus itself becomes indispensable and inevitable. As it thus revives the possibility of a living language that can match words to our imaginations, literature discovers for itself the function of giving its culture words that permit it to speak as if for the first time. What a literature says is what it sees, even if what it says and sees is unsaid and unseen outside the enabling act provided by the aesthetic mode. For only *in* the seeing and saying can its world exist, can the signified survive in the signs that create as well as carry it—indeed, that embody it.

It should now be seen that, as must have been unavoidable, I have been providing not so much a definition of literature as a definition of the only sort of literature I believe I can justify. From the outset I warned that my proposed definition would be normative and even honorific, enclosing only those kinds of literary works which it is designed to find successful. Obviously, it prefers works of closed form, as in the critical tradition we can trace from Aristotle to post-Coleridgean organicism, to the exclusion from literature of so much else. But there is also in the definition the requirement for works to turn on themselves and their own closedness, and for them consequently to open to the world, if only by negation. Thanks to self-reference—that self-consciousness which illusion reveals about what it is and is not—

the totality of self-assertion for the sake of illusion is to be matched by the totality of self-immolation before an unyielding if unenclosable reality. Both are totalizations, although the simultaneous reversals of possibilities in them leave them free from the metaphysical consequences of holism. Further, however narrow one may think the inclusions permitted by my definition, it should be remembered that only the most uselessly non-restrictive nominal definition could try to include everything to which someone might wish to attribute the name of "literature." As in all definitions, it comes down to a choice among exclusions.

I return also to another earlier warning: that this occasion would permit only a hasty summary of the elements of my proposed definition, with little opportunity to do more than state them baldly, essentially without argument. Yet what I have had to state baldly is a series of apparently self-contradictory propositions about illusion and reality in literature, about both its self-enclosure and its consciousness of self-enclosure which opens it outward, pointing it toward all that is outside it, toward all that it is *not*. The propositions, in denying themselves, deny their appropriateness as defining tools for this object of definition. I have tried to speak firmly, definitively, about the will-o'-the-wisp literature, whose very being undoes this mode of dealing with it. Its duplicitous way of functioning makes a myth of every claim. In taking itself lightly as discourse, it forces all discourse—even the theoretical—to take itself lightly in pursuit of literature. I feel like the lover in my epigraph from Wyatt, who cannot find the equipment appropriate to his beloved quarry, and finally retires, exhausted: "I leave off therefore, / Since in a net I seek to hold the wind." But as I do, I remind myself that the elusive deer in Wyatt's sonnet was very likely —as poetry is for me—his mistress and a queen.

13

Theories about Theories
about *Theory of Criticism*

LIKE THE OTHER contributors to this issue, I confront an occasion fraught with temptation. Professor Hernadi has provided all the stimulus one could wish for the desire, which sensible authors have learned to suppress, to answer all those "unjust" (which is to say unfriendly) reviewers for all their misreadings or out-of-context attacks. We are here being licensed—indeed encouraged—to give vent to all our aggressive-defensive gestures as a response not only to our maligners but also to those whose praise has been too faint or inconstant: the book, via its author, is encouraged to glare back at the fish-eyes which have been viewing it too coolly.

Yet, beyond these frivolous temptations, there is the more serious opportunity to write some afterthoughts to one's completed work—to make clear certain methodological underpinnings that seem not to have been grasped by those readers who have recorded their reactions. And if, submitting to trivial temptations, I were to detail my many

This essay was written for an issue of *The Bulletin of the Midwest Modern Language Association* (Spring 1978) in which several authors of recent books were to review the reviews of those books. I am of course dealing with reviews of *Theory of Criticism: A Tradition and Its System* (Baltimore: Johns Hopkins University Press, 1976).

197

inevitable complaints against my reviewers, there would be little space to develop these more consequential matters. So I shall make this response more in the nature of a general extension of the book and—except for examples I can introduce in passing—let go my chance to talk back in a point-by-point way to those who have so far reacted in print to my work. I prefer, in other words, to use this assignment calling upon me to review my reviewers to look through what they say toward a re-viewing of the book itself.

I find one recurrent concern running through the reception of *Theory of Criticism* so far, one which the very organization of the book—as well as its final polemic—perhaps asks for. It is the relation of my career to the New Criticism, which soon turns into the relation of this general systematic statement (in the present book) to my own earlier work as a theorist for (or critic of?) the New Criticism. By implication or open statement, this concern leads to suggestions about the continuing relevance (or, by contrast, the obsolescence) of my sort of system in its relation to the current theoretical dialogue. Obviously, the judgments made on these issues depend on the friendliness of the reviewer—although friendly reviewers turn out to be well disposed either because they think of themselves as reactionary and welcome me as a theoretical defender of their position or because they see my work as less bound to older orthodoxies and welcome it as a still vital alternative in a changed universe of theoretical discourse. Obviously, I prefer the second attitude, although I confess that I would prefer either of the two to those who, seeing themselves as being carried along in the new wave, relegate my work to quaint nostalgia. Though I have been impressed (and, I admit, pleased) by the general respectfulness and cordiality of my reviewers, without exception, I clearly am more pleased by those who would still count me among the living.

Theory of Criticism, as my most recent book and my attempt to formulate a total poetic, comes twenty years after my first volume, *The New Apologists for Poetry*, which is my only other book devoted exclusively to theory, while the several books in between the two treat specific literary issues which were to influence and reflect the various theoretical changes I thought I was undergoing. So what naturally must bother me most—as I contemplate a writing career of a quarter-century which I must hope reflects considerable development and growth—is the ungenerous observation that my new book reveals my position to have undergone little if any change, even if we go back for comparison as far as *The New Apologists for Poetry*. Thus, after these many years and writings in which I tried to draw careful distinctions between the New Criticism and me, I am especially (and weariedly) disheartened, if not offended, at the disdainful title of a review of

Theory of Criticism which carries its complaint on its face: "On Going Home Again: New Criticism Revisited."[1]

I recall in the past being disowned by both René Wellek and the late W. K. Wimsatt, two distinguished historians and theorists we associate with New-Critical theory, who saw me as one who deserted the movement to embrace other modernist tendencies.[2] Nor do I feel that their rejection of me was totally undeserved. Yet in his review Weinsheimer speaks from the first of my continuing "allegiance" to the New Criticism, confident as he is "that Professor Krieger's theory does not seem to have changed in essentials during the last two decades." Robert Scholes similarly freezes my position in his review in the *New Republic*:[3] "Since *The New Apologists for Poetry*, which he wrote twenty years ago, Krieger has been trying to provide a consistent theoretical justification for the interpretive practices of the New Critics," with "the present book" providing "a kind of summary statement of this theoretical position." If this position represents "old verities," instead of them "we need new truths." Even Denis Donoghue, who shrewdly follows some of the complex arguments which I see as differentiating me significantly from New-Critical orthodoxy, brings me back to it in his final judgment: "But when all is said, I cannot see that Krieger's position differs very much from, say, Ransom's."[4] And yet more friendly, O. B. Hardison is anxious to enlist me in the traditional defense of poems as objective synchronic systems and consequently laments any tendency I show to complicate my own allegiance to it.[5]

Having permanently tied me to the New Critics, Weinsheimer condemns me with them, invoking much as Scholes does the need for newer and more fashionable doctrines. Thus is historical determinism introduced to rationalize our current modishness. Weinsheimer complains that my theory, which he charges with not having changed, "is no longer tenable," recent movements—such as those reflected in the School of Criticism and Theory (of which I am the director)—having "cast the most serious doubts on [its] viability."

[1] A review article by Joel Weinsheimer in *PTL: A Journal for Descriptive Poetics and Theory of Literature* 3 (1977): 563–77.

[2] See, among several places in their writings, Wellek, *Concepts of Criticism*, ed. Stephen G. Nichols, Jr. (New Haven: Yale University Press, 1963), p. 341, and Wimsatt, *Day of the Leopards: Essays in Defense of Poems* (New Haven: Yale University Press, 1976), pp. 188–89.

[3] In the issue (vol. 175) of October 23, 1976, pp. 27–28.

[4] In the *Times* (London) *Higher Educational Supplement* (March 4, 1977).

[5] O. B. Hardison, "Krieger Agonistes," *Sewanee Review* 85 (1977), cxv-cxviii.

Since it is undiluted New Criticism, "the paradigm of interpretation it represents no longer speaks to us." Presumably this New-Critical paradigm presupposes a fixed literary object which is out there for all critics to respond to and which stands immutably and absolutely as the judge of each subjective response. No wonder, then, that the paradigm cannot speak to critics who have become epistemologically, psychologically, and linguistically more sophisticated, as critics have presumably become in the post–New-Critical years. I am charged with accepting this paradigm "by adhering manfully to a notion of absolute objectivity," treating the poem as a static object and placing it normatively (and without a trace of critical epistemology) before each critic, insisting "that the aim of the responsible critic is to recover the poem as it was before he imposed on it all the personal quirks and dead generalizations that comprise his critical apparatus."[6] Thus, guilty of "a mimetic theory of reception," I am, in effect, categorized—like the New Critics—as a naive epistemological realist,[7] who grants an uncritical ontological status to the poem as absolute object. I suffer this placement despite my explicit denial— made increasingly as the book develops through its dialectical pattern —that the object, in its illusionary character, can ever attain more than a phenomenological presence.

Now in the last couple of pages of his review, Weinsheimer introduces an acknowledgment of a second side of my claims that turns my theory into sets of "intentional self-contradictions Professor Krieger has developed into a method." It is unfortunate that Weinsheimer did not read this acknowledgment back into his earlier pages so that it could have qualified his more simplistic version of my still-blooming New Criticism in the major portion of his comments. But this fuller sense of a certain systematic duplicity in my thinking is, I would judge, a more adequate representation of what I am doing. In its distance from the static and absolutistic positions associated with the New Criticism, I would expect that this duplicity would create complications that might make it less irrelevant to some of the theoretical debates still very much alive among us.

[6] Weinsheimer complains—because of its "most regrettable consequences for the concept of criticism"—about the notion (which he claims I maintain) of the poem's "logical and temporal priority to the reader" (p. 567). Yet, in trying later to produce an antidote to his version of my position, he categorically states as his truism, "A poem is temporally and logically anterior to a reader's consciousness" (p. 574). Not that I would wish to dispute so *prima facie* a claim, but why—earlier—should he?

[7] Thus, while Weinsheimer's argument should lead him to call me an epistemological realist, he strangely pursues his argument by associating me with the opposite tendency, nominalism (see p. 566). Had he been aware of this inconsistency, he might have questioned the limited terms he was using to describe my own argument.

I would like to believe that my more astute reviewers are alive to a vital relationship between dominant currents in present theory and my own work, and that they see my work finding its shape at least partly as a result of that relationship. Instead of relegating my function to that of an embattled rear-guard action (to be expected of a late-lingering, hold-out New Critic), which is pretty much what Weinsheimer and Scholes unhappily and Hardison supportively suggest, a reviewer like Paul Miers places me in a far more ambivalent position with respect to my fellow-theorists.[8] He concludes what I take to be the most searching and accurate (though hardly the friendliest) review I have yet received by dwelling upon the complex role which Jacques Derrida plays in the book, one which far exceeds that of simple adversary:

> If Derrida and the post-structuralists did not exist as the antagonists of the humanist tradition, Krieger would have needed to invent them in order to give his system the dialectic power it lacks by itself. Derrida serves as Krieger's shadow. . . . Krieger's problem is not to refute or imitate Derrida, a mistake he avoids making where others have not, but rather to evade Derrida's own shadow. So Krieger and Derrida dance around each other in the play of critical thought, around a word both present and absent.

Hazard Adams, in his review of the year's work in literary criticism, uses more striking language to observe much the same relationship taking place in the book between Derrida and me: the book, he says, "ends in a clash with Derrida in which, as in Yeats' dance plays, the swords never quite touch, the duel being as much dance as battle."[9] And Robert M. Strozier similarly (and, I think, with equal justness) claims, "Derrida and Krieger are roommates if not bedfellows, though they turn in opposite directions."[10] Though Strozier must acknowledge that my theory is disquieting since its challenge seems "to entail our rejection of a great deal of the critical theory of the last fifteen years" (and in this his placement appears to resemble Weinsheimer's or Scholes's), he proceeds to mark off my differences from that theory in far more delicate strokes—as the quotation about Derrida, above, indicates—so that he can see my own skepticism endearing other critics to me, as well as estranging me from them. Finally, if I may cite an essay which, while not a review of the book, does review the relation-

---

8 In *Modern Language Notes* 91 (1976): 1634–38.

9 In "Hazard Adams on Literary Criticism," *New Republic* 175 (November 27, 1976): 29–30.

10 In *Criticism* 19 (1977): 275–78.

ships of several current theoretical movements to one another, Wesley
Morris uses this book as one of several refracting lenses through which
a number of positions illuminate one another in complex and unexpected ways.[11]

If I do continue to have a living relationship to the dominant
movements in current theory, it is because I have worked at it, trying
to keep my own position in motion, whatever the fidelities which I
tried to retain. Though I have always been self-conscious about my
debts to the New Criticism and anxious to exercise a continuity with
the tradition out of which it grew, I have constantly been alive to the
need to open doors outward from it. I thus would argue for the accuracy
of the observation by Miers that "Contextualism has served Krieger's
purposes well as a critical umbrella he can expand or contract in order
to maintain contact with his origins in New Criticism and yet avoid
the narrowness that has driven that tradition into disrepute."[12] My
actual origins in the history of my career should not be mythified into
the fallacy of origins which would confound them with the circular
beginnings and endings which weave (and unravel) my system.

As I look back, I see that mine has been a cautious and cumulative
—if not conservative—theory. As it has developed, built (I hope)
on openness to other theories rather than on easy rejection of them, I
have tried to add ever newer ways of coping with antagonists as I have
seen them coming—trying to convert possible duels into dances, as
Adams has suggested. In other words, more than most theorists, I have
worked in accordance with what counterpositions (to mine) in the
history of theory and in the work of my contemporaries have forced
me to take account of, but to co-opt them, to incorporate them without undoing my own construct, (if I may be dangerously candid) to
see how much of them I could swallow without giving myself indiges-
tion. So I appear guilty of trying to turn what appear as inimical
elements into cooperative supports for my theory, although I also try
to make that theory an extension of what I have seen as the traditional Western poetic from Aristotle to Kant and Coleridge to literary
modernism as represented—say—by Wallace Stevens. My pragmatic
assumption is that—at least through modernist literature—the works
themselves seem to demand such an aesthetic if the continuing presence of the best of them is to be accounted for. Perhaps post-modernist
literature, with its anti-artistic and anti-verbal bias, will require another aesthetic—one much like the "decentering" theories now

11 In "The Critic's Responsibility 'To' and 'For,'" *Western Humanities Review* 31
(1977): 265–72, esp. pp. 266–68, 272.

12 Miers, in *Modern Language Notes*, p. 1635.

flourishing among us[13]—though I see this revolutionary aesthetic as inadequate when confronted by the long history of our most elite works, those whose brilliance creates and earns our sense of their privileged status. This is the privilege that requires the delicacy of critical treatment which my sort of theory sanctions.

In my book, with its detailed exposition of the theoretical tradition *and* the (I hope) systematic extension of that tradition into not always likely shapes, I have tried to demonstrate the power of the traditional aesthetic to accommodate alien perspectives and yet to thrive. But finally, for its preservation, it must insist—with all its newly won self-consciousness and self-skepticism—on the illusion of verbal and aesthetic presence in that beckoning structure that confronts the reader-critic. So I have tried to outmaneuver anticipated contradictions (as I have tried to account for alien elements forced upon me by history and by my contemporaries) by including them within the terms of a paradoxical model. Somewhere in my argument I have anticipated most objections by trying to include them too within my paradoxical contours in advance—if one can accept my tactic just at the outer edge of what may be permitted to argument. The reviews indicate that some will not, although I prefer them to object to my two-sidedness rather than to cut my position in half by reducing me to one side only, however more neatly systematic it would then appear.

Paradox may well be less acceptable in critical discourse than it is in poetry, but in my defense I can say only that I can do no better and can do no less if I am to do justice to what I find our literature requiring of its critic. For critical theory, I feel, should always yield to the art for which it vainly seeks to account. It is in this sense that I mean both my starting point and justification to be empirical and practical rather than self-sufficiently theoretical: what is the scholar-critic to do about the literary corpus—as his "given"—which is in his charge as teacher and writer concerned with the Western literary tradition? The corpus, even if it is a shifting group of works easily added to or subtracted from, is of course enormously limited and limiting, although it is his professional world, the world for which he is held to account. It is, alas, ethnocentric surely, and surely elitist too, in that we recognize from our shared experiences of them that—as they func-

[13] But only "perhaps." It has been the case in literary history before that literary works were perceived by their contemporaries to evade the receptive possibilities of existing manners of response, so that they were seen as demanding a revolutionary aesthetic—except that later periods came to see them as being less discontinuous with their predecessors than they were intended to be or were originally read as being.

tion for us and should be taught to function for students—the works in that corpus (and perhaps this is the criterion for admission to it) do indeed appear to claim privilege. So if, as such a scholar-critic, I can construct a theory to account for them and the privilege in them, that is objective enough for me. If such are their apparent qualities within our habit of response to them, then we should try to account for them and their effects on their most faithful readers. They seem to demand privileged treatment, the delicacy and complexity of criticism many of us practice, and they *are* responsive to it—which is to say that we are responsive to them. If, in our commodity culture with its egalitarian reductions that turn poetry into just so much *écriture*, we produce an anti-art that insists on its anaesthetic character—with its denial of the power of the word—then such products may give rise to another sort of reader intentionality which may be more appropriately productive of another criticism and another theory. Yet probably behind my theory and what I claim to be its empirical sanction is an anxiety— finally, I suppose, a moral anxiety—to keep active within our tradition the capacity to read the major works within our corpus lest we lose what man at his most creative is able to do with language for other men—lest, that is, we lose our sense of all that language can mean and do.

So there are several major paradoxes which I find our literary experiences to suggest—paradoxes in which I can see neither side yielding. As I state them baldly here, they may overlap one another, but I believe each is worth mentioning separately. In the book I have tried to hold fully and press simultaneously both halves of the following oppositions: both the poem as object *and* the poem as *intentional* object; both the concept of a discrete aesthetic experience *and* a notion of *all* experience as indivisible and unbroken; both the discontinuity of the poem's language system *and* the continuity of all discourse as *a* system; both spatiality *and* temporality, mystification *and* demystification in the work's workings upon us; both the poem as self-willed monster *and* the poet as a present agent subduing a compliant poem to his will; both fiction as reality *and* fiction as a delusive evasion of reality; or, put another way, both a closed, totalized, metaphoric reduction seen as our autonomous world *and* an open fullness of reality that resists all reduction and gives the poem the lie. Finally, then, both the verbal miracle of metaphorical identity *and* the awareness that the miracle depends on our sense of its impossibility, leading to our knowledge that it's only our *illusion* of identity held with an awareness that language cannot reach beyond the structuralist principle of difference. We both learn to see *and* distrust our seeing, as we view poetic language both as breaking itself off from the normal flow of discourse to become a privileged object, worthy of idolatry, *and* as language self-deconstructed and leveled, joining the march of common *écriture*.

So one may well complain about my method, as Weinsheimer does, since it makes no secret of trying to have most things both ways, but—whatever *those* complaints—I do not expect to be surprised by complaints either that I have deluded myself or that I have stumbled into unforeseen contradictions; for I have depended on bringing them up in advance to anticipate objections that may be made by those who notice only half my story at any point. Nevertheless, I hope that there is more than this doubleness to my theory. I have intended the doctrine of self-reference——which bestows upon the literary work a fictional self-consciousness—to exploit the nature of metaphor so as to create for the literary work a single, overriding form which unifies (as it exacerbates) tendencies to paradoxical inconclusiveness. For, as I see metaphor, its self-consciously illusionary status requires it to make an affirmation of miracle which—in the very act of affirming—is affirming also its own self-denial. As it affirms itself, it constitutes itself as the world, in an act of closure that excludes all else; although as it affirms itself as fiction, it obliterates its own "reality" in order to open the way outside its own linguistic trap, suddenly seen also as no more than trap. In permitting us both visions at once, the metaphor becomes an enclosing unity which contains the opposing elements it sustains. It serves as both the essence and the transcendence of the paradoxical.

I do not share the concern others have shown for my invocation of paradoxical or self-contradictory elements in my discussion of metaphor and the literary work as master metaphor, for I see these elements as fused in what the metaphor, as a fiction, does and has been seen to do by generations of readers. Metaphorical closure functions under the aegis of aesthetic illusion although we remain aware (and its fictional self-consciousness helps remind us to remain aware) of its illusionary character. This is to say that even while it functions it gives way to the demystification of an epistemological breakdown or a phenomenological reduction that shows it up for what it is, though what it is is glorious and *enough*, so long as we are under the aesthetic dispensation. This is really no more contradictory, in the end, than the double sense of reality-unreality which we feel as we watch actors (or are they "characters" or even "actual" people?) on the stage or as we indulge in equivalent illusion-making in the silent reading of nondramatic fictions. I am referring only to our dual capacity to believe and disbelieve literary fictions, as I am appealing to the primary element of *aesthesis*, of *Schein*, which theorists have long associated with our experience of the arts. Is it not just this venerable response which I call up with my notion of the metaphor as the miracle in which we can believe only because we know that, as miracle, it cannot "really" occur? So I must claim that here, and in my more detailed exposition and poetic examples in the book, my argument is not itself reduced to the paradoxical doubleness which it will not permit the metaphor to give up. But whether I achieve more than mere doubleness I must leave to others to say—even if I have seized this occasion to quarrel with their conclusions.

It is this attempt at a systematic duplicity both yielded to and overcome which marks my major differences from the New Critics as, over the years during which I have grown in response to a succession of new theoretical impulses in our midst, I have either increased my distance from the New Critics or become increasingly aware of a distance that had been implicitly there. The first major difference is that, while they must be exclusively committed to an aesthetic closure that substitutes the work for the existential world, I claim that the apparently self-conscious character of this closure—its fictional self-referentiality—leads it also and at the same time to deny itself, thus opening itself outward to the existential world which it would exclude but now, by negation, must include. So for me, the paradoxical character of metaphor permits a total closure that also is a self-abnegating opening. The synchronic illusion need not preclude the diachronic, but rather insists on it. In its self-demystification, the illusion that knows itself as such does not undo the totalizing power of metaphorical reduction; it rather doubles back upon itself in an anti-metaphorical thrust that denies the power of language and metaphor even while the metaphor and its language offer testimony to that power. Metaphorical speaking identifies—as it polarizes—linguistic identity and polarity in words and their existential references.[14] My second major

14 With these claims I am invoking an alternative model to the popular version of Hegelian synthesis in that the unity of method which I seek through metaphorical analysis is one that denies that differences can be modified into a joint reconciliation. Instead of a compromise union, as in the usual model of synthesis, I am urging the paradoxical model of at once *both/and* and *neither/nor*, representing the simultaneous pressure of both polarity and identity, polarity *as* identity. In pressing forward from these notions (esp. in chap. 7 of *Theory of Criticism*) I perhaps did not relate them as explicitly as I should have to the anti-synthetic methodology out of which I built my earlier book, *The Classic Vision* (Baltimore: Johns Hopkins Press, 1971). I now do so in my tenth essay, above, "Poetic Presence and Illusion II: Formalist Theory and the Duplicity of Metaphor," in which I borrow my diagrammatic description of the synthetic and anti-synthetic models from pp. 24–27 of that volume. What I am suggesting in this essay is that the New Critics, with their total commitment to organicism, cannot and would not move beyond synthesis.

difference from the New Critics is involved in the first: they must assume a fixed ontological place for the literary work as object, freezing our radically temporal experiences of it into the stasis of spatial thereness, while I can invoke the notion of illusion, in the manner of Gombrich, to convert the object to a phenomenological object— conscious of the fiction which gives it its as-if existence—and this permits us to indulge in the mystification about its presence only as we know it to be a mystification and thus place ourselves outside that indulgence. Its sounds disappear in the sky as they are spoken, or its black marks off the page as they are read while aesthetic intentionality leads us to arrest them. The metaphorical and linguistic system which is the work seals itself off from a general discursive system, and yet the first flows into the second, as it is reduced to it under the egalitarian principle that levels both language and experience into a single continuum.

These differences from the closed and exclusivistic formalism and even aestheticism often associated with the New Criticism derive from the doubleness of my treatment of metaphor—within a definition of each literary work as a master metaphor. And this doubleness, in turn, derives from my commitment to the existential as that which—like the death of each of us—is outside metaphor, indeed outside language. And, however closed in its totalization, the metaphor should keep us aware—by the negation fostered by its self-referentiality—of that outsideness. So my differences from the New Criticism should permit the criticism sanctioned by my sort of theory to open literature to the existential as well as to contract it to those enclosed metaphorical mini-worlds which become man's reduced moments of vision, representing what the world has become for a given moment in culture. In light of these differences it is painful to read charges that my theory "suggests that all poems are autoreferential and thus irrelevant to the world," or that my denial of "truth" to poetry "reduces literature to vapidity."[15] As some of my reviewers recognize, though none more perceptively than Harold M. Watts,[16] the most important element in my "systematic extension" to the theoretical tradition is the argument

---

[15] Weinsheimer, p. 573 and p. 567, respectively. Perhaps his misunderstanding derives from his own inability to recognize that poetry can have meanings and can relate us to experience without having to state truths. Weinsheimer is thus led to the extreme position (and, strangely for him, extremely reactionary position) of arguing that poems must state truths that are "falsifiable." "What cannot be falsified is worthless, vacuous, and inane," as obviously poetry is *not* (p. 572). When he so identifies poems with propositions, it is no wonder that he is unhappy with my attempt to distinguish poems from other forms of discourse.

[16] In *Modern Fiction Studies* 23 (1977): 307–10.

I make, in chapter 7 ("The Aesthetic as the Anthropological: The Breath of the Word and the Weight of the World") for the visionary function of metaphor.

That argument is based on the doubleness of the metaphor's affirmation and denial, of its closedness within its own world and its openness to the pre-poetic world of experience—the doubleness which I have tried to expound here. If the literary work seeks to enclose a segment of experience within the terms that create its reduced totalization (the argument runs), it also—by virtue of its fictional self-consciousness—points, through negation, to the broad world of experience that it excludes. And both its inclusions and exclusions serve us as ways into a moment of vision which the poet provides his culture. If we do not find propositional truth here, we do find what a culture, by way of its poet, constitutes as its truth, together with a grudging acknowledgment of its limitations, of that world beyond in which the non-linguistic fact of death withstands all metaphorical reductions and transformations.

In his review of my book, Hardison laments my failure to be sufficiently faithful to the Kantian perspective (an accurate observation made by none among the other reviewers who term me a Kantian); he rejects my insistence on the lingering reality of existential fact outside the realm of the human vision into which it has been transformed by our symbols.[17] If we agree (as Weinsheimer would not) about the self-sufficient value of symbolic vision as the prime content of man's earthly story, my double view requires me to disagree with the claim that it is all the reality there is, however much our solipsism may cherish it as such. It is in this expansive and yet self-limiting sense that I claim for literature revelatory powers, illuminating both what man sees and what he endures, as private man and as communal man.

Only after exploring this duplicitous function of metaphor, and the work as master metaphor, can I move, in my final chapter, to my now-you-see-it-now-you-don't notion of "the presence of the poem." Thus do I bring the humanist theoretical tradition into a perhaps unexpectedly ambivalent relationship to the structuralist and post-structuralist movements. In this sense the presentation of my poetic is completed with chapter 7, so that chapter 8 serves, essentially, as a polemical conclusion. The book, beginning in that humanist tradition and trying to develop a systematic poetic which could grow outward in the hope of speaking to other contemporary movements, had an introduction that was anything but polemical. From the exposition

17 See Hardison, "Krieger Agonistes," p. cxvii.

of that tradition it extends itself dialectically until its later stages create complications which, read back, qualify significantly those earlier definitions which were apparently made without the intrusion of ideas potentially alien to the tradition, which is now being forced to absorb them.

The structure of the book should then be evident, although it seems not to have been so to Fabian Gudas who, though otherwise writing a very favorable review, warns the reader not to expect in the book "a systematic presentation of a fully articulated poetics."[18] I believe the presentation is quite systematic and my poetic articulated as fully as I am capable of doing. Gudas agrees that my early chapters (especially the second) examining the several areas to be covered by a theory do indeed constitute a "systematic survey" of my position. He has high praise for this survey, recognizing it (in language similar to what we have seen in other reviewers) as "essentially similar" to what I have been urging since *The New Apologists for Poetry*. Seeing this portion of the book as so satisfying and consequently as conclusive rather than (as I suggest) only preliminary, Gudas sees the remaining five chapters as mere "refinements" or "a filling in of gaps," hence lacking in systematic presentation. Had he been less satisfied with my early statement, had he understood that my "preliminary questions and suggested answers" (which indeed restate many of my older positions, though in small ways preparing for later modifications) were indeed preliminary, he might have discovered that the historical and problematic explorations which follow must open into a fuller, if more complicated, statement that seeks to incorporate positions with counterpositions. And if their organizational interrelationships are not explicitly announced, I think they are clearly enough there. The four crucial issues I delineate in chapter 2 are the act of poetic creation, the poem as object (if it is one), the peculiarly aesthetic response (if there is one), and the function of poetry in culture. The four chapters which follow trace historically and extend theoretically the provisional suggestions made in my preliminary discussion, each chapter devoted in turn to one of these issues: mimetic and expressive theories (in chapter 4) relating to creativity, the role of form (in chapter 5) relating to the poem as controlled by its poet or breaking free of him, and the problem of fiction (in chapter 6) relating to the reader and the kinds of reality he surrenders or discovers as he experiences the poem. As I have already argued at length, chapter 7 seeks to determine the grounds on which the poem may or may not be

---

[18] In *Journal of Aesthetics and Art Criticism* 36 (1977): 480–82. The quotation appears on p. 481.

returned to its culture (and ours); and, with the poetic articulated as fully as it is going to be, chapter 8 uses it to make its polemical conclusion.

But I have been too long in using these remarks by reviewers as an opportunity for afterthoughts of my own. Obviously, if I had made many of these points more clearly in the book, I would not have had to work over them now since my reviewers would not have read me as they did. This is my way of saying that I am grateful to them for showing me what I had left less clear than I intended, and it is my way of apologizing for some suggestions made earlier about what they have missed when I should rather have spoken about what I failed to put in the book to be found. To the extent that such is the case, I must thank them for stimulating me to make perhaps a clearer case for my position on this occasion, as I must thank Professor Hernadi for seeing the potential value in providing the occasion. I feel fortunate in my reviewers: they have shown themselves to have both respect and good will toward my work, even where they wished it would have taken other directions, and they have without exception said kind things about my role in the recent history of critical theory, whatever their thoughts about my role in its present debates. Finally, whether from a keenness of perception (exceeding my own) or from their failures of perception, they have provided me ample opportunity to make these supplementary remarks which I now feel my book needed. Though I obviously have my own ideas about which are which, I leave to the reader the task of distinguishing keenness from failures of perception, theirs and mine.

14

A Scorecard for the Critics

I REMEMBER, when I was a boy who attended baseball games with the frequency of an addict, that I used to resent the confident claim shouted by the vendors as they hawked their wares: "Buy a scorecard! Can't tell a player without a scorecard!" They seemed to be insisting that I needed to use their code book, which matched the numbers on the backs of the players' uniforms to their names, the positions they played, and their histories, before I could bestow any identity upon them. Such a minimal placement seemed contemptibly trivial and superficial to me, who had observed every idiosyncratic detail about the way each batter placed his feet and held and swung the bat, the way each pitcher prepared for and took his wind-up, the way each fielder took his position and moved for the ball. (Little did any of us know that history was to justify my impatience: some years later fans would be empowered to "tell a player" merely by reading his last name which was added to his number on the back of his uniform.)

There was another function which the scorecard was to serve. A

This is the introductory essay to a collection of essays, which I organized with the title *Directions for Criticism: Structuralism and Its Alternatives*, with essays by Edward Said, Hazard Adams, Hayden White, René Girard, and Ralph Freedman. It appeared in 1976 as the summer issue of *Contemporary Literature* before being published as a book by the University of Wisconsin Press (1977).

system of minuscule boxes with diamond-shaped inserts next to the players' names permitted one, through the use of an elaborate base-ball shorthand, to make a record of every play every inning. Thus the enthusiast could preserve—as he tried to create for himself—a unique historic occasion. But here, too, the scorecard frustrated me: in my anxiety to make my transcription detailed enough to jog my future memory with nuance as well as with the crude abstraction of conse-quences, I continually overran the boxes, extending my coded mark-ings until they produced a jumbled mass on a page where no blank space remained to separate the individual actions or the actions grouped into individual innings. All that remained legible, in the end, was the coarsest reduction of all—the cold numbers isolated at the bottom of the page reporting, for each inning, the runs, hits, and errors. In the end I was as exasperated with myself as with the score-card—as much with my incapacity to accept the need to discriminate and to omit as with the procedure that made it necessary for me to do so. It may have been true that everything really counted, but it was also true that the scorecard ritual required that less than everything be recorded. Some placement of the players, their actions, and the consequences of those actions for the team and the game was needed, though the nominal labels that went with the numbers on their backs hardly characterized the players any more than the rude numbering of their runs, hits, and errors constituted that delicately maneuvered game they played. So, despite the inadequacies that troubled the observations of a self-confessed expert witness, the scorecard process—however misleading here and there—was a helpful and not altogether inaccurate one.

I make this personal recital because I see this essay as having something of a scorecard function—of placing (if not labeling) our critics and trying to keep count of their runs, hits, and errors—and I see myself as probably the wrong man to play the scorecard-keeper's role. When Professor L. S. Dembo asked me to organize and act as editor for this number of *Contemporary Literature*, we conceived it as a kind of scorecard to track the varieties of recent criticism. However, to the extent that this conception was realized, it becomes my task, in this introductory essay, to keep score of the scorekeepers. If each of them felt licensed to judge as well as to observe, to press forward certain attitudes toward literature and its criticism at the expense of others—in short, to be polemic as well as descriptive—it is clear that my position as scorekeeper-once-removed requires me to be more re-strained. This need for me to suppress my own preferences and to resist climbing into the theoretical arena is the more oppressive in view of the fact that I have just completed a book (to appear at just about the same time as this issue) whose title, *Theory of Criticism,* should not mask the parochialism of its commitments. Still, I have tried to permit that work to remain the repository of my partisanship for this moment, as I have struggled toward a disinterested transcendence in playing my role here. Like Pope's dispassionately rational God, I was to see "with equal eye" the making and unmaking of systematic worlds and bubbles: in short, the scorecard-keeper was to replace the partisan fan. Since this is a difficult role for mortal man to play—especially for me, especially at this time—I felt it necessary to warn the reader of this additional disqualification which I bring with me to my task, one for which my irritation with labeling and generalized defining already renders me unfit.

It occurred to Professor Dembo and me that our theoretical spectrum these days was in considerable need of whatever demarcations could be made within its graded variations by knowing and intelligent observer-participants. The classifier of methodologies could look back nostalgically at the simplicity of his problems in the limited warfare only a few decades back among New Critics, biographical and historical scholars, neo-humanists, neo-Aristotelians, and old-style Freudians and Marxists. How much more problematic these days are the challenges and cross-challenges not only to critical method but to the very assumption that there is an object or a language for criticism, as we move through the baffling array of structuralisms, post-structuralisms, and phenomenologies, as well as the still-lingering versions of older positions now modified to confront these revolutionary alternatives, largely continental, which could not have been anticipated even a short while back. So we thought any effort toward classification and commentary would be useful, although all my skepticism from my scorecard-keeping days warned me that, given a complexity in which almost everything was constituted by differences and difference itself was elevated to a principle both metaphysical and anti-metaphysical, such an effort—in its necessary simplifications—would be misleading as well. But we still decided to try, proposing to call the joint effort *Directions for Criticism: Structuralism and Its Alternatives.*

Our selection of theorists was meant to display a variety of methodological commitments and areas of humanistic and literary interest—at least as much variety as one could reasonably expect from only five authors whom we also wanted to be distinguished commentators on theory and makers of theory. Since at much the same time we at Irvine were organizing a Board of Senior Fellows for our planned School of Criticism and Theory, basing the selection on much the same criteria, it should hardly be surprising to find that our authors are members of that board. Regarded in this light, our collection of essays here has another and more immediate function: it serves to delineate the current situation in critical theory against which any such institution must measure its mission. Since that institution is just now in its first summer session, the appearance of this journal is most timely, and the writing of these essays for it has been an appropriate way to prepare to guide the work of the school.

Once our authors were chosen, there had to be a fictive occasion created to stimulate them to produce studies that would reflect on one another and on the state of criticism. I therefore projected a make-believe symposium: we would suppose ourselves seated around an imaginary table, on which we found a number of anthologies which have collected, according to various principles of selection, recent essays in critical theory. Then each of our authors would react to issues raised by them, and I would try to group their reactions. Even though there are obvious shortcomings in anthologies (such as have been pointed out in the essays that follow), it seemed wise to me to avoid the sort of squabbles over critical personalities and the hierarchy among them that might ensue if I chose books by a limited number of arbitrarily chosen theorists. Better to have an arbitrary choice of anthologies, with their arbitrary choices of essays or chapters of books, in the hope that, among them all, enough representative work would be assembled to produce significant responses in our authors. So, with the cooperation of the publishers, the following books were distributed:

> *In Search of Literary Theory*, ed. Morton W. Bloomfield (Ithaca: Cornell University Press, 1972).
> *European Literary Theory and Practice: From Existential Phenomenology to Structuralism*, ed. Vernon W. Gras (New York: Dell, 1973).
> *The Languages of Criticism and the Sciences of Man: The Structuralist Controversy*, ed. Richard Macksey and Eugenio Donato (Baltimore: Johns Hopkins Press, 1970).
> *Velocities of Change: Critical Essays from* MLN, ed. Richard Macksey (Baltimore: Johns Hopkins University Press, 1974).
> *Issues in Contemporary Literary Criticism*, ed. Gregory T. Polletta (Boston: Little, Brown and Co., 1973).
> *Modern French Criticism: From Proust and Valéry to Structuralism*, ed. John K. Simon (Chicago: University of Chicago Press, 1972).

As will be apparent in the essays that follow, we did not solicit mere surveys or reviews: there was no requirement or even suggestion that the entire spectrum of work represented in these anthologies be responded to, or that the issues arousing the response be broad rather than narrow, shared by many rather than by a few. We hoped for a distribution and breadth of focus. But mainly there was the hope that each of our essayists would find something or many somethings that would provoke him to contribute to our awareness and our understanding of questions currently seeking responsive gestures from those helping to shape where criticism is and is going. Whether stimulated by a wide array of essays, authors, and theoretical positions, or by just one (or by anything in between), each was to use that as his point of origin leading to some more general observation about the state and the tendencies of the theory around us. Unfortunately, circumstances prevented us from allowing for any interaction among our five major authors, so that each essay stands independently of the others, neither reflected in them nor reflecting upon them. Nevertheless, I claim to find areas of debate among them in my essay, the only one written after the others and in reaction to what they were doing. Hence I try to restrict my reactions to them instead of reacting on my own to the anthologies. If my remarks alone have the advantage of being a response to those of my colleagues, then I must be the more restrained, taking care to maintain the disinterestedness I find so hard to cultivate. It is also true that, just as the completed scorecard can normally be seen only after the game has been played, my comments should perhaps be read after, rather than before, the five essays. But there is an introductory function to be served here also, as I search for a structure of dialogue that can contain as well as place them in advance.

I shall proceed in the most obvious way, dealing with our five authors one at a time, beginning with those who survey the widest field of issues and theorists and moving to those who concentrate on just a few specific problems and writers. But in the end none is narrow in the consequences he draws from his observations. Further, none is merely a reporter, all are argumentative; but the centers toward which their arguments gather differ in the range of current critical practice they encompass. Edward Said and Hazard Adams come to very different conclusions about a large collection of critics and writings in these volumes: they do not agree about how to group them or, more important, how to judge those groupings. Hayden White is most concerned about the post-structuralist theorists, although he still cuts a very wide swathe among them—and others he discusses by way of contrast. René Girard seems to draw his argument exclusively out of his concern with Lévi-Strauss, except that his conclusions spread out to affect our view of structuralism and post-structuralism, as well as of his own quite original alternative. And Ralph Freedman restricts his interest to the phenomenological tradition in criticism though he ends with wider and more ambitious claims.

I

Edward Said seeks to provide historical placement both for recent critical schools and for individual critics whose common interests often blur the apparent differences in the schools that are sometimes seen as claiming them as members. For his interest in placement is subordinated to his interest in returning literature (as well as criticism itself) to its social nexus. Indeed, so anxious does he appear to return literature to the historical and social dynamics which give it its shape that he broadens the common attack upon the formalism of the New Criticism to include mainline structuralism within its range.

Early in his essay, he marks off the *new* new criticism (mainly continental criticism) by its rejection of the mere "object-ness" of "a confined text," which we usually associate with the old New Criticism —a claim with which many would readily enough agree. But, despite this claim, he argues that in "most of the anthological materials" we "will find the critic talking about what a text does, how it works, how it has been put together in order to do certain things, how the text is a wholly integrated and equilibrated system." In view of the obvious fact that our anthologies are post–New-Critical and heavily continental in their inclusions, we may well find this observation a baffling one. Said properly traces this attitude toward the text back to "the advent of American and English New Criticism," a "functionalist criticism" that grows out of "a rigorous technical vocabulary based mainly upon linguistic terminology" which, in later critics, sharpens itself at the expense of the poem, "since one aim of functionalism is to perfect the instrument of analysis as much as one's understanding of a text's workings." Surprisingly, the next example of such functionalism is Barthes, latest proponent of the "critical ingenuity" that transposes "the work—any work—into an instance of the method."

Said finds that critical ingenuity—and arrogance—that can create common cause among writers from the old New Critics to Barthes is rooted in their need to center and isolate "the text." If he now claims such alliances, then, as I have suggested, it is difficult to reconcile this common commitment to a text and its functioning with Said's earlier claim that recent continental criticism is marked by its turning from the text as its object, rather seeing the object elide itself by sliding into an activity. Yet he mainly—at least in the cited passages—prefers to ignore this major difference between those committed to literature as object and those committed to literature as activity: he rather comes to group together philologians, New Critics, and structuralists (his "constellation" includes Auerbach, Spitzer, Blackmur, Barthes, Genette, and Benjamin, and he will add Frye and even Poulet), seeing them all as readers "whose learning is *for* the text, and whose method is *from* the text." He must surely grant the great differences among them in their notions about what a text is—some restricting the privilege to literary fictions and others broadening it to an indiscriminate coverage of *écriture*—but above such differences he holds their common concern for "how language signifies, what it signifies, and in what form." (Though Said has shrewd strategic reasons for his groupings, one might wonder how comfortable the structuralist would be with a characterization that has him as concerned with "signifieds" as with "signifiers." Or one might wonder how much Poulet's commitment to a fluid consciousness would have to be altered before it could be fastened to a fixed object, a text.)

The motive for Said's exaggerated effort to find common ground among so motley a group is his theoretical need to find an alternative to their centering attention upon a text. By lining up these varied voices he thinks he can expose what he sees as their similar neglect of social forces, first, because they are devoted exclusively to the text as a privileged document and, second, because they fail to root such texts —as well as their own work—in the historical realities that feed and shape them. Thus he clears the way to proposing another group of critics as antidotes to such elitist oversight.

Since Said echoes the frequent complaint uttered by different people at different times against both structuralists and New Critics— that they are ahistorical, gaining the synchronic only by denial of the diachronic—he can introduce, among others, Foucault and Bloom (or, as parallel cases, Schwab and Bate) as exemplary figures who seek to restore literature to its place as part of our social reality in time. The dynamic restlessness of existential sequence, through such as these, sweeps over the text, making it part of its own continuity, submerging all contours. While Said acknowledges that such a notion of literary history makes it exclusively a continuous unfolding, an unbroken linearity of dramatic change, and while he therefore concedes the need for some balancing notions of "stabilities," structured in repetitions and in cultural institutions, he clearly feels that the change in emphasis is so necessary that even such excesses are welcome. For in contrast to the "worldless" criticism he rejects, this criticism is "about, and indeed is, the text's situation in the world."

Here again, with Foucault and Bloom, Said—as he concedes—has created a strange alliance. Between the two there is the difference between a historical concern that sees all discourse struggling to find itself as part of the culture's archive and a historical concern that sees all poems struggling to create themselves out of opposition to, and in competition with, the earlier poems that seek to determine them. Bloom is unlike Foucault in that he sees antagonism rather than cooperation between text and archive, but also in that his archive is a literary one: he dwells on the special sort of familial relations between a poet's text and those of his poet-ancestors rather than on the uniform relations between texts of whatever sort and the collective system they make up.

This latter difference may well remind us of the difference we remarked earlier between structuralists and New Critics—between the dedication to a text as part of *écriture* and the dedication to a literary text as a uniquely aesthetic entity. One might well view Bloom and the New Critics, however great their differences, allied (against Foucault and the structuralists) as literary devotees concerned about those who would deny them a specially discernible object, while on their side Foucault and the structuralists might bury their differences long enough to assail any such attempt to lift poetry out of the common domain of discourse on the assumption that it required distinctive treatment. These pairings may seem no more difficult to establish (if no less so) than Said's cross-pairings. That he insists on making his, in spite of the internal differences that undercut them, is indicative of his exclusive concentration on the need to return literature and its criticism to their places in the world of action. So he concentrates on the common historical commitments of Foucault and Bloom that distinguish them from structuralists and New Critics, respectively. The two work in their different but equally history-conscious ways to deny the text's presence by dissolving it into the no-longer-absent past. It is this notion, Said's argument reminds us, that permits Bloom to find a community of interest with post-structuralist continental theory.

Thus Said calls for a concern with what we used to term the sociology of literature, an interest in such extra-literary circumstances as condition every element of a text from its beginnings to its currency with readers at one moment and its neglect at another. (Said exemplifies his own precept in his recently published volume, *Beginnings: Intention and Method.*) Those familiar with the criticism of this past century may well view as a return to old-fashioned pre–New-Critical enquiries such investigations into linguistic, social, and cultural history as sources for the creation of a work or investigations into the circumstances that—after the work has been created—make or unmake its reputation. But Said argues that Foucault's archaeology provides for the renewal of such studies within an original and productive framework.

More significantly, Said extends his plea for worldliness from an active role seen for literature to an active role seen for criticism itself. He summons criticism not only to treat literature as a social act, but to join literature by itself being undertaken as a social act. He thus willfully blurs criticism and literature in accordance with his own doctrine of an unprivileged *écriture*, one that enacts its social role through the text, trying to win freedom *for* society instead of freedom *from* it. So the critic has this as his independent obligation—independent, that is, of the text. He is to act in his own behalf: his work is to be conceived as an action in the world.

Said welcomes, as the consequence of such a notion, the claim that criticism is in competition with the literary text as an original act, that it has its beginnings in itself—that, in short, it is constitutive and sovereign rather than derivative and subservient. He speaks with some contempt, then, of the "simplistic opposition between originality and repetition" that holds for most critics who bow in humility before their object. As in all writing, he asserts, criticism should begin by creating its object, not by finding it. Traditional criticism forgoes "independent creation in criticism" because of naively realistic assumptions that lead it to mythologize the literary work into an object before which it modestly submits, as secondary submits to primary. Said's doctrine of universal autotelism in writing, all devoted to becoming modes of action, may seem to fly in the face of the critic's conventional common sense of his relation to the poem—of his very *raison d'être*—but it follows logically, even necessarily, from the denial of a privileged status to literature and the granting of an equal place for all writing in our culture's archive. The denial to criticism of its external object is of a piece with the denial of objects to all writing (including what we used to term literature or *poesis*). It appears to reflect the structuralist's insistence that no signifieds exist for the empty signifiers which we choose to turn into any kind of writing we address (though self-deceptively) to any object (or to whatever we reify into an object).

But criticism for Said, having a historical commitment, must go where structuralists disdain to go—into the world of time to make itself felt. Toward those he sees as critics centered on the text—structuralists, New Critics, or other non-activists—Said feels his own disdain: "Contemporary criticism achieved its methodological independence by forfeiting an active situation in the world. It has no faith in traditional continuities (nation, biography, period); rather it improvises, in acts of an often inspired *bricolage*, order out of extreme discontinuity. Its culture is a negative one of absence, anti-representation, and (as Blackmur used to put it repeatedly) ignorance." Thus

Said constructs an archaeological placement for this criticism, accounting for it by showing its negative relation to the world. He has
performed in accordance with the alternative criticism he proposes—
one that would find, within a unified historical field, continuities
among writings which, in constituting themselves and their objects,
also constitute a cultural archive. Free from a world of objects, such
criticism—as an equal among those writings—yet leads us to the world
as it takes its place in it.

II

Hazard Adams, as an observer of the contemporary critical scene
reflected in the anthologies, is a self-conscious partisan for the kind of
criticism Edward Said rejects. But, as we should expect, he shifts the
philosophical ground to one which, in supporting him, would force
the collapse of the structure of recent continental thought. He views
"the so-called crisis of language" imposed upon us by this thought as
one in which "criticism threatens to break down all boundaries and to
rival (by obliteration) literature itself." This is an apt description of a
central assumption of Said's essay. In words that echo the mood of
that essay, Adams complains that "the critic seems tempted to compete
with his texts, to surpass them, and in his most ebullient moods . . . to
deny the existence of literature entirely." But this is the very critic
Said hopefully invoked, so that he would hardly take Adams's words
as a charge to be answered. (Curiously, Said complained that such
critics were more to be invoked for the future than presently to be
seen, while Adams observes them in large and influential numbers.)
From the opposite perspective, Adams is quite willing to place himself
among those who express "profound respect for the unmeasurable
distance between criticism and the poem"—the very attitude which
Said saw as "simplistic" in its relegation of criticism to the role of a
distant and inadequate attendant to the poem.

Indeed, the argument that grows out of Adams's observations
springs entirely from his sense of this distance which Said denies—the
awesome gap he points out between criticism and the poem which is
its object. From the beginning Adams emphasizes (citing arguments
in Vico and Cassirer) that the philosopher's language makes it difficult
to speak of poetic or mythic thinking "from its own point of view,"
"from inside itself." Adams continues, "The problem with respect to
poetry is the same as that with myth: even the most careful of discursive approaches betrays an alien perspective." If this distance between
poetic discourse and the critic's discourse about it depends on a sense
of the difference in the language of the two entities, then what must

follow is the claim that the poem is a most privileged discourse. Yet Adams is very cautious in making this claim, even at times coming close to rescinding it. For he is aware of the indefensibility of an absolute distinction between poetic and "normal" or "ordinary" uses of language, just as he is aware that the notion of a baldly referential, normal discourse is an unreal fiction. So whatever the critic must say about the poem as a privileged discourse, with a special power for radical creation in language, he must say with an irony that bears within it a sense of mere fiction. Yet, in contrast to Said, for Adams the text is primary—and a poetic text at that.

Adams cannot launch his theoretical counterattack upon continental theoretical fashions without assaulting head-on the omnibus conception of language in accordance with signifier-signified analysis. And it is both the analysis, and the fact that it is indiscriminately applied to all language, that he finds open to challenge, a challenge launched by the humanist against a threatened intrusion by a positivism dominated—consciously or otherwise—by the perspective of the social sciences. The opposition between signifier and signified, as Adams views it, can occur only within a crudely and archaically mimetic notion about how language functions, with its signs pointing to things or concepts; and he finds this true even of the structuralists who, having made the analysis, go on to claim that there are really only signifiers, making patterns among one another, since all apparent signifieds are the product of our mythologizing reification. If such be the case, then all language represents the futile effort to capture a world that forever eludes it. It is not a long step from here for Adams to account for Paul de Man's notion of poetic allegory as the dominant mode for the romantic poet as ironist—the acknowledgment of the failure of the poem's words to leap across the distance that separates them from the things they would enclose. The poet's consciousness of his empty signifiers leads him to make his poem the representative utterance of the structuralist limitations upon all our language.

Adams sees the sign-thing or sign-concept dichotomy for all language as resting upon a naive epistemology that ignores all that we have known since Kant (if not Vico), and he sees the sign-thing or sign-concept dichotomy as especially disabling when we try to speak of poetic creation in language. For him the poetic is representative of the inherently creative capacity of all language. This is to say that Adams can conceive of "the idea of language as creative of such *signifié* as it has," as he seeks, "borrowing from Vico and Cassirer," "a theory of radical creativity in language that gives priority to the poetic." He projects a language continuum moving from a "poetic center" "outward through the zone of ordinary language" to a "mathematic circumference." The monistic heart of the word-making process reveals the creative principle that is central to all language usage, even if—as we often witness and participate in it—it has degenerated toward the passivity of a deadly dualism. He thus denies the norm of an ordinary pointer-language (with its sign-referent dualism), from which poetic language would represent a deviation, arguing instead for the centrality of the poetic as the vital creative norm from which all else is a falling off. Language is constitutive of its world, even—alas—when, using its dying elements, we create only a dull world with it.

Can such a continuum support the opposition between poetic and ordinary language which Adams sometimes seems to need even though his epistemology requires him to reject it? When we ask whether or not Adams believes in an opposition between poetry and ordinary language, we find two answers. First, he must deny it at the theoretical level: as poetry is the central human way of speech and writing (being logically—and perhaps even historically—prior, in the manner of Vico and Shelley as well as Cassirer), all less-creative speech and writing are gradations away from it. So, "from its own point of view," "from inside itself," the answer is that there can be no such opposition. But secondly, he must allow it in the back door as a practical necessity for the unpoetic critic: as he, with his fallen language, talks of poetry from his "alien perspective," he must create the fiction (with an ironic self-consciousness about that fictional status) that the poetry–non-poetry opposition appears to criticism to exist. It is, consequently, in this sense that we can speak of allegory as the critic's method of describing what, from inside the poem, is a symbolic unity. Here is the ground of his argument with de Man: the distance which de Man claims to find between the poetic word and its object Adams claims really exists only between the critic's word and the poet's. For the poet's word is creator and container of its object for Adams, so that the allegory is not the poet's (as with de Man), but the critic's.

It would seem, then, that Adams will admit a phenomenological opposition between poetry and ordinary language (which includes the critic's language), while denying on epistemological and even metaphysical grounds that such an opposition—or even a concept like ordinary language—can exist. "It is necessary here to state that the theory of radical creativity, though it refuses to draw a line *measuring off* poetry from other forms of discourse and argues for the creativity of all language, does not quarrel with our needs as critics to create an ironic fictive opposition where a continuum is the reality." Adams is aware that such a claim (and we must note his giveaway term "reality") has ontological implications and is thus vulnerable to continental demystification, the dissolving of his myth of origins. One may, I think, properly wonder whether he needs the Viconian or Blakean epistemology in order to make his phenomenological—his fictive and ironic—claim. One may wonder also what advantage he gains as a theorist of literary criticism to insist metaphysically on a continuum, when poetry looks upon itself from within, in view of his admission of discontinuities and oppositions, when poetry is looked upon by the critic from outside, which is the only side from which he can look or speak.

What remains important about Adams's position, as we see it distinguished from Said's, is the insistence that, under the poetic dispensation (whether seen as universally constitutive or as constitutive only within verbal works of art), words be treated as symbols rather than as signs, that signifiers be seen not as empty but as full of the signifieds that they create in order to contain. Such words, of course, cannot be viewed as "worldless"—which is how Said claimed modern text-oriented critics viewed them. Adams thus reminds us that, in lumping all text-oriented critics together, Said failed to distinguish those who saw words as cut off from the world from those who saw words as opening us up to the world. Adams would claim that his way of focusing on the text leads to our apprehension of the world it constitutes. Such are the far-flung theoretical consequences of his antistructuralist refusal to start with a concept of language based on signifiers at a distance from, and only arbitrarily related to, their signifieds.

Thus Adams can, on *his* grounds, join Said in pleading for a criticism that helps make it possible for both literature and itself to play a historical and anthropological role. But Adams would complain not only about structuralists as "worldless" but also about diachronic critics like de Man (or, might he add, Said?) who—despite their distance from structuralism—are like structuralists trapped by the binary opposition between signifier and signified and by the positivistic assumptions which make that opposition a monolithic one. Hence they cannot, like him, show how truly world-ful the poem can be. Adams joins in the Goethean "insistence on the poet's connection with the concrete and particular, with earth. . . . Goethe does verge on asserting a positive cultural role for poetry, moving from the negative enclosure of the Faustian study to establishment of the poetic power, not of transcendence, but of building on earth, presumably in language." Adams similarly rejects the "negative enclosure" of the structuralist view of language. As if answering Said's call, though in alien terms that lead him in directions which Said would prefer to

shut off, Adams sees the word, like the human poem it constitutes, "as
potentially creative of cultural reality, which is of the earth, but an
earth of man's making and remaking in symbolic form."

III

The differences I have been marking in the positions of Said and
Adams are accounted for in Hayden White's ambitious historical
undertaking, which attempts to place all the varied phases of recent
literary theory, relating them to one another and to the culture that
both produced them and determined when they would come into and
go out of fashion. Adams and Said are surely worthy representatives of
White's "Normal" critic and "Absurdist" critic, respectively. With the
historian's transcendent dispassion, White traces the several moments
of each, as the two wrestle for dominance of the contemporary critical
scene. The "Normal" critic holds the traditional view that criticism
can illuminate the meaning of a text and assess its value; and such a
criticism assumes the possibility of literature—of a literary text that
contains such a meaning and value. On the other hand, the "Absurdist" critic at the least calls both literature and, therefore, criticism
into question and at the most denies the possibility of either to exist
as containers of meaning.

While it is obvious what makes the first group "Normal," White
argues for the second as "Absurdist" on the ground that they write
and continue to write "at interminable length and *alta voce*" about
"the virtues of silence": they "criticize endlessly in defense of the
notion that criticism is impossible." Such reflexive contradiction constitutes a position that "is manifestly Absurd." But if the absurd "is
simply that which cannot be thought," when someone like Derrida
"not only thinks the unthinkable but turns it into an idol," he is
"Absurdist." Finding the source of Absurdism in Paulhan, Bataille,
Blanchot, and Heidegger, White sees it carried "to its logical conclusion" in Foucault, Barthes, and Derrida. And it is clear that he would
find Said's definition of the critic's plight and opportunity—as I have
observed it—well within his Absurdist camp. On the other side,
Adams would be for him a splendid summoner to a return to critical
normalcy. Indeed, White would see him not only as "Normal," but as
representative of the most fetishizing subgroup of the "Normal"—the
"Inflationary" critics.

Perhaps I should trace briefly the several subgroups of these two
general tendencies which White gathers into a dramatic parade of
critical fashions from the latter part of the last century until today—
with the unhistorical implication that there may be no tomorrow. The

first version of "Normal" criticism, as its practice comes into the twentieth century through the First World War, he terms "Elementary" criticism. It moves out of a naive acceptance of the function of criticism to discover and communicate textual meanings and aesthetic value and, by doing so, advances culture and civilization. The privileged status of literature is thus assumed, although the untroubled process of criticism precludes mystery. A countermovement arises between the wars—"Reductive" criticism—spawned by the new would-be social sciences (Marxism, psychoanalysis, sociology of knowledge) and devoted to stripping the text down to its "hidden, more basic, and preliterary content," to merge literature with "life." It thus springs from an anti-elitist impulse but is still "Normal" in that it does not question the capacity of literature to hold meanings and of criticism to uncover them.

Yet another reaction asserts itself, producing in the post–Second-World-War years a newer version of "Elementary" criticism, but this time self-consciously theoretical and defensive, having learned the hard lessons imposed by the "Reductive" ascendancy. What emerges is a third variety, "Inflationary" criticism, an alliance (despite differences) among New Critics, "practical" critics (White cites Leavis and Trilling), and "formal" critics (he cites Frye), dedicated to literature as little less than a sacred object embodying "high culture" in its transformation of mere life. Its "objective" methods were to bring "Normal" criticism to a new completeness. (We can see at once that Hazard Adams fits the "Inflationary" category very well.) We are ripe, at this point, for another reaction against an autotelic and privileged notion of art, and the existentialist critics, like Sartre and Camus, provide it. But this time, as art is related (and perhaps reduced) to human need, as it was earlier by "Reductive" critics, its very existence —like that of criticism—is brought into doubt. The problematic of literature and of criticism enters our scene for the first time. And we are ready for this problematic to be systematically—indeed, even programmatically—pursued in our next variety, "Generalized" criticism, as jointly developed by phenomenological and structuralist theorists. Criticism is generalized in that literature becomes no more than a part of language-in-general, which is a universal system of signs, a uniform (if uniformly inadequate) projection of consciousness. Both literature and criticism are first blurred and then lost in a unified field theory. What remains is the final stage, "Absurdist" criticism, which dares to take the consequences of such "arbitrary" workings of an empty language system and, thus, to accept the reflexive impossibilities of both the poetic and the critical act.

Yet, in this final reversal of "Inflationary" criticism, mystique returns, in whatever negative guise. White calls our attention to Said's acknowledgment that, for the structuralist, "everything is a text . . . or . . . nothing is a text." But in the discussion that follows, White seems to replace the "or" with an "and," making it clear that, for the Absurdist, both possibilities are maintained at once. As a consequence, " 'the act of reading' could become fetishized, turned into a mystery which is at once a fascinating and at the same time cruelly mutilating activity." Such paradox is cause of a further one: the denial of privilege to any text does not prevent the implicit claim that there are privileged readers, with access to the mystery of all and/or nothing, and to the complicated discourse in which such mystery is set forth and discussed. And this becomes yet another paradox: such tortuous discourse revolves endlessly about a subject whose very existence it precludes. Yet, despite or because of the cultivation of such paradoxes, here is where—for White—criticism now finds itself, strongly backed by current intellectual fashion.

The very trimness of White's scheme, which finds one critical fashion replacing another at center stage, naturally invites the claim that the errant facts surrounding the actual work of theorists and groups of theorists are in some instances at odds with the design of his chronicle. These are the necessary risks the historian must run if he has the courage and the largeness of vision to undertake the organization of such resistant and complex data. For example, it is not altogether accurate to portray the New Critics as reacting to the Reductive critics and reviving—in more sophisticated form—the literary devotion of the Elementary. One might argue that they were at least as much a reaction against Elementary critics, like the so-called impressionists and neo-humanists and historical scholars, as the Reductive critics were. Indeed, it may be that the New Critics were more anxious to react against such Elementary critics than they were to react against .the Reductive critics. White would thus have to move back his placement of this variety of Inflationary criticism to well before the Second World War, seeing it in the thirties as being as much an extra-academic movement as he found the Reductive critics to be.

Or again, it is hardly likely that existentialist critics like Sartre or Camus were aware enough of Inflationary critics of the sort White deals with for them to come into being as a reaction against Inflationary criticism. Nor is the relative timing of the two movements such as to support a cause-and-effect relationship between them. But White needs the anti-Inflationary consequences of existentialism in order to move toward the anti-elitism of his Generalized critics—the phenomenologists and structuralists he views as post-existentialist. Further, his attempted union between phenomenologists and structuralists forces him to join the primary interest in "human consciousness" to the primary interest in a "universe of speech acts" as if they were one interest, when the antagonism between the two groups stems from the fact that they can be opposed interests. Thus, as we have noticed before—for example, in dealing with Said—a special way of viewing the schools of critics and the drama played among them requires the marshaling of groupings that may, from alien perspectives, seem difficult to defend. (We can recall that, whereas Said grouped Barthes with Spitzer and Blackmur, White groups him with Derrida and Foucault—and that White sees these last two theorists as mutually reinforcing while Said set them against one another.)

There is another risk that the historian must take as he constructs the cause-and-effect pattern out of which his story emerges. When we review White's drama of this sequence of critical moments in a rapid-fire summary such as mine has been, we find that he has imposed several shaping structures to control that sequence, perhaps to overdetermine it. He sees the causal relations between one critical moment and the next turn into a repetitive pattern of reaction, counterreaction, and then yet another reaction that is the first one returned in a more sophisticated form, thanks to the lessons of the second—and so on. It is something of a Hegelian succession—a method of description strangely at odds with the decentered way the succession ends (though the notion of a decentered ending is self-contradictory). What is suggested is a series of linked and opposed movements and a systolic-diastolic rhythm established by them. The Elementary and the Inflationary critical modes are interlaced with the Reductive and the Generalized modes in a sequence in which the idolatry of art alternates with the desire to demythologize and level it. Naiveté breeds reduction, reduction breeds inflation, inflation breeds egalitarianism. But also, fetish breeds fetish: Absurdism, the fifth moment, has echoes within it of both ally and antagonist, being a "fetishization" of the structuralism it succeeds and yet—as a fetishization—answering the counterfetishization of the poetic object in Inflationary criticism. So echoes are either of similar critical values or of similar critical dispositions at the service of opposed values.

The rhythm has been kept moving by the repetitive principle of reaction, so that each movement is seen as calling forth its answering opponent-successor. In effect, each movement gets what it had coming to it, and all of us and our culture get what we have had coming to us as Absurdism becomes history's vengeance upon us: "In Absurdist criticism, the dualism of Western thought and the elitism of Western social and cultural practice come home to roost." Since dualism and its consequent elitism have, White acknowledges, been with us since

Plato, "this Absurdist moment was potentially present from the beginning of modern European humanism." The previous critical moments of ours which he has traced, however seemingly resistant, are
the final avenues to the Absurdist apocalypse we have been building
toward: "Now dualism is hypostatized as the condition of Being-in-
general and meaninglessness is embraced as a goal. And elitism is
stood on its head."

So the historical rhythm does more than just alternate. It has an
objective, however destructive: as the revolutionary answer to the
hierarchical habit of an obsolete society, it means to undo an elitist
cultural tradition. We may begin to sense that, as he has constructed
this anti-teleology, our historian has been complicitous with his history in leaving us where he does, however unhappy he may claim to
be about it. The cool dispassion which distances his pain helps disguise the extent to which he has been in control of the drama. We
must remember also that he further justifies this perverse revenge,
which our culture has asked for and has had visited upon it, by
pointing to our gross economic reduction of all things to an equivalence of mere "commodities." Thus all our cherished notions of value
must now be seen as myths which our culture has fraudulently used to
disguise the egalitarian march of familiar signifiers. It is appropriate,
White suggests, that our criticism, in its primary concern with value,
should now level all our precious objects to the "arbitrary" indiscrim-
inateness of the commodity economy. (One may wonder whether, in
attempting to account for the emergence of Absurdism by applying
such economic metaphors to the critical realm, he may himself be
joining the Reductive critics whom he placed some decades back.)
The undiscriminating commitment to arbitrariness in our culture is,
for White, a major force in the triumph of Saussurian linguistics, with
its arbitrary relation between signifier and signified which we have
seen Adams reject and White deplore. But, given the implied determinism of White's scheme, he cannot join Adams in trying to conceive
for our art a language whose creativity would permit it, as signifier, to
constitute its signifieds in and through its very form, thus converting
the arbitrary into the inevitable. For this would suggest a privileged
sanctuary for language which the economic metaphors that shape our
culture would preclude. Better the Absurdism, whatever the blankness of its vision, as the fitting deconstruction of the monstrosities we
have constructed.

It is not surprising that White feels required to end by admitting,
despairingly, that the questions of the Absurdists "put the Normal
critics in the position of having to provide answers which they themselves cannot imagine." The questions sustain all the levels of the

reflexive problematic that—short of contradiction—should have precluded the Absurdists from asking them. How, possessed as they are of a more-than-arbitrary commitment to language, can Normal critics imagine answers to questions which presuppose a reflexive problematic, one that precludes the possibility of their ever having been asked—even by Absurdists? Such is the box in which White sees them enclosed (or in which he has enclosed them). For, as so often happens with daringly ambitious historians, it is difficult to tell whether the box is his or history's.

White's apocalypse reaches out from the history of literature and its criticism to enclose our entire culture, our world itself. He partly fixes the blame for this extension on Derrida who, guilty of what Frye called "existential projection," "fetishizes" the structuralists' dualism "and treats [their poles of language] as the fundamental categories of Being." But partly too, we have seen, it is the guilt of our culture itself which invites the Absurdist conception of language to destroy not only its poetry but its very being as a meaningful construct. As Pope, in the apocalyptic close of the *Dunciad*, reached beyond his grim picture of the contemporary literary world to envision the fearful destruction of the contemporary world itself, so White seems to end by shrinking from what he has justified. In Pope's language, under the burden of the "uncreating word," "universal darkness buries all."

IV

Others, of course (we may think at once of Edward Said), will agree with White about the revolutionary implications and consequences—both literary and cultural—of post-structuralist thinking without sharing his dark view of its influence and of that culture's present and future. They may well claim to find injustice in his treatment. Still others may be as unsympathetic as White, while rejecting the notion that this movement represents a dead end. For example, René Girard shares much of the antagonism to structuralist and post-structuralist thinking, though he retains the hope of working through it to an alternative that is anything but nihilistic. Girard and Freedman, our remaining critics on this occasion, are not so wide-ranging, both choosing to narrow-in on more limited issues, though issues that are still central to some of the major writers in our anthologies.

Girard concentrates his criticism on the structuralists' linguistic doctrine of difference. He sees this doctrine, in the work of Lévi-Strauss, as being inflated into an absolute principle of both theoretical method and metaphysical substance. The structuralist attachment to such a principle leads Lévi-Strauss to elevate myth (based on differ-ence) and to reject ritual (based on undifferentiated immediacy). It is at this point that Girard levels his attack. He sees Lévi-Strauss's dis-tinction, invidious as it is to ritual, as deriving from a dualism inherited from Bergson: with all methods and all experience divided into the differentiated and the undifferentiated, Bergson's exclusive championing of the undifferentiated is answered by Lévi-Strauss's exclusive championing of the differentiated. But Girard sees the two of them as clinging, with equal metaphysical fervor, to a universal principle, whether that of differentiation or that of undifferentiation, each rejecting the other. Girard's concern is to deny polarity and the dualistic metaphysic that allows the inadequacy of either pole. Hence he argues that not only ritual, but myth itself, reveals both undiffer-entiated and differentiated elements in conjunction, claiming that only Lévi-Strauss's unempirical devotion to a positivistic view of language permits him to ignore the undifferentiated elements in myth and the differentiated elements in ritual. This argument opens out into his attack against the more general inadequacy to experience which he finds in the positivistic commitment to linguistic difference. (I am reminded of Adams's attack on the positivistic basis of struc-turalism and of White's treatment of post-structuralism as the furthest reach of the Western dualistic tradition.)

The central role of myth as Lévi-Strauss's agent of difference prompts Girard to use it as his weapon to turn structuralism against itself. He claims that Lévi-Strauss treats myth "not as 'differentiated' solely, as any text would be, but as differentiation displaying itself. Myth is not simply structured, it is structuralist." Thus myth is seen to be a paradigm of the symbolizing process as differential. In its com-mitment to the single process, "the all-purpose differentiating ma-chine" endangers its own nature with the uniformity—the very sameness—of its application, whatever the objects on which it oper-ates. Such undifferentiation produces a self-contradiction. And it leads to the unprivileged equivalence among all its differentiated objects, appropriate to "the *société de consommation.*" This phrase recalls White's language about commodities and the indiscriminate reduc-tion of all things to that status. For Girard it is the way in which difference undoes itself: "We cannot respect all differences equally without in the end respecting none."

But, unlike White, Girard is not ready to resign himself to the triumph of the fashion of differentiation turned into a metaphysical principle; instead, he belligerently tries to supersede it. For he feels he can renew the defense of religion and its source in ritual only by emphasizing those elements—mythical monsters, incest, sexual or hierarchical inversions—which disrupt the order that society's rational distinctions create, and *un*differentiate their communities. Perhaps the most basic of such undifferentiating rituals is the scapegoat. This arbitrarily chosen victim serves his community most ambiguously: through being uniquely differentiated from the others, he brings undifferentiated unity to the rest, and what was an arbitrary selection becomes necessary and indispensable through his function. In this manner the victim overcomes the arbitrary role of signifier to which a differential linguistics would relegate him. Such are the "rebellious phenomena" "that do not respond properly to the structuralist method." Only a stubborn positivistic allegiance, fearful of confronting human disorder with its irrational propensity to violence, would evade such rebellious phenomena or demythify them away by subjecting their irreducibly undifferential elements to "the all-purpose differentiating machine."

Once Girard has fastened onto victimage as the exemplary ritual which exposes the inadequacy of structuralism, he can claim that structuralism must respond to the threat posed to it by turning ritual itself into its victim. Once again structuralism is turned against itself: with Girard as our guide, we find Lévi-Strauss enabled to define myth as he does (and, by negation, to define ritual as he does) only by first enacting the ritual of expelling ritual as *his* victim. We are to understand that "the arbitrariness which characterizes the treatment of ritual . . . duplicates exactly the arbitrariness of the victim. . . . Ritual is expelled as the sole and complete embodiment of the undifferentiated. This expulsion is supposed to rid us once and for all of this 'evil mixture.' " What could be more persuasive proof that victimage is the most basic of symbols and the very source of our symbolizing power—whatever structuralists may say—than the fact that structuralism itself, in order to define myth as the source of its differential symbol making, must indulge in the ritual of victimage through the expulsion of ritual? Through this act the priority of symbolization is granted to ritual, so that Lévi-Strauss is unwittingly proving Girard rather than himself right. Structuralism thus engages in the ritual that disproves its own first principle of universal difference: "Since the undifferentiated is supposed to be entirely contained in ritual, it is entirely expelled by the expulsion of ritual." So myth is purified as an exclusively differential entity, except that the purifying act has undermined the ground on which it would stand.

Girard can now generalize his observation about Lévi-Strauss's ritual act: "The horrified recoil from primitive ritual and religion stems from the same impulse as religion itself, in the new circumstances brought about by this very religion." It is this claim which enables him to resist the resignation I have sensed in White, who perceives, in those who follow from structuralism, a final stage, an ultimate revolutionary method, that undoes—while it consummates—our culture's history. For Girard prefers to regard them as too rigidly attached to just another privileged metaphysic—the negative principle of difference—which post-structuralists like Foucault and Deleuze institutionalize into an "epistemological nihilism." Thus "Foucault correctly appraises the limitations of this system [the structuralist] but he confuses them with the absolute limits of human language and of our power to know." Here, then, is a "particular scholar who seems primarily intent on a most scholarly burial of scholarship itself." These judgments echo somewhat those we have heard in White's essay, except that Girard claims to have found a way out of this dead end with his proposal of victimage as a ritual that is the true source of symbolization. Does he mean his essay itself to initiate such a move by its performing of the ritual expulsion of structuralism? If so, Girard himself has no obstacle in *his* system to prevent him from resorting to a ritual cure.

When he turns to the more exclusively literary sphere, Girard sees the same structuralist reduction at work, to the neglect (or should I say the expulsion?) of the less orderly stuff of human experience. Thus he calls for the approval and encouragement of works "which suggest some relationship, however indirect and tenuous, between human conflict and the principle of form, or structure." He finds hopeful examples in Derrida and Frye, and healthy earlier anticipations in Kenneth Burke. On the other hand, he sees Poulet's work on the circle as reflecting in literary criticism the unfortunate "process of anthropological neutralization," which ritualistically expels from his abstract mathematical analysis the disordering elements of human ritual, itself full of expulsive intent. What is needed instead is literary analysis that respects the "true mystery" of language: "The true mystery is that language is both the perfectly transparent milieu of empiricism and the prison-house of linguisticism."

As Girard orders his sequence of arguments, he leads us toward an infinite regress of ritual victimage. The expulsion we find in literature is expelled by an inhospitable theory of language, and this theory is in turn expelled by our theorist ritualistically defending the ritual of expulsion. Through this reflexive series we come to the primitive origin of expulsion, with the victim's ambiguous function as the root of all symbolization. Having returned us here, the theorist would have us begin the symbolizing chain again, this time less puritanically, less positivistically. This is, of course, to place an enormous burden on victimage since all symbolizing is to emerge from it and to repeat its

essential pattern on increasingly sophisticated levels. Such a uniformity of pattern, continually susceptible of being reduced to its
origins, is unhappily suggestive of the structuralist analysis from
which it is supposedly exempt. Yet the residue of arbitrary violence
persists, though rescued for order and community. But it cannot surrender its irrational nature even if the structuralist again tries to read
it out of existence.

V

In our final essay, Ralph Freedman restricts his attention to a
phenomenological interpretation of intentionality which he makes in
the interest of reconciling modes of criticism often seen as disparate.
He seeks a common intentionality which can fuse the poet as live
person with the poem as his verbal object seen as such by living
readers. Freedman, then, is one of White's "Normal" critics, firmly
and imperturbably Normal. He tries to accommodate within his
normalcy most of what our other critics have seen as threats to criticism. In this way he can, by means of his attachment to Valéry, become "Inflationary," and then can even expand to the "Generalizing"
mood induced by his interest in Heidegger, still without letting go of
that normalcy. Even with Heidegger he is never troubled by the
temptation toward "Absurdism," though he does reject Barthes and
what he sees as the structuralist tendency toward the dissolution of
criticism. Only structuralism seems unaccommodatingly beyond the
friendly and expansive confines of a Normal criticism that can embrace even the Heideggerian enlargement of consciousness to "conversation," while holding onto the sober commitment to the poem as
verbal object.

Freedman presents four historical moments which portray para-
digmatically the development of the fused intentionality he seeks.
First, by way of the *dizain* of Scève, he shows how, through the
Renaissance "emblem," the poet's feelings can be "neutralized and
turned into literary objects while at the same time evoking a living
mind." With no epistemological problem to haunt it, this poetic theory can use the emblem to lock the subjective into the object for
permanent display. In Freedman's second moment, Diderot intrudes
the temporality of the empirical self upon the lingering spatiality of
the emblem. In a paradoxical awareness typical of the eighteenth
century, he sees both the inner states of consciousness and a verbal
object which alternately dissolves into time and retains its claim to
spatial there-ness. Intentionality here is double and unreconciled. In
the third moment, Freedman arrives, by way of Kant, at Valéry, whom

he sees as completing the aesthetic prepared for by Kant. Kant resolves the dualism represented by Diderot, though he retains too much epistemological sophistication to *dis*solve it. Still, he frees himself to portray "an objective order . . . as an analogy to a structure of the mind," and thus frees modern criticism to develop theories of intentionality that can reconcile subject and object. Freedman sees Valéry as going farthest toward realizing these possibilities: the poet's self, moving through the *"état poétique"* to the "abstraction" that creates the object's world, retains that self in an utterly transformed verbal reality. "A relationship between the mind, the organization of the world, and the work of art exists, creating an order in which they all can cohere." But the order is firmly in the realm of the literary object. As Freedman puts it, to Valéry "the dance of the mind among things and the dance of things among minds . . . are caught in the verbal dance of poetry."

But there is yet a fourth moment, for Freedman is aware that, in Valéry's total commitment to the object, the delicacy of the Kantian balance may be unsettled. So he turns to the phenomenological tradition from Husserl to Heidegger in hopes that he can restore the centrality of consciousness while retaining the verbal object as its embodiment. He sees the notion of intentionality as providing for "the reciprocal relationship of subject and object *within* consciousness." Yet it must move outward as well. In Heidegger's essay on Hölderlin he finds the movement outward from the poem which does not lose it as poem. It is a movement from consciousness, via the poem, to other minds, to existence, and to historical existence. It occurs through the communal act of "conversation" in which "we" engage. But, for Freedman, so long as there is the need to return to the verbal notion of the "conversation," the poem is preserved: "In a poetic text we discern how a mind deals with its objects and confronts other minds, while remaining a single text in which all these relations are absorbed." Even the image in the Scève poem can be reexamined and used to reinforce this fourth paradigmatic moment. The mutuality between the lovers and the hair, in the language that constitutes that relationship, becomes an allegory of the Heideggerian conversation: in it "subject and object are therefore both separate and unified, for they exist in an identical realm of consciousness while reciprocally acting upon one another." Do we hear an echo of Girard in this claim to the coexistence of identity with difference?

Having come through our other essays, we should by now have noted that the price of this theoretical expansion has been what White referred to as the "generalizing" of criticism. The notion of "existence as a single conversation" collapses all of history into poetry in a way that certainly explodes the Normal critic's concern with actual poems. Freedman is himself aware that poetry is becoming synonymous with man's generally creative capacity as verbal creature, as the following description of Heidegger's position makes clear: "When man in general becomes a poet and language in general becomes poetry, a conductor from consciousness to Being by way of the existent may have been found. Poetry, then, is the language of history and existence." Earlier we saw that this neo-Kantian view of language, which would have it constituting all our reality, gave Adams reason to be wary, though not always—I then feared—wary enough. Nor does Freedman seem sufficiently concerned about the potential conflict between the "Inflationary" tendency of his version of Valéry and the "Generalizing" tendency of his version of Heidegger. Once expanded to conversation, can poetry ever again contract to the poem as he found it in Valéry?

The dominant theoretical mood in Freedman is one of reconciliation, perhaps more pleasant and appropriate for our final essay than the more embattled mood in the critics who preceded him. Would that we could blend our theories instead of having to choose ineluctably among them. But, as I have suggested, reconciliation has its price—usually the smoothing over of rough differences that turn opponents into allies. It is, Girard would remind us, a triumph of the undifferentiated over the differentiated—except that the analytical faculty of the theorist, in its search for order, overlooks differences at its peril. We may be worried about accepting the resolution Freedman finds in phenomenological criticism when we find that criticism to include—without distinction among them—a variety of theorists stretching "from Merleau-Ponty to Poulet, from Heidegger to Staiger." Poulet, in particular, hardly seems to warrant the designation as phenomenological in the way others may—especially the Poulet we have seen in discussions by our other critics. The inclusion of Poulet is the more troublesome when we see phenomenological criticism characterized as "hybrid formalism," in which "the uniqueness of the literary text is retained," so that, if "it seemed to solve the problem of the formalist isolation of the poem from life," it does so "without abandoning the inviolability of the poetic text." I fear that, as it applies to Poulet and to some of the others, this claim holds more hope and good will than truth. Freedman's commitment to Normal criticism, in its Inflationary mode, has persuaded him to broaden his fellowship to an inclusiveness in which theoretical incompatibilities may be overlooked. Only structuralist criticism, in which "the literary object is entirely eliminated," remains expelled—by Freedman as by Girard. He does not explore the fact that his reason—that "most structuralist theories . . . reach . . . toward that view of imagination which dissolves *all* art into life, and language, in general"—could be applied to some of those whom he termed phenomenological and whom he used to complete the merger between self and other, between self and text, which he sees as the achievement of the new intentionality. As perhaps a half-confession of the truth of what I have been suggesting, Freedman fittingly permits Valéry to return to have the last word about the *état poétique*.

VI

As I look back on what I have done, I feel that I must remind the reader of the relative safety of the scorecard-keeper. As he watches the play, he can point out flaws and still be lost in admiration. For he knows that he is not to be confused with the players and their greater risks, since he does not independently confront their tasks. Neither is his criticism subject to their overseeing. What I have found in these essays is a series of contrasts and parallels and overlappings too complex to mark them off briefly here in my conclusion. (I warned earlier of my impatience with scorecard shorthand.) But I did try to note some of them along the way. One generalization I must permit myself: there is among these critics no partisan—indeed there is little sympathy—for structuralism. I may have thought of these "directions for criticism" as dealing with "structuralism and its alternatives," but while there are plenty of alternatives, there is not much structuralism. It is, of course, frequently enough discussed (indeed it is treated prominently by all our critics), but only to be rejected. Either it is passed by on the way to post-structuralism (as in Said), or it is seen as too generalized a view of language which needs some supplementing (as in White or Freedman), or it is expelled altogether as a misleading theory (as in Adams or Girard). There is a general distrust of the projection of linguistic principles into a privileged metaphysic. Further, our authors share a concern about the positivistic element of reduction in structuralism, that which denies existence in its temporal fullness. The density of cultural data is not to be "signifier-ed" out of existence, signifying the decline of structuralism instead. And time is on their side. As for the alternatives to structuralism, those are what these pages have mainly been about.

An additional common feature of these essays should be noted. With the exception of Freedman, all of them at some point either have criticism turn on itself or discuss that criticism which turns on itself. They are, in other words, aware of the problematic of criticism, of criticism as a reflexive act that becomes its own object as well as—in the "Normal" sense—being a subject with another work as its object. Whatever their sympathies to this disposition in recent criticism (and they vary from participating in it to disdaining it), they recognize its revolutionary consequences, even (as in White or Girard) its tendency toward infinite regress. But most of all they are concerned with the loss of privilege suffered by the literary work in this reflexive dimension accorded criticism. And they must come to deal, as Said or White does, with the newly introduced competition between criticism and poetry—except that both arts have lost their discrete names and characters in the common democracy of *écriture*. About this problem all our critics concern themselves in ways that we have seen reflect their theoretical allegiances.

In thanking Professor Dembo for making this issue of *Contemporary Literature* available to us for tracking recent criticism in our several ways, I am really expressing my gratitude to him for recognizing criticism as a major form of contemporary literature, worthy of being studied as an object in its own right. This is to justify criticism as an "independent creation," as Said did; it is to justify works of criticism as appropriate replacements for the contemporary literary works normally treated in this journal as objects by a criticism functioning as what Said condescendingly called a secondary art, a subject serving its poetic object. But now I am using the ritual gesture of thanks as an occasion to press further that reflexive tendency in our criticism which, in its autotelic arrogance, threatens to do away with any object but itself. And I confess myself too much Hayden White's "Normal" critic not to counteract that tendency—to see it as a tendency to usurpation. Indeed, it is with some comfort that, as a "Normal" critic, I contemplate the return here, with the next issue, of properly literary objects of critical concern. I would say that it is an occurrence which should put all us critics in our place, were current criticism otherwise than it is, as we see it reflected in this issue.

15

Literature, Criticism, and Decision Theory

Humanism and the Theory of Rational Choice

Please
for
give
me
for
eating
your
dog
biscuit

ALTHOUGH DAVID BRAYBROOKE's paper[1] seeks to force the theory of rational choice to confront "humanist misgivings" about it, it is clear

[1] "Humanist Misgivings about the Theory of Rational Choice," in *Problems of Choice and Decision: Proceedings of a Colloquium held in Aspen, Colorado, June 24–July 6, 1974*, ed. Max Black (Ithaca and Aspen: Cornell University Program on Science, Technology and Society, and Aspen Institute for Humanistic Studies, 1975), pp. 1–50. My essay here is a revised composite of my several contributions to that colloquium which appear in that volume on pp. 55–67, 398–431, 441–48, and 578–86.

that he has confidence in that theory's capacity to broaden itself to accommodate them. Since much of his paper arises out of poems that are apologies (like the one I have quoted above), it is perhaps appropriate for me to begin in the apologetic vein. For, as an unregenerate critic and theorist, I am hardly a fit commentator for the paper. In the nicety of its distinctions, its carefully manipulated complications which couple progressive eliminations with accumulated refinements, it both demands and deserves someone trained as I am not. I have been concerned with recent versions of formal decision theory only from the time of my invitation to this colloquium. And no one has taught me more than Braybrooke, in his companion essays as well as in his colloquium paper, which, despite its qualifications, I therefore treat as my representative sample of decision theory. So it is unseemly for me as his student thus presumptuously to respond by confessing that I am far less sanguine than he about the capacities of any theory of rational choice. Yet as a humanist with misgivings still unallayed, I must so confess. Unfit as I am by training and by inclination, I must yet ask our author to suffer these impatient responses to his work. In the spirit of those little girls who wrote those splendid poems he borrows from Kenneth Koch's young students, I apologize for munching upon biscuits other than my own.

To permit myself some assurance, I begin by briefly reviewing the paper's major sections. First there is a definition of both major components of the title, humanists on the one hand and the theory of rational choice on the other. Then Braybrooke argues for the generality of the theory, both as to the goods to be chosen and as to the motives behind the choice. With such generalization established, the theory would seem to have its hegemony guaranteed within its domain: it solves problems of actual choice-making in accordance with what it treats as our internal "preference maps," leaving to humanists the role of seeking to improve the quality of what those preference maps turn out to be.

But Braybrooke acknowledges five areas of humanist misgivings against the theory and its hegemony, with charges that can produce "concessionary modifications" without undoing the theory and its sway. At least he can suggest such modifications with respect to the first three of the charges. First, the theory's claims of "optimization" can give way to the more modest notion of "satisficing" through combinations of minimal requirements. Secondly, any mutually exclusive alternatives can, at the sacrifice of drama, be translated into non-exclusive ones. Thirdly, the primacy of self-interested calculation can, thanks to the humanistic notion of "intervals of abundance," yield to "engrossment," that absorption of self which momentarily banishes self-consciousness and, with it, narrow self-interest.

Two further charges remain, serious and profound, although modifications to appease them cannot be advanced. The fourth points to the failure of the theory to take account of the function of socially shared structures—whether one calls them "idioms" or "habits" or just conventions—in determining most choices. The theory rather sticks to the behavioral prejudice of regarding the chooser atomistically, defining him solely in accordance with a preference map determined by calculations of private self-interest. The final and most explosive humanist misgiving laments the theory's need to preclude development and innovation—in a word, novelty—since the very possibility of surprise or spontaneity would destroy the theory's primary function of providing a general structure for predictions that are characterized by determinate specifications.

Braybrooke concedes that the very ground-rules on which the theory and its mission are based prevent it from addressing such misgivings as these final two: "I do not know what [concessionary modifications] could be brought forward, except a confession that general though it may be as to goods, and general as to motives, the theory of rational choice is not general enough to cover all choices in determinate detail." Still his self-critical good humor and the balanced good sense of his generous liberality, here as elsewhere, carry him past such obstacles to the undogmatic sense of compromise in his final paragraphs. The misgivings remain, but so does the theory of rational choice, the misgivings persistent though not wholly unsatisfied, and the theory bent not quite out of shape and still standing.

A less yielding humanist than Braybrooke (and my own paper will quickly show me to be one) is likely to be more demanding and less generous. Surely he would be less willing to put up with the notion that any "hedonic calculus," however undiscoverable, is a worthy scientific objective or can have any moral authority. Yet the theory of rational choice itself, with its preference maps, must rest upon such a notion. But the humanist's argument is not with optimization or with the mutually exclusive nature of alternatives (indeed humanists have always wallowed in ineluctable alternatives), but with the assumption that private preferences are the automatic bestowers of value, that life is a supermarket, with its preferred goods properly "good," so that economic terminology and criteria become moral ones. The humanist's quarrel, then, may be with the argument that the theory can be generalized by quantification to include all goods and all the motives of those whose tastes prefer them.

Of course, to the extent that I am complaining that such general claims override human particularity, thanks to the power of prediction that resides in the notion of preference maps, Braybrooke has anticipated me with his final misgiving about the exclusion of novelty, which I believe—more than he does—explodes the theory. For me, schooled as I am by the great fictions in our literature, particularity, with its unpredictability, involves also a component of the potential irrationalism that undoes self-interest and puts land mines on anyone's preference map. And unless the theorist of rational choice is willing (as he dare not be) to prescribe that we *ought* to prefer what his maps describe us as preferring (that we ought, in other words, to be rational—that is, ought to be motivated by self-interest), he may be forced to give up cartography altogether.

All this does no more than return us to the old concern about the relation of fact to value and to the theoretical paralysis that ensues when we try to be consistent, as in the end we never quite are, about reducing values to facts. Given the economist's model, we cannot ask whether anyone's desires are worth fulfilling any more than we can question the goods we prefer to purchase. Each is master of his own purse. There is at no point anything but a statistical acceptance of what is preferred; yet there is, to be sure, an assumption of the consistency in our preferences, which is identified with the rationalism which *ought* to be displayed in order to conform to the model created by the theory. And so the *ought* of consistency and rationalism is smuggled in, at whatever cost to the theory's own consistency.

Besides enforcing the claims of particularity over universality and of value over fact, this humanist has a quarrel with the theory that Braybrooke seems not to share. Indeed, my quarrel may be as much with his misgivings. Rather than the everyday choices which exercise our preferences, I am concerned, perhaps because our greatest literature has taught me to be, with those extraordinary dilemmas that seem to defy resolution. Instead of the routine center of existence, it is the extremity at the outer edges which is in direst need of help in decision-making, served as it is now only by the profound but untransferable resources of literary casuistry. But Braybrooke seems to concentrate on routine decisions instead of those made under conditions of risk or uncertainty. Even more to my point is Braybrooke's dismissal, in a recent article ("From Economics to Aesthetics: The Rectification of Preferences") of what he terms "moral cases," helpful or harmful to others, and "prudential cases," helpful or harmful to oneself. He excludes such cases from his argument "as exceptions requiring special treatment." In their extreme forms—those which would interest me—they *are* exceptions and, as such, *are* deserving of the special treatment, well beyond theories of rational choice, which they find in works of literature.

It is as a result of his exclusion of moral and prudential cases that Braybrooke, as theorist of economic preferences, is able to confine his interest, in the same article, to what he broadly refers to as "aesthetic" matters. His characterization of the aesthetic stems from precisely its non-moral and non-prudential character, in the traditional Kantian sense of the aesthetic as the disinterested, free from interest, involving in effect the suspension of the will, agent of practical judgment. But for those of us concerned with the usual humanistic connotations of decision-making, this exemplary use of the aesthetic may seem eccentric. For, if what characterizes decisions is the operation of an interested will, as practical judgment, and what characterizes the aesthetic is the disinterested, freely playing suspension of the will, then the distinction between the two realms would seem to preclude the second's being used as a crucial example of the first. The aesthetic, described by Braybrooke in the present paper as functioning during the poet's activity, requires just that spirit of free play, of experimentation which declines to choose definitively between alternatives, thus avoiding the awesome finality of a choice made and to be lived with.

But how to choose without being locked in, shut off from the alternatives one has not chosen? It is like asking how to choose without choosing. The poet can do it: he can have a character make the choice and yet himself see around that choice either through the presence of his own voice in the poem or through other choices revealed in the dramatic structure which surrounds the character; for example, by having an analogue of that character *not* make it. But, away from the world of fiction and its freedoms, we are usually like its trapped characters, with little chance to have it both ways in the existential world of both common and extraordinary decision-making. It is why the doctor, who normally can go only one way at a time with a patient, envies the laboratory scientist his control groups, which permit him both to do and not do something at the same time. Unlike the doctor, such an experimentalist, who is for the purposes of this occasion unconcerned with the individual worldly weal or woe of the creatures he uses, is in effect operating within a fictional structure, not altogether unlike that of the poet in its freedoms from the ineluctable aspect of decision-making.

Braybrooke's dependence on the aesthetic for arguments he makes within the moral realm helps him enormously when he comes to introduce notions like "intervals of abundance" and "engrossment" in support of his humanist misgivings. Nor should it be surprising that he calls upon the precedent of Dewey to support him, since for Dewey, who could brook no distinctions of kind within the continuity of experience, the aesthetic was a major component of choice-making. To preserve the potential experiential benefits of choice-making, we are not to foreclose the expansiveness that free play can provide: we must open out, not lock in. In effect, even in choice-making, the will is never to be permitted to sustain itself by eating up the imagination. Again, since aesthetic examples will serve more easily than urgently moral ones, Braybrooke quotes an art critic, Edgar Wind, for support, using his insistence—in the spirit of Kant and Schopenhauer and beyond—on the artist's need to suspend his personal will in the moment of creation. Part of the artist must remain outside his commitments to provide an aesthetic, a more than willful, context for them. I may agree; but the question remains, Dewey perhaps to the contrary notwithstanding, whether, as non-artists, we can thus suspend our wills in that final moment that precedes the decision we make.

We must worry, it seems clear, whether, any enriching of the decision-making process can alter our anxiety about the decisions made. Having chosen one alternative, we are no longer free to choose, and *its* consequences are the ones with us from now on, in that room into which we have locked ourselves in choosing. Nor is there a poet to place us and our choice within a broader canvas on which he plays. There is an enormous difference, in a fiction, between the character's existential need to choose absolutely, even as we sometimes do, and the poet's provisional aesthetic choices of ways in which to dispose that choice within the play of his total construct. By concentrating only upon the poet's choices and not the character's, Braybrooke has, I believe, failed to mark this critical distinction and thereby failed also to mark those aspects of literature that are intensely, if casuistically, choice-laden in ways that have moral, and not just aesthetic, consequences for us all. His not pointing out this distinction is, I fear, a necessary convenience for his argument, which seems to shy away from those more morally urgent aspects of choice-making. Thus I would argue that his attempt to transform mutually exclusive alternatives to non-exclusive ones, and to transform self-interest to engrossment, cannot succeed if it rests on the poet's aesthetic need to exploit inclusive abundance, without recognizing the fictional character's need (or ours, as existents) to live with the exclusive meagerness our choices provide.

Yet Braybrooke is crucially correct in allowing the poet a place inside and outside and all around the decisions and counter-decisions of any dilemma, as he thus reveals the limitations of practical judgment and its necessary consequences. As he suggests, the poet enjoys his freedom, playing even with his words in order to create an optimal object. But I would insist, more than Braybrooke does, on the poet's need to optimize his language. In dealing with the poetic apology to the dog and the biscuit, he settles for "satisficing" and for meeting "minimal" demands, rather than for optimizing. If in her verbal decisions the young author refused to settle for less, "would not the enterprise of poetry-writing, which [she] took up with so much joy, have become impossibly laborious and tedious? And so exacting, because of the pressure latent in the idea of finding an optimum, as to jeopardize [her] spirit of freedom?" Now this argument may be adequate in the case of Lorraine Fedison (student author of the poem), who is functioning within the goals of an educational experience rather than as an incipient "great poet." But what would be our culture's repository of artifacts if our Michelangelos and Shakespeares and Bachs had similarly reduced their demands, instead of prolonging their creative acts unduly: if they had satisficed instead of optimized? We are, in effect, back to the problem we had with Dewey a little while ago, this time with poems instead of decisions: are we primarily concerned with the poetry-making experience or with the poetry that is made?

Braybrooke himself acknowledges a moment of optimization in the poem I have quoted, where the word chosen has more than minimal reasons to justify it in preference to alternatives. Let me repeat the poem addressed to the dog:

> Please
> for
> give
> me
> for
> eating
> your
> dog
> biscuit

Braybrooke rightly points out the advantage of repeating "for" ("*for*-give me *for* eating") as "the uniquely best choice of a word to fill the gap." He does not explain why it should be "uniquely best," although the general syntactic preferability of "for" to other constructions is clear. Let me, however, suggest an alternative wording that seems to me to approach being optimal at this point, as the original does not:

Please
for
give
me
for
giving
myself
your
dog
biscuit

However trivial, the optimization here could be specified by the complications introduced by semantic overlappings and conflicts in the syntactical repetition-with-variation of "forgive" ("for give"). In my alternative version ("forgive me for giving myself" rather than "forgive me for eating"), possibilities of meaning are multiplied and deepened as playfulness leads to word play, the pun that converts phonetic accident into semantic substance. In this strange philological creation, as part of even so slight a poem, word play as pun seems to become teleological necessity, at least for this aesthetic occasion, which is never altogether unplayful.

Such suggestions of a substantive level of language remind us of the extent to which what we take to be our experienced reality is a world we create through our metaphors and our verbal mistakes and self-indulgences. We wonder, consequently, how nakedly empirical our experiential world is, and how filtered by our schemata (as Karl Popper uses the term) our acts of will can be as they seek to respond to that world. If language is our primary schema, creating our situations for us, though we think and act as if we are encountering and judging raw experience, then the symbolic philosopher can make fools of the would-be empiricist in us all.

With this notion in mind, I turn again to the economic, marketplace model for decision preferences. In referring to Wicksteed's phrase, "the market of life," Braybrooke assures us it is intended "innocently." The view of language I am suggesting permits no such innocence. I must suggest, of course, that such a phrase is not idle rhetoric, an empty metaphor, a superficial manner of speaking; instead it is a total manner of meaning, a key to the man's vision—especially when we put it in the company of other economic terms and metaphors used by him. However noble or well-meaning Wicksteed may be, do we not find the competition among our values, as we seek to make our major decision, reduced in him to market preferences, as his metaphors constitute our realities? Indeed, might we not even claim that Braybrooke's general use of the economic term *goods* in a moral context suggests that, as the objects of our preference, they are all that is "good," and that what we do not prefer are, therefore, "bads?" Cannot a literary critic (or should I say a literal critic?) find that, in such reductive language-as-vision, economics literally *becomes*, by absorption as it were, all the morality there is? If we learn that our words, like ourselves (or should I say our words *as* ourselves?), are never innocent, then we have taken on humanist misgivings that lead us to distrust all theories, together with ourselves.

Literature, Vision, and the Dilemmas of Practical Choice

I prefer, as my example of recent decision theory, Howard Raiffa in his *Decision Analysis: Introductory Lectures on Choices under Uncertainty* (1968). As a literary man, I find in Raiffa's concern with decision-making under conditions of risk and uncertainty (what I would call conditions of extremity) a concern in which I can take greater interest than I can in the more routine, economically determined models which concern Braybrooke. Yet in Raiffa we find a similar rational need to organize and systematize our thinking—as the author puts it—for difficult decision-making situations, the need to measure "viable options," to make series of "calculations" so that one may "fix on a . . . strategy" keyed to "utility values." There is the helpful invocation of probability theory and of game theory; and there is the usual polemic between so-called intuitive or subjective judgments and so-called objective ones. But even Professor Raiffa, as subjectivist, must build his argument on the claim "that there is a structure of abstract elements that is common to all these illustrative decision problems under uncertainty." Another hold-out with misgivings ends by being enlisted under the banner of rational decision theory.

His claims seem eminently reasonable, of course. But, as a literary critic, I must be aware of the fact that our major literary works provide a far less reasonable—and yet a more humanly candid—view of the prospects and consequences of decision-making. More than anything else, a reading of such works forces us to despair of any confidence "that there is a structure of abstract elements that is common to all" decision-provoking problems. But without such a structure, how can we provide models for dealing with these problems? How, in other words, can we hope to discover and promote rational procedures for resolving them?

To ask such questions is to drag in that antique debate about universals and particulars. For just as surely as any procedure like Professor Raiffa's must depend on the assumption of universals (the "structure of abstract elements common to all," or at least many, problems), the peculiar casuistry of the literary work must insist on the irreducible particularity of its "case." Of course, Professor Raiffa would rightly insist that he has not claimed to find a universal structure common to all decision-making problems, but only one that is common to his *illustrative* problems. He has, in other words, *pre*pared his problems (pared them down beforehand, a priori, that is) in order for them to serve, to support, that structure of common "abstract elements." It is just this illustrativeness that literature, at least according to literary theory in the wake of Kant (and we are still awash in that wake), must reject in favor of uniqueness.

Here is the major difference between Renaissance and neoclassical literary theory on the one hand and theory of past two centuries on the other. For the theory of older, philosophically more secure times was content to allow poetry to reflect universals or the "abstract elements" "common" to particular human problems. Confident of the "truths" of its philosophy and confident too of the authority of those philosophical universals to bring particulars into line, the theory could assign to literary works the role of furnishing, in their particular cases, exemplary demonstrations of those general truths. Here indeed was an illustrative function for literature, not essentially different from the function performed by the skeletal examples furnished by Professor Raiffa. Nor can the difference in the degree of flesh on the skeleton in the two cases become a difference in principle, so long as true particularity is similarly denied. These days a unity of method has merely replaced an older and more naive sense of the unity of truth: just as an older philosophy assumed its hegemony over an often resistant experiential world, so the would-be scientific purveyor of rational method must have assumed before beginning that his common procedures can accommodate a variety of special possibilities, provided we know how to reduce their specialness out of them. But in neither case have we really had a solution to the problematic relation between universals and particulars. Instead, the dominance of the universals has been made so complete that the particulars have been done away with—at least so far as their particularity, which is their defining characteristic, is concerned. In literature, we are to find logical (which is to say universal) argument accompanied by a rhetorical overlay. The bait of a particularized fiction must hide the trap of moral philosophy: as Scaliger says, the poet is to "imitate the truth by fiction"—a far cry from the use of an autonomous fiction as itself the model, as the ultimate particular.

No, for the Renaissance as for the modern social scientists (dare I say "human engineer"?) the particular can be seen as a pseudo-particular that is no more than a mask for the universal. Technically, of course, we can admit that it is enough to satisfy the definition of particularity if the particular serves as a single, representative instance of many occurrences which can be described by a universal model. But the existential view of the particular would insist on defining it by those unique characteristics which are not susceptible of reduction to the universal. If the particular functions only as a common example of the universal, so that it is defined only by "illustrative" characteristics, then the existential views it as no more than a mock-particular, one that is intent on deceiving us (and itself!) about its slavish role that denies its proper autonomy: a pretended free subject in a democracy is really one among many ruthlessly disposed objects under totalitarianism.

Finally, we must return to Kierkegaard's quarrel with Hegel: either, as with Hegel, the universal has an absolute sanction and the particular must succumb by denying its nature as particular, or, as in Kierkegaard, the particular has an absolute sanction and can make good its secession from the universal in order to go it on its own. In the case of Hegelian man, as Kierkegaard puts it:

> the particular individual is the particular which has its *telos* in the universal, and its task is to express itself constantly in it, to abolish its particularity in order to become the universal. As soon as the individual would assert himself in his particularity over against the universal he sins, and only by recognizing this can he again reconcile himself with the universal.[2]

But the subjectivity of faith can produce the Kierkegaardian alternative, in which the dissident particular, having seceded from the universal, replaces the universal as having the authority of the absolute:

> the individual as the particular is higher than the universal, is justified over against it, is not subordinate but superior—yet in such a way, be it observed, that it is the particular individual who, after he has been subordinated as the particular to the universal, now through the universal becomes the individual who as the particular is superior to the universal, for the fact that the individual as the particular stands in an absolute relation to the absolute.[3]

Of course, Kierkegaard knew that such radical particularity resists our language, with *its* universal properties, just as it must resist the uni-

---

[2] *Fear and Trembling*, trans. Walter Lowrie (Princeton: Princeton University Press, 1941), p. 79.

[3] Ibid., p. 82.

versals of the rational realm. Literary theory that shares this attitude has viewed literature as the only discursive equivalent for this experiential particularity: that is, it is more faithful to our experience in its infinite contingency, the only language created as a match to that experience. Hence the individual literary work, in its dealings with the problems of moral choice, would be obliged to resist the rational requirements of any systematic decision-making science.

The humanist, with an instinctive existential bias,[4] often proceeds in sympathy with Kierkegaard's anti-scientific slurs:[5] he feels the need to protect the irreducibility of the unique case, thus resisting the calculating manipulations (of the sort presented by Professor Raiffa) that rightly must accompany the search for universal models. Dostoevsky's "underground man" perhaps is the spokesman for this humanistic irrationalism in his idolatry of the person's uniqueness. The perverse willfulness of the fictive author of *Notes from Underground* springs from his need to assert himself against "the stone wall" constituted by "the laws of nature, the deductions of natural science, mathematics."[6] He refuses to accept the fact "that two times two makes four" even if it is true, because it is true whether or not he wills it so. In other words, as Kierkegaard would put it, just as impatiently, it is true objectively, with or without me, so that it can have no relation to my subjectivity. For one to respond to these laws, subjecting his private decisions to universally operational principles, is for him to prove that, instead of being a man, he is "nothing but a piano key." And since our underground writer must at every point "convince himself that he is a man and not a piano key," he must act in a way that we might consider perverse, since it runs counter to his self-interest. In order to deny the rule of Benthamite law, he has, in effect, replaced self-love with self-hate, thereby introducing new and other-than-rational complexities into the grounds of decision-making.

It is precisely these complexities of decision-making with which

---

[4] By using this phrase ("instinctive existential bias") I mean to distinguish this attitude from the formal philosophical program of any particular "existentialism." All that is required here is the antipathy to universals, or—to put it another way— the anti-ontological cherishing of the uniqueness of the person and his experience, as well as his dilemmas.

[5] Kierkegaard's key text here is his *Concluding Unscientific Postscript*.

[6] Of course, Dostoevsky's concept of "the laws of nature" is an obsolete one based on a naive philosophical realism. But the "operational models" of the modern scientist, though unaccompanied by ontological assumptions, would be no more acceptable to him. He would reject them as arbitrary ones posited on a dehumanized and depersonalized assumption about nature and man. Whether they are laws of nature or only laws of method, objective and absolute or only tentative and operational, he would damn them.

literature busies itself in the unique cases which its fictions embrace. At least this is so as literature is viewed by much criticism since Kant and Coleridge. It is not, then, as an older criticism would have it, that a fiction furnishes us with examples of universal moral problems and samples of model behavior; rather the fiction provides a case for us so extreme in the refinement of its intricacies that, while its uniqueness hardly permits it to duplicate our own moral problems, its endlessly contingent nature sharpens our awareness of the multiple involvements within those experiences of our own which, without literature, we are likely to oversimplify. Through such works our look-outs become alerted to probe the fastnesses of experiential depth. We are given, then, methodological and structural models for moral experience, though not substantive ones. The complexity of that fictional case awakens us to the complexity of our own, though the configurations in each case are utterly different, with each gravitating around its own special disposition of warring particulars. As Samuel Johnson put it in his "Preface to Shakespeare," "The reflection that strikes the heart is not, that the evils before us are real evils, but that they are evils to which we ourselves may be exposed."[7] For what it offers the spectator or reader is a model of "what he would himself feel, if he were to do or suffer what is there feigned to be suffered or to be done." And it sensitizes him to the nuances of response which, as moral agent, he must not overlook in his quest for authenticity.

The introduction of the criterion of authenticity returns us to what has been with us since the irrationalist arguments we have seen in Kierkegaard and Dostoevsky: that, as we seek decisions, the externally and "objectively" measurable criterion of any interest-theory of value gives way to the personalistic criterion that declares the primacy of our willingness to confront the dilemma in all its ramifications and to confront as well our awareness of the incompleteness of any response we can make. In other words, what is primary is our establishing a relation between us as complete persons (immoral as well as moral agents) and *it* as an unrepeatable dilemma whose unique configuration forces any single, clear choice based on universal considerations to appear as a lie and a cheat. We thus convert the dilemma and the people it involves from objects to be disposed of into persons whose uniqueness is to be cherished. Since, as Kierkegaard insisted, subjectivity is all, then this interpersonal relation (I-Thou rather than I-it), in its completeness, its utter candor, is what counts, even more (nay, *especially* more) than that act-in-the-external-world which is the result of the decision itself.

[7] Johnson, *Selected Prose and Poetry*, ed. Bertrand H. Bronson (New York: Rinehart & Co., 1952), pp. 255–56.

Taking their lead from the Kantian injunction about the required distinterestedness of the aesthetic realm and from the Coleridgean definition of the poet's imagination as that which expresses itself as "the balance and reconciliation of opposite or discordant qualities," some modern critics have found a formal justification for what in our practical context we might think of as a literature of *in*decisiveness. Further, this was to be the model for all our best literature. The suspension of any private interest would easily lead to the notion that a balanced presentation of warring options for action means there can be no declared winner at the expense of a loser, but that both would be maintained at equal strength. Thus the best, or most authentic, literature would be less a prerequisite for action than an enemy to action, standing for our contemplation of the impossibility of deciding cleanly, culminating in the blockage of action—perhaps moral paralysis itself. We can thus see how, from Kant onward, the "will" becomes an inimical faculty for art in that it would prevent the requisite disinterestedness; for the will strives for the gratification of individual interest, leading surely to an interestedness. The crescendo of attacks upon will culminate in the assaults on it by Schopenhauer and, through the influence of Schopenhauer, to the early Nietzsche and Bergson, each raising up the suspension of the will in true imagination or intuition as they cast down the onesided decisiveness (and consequent visionary blindness) of the will. Since seeing is better than doing (or rather, inclusive seeing would prevent doing since action requires partial blindness), vision is to be all. The call to contemplation, and to art as that which fosters contemplation, thus rises as the call to action subsides. (Of course, that these philosophers are re sponding to an increasingly action-oriented culture is obvious enough. It may also appear to the literary mind that they are only catching up to insights long before provided by our best literature.)

Modern critics, inheriting all this, founded, as I have said, a criticism based on formal principles that emphasizes precisely this suppression of the will. Perhaps the epigraph for them all is Yeats's famous derogation of rhetoric as a pseudo-poetry to be rejected when he asked, "What is rhetoric except the will trying to do the work of the imagination?" Yeats's attack on will comes in a parallel way from Blake and the Symbolists rather than from Kant, but from it we see just as clearly the misuse which poetry must not permit itself to undergo. Such a need to demonstrate the balanced and disinterested view has led critics since T. S. Eliot and I. A. Richards to emphasize poetry's *im*personality and its *in*clusiveness, respectively. Richards expressly rejects a poetry of *ex*clusion, which puts forward one set of values at the expense of another set, and instead calls for a poetry of inclusion, which embraces opposed alternatives with a stance that no term describes better than does his "equilibrium." Although Richards speaks of the balancing of normally opposed impulses in order to achieve psychic fullness, it is clear that it is action (as well as the will from which it springs) that is being suppressed. For Richards sees action as involving the satisfaction of a single group of impulses at the expense of all competing groups, while the blocking of any single decisive action by sustaining other groups of impulses at equal strength would allow the inclusive psychic satisfactions that Schopenhauer and others would attribute to rapt, will-less contemplation, almost Oriental-style.

This notion easily leads to the celebration of ambiguity, irony, paradox, and tension as major literary devices to induce this inclusiveness of presentation and response: ambiguity which offers two possible meanings without choosing between them, irony which requires that every claim carry within it its own self-denial, paradox which suggests self-contradiction, and tension which is the general term, inclusive of the others, that precludes any resolution in one direction or another. Such critical tendencies become refined into the brilliant virtuoso displays of the New Criticism, which reinterprets the history of English literature through revaluations performed in the interest of such inclusiveness as the transcendence of mere willfulness.

It would seem that the interest of this criticism, however, is formalistic rather than existentialist. And indeed it is true that its procedure does intend to discover its principle of literary form in the structure of oppositions, consistently maintained and developed in the literary work, in contrast to normal discourse (more properly the work of will), in which one side would give way to the other. But complexity as a principle of literary form necessarily has thematic consequences that lead to complexity as a principle of our moral experience. This, then, is a cognitive claim which permits the critic to maintain that literature, through its inclusiveness, can confront experience more honestly, can permit an existential candor that is prerequisite to authenticity. The uniqueness of its formal structure enables the literary work to become the discursive key to the uniqueness of our lives, as the particular work's resistance to the exclusiveness of will reflects the particular person's resistance to the exclusive sway of moral imperatives, of decision-guiding universals. In this way a movement that has crossed over from philosophy into formalistic literary criticism has consequences that lead it to cross back again. The attack on the will and its universals in favor of contemplative disinterestedness is transformed into a defense of an inclusive, tension-filled literature that disdains simple resolutions; and that is in turn transformed into a defense of an irrationalist view of our moral life that elevates vision and its existential candor at the expense of the practical necessities of choice, and of the action choice requires.

There are many works which furnish paradigms of the kind of anti-universal wrangling that precludes the extraction of a moral proposition upon which decisions can be based. (One hardly has to remind critics at this point that they are on the verge of that self-contradictory trap: making a universal proposition of the claim that there are no universal propositions and then using several fictions as examples of the claim after insisting that each is unique and not exemplary. By way of defense I can do no more than repeat my earlier statement that the works are "methodological and structural models for moral experience, though not substantive ones": they are to remind us of the impossibilities of clean decision-making without prescribing any action or inaction in a particular case.)

Perhaps the most obvious paradigm is the story of Abraham's willingness to sacrifice Isaac, as related by Kierkegaard in *Fear and Trembling*, which is—most philosophers will gladly grant—a work closer to literature than to philosophy. In it Kierkegaard traces, with an almost maddening patience, the endless involutions of Abraham's plight as he seeks to measure God's apparent command against moral and social law. Again and again he goes over, from every perspective and within every shading of each of them, the absurd demand made upon him to transgress the profoundest ethic he knows. Here surely is the case a fortiori for the inadequacy of universals: even so unarguable an ethical commandment as that which would absolutely forbid his murdering his son is not untouchable. Kierkegaard makes the case as absurd as possible when to this apparently uncontingent law he opposes God's word—or rather Abraham's belief about the word he attributes to God. After all, as Kierkegaard is at pains to remind us, Abraham has no way of assuring himself that it is God who has spoken to him and not the devil within himself who is tempting him.

Nor can the private visionary ever know whether he is saint or demon, once he has forsaken the safe mediation of rational universals. For in forsaking universals he is forsaking all that can be known, all that can be appealed to outside himself, all that holds for any besides himself. What he is rejecting is mediation, as he comes to discover that even the safest of universal moral laws (agents of mediation) cannot withstand the self-persuasions of subjectivity. The either-or is absolute: either the external proposition that holds societies together or the inner voice that threatens to tear them apart. Deprived of all the security of communal certainty, he is deprived even of the possibility of communicating the subjectivity of his inner faith that risks everything: for he has seceded from the universal which is the domain of language. Hence it is that, as the particular asserting his radical particularity, he requires "the teleological suspension of the ethical" by resolving the dilemma in the direction of private absurdity, whatever the risk. For existential risk is at the root of such utter self-assertion.

Compared to the major dilemmas that mark our greatest fiction, Abraham's seems utterly out of balance. After all, the rational weight in favor of refusing to sacrifice his son is countered only by his unsupported private conviction about the voice he has heard and the outrageous command it has given him. It is precisely the imbalance between these forces that allows Kierkegaard to use this as his argument a fortiori on behalf of the particular's need for self-assertion and for secession from the universal, whatever the private demonism to which it exposes us. The alternative is the automatic responsiveness of Dostoevsky's piano key. The literary works we shall be looking at will provide dilemmas far more troubling to rational man. For whatever his tendencies toward the literary, Kierkegaard is still a religious philosopher. As such, he can finally depend upon the self-justifications of undemonstrable (even unobservable) faith. Indeed, the power of faith, as the belief in things unseen, must rest precisely on such undemonstrability and unobservability. The literary work, in contrast, must "earn" its credibility from inside, the credibility, that is, of its dilemmas as these resist simple dramatic resolution. Furthermore, Kierkegaard had Abraham resolve his dilemma on the side of faith, at the expense of the ethical, so that he is not locked in the unresolvability of unyielding tensions as is the pure poet, who is dedicated only to experiential complexity, with no prior commitment to a resolution imposed by a transcendent faith. Thus the literary work is rather likely to hang on the impossibility of ethical resolution, balancing its revelation of the inadequacy and the visionary blindness of the universal claim with the risks of demonism in the candid confrontation of private vision. But to hang this way is to render the ultimate critique of decision-making: it is not that decisions are not made in great literature (they are indeed, and even in cases when they are not, then we discover how profound a decision is the decision not to decide), but that the entire work renders a most ambiguous judgment on what the protagonist, often quite single-mindedly, decides.

A more illuminating *literary* instance is that of Starbuck confronting his opportunity to murder Captain Ahab before the final commitment to destruction in *Moby Dick*. There is, by this point in the novel, no longer any question in Starbuck's mind about Ahab's madness, his monomania that no longer has any restraints in its destructive commitments. With Ahab thus possessed and in control of the ship if not of himself, the ship and its crew are surely doomed to a blasphemous and suicidal mission, and Starbuck knows it. At such a moment he comes upon a remarkable opportunity, with the rifle and the unguarded Ahab most fortuitously coexisting. The chance will not come again. But it is here that Starbuck proves that it is not for nothing that he has been characterized as being, in an emergency, a man of "mere, unaided virtue." And he is powerless to act, though for the best of reasons, even as we know his failure opens the final door to catastrophe. It is not only practical to kill Ahab; it is necessary to kill Ahab. But, if he kills Ahab, Starbuck will no longer be Starbuck, and in the transformation caused by the act the savior will turn out to have been a monster, prompted by a malice more sinister than the open malice of Ahab. And the saved world will not have been worth the saving, at the price of transforming it utterly. It is the old moral dilemma about ends and means, one which "mere, unaided virtue" cannot resolve in the direction of action, and, however he has failed his fellows, his is a response that redounds to his glory. The Ahabs count on that failure, admire as they contemn it—and profit from it knowingly. Melville never permits us to forget that the virtue Starbuck has is "mere" and no more, though virtue it is.

The scene in which Starbuck is given the chance to kill Ahab, considers doing it, and decides not to, is obviously reminiscent of the scene from *Hamlet* which probably inspired it: when Hamlet is tempted to murder Claudius at prayer, but doesn't. The issues are more explicitly defined in the scene from *Moby Dick* and the consequences of not acting more immediately explosive, but the elements of the dilemma are similar. One should remember also that Melville was the product of a literary culture in which the romantic interpretation of Hamlet as "the man who couldn't make up his mind" to act was a commonplace notion. It is not unlikely, then, especially in view of the Shakespearean flavor of much of *Moby Dick*, that the central conception of Starbuck and his virtuous inability to act to save himself and his community is explained and given depth by his inheritance from Hamlet. The need to act decisively, the inability to act, the fearsome consequences of the action which is rejected, and the catastrophic consequences of the inaction which is decided upon—all achieve a masterful dramatic coexistence here.

In an extreme situation, what we have, in short, is the impossibility of making a right decision, and chief among the options is the decision not to decide, which is a decision as devastating as the rest. Whatever possible universal principle might be invoked, the peculiar concatenation of circumstance, of character, and of the sets of oughtness renders it as inadequate as its contrary principle would be. Our intense vision of the particular dilemma forces us to recognize that, behind the facade of our universal ethical models, is a chaos of mutually contradictory particulars which undermine every choice, converting would-be wisdom into pride, and every apparently right action into a deadly one. The god we create in the name of ethical probity comes, in spite of (or because of) our best efforts, to wear the Manichean face of reality that confronts our most candidly searching vision of existence.

It is, then, in accord with the increasingly skeptical attitude toward the possibility of honest action decided upon by the application of ethical universals, that we find Joseph Conrad's protagonist in *Victory*, Axel Heyst, saying,

> I suppose I have done a certain amount of harm, since I allowed myself to be tempted into action. It seemed innocent enough, but all action is bound to be harmful. It is devilish. That is why this world is evil upon the whole.[8]

Later in the novel he pursues this thought by explicitly tying action—together with the illusion of ethical decision-making on which, in the best of cases, it is undertaken—to Adam and the original Fall of Man. He concludes,

> Action—the first thought, or perhaps the first impulse, on earth! The barbed hook, baited with the illusion of progress, to bring out of the lightless void the shoals of unnumbered generation!
>
> "And I, the son of my father, have been caught too, like the silliest fish of them all," Heyst said to himself. (p. 174)

The entire novel spins out of Heyst's inconstant ability to remain true to his father's teachings: the story derives from his momentary lapses from the philosophy of detachment, and it plays itself out tragically under the unsympathetic supervisory presence of the dead but still disdainful father, embodied in his overseeing portrait. Under his aegis, Heyst has withdrawn from the commitment to human relations which would lead him to the need for decisive and risky action. But his incompleteness in willing this withdrawal leads to only minimal involvement, though even this is enough to draw him irrevocably in. He is led into his strange partnership with Morrison by that coolest of emotions, a half-contemptuous pity, but he has now been trapped by

---

[8] In this and the following example I am recapitulating discussions of works treated in a book of mine with which this audience may not be familiar (*The Tragic Vision: The Confrontation of Extremity*). This passage is from *Victory* (New York: Doubleday & Co., 1939), p. 54.

life and readied for that more fateful partnership with Lena. And even that slight immersion in the world in his business relation with Morrison has the consequence of arousing in the jealous Schomberg the malicious slander that sends Jones and Ricardo as agents of destruction to his and Lena's magic isle. Neither wholly engaged nor wholly withdrawn, he is incomplete in every way. Having, however half-heartedly, made the decisions which enmesh him in the need for further protective action, Heyst naively believes that Lena and he can still withdraw to be alone together. When he learns that, the commitment once made, there is no longer any chance for a pure withdrawal, he finds himself unable to respond to the need to save what his prior, minimal action has brought him. He is paralyzed, and his indecision in the face of the unmitigated immoralism of his antagonists leads to the catastrophe, however modified by the vain heroism of Lena. He can only pay her the tribute of the final purgative fire which is his own suicide, testimony also of the impossibility of his incompleteness. If *any* action is the agent of evil, utter disengagement is coldly inhuman, if not unattainable. Heyst is too self-aware not to know and condemn the insidious consequences of human action, upon oneself as well as others, but he must condemn equally the ruthless dispassion of his father's analysis which produced that self-awareness in him. Knowing the risks of decision-making, then, he has tried from the start to decide only to avoid the commitment that makes decision-making necessary, but he is not consistently enough on guard to make even that decision a definite one.

His problem is not altogether unlike that of Byron Bunch in Faulkner's *Light in August*. Bunch also seeks non-involvement, once more under the influence of a mind more philosophic than his own. Reverend Hightower serves as his guide much in the way that Heyst's father served Heyst. But, working by himself on a Saturday in order to ensure his isolation, he is—ironically—available for being captured by his Lena (Lena Grove) much as Heyst was captured by *his*. And Byron's decisions from this point are marked by the same waverings we have seen in Heyst, although finally—less deeply shaped by Hightower than Heyst was by his father—he is able to land with conviction on the side of affirmation. Unlike Heyst's father, Hightower is for us a live character whose continuing comments on Bunch's new commitment on the side of action give us an important alternative view. We have also been shown that Hightower achieved his own retreat from living as a consequence of what he discovered of himself and the world during his earlier phase of total engagement. His youthful earnestness in his engagement with his painstakingly chosen fate led him only to a dark recognition of the depravity of his wife, the potential demonism in himself, and the ugly shallowness of understanding in his congregation. So he dropped them all in a total retreat, with a thoroughly worked out philosophic justification based on a Heyst-like condemnation of the inevitable consequences of action: "Man performs, engenders, so much more than he can or should have to bear. That's how he finds that he can bear anything."[9]

All this negation he has thrust upon Bunch as his lone disciple, and when Byron breaks free of this shell of rejection and decides to pursue his championing of Lena actively, Hightower turns on him in moral condemnation, forcing him to acknowledge the likelihood of unworthy motives beneath the claimed nobility of his action. Hightower is shown to be correct in claiming that, once Byron has committed himself to Lena and to hope, he has exposed himself to the self-interest that is the father of all lies, especially the lies that deceive oneself about his good intentions. When Hightower observes, simply from Byron's demeanor, from his carriage as he walks, that he has made his decision and that he has acted, Hightower is cetain that, like any agent, Byron has become the agent of the devil. Although Byron must believe that what he is doing he does for Lena, in order to reunite her with the father of the child she carries, Hightower with justice can see it as a surreptitious attempt to advance his own hopes by displacing Brown at her side. Nor is Byron in a position to deny the charges. By committing himself to action and hope, he necessarily runs the moral risk of doing what he does out of self-interest, whatever the disinterested service in behalf of which he may claim, or even appear to himself, to be doing what he does. Such is the price of his firm and decisive course: all this he "performs, engenders," and all this he will have to bear. That Byron is ready to bear it all, whatever the price, is indicated by his persistence in this course of action, however persuasive Hightower's moral revelations may be.

These revelations of the moral underside of Byron's actions rest on an insight into his self-deception, which prompts him to claim he has decided to do "what is right." Such a claim, of course, assumes, first, that there *is* a universal principle that properly applies to this particular instance and exhausts its possibilities and, secondly, that as the agent, he knows the principle and is applying it appropriately (*and* absolutely). More self-righteously, such a claim assumes also that the agent is sufficiently devoid of self-interest to recognize this principle and to bring it to bear upon this situation disinterestedly, in effect as a *deus ex machina*. It is the human impossibility of living up to such assumptions—or at least the inability to trust oneself to do so—that

9 *Light in August* (New York: New Directions, 1947), p. 283.

justifies the skepticism about all action that we have observed in both Heyst and Hightower.

But, as if in answer to Hightower, Byron Bunch does act: he "performs, engenders," and as a consequence comes to bear "more than he can or should have to bear." But he chooses at last even to bear all:

> It seems like a man can just about bear anything. He can even bear what he never done. He can even bear the thinking how some things is just more than he can bear. He can even bear it that if he could just give down and cry, he wouldn't do it. He can even bear it to not look back, even when he knows that looking back or not looking back wont do him any good. (*Light in August*, p. 401)

But he chooses to bear even the looking back and what he sees re-involves him with Lena and transforms the tragic story of Joe Christmas into the comic ending of the new bastard child on its open picaresque journey on which it is being squired by Lena and Byron. So Byron acts, engenders, bears—and even wins, if only to have to bear some more.

Further, prompted by Byron, Hightower half hounds himself out of his retreat: the teacher is taught by his renegade disciple. For it is he who delivers Lena's child, having been trapped into involvement after he had angrily resisted Byron's urgings to play a hand in the unfolding events. And he feels proud and strong of his midwife's role. Though it is now too late, he even decides to try to save Joe Christmas by lying to give him an alibi for the night of the murder, just as Byron had earlier pleaded in vain with him to do. He is in it all the way. But it is too late for him as well as Christmas, and he dies alone again, though dreaming of another's historic action that had long ago deprived him of the chance for his own.

Now nothing in *Light in August* denies the justness of Hightower's vision of the necessary expense of action—indeed, an expense that does not stop short of moral bankruptcy. But the sins of contemplative inaction are no less. So Bunch may have to bear the expense of acting, knowing how little choice there is and how much less it matters. Action, the commitment to moral (which is to say immoral) choice, *is* possible and—what's worse—necessary after all, though he can be neither proud nor hopeful about any victories it may promise.

Here again we see that, even at its most skeptical, the literary work does not opt for inaction: the completeness of its vision rather reveals how completely inaction too is but a form of action, for which we bear as much responsibility as for any other. Though action remains necessary, then, the work *is* ruthlessly candid in exposing the illusions upon which decisions are based. The major illusion is that it is a rational decision, with competing elements of self-interest and social interests carefully measured: that there are clear measurements available and universal principles against which they can be matched, that we are disinterestedly capable of making the measurements and the matchings, leaving the insidious influences of our underground selves out of it.

An even prior illusion is the assumption (made in fact even if denied by our sophisticated epistemology) that we can behave *as if* we lived under the aegis of a universe grounded in a naive philosophical realism, in spite of what we know after the epistemological skepticism of well over two centuries of critical philosophizing. What we have become increasingly aware of is—at least since Hume—that these universals are our projections rather than external discoveries and—since Kierkegaard—that we impose them upon our chaotic subjective experience in order to make it more manageable, reducing the fullness of vision in order to guarantee the simplicity of living at the decision-making level. One might say that this pragmatic imposition is the price of moral and social sanity, but it is not to be mistaken for existential reality. Yet we reify these universals, treat them as if they existed out there, a priori, and then reduce our experience to make it serve them.

We have observed literary works, in their obsession with the irreducible particularities of ineluctable dilemmas, forcing us to confront the illusory nature of our reified universals and to acknowledge that, in making these invented universals absolute, we have reversed the existential priorities. For these universal principles, as the bases for rational choice, have not been derived from experience but have been interposed as a veil between our experience and us in order to protect us from having to confront that experience in its chaotic particularity. For, as decision-making animals, we must act upon our experience rather than seeking to know it fully, since such fullness of knowledge would inhibit the simplicity of an action in which we can believe. And our egos want us to feel righteous about the acts we perform, lest, like Byron, we face the need of having to bear, half guiltily, the consequences of what we have wrought.

But the literary judgments we have been witnessing, however balanced their vision and self-distrustful their claims, finally do not—if we view them in all their delicacy—constitute a philosophical defense of anti-action, to decision-dodging, to moral paralysis. (It was for this reason that I ended with the modest affirmation, modest but earned, of *Light in August*.) They serve rather as existential reminders of the heavy cost of action and the uncertainties of choice. They thus serve the humanistic objective that forces us to keep the fullness of vision with us as we undertake our versions of action, playing those practical roles which no man—not even the Hamlets or Starbucks or Heysts or Hightowers—can avoid. And the decision once made, the clarity and simplicity of the one act that precludes all competing possibilities are forever established. Our freedom is now foreclosed, and we are locked in. But our humanity reminds us of our need to remain free by retaining the openness and fullness of vision that sees through and beyond the decision that practically closes us in. It will soften the decisions we make and how we make them.

It is here that literature functions for us profoundly. But it functions as literature only to the extent that it resists falling into line as a false particular that exemplifies the universal. It must not ape the clarity and simplicity of the world of practical choice if it is to provide us with the mysterious underside of the surfaces of experience with which action must be concerned: it brings its light and its play to the dark side of the moon. Thus literature must avoid becoming mere rhetoric in disguise, "the will trying to do the work of the imagination." There is enough of mere will and its half-blind, coarse judgments in the workaday world: if it is to serve our needs, literature must resist the all-resolving propositional formula, hovering instead at the level of the contradictory elements which surround particular experience.

The "play" of our profoundest "fictions," those strange versions of an extreme rather than a merely representative casuistry, allows us the freedom to probe within and all around the delicate contours of decision-making. As decision-makers ourselves, we may come to the acute self-consciousness and self-distrust that lead to caution, to the humanizing of the ruthless act of deprivation that subsumes particulars to universals in the act of choice. Since act we must, will this self-consciousness and self-distrust impair our capacities? I think not: what must be lost in pointed vigor is gained in breadth of humanity, however less efficient. For in action thus modified we discover our person and the person of every "other."

Tentative Summary

The full weight of the literary sensibility responds with distrust and fear to the expectations of such a colloquium as ours, even as it recognizes the need to continue making decisions and the desirability of making better rather than worse ones, more rational rather than less rational ones. I list a few areas of this distrust and fear. I am aware that there is a great amount of overlapping among them, that each may be only a different way of saying the same thing. But there is a difference of emphasis among them that I think is worth observing.

1. The literary sensibility distrusts the assumptions behind any hope for a calculus of rational choice, fearing what the agreed-upon objectives ignore about human subjectivity and its caprices.

2. It distrusts any hope for a model process or for generic criteria, fearing that such universalizing of dilemmas denies the radical particularities that characterize every dilemma in its private dimensions.

3. It distrusts any suggestion that the need to err in decision-making should be denied, fearing that to preclude such erring—though error be costly—is to preclude true freedom of choice, of the human need for the gratuitous.

4. It distrusts the projection of universal desiderata as if they really existed (despite a sophisticated epistemology that projects them on the most tentative of operational grounds), fearing that such impositions of commonplace and reductive creatures throw a veil over subjective experience, a veil that disguises the shape of its flowing. For the literary sensibility believes in existence and believes that its immediacies—and not our reductive universals—are real.

5. It distrusts the confidence in one's decision-making that neglects the importance of distrust of oneself as an agent with clean hands, fearing that such neglect leads one to forget that it is crucial for one to suffer from the option of not being able to decide or not having the right to decide, even as one knows that not deciding can be the most decisive choice (and the most risky) one can make.

6. It has a thoughtful reader's distrust of any clear prescription for making a decision, out of fear for the lessons taught by authentic literature (in its uncensored power to reveal the awesome depths of experience) about the inherent damage inflicted on agent and patient by a critical decision-making situation—whether one makes any of the choices or forgoes the act of choosing altogether.

Postscript

I have some afterthoughts, as a result of our discussions, about the peculiar ways in which fictions relate to the openness and closedness of decision-making desires and the decision-making process. I am thinking especially of the claim made around this table that empirical evidence suggests that a subject usually wishes to decide in a way that keeps the decision-making process open. In other words one wishes to keep from deciding ultimately, to avoid an absolute decision that locks one in. It is an element in the un-extreme decision to "satisfice."

The fictions I discuss in my paper clearly insist on the absoluteness, often tragic, of the extreme decision that does lock the character in.

The classical formulation of the Aristotelian fable is precisely of this sort. The lines of probability begin as multiple and fan outward until the climax or turning point, when the alternative conclusions are eliminated, one by one or several at once, and the utter closedness of form, sealing the character's fate, is assured. It is precisely this feature that for Aristotle transforms history, with its loose ends, into the tightness of poetry. The character is not so shrewd as the poetic form that encloses him: he often believes that many freedoms of choice yet remain for him (reflected in the fanning out of alternatives prior to the climax), although the poem itself is narrowing its way toward its and his inexorable close.

Such a plot form emphasizes the transformation of the casual into the causal, the transformation of what seems to be done freely, without commitment and without expectation of necessary consequences, into the interlocking chain of cause and effect which initiates and concludes the deprivation of options. This is just the point I tried to make about Axel Heyst's condemnation of action and his recognition of the necessary doom he has unwittingly set in motion. His initial decision with respect to Morrison is utterly casual, made in the expectation that he can withdraw at once, free from further commitment. Instead, it forces further decision after decision, with ever-narrowing alternatives as the world closes in.

At the other extreme, I might have used the example of *Lord Jim*, in which we have a protagonist committed from the start to seek an ultimate act. But it must be nothing less than absolute in its heroic dimensions, as if to assure him that there need never again be a choice about the direction of his decision-making. But how to recognize the situation which presents so absolute an opportunity for action? When the crucial moment occurs, it does not seem to him quite yet the right one, and he demurs. It is as if he must reserve his chance for the absolute act until that one signal opportunity in the future when circumstances announce themselves as being utterly dire. But of course opportunity does not usually signal; his chance is lost, with the dream of heroism replaced by the reality of cowardice. When, much later and after long anguish, Jim believes he has another chance—one he does not dare miss—he accepts it with a certainty of his death, though for reasons that friend and author alike see as illusory. Despite Jim's commitment to decisive action, the novelist is emphasizing our desire to keep the process from closing at this moment by looking beyond its limited dimensions to a later apocalyptic moment. As his own person, the novelist himself, by transcending and seeing around the problems of his surrogate—the protagonist—manages to have it several ways, thereby putting off any need to make up his own mind.

With such additional complexities introduced into our observation of the decision-making moment, we can understand why the empirical data resulting from thousands of game-theory experiments should be inconclusive, why Prisoner's-Dilemma models—for example—create fictions that, for their lack of contingent detail, fail to describe what leads us to decide what. At the same time the fictions I have been describing portray the fears which our imaginations have about deciding as well as their need to have the fulfillment that comes with a decision firmly made. The ambivalent act or failure to act springs from what we fear as well as what we seek in ourselves as we move in the human world about us.

It is all these crevasses which the cool rationality of recent decision theory must override, and which literary criticism must dwell upon endlessly. Yet I hope that my remarks are not thought to be un-friendly in tone and implications toward this conference and toward decision theory in general; distrustful, yes—unfriendly, no. But I do mean to suggest the risk behind the one decision that is indispensable to our colloquium: the metadecision to seek a theory of decision-making. And I know of no metatheory that convinces me of the wis-dom or unwisdom of such a decision: our attitude toward it may very well depend totally upon our individual or collective "preference maps." My paper argues for the high price of making the decisions we must make; I am suggesting now that the existence of my paper itself, with its skepticism, testifies to the high price of deciding to undertake a systematic study of our subject, and of inviting me to help.

In the paper, I assume the kind of fictional art approved by the aesthetic value structure of that segment of modern criticism with which I associate myself. I trace the development in criticism of the argument that values most highly those literary works which treat existential problems in their full complexity, revealing both the need of a given course of action and of its reverse, and of the high cost of both—high enough to argue against either of them. I use the Kierke-gaardian example and dismiss it: I find it finally unbalanced in its alternatives and the rational persuasiveness of each, and I find that it ends by imposing a resolution as a kind of *deus ex machina*. It is an unearned leap of faith that is an imposition from the outside of the dilemma it so profoundly traces again and again. I turn rather to works which earn their credibility internally without any intrusion by an external propositional resolution. This may, let me confess, mean in the end that no resolution at all can be found, or at least no thematic resolution; for it remains the poet's responsibility to provide an aesthetic resolution.

With these assumptions, the major purpose of my paper is merely to insist upon the function of fictional casuistry to force us to realize the contingencies within a particular decision made under the conditions of extremity. Such contingencies and particularities do not merely fill in our generic models for decision-making, but may very well undo them: (1) they create an equilibrium between alternatives such that any decision leads to futile, and probably destructive, ends —even the decision not to decide; (2) they put the protagonist into the situation of ultimate choice even when (like most of us) he tries to avoid it: he is sucked into definitive closure by what unfolds—as Aristotle puts it—"in accordance with the internal laws of probability and necessity," an inner teleology in which every casual touch is eventually translated into the potentiality of the final grasp. The author wins his freedom by denying the character his (turning the act of composition also into a moral—or amoral—act); (3) the protagonist discovers or reveals to us, in the course of the fiction, the flimsy ground of his claim to being a free moral agent, one who is sufficiently disinterested to identify himself honestly and without self-delusion with a moral universal.

Were there time I could cite an example like that of Melville's *Pierre*, whose protagonist makes a decision that sacrifices everything to serve a moral universal, only to discover that he has been serving his own perverted desires. (And what desires of the author has this decision served?) In such a work the central concern is the consciousness of guilt and what it does to the morally righteous claim. Even the individual Prisoner's Dilemma, as he measures his own fate against that of his confederate, is subject to the literary man's vision that turns it from an experimental model into a condition of moral existence: one's sense of one's own moral duplicity, and that of the mirrored other, affects crucially his sense of his right to be better or worse off than the other, more or less rewarded or punished.[10]

Behind all these considerations is the overriding question about the relevance of such irrationalist cases. I am reminded of a colleague of mine who once said to me, not altogether in jest, that the trouble with all the protagonists modern critics worry about at length is that they are self-important fools: they take themselves and their problems

[10] It now seems to me—in light of the pages that follow—that the series of Prisoner's-Dilemma games, each of which combines doubling with duplicity, reflects the emblem and its epigraph which appear opposite the title page of this volume. Once seen this way, the Prisoner's Dilemma, with its inevitable mirrorings, can become the ultimate, if fearsome, model for fictional creation itself.

too seriously, refusing to compromise as we all have to do, so that the sooner we dismiss them as fools and madmen the better. It is like the teacher I knew in a humanities course who, as his class moved from the study of the *Brothers Karamazov* to the study of *Tom Jones*, rejoiced that they were moving from barbarism to civilization. What we have to decide, really, is the extent to which we must commit ourselves to the healthy and civilized avoidance of the ineluctable in decision-making, what I call the retreat from extremity, rather than the more romantic willingness to acknowledge the significance of the tragic confrontation of extremity. It is a question of whether the vision and awareness made available to us at such great cost to sanity by confronters of extremity produce the indictment of the partial blindness we need if we are to undertake the necessary compromises, the moderations, that allow us to act. Decision theory is an optimist; our profoundest literature is not.

A Playful Postscript to the Postscript; or, a "Satisfiction"[11]

I have, luckily, come upon a document from a source I prefer not to name, which narrates an absurd story that presses these issues forcefully and echoes many of the themes of our colloquium, with its emphasis on game theory models and Prisoner's Dilemmas. I shall, of course, have to be far briefer and less detailed than my source, so that I must ask you to assume that the incidents I am to relate can and need to be fleshed out by your imaginations, the fiction writers in you all. But I must ask you to believe every melodramatic word, and not to suspect a plot.

A young man from an urban ghetto emerges, after a youthful misdemeanor, from a reform school thoroughly reformed. He gets an honest job, marries a decent wife, and—in accordance with a promise conscientiously made to her—forgoes all his former associates and way of life. Their continuing union depends upon his carrying out this promise, and for several months he does so. One day, inevitably, he meets an old friend who at considerable risk had saved his life during a reform-school brawl. For various reasons which I shall not here take the time to specify, the friend is in dire need of his help in a small-time and apparently simple robbery. The friend persuades him (1) that, in view of the exigencies of time and other circumstances, only he can be the needed partner in the crime, (2) that it is guaranteed to

11 I have derived this term from an invented Latinate past participle (*satisfictus*) of that ugly coinage, "satisfice." Having satisficed, I invent this "satisfiction": it should be *fiction enough*. I'll be satisfied if one coinage leads to the doing away with the other, for I can do without both of them.

be a one-shot and minimal risk episode, and (3) that, while there is no question about the friend's right to call upon him in view of what the friend has done for him, the debt will be totally discharged with this single slight payment.

Our protagonist is deeply troubled: he has become too decent a person not to remember that his friend risked his own life to save his, thereby making possible the transformation that has occurred in him and the happiness it has brought. At the same time, of course, he respects the promise made to his wife both for itself and for the possible consequences of breaking it. In addition, he despises for itself the way of life characterized by the act the friend is pressing upon him.

Even in the little time given him for decision, he weighs carefully the risk of deceit and crime on the one hand and the debt as well as the guaranteed singleness and minimal risk of the occasion on the other. His moral perplexity and his responses to it suggest that his very reformation contributes to the moral depths of his decision-weighing and to the painful decision itself. He comes to feel that the risk *is* small, that there would be an enormous relief in being utterly quit of this moral debt from the past. It is as if his rebirth could be completely disencumbered by any trace of the past, which now still falls like a shadow upon him and his new life. We do not know whether there may also have been a fear of vengeance if he failed his friend, so that we cannot know whether, or how much, egoistic motives were mixed with altruistic ones.

On the other side, he convinces himself that the singleness of the episode and its minimal risk would make it most unlikely that his wife would ever learn about it, so that his promise to her—so far as she knows—would be unbroken. So he throws in with his friend, though with grave misgivings. He believes he is, in effect, "satisficing": he is neither being so unrealistically absolute in his commitment to his promise that he forsakes all obligation to his friend (perhaps also risking possible vengeance), nor is he committing himself to a life of crime, since he is to cut off after one occasion. (Of course, I think smugly, this rationalization for his "satisficing" is itself a "satisfiction.") He believes that his current domestic life is optimal, but he cannot adhere to it or secure it on this occasion without compromise. His decision then appears to him to keep more avenues open by resisting the absoluteness of a totally exclusive choice.

Despite the high likelihood of success, the robbery fails and the two men are apprehended after fleeing the scene. The failure was caused mainly by the overcautiousness and uncertainty in our protagonist's behavior, thanks to the incompleteness of his commitment and his anxiety about having made it. The police question the men in separate rooms, trying to persuade each to confess and implicate the other; for the men fled empty-handed and were captured later with no evidence on them. Each is promised his freedom if he agrees to turn state's evidence against the other, provided the other refuses to confess. Our protagonist hesitates not a moment, certain of the mutual loyalty between the friends, and declines to say anything. The friend just as quickly confesses, naming our protagonist as the instigator and thereby earning his own freedom. Our protagonist is sentenced to jail for a lengthy period. His wife comes to see him in tears, is unmoved by his explanations, recognizing only the breaking of his vow and her consequent helpless abandonment, and declares she is giving up on him. He has lost his wife, his freedom, and his way of life upon his release.

He emerges from prison transformed once again, now committed, misanthropically, to the life of an outlaw. After a few successful crimes, he and another partner (working within a criminal syndicate) are apprehended, once again without evidence and once again with each given an opportunity to confess under conditions like those we have met before. Our hardened protagonist this time of course implicates his partner at once. But this new partner has too profound a hatred for the police, as well as too strong a commitment to the syndicate's code of silence, to talk to them. So our protagonist is set free and the partner sentenced.

The partner, furious at being double-crossed, gets word to the Master Criminal running the gangster ring. The Master Criminal claims that such infidelity can lead to the destruction of his crew and so arranges to have our protagonist shot. He decides that it would be easier and more effective for a woman to do the job and, with malice aforethought, calls upon one of his more effective trigger-girls, who of course turns out to be our protagonist's former wife. Desolate and help-less after his initial arrest, she had turned increasingly bitter and—unknown to our protagonist—herself entered the underworld where she has become an increasingly violent criminal. She is told where to be and when and whom to shoot, without being told the identity of her prey since the Master Criminal has given his order in full knowl-edge of what he is doing. When, under the street light, she sees who her victim is as she is about to pull the trigger, she is horrified, mo-mentarily paralyzed by memory and shock. Her former husband is certain that her recognition of him has saved him; but his sudden confidence in his safety so infuriates her that, in a paroxysm of anger, she shoots him, screaming, "Here's your 'pay-off'!"

While she kneels tearfully at the body as he lies dying, she is suddenly joined by a man, tape-recorder in hand, the all-observing Master Criminal (who is also the chief of police)—and a famous experimenter in game theory. (I shall hereafter refer to him as the M.C.) He is aware that he has arranged the entire matter from the beginning and is now anxious to complete the game by recording the inmost responses of this "Prisoner" who has been put through these successive "Dilemmas." Our dying protagonist, now re-reformed, insists, "It was all a result of the decisions I made and of the deceits and bad faith I practiced on others and myself." (It seems to me that he is right.) But the M.C. answers, "No, it was all in my arrangements and my desire to refine my methods. But tell me—" (I interrupt to say that it seems to me that he also turns out to be right.) Our protagonist also interrupts: "If this be so, then, as flies to wanton boys, are we to the gods. They kill us for their sport." Thus muttering, he dies without another word for the scientific record. The M.C., frustrated, responds to the body, "I've heard that before out of fancier mouths, and it smacks of unscientific moralism. You seem to be suggesting that the Prisoner's Dilemma is an existential rather than an experimental model!"

I now believe I see the police arresting the murderer-wife and the M.C., and interrogating them in separate rooms. But I may be wrong. For now I have put myself into the story and have entered the scene as creator-collaborator: perhaps what I see is that it was the wife who fled the scene and it is the M.C. and I who are found and are being separately interrogated by the police. I have been no more honest than he, as I have been pursuing my metagame of fiction about his game of decision making. All the arrangements and manipulations were mine before they were his—and for what questionable moral purpose? Perhaps what I see is both of us in separate interrogation rooms, not at the police station but in the higher court of divine justice where, asking identical questions of us both, heavenly "fuzz" play the metametagame, playing with us about his guilt and mine.

I cannot know, since I am alone in my room (is the M.C. in his?), now that I have finished writing the document which I deceitfully said I found. But I hear a brusque step at the door, a harsh and demanding voice, and the doorknob turns. Thoughts of our on-again-off-again criminal, his wife, the M.C., and my own forged document race through me. I shudder—and turn to face a uniformed intruder.

16

Mediation, Language, and Vision
in the Reading of Literature

I

IT IS A SPECIAL opportunity, and a special challenge—on an occasion
sponsored by The Johns Hopkins University—for me to discuss the
problem of language as mediation in literature, a problem increasingly
at the forefront of recent theoretical discussion. I hope it is not also a
presumption for me to do so. For it is largely through the intellectual
activities that have been going on at Johns Hopkins that theorists and
critics in our country have become concerned about the very applicability of the term *mediation*. This concern opens to a broader one:
the critic is to concentrate on the person and his vision or self-

This essay is comprised of two lectures delivered in April 1968 to the Humanities
Seminar of the Johns Hopkins University, which that year was devoted to
"Interpretation: Theory and Practice." Today, more than a decade later, when the
coordinates within which our critical theory moves have changed so radically, I
would of course alter my emphases considerably. Indeed, the characterizations in
my opening paragraph (and later ones) reveal, in what would be their inaccuracy
today, how profoundly different the positions of some of our leading critics—or our
perceptions of them—have become. Still, the reception which this essay has enjoyed
persuades me that there is considerable value in leaving its original context
undisturbed. It may also be useful for the reader to see earlier versions of ideas
which I develop in the later essays that have preceded this one in this volume.

consciousness that shines through the literary work, in contrast to the previous, New-Critical obsession with the persona and the "impersonal" vision objectively structured *in* the work. This has been the source and has supplied the nourishment for both so-called phenomenological criticism and structuralist criticism as these two movements have—in their different, if not totally opposed, ways—supplanted the so-called New Criticism or contextualism that went unchallenged for so long. It was Johns Hopkins that was this country's forum for Georges Poulet; and it is at Johns Hopkins that we find such productive younger protagonists of these movements as J. Hillis Miller and René Girard, with Paul de Man shortly to arrive as a brilliant reinforcement. No wonder commentators begin to be tempted to speak of the Hopkins school.

Let me admit that I offer myself as a new offshoot of that contextualist movement, now perhaps deservedly displaced among those doing our most adventurous theoretical probings; I hope to find a new life (or at least liveliness) for it by trying myself to do justice to the serious misgivings about language as mediation which critics like Poulet have shown to us all. Surely in these late days criticism can no longer dare to assume the validity or the value of its discrete analyses of literary works, or of its arguments defending the exhaustive study of unique forms as unique language systems. As the person of the poet threatens to undo the persona, so his consciousness threatens to undo the work's telic self-sufficiency: as the person threatens to undo the persona, so his body threatens to undo the word-as-body, so the world threatens to overwhelm the word.

> the modern [poet] either does not acknowledge or does not know a mediator for his orphic journey. He passes through experience by means of the unmediated vision. Nature, the body, and human consciousness—that is the only text.[1]

These words are taken from *The Unmediated Vision*, a remarkable volume by Geoffrey Hartman (recently a close colleague and cohort of Paul de Man). It was fitting that in 1966 this early work of Hartman's was at last reprinted and that it appeared with a freshness that suggested original publication. It was not only fitting but seemed to be a necessary accompaniment to the recent flourishing of criticism directed at denying or overcoming the mediating nature of poetry in order to get us to the thing itself. Indeed, in view of all we thought we had learned since 1954 (its original date of publication), and from

---

[1] Geoffrey H. Hartman, *The Unmediated Vision: An Interpretation of Wordsworth, Hopkins, Rilke, and Valéry* (New Haven: Yale University Press, 1954), p. 155.

more recent European writings, we surprise ourselves with the reminder of its date and of its being composed by a young American
scholar (though by one clearly indebted heavily to European sources).

We may remember also that our recent fantastic, Norman O.
Brown, in his Neo-Freudian apocalyptic plea, *Life Against Death*,
recognized in kinship that *The Unmediated Vision* was a revolutionary work of criticism which bypassed the word for the body. He saw
that, for Hartman, the poem is no longer to be conceived as "other" or
as object; it is to be absorbed into the poet's (and, ultimately, the
critic's) self as subject. In the modern world, now bereft of all mediation—of the Christian miracle in which Word did become flesh—
there can be no verbal text for our study; instead, "the only text," as
Hartman tells us, is "nature, the body, and human consciousness."

It is just the notion of the poem as object, as an "insensible It,"
that—by way of reaction against it—impels the anti-critical crusade of
Ihab Hassan, literary follower of Norman Brown. Despite differences
between the European phenomenological tradition behind Hartman
and our native irrationalist, anti-establishment radicalism, this connection between Hartman and both Brown and Hassan reveals them
serving a similar tendency to deobjectify and repersonalize literature.
The similarity deserves to be noted, as it has not been, for it points to
a common need in our theoretical climate. Neither Hartman nor
other phenomenological critics are likely to travel with Hassan to the
logical extreme of maintaining that action, rather than contemplation, is a "legitimate response to art" once a presence—not depersonalized—has replaced the coldly viewed object as the stimulus of
that response. But one might well claim that such an extreme is a
proper consequence of those aspects of the neoromantic theoretical impulse which they share.

These attitudes toward literature, seemingly revolutionary to those
of us who grew up under the unchallenged dominance of the would-
be classicism of New-Critical analyses of discrete poems, achieve their
force and the momentum of their influence through their being a
moving alternative to that criticism. Ever since the earlier revolution
in the academy effected by the New Criticism, the abundance of discrete critiques in our books, our journals, and our classrooms has
prompted the wearied cry "Enough—and too much." So convergent
has been the focus on the discrete work that we must have expected, as
an inevitable humanistic reaction, the impatient demand to have literature returned to the humane matrix that fosters it and is in turn
fed by it. As critical method, fed less and less from a source of theoretical justification, seemed more and more to feed on itself, it multiplied its increasingly mechanical operations and its consequently

lifeless products. The living body of the poems it dealt with was made more and more into a corpse: the critic's role, no longer the humanistic one of renewing the vitality of our verbal heritage, was becoming the pseudo-scientific one of post-mortem, dissection become autopsy.

There has, then, been the inevitable reaction against this sort of critical establishment by those determined in their own ways to restore life to literature, to reassert the critic as midwife instead of as coroner. Some would destroy criticism itself by opposing mediation: by seeing its mediating function and the mediating function of poetry as suspect, as precluding life, draining that life from an object left on the dissecting table. This attack on criticism as it is restricted to single works is an attack on the objective hopes and disinterested pretensions of the critical exercise. Under attack here is the detached critic—the critic as analyst and judge—the critic coolly operating a mediating (meddling) enterprise. Distance between the critic and the work is to be destroyed as that which replaces human response with dehumanized analysis: distance creates the space for analysis and, consequently, the claim to a would-be scientific objectivity. But the critic's destruction of space or distance can be accomplished only by his following the precedent of the poet, who must be seen as destroying the distance an "impersonal" theory of creation would impose between him and his work. If the critic (or, rather, anti-critic), thus dedicated to process rather than product, must deny the distance between the work and its author, then poetry, too, comes to be seen as the enemy of mediation, of the mediating nature of language. The poem is at war with discourse as mediator. The poem is that paradoxical discourse dedicated to denying its own nature. It is to transmit immediacy, obliterating its own presence, a presence that threatens to deaden immediacy by freezing its dynamic flow into a static object. Instead, the work melts into an instantaneous union of "unmediated vision," shared among work, author, and critic, an undemarcated flowing of the vision among the three. And the spectacular—even apocalyptic—breath of life returns to inspire, as it rehumanizes, our traffic with literature. Thus it is that the central and detached concern with the object as a self-defined structure comes to be rejected because of its flight from the human contact with the object, the human contact that not only comes before and after the object but becomes the object, by merging with it, giving it its life.

The attack on the mediating properties of poetic structure and of the critical language seeking to fix that structure has taken several forms. The so-called phenomenological critics here and in Europe, perhaps most extremely represented by Georges Poulet, who, as Hillis Miller has shown us, is not really phenomenological at all—such critics (let us rather call them critics of unmediated self-consciousness) blur the work into the author's consciousness and ours, substituting a pulsating "interior distance," as subjective as human time, for the flat contours of spatial form, searched out by conventionally "formalistic" critics. Poulet's conception of form as static and dead—as objective—makes his anti-formalism explicit. The disregard for the single work as a discrete whole, as well as the impatience with the critic who painstakingly fusses over such works, must follow—and normally does. The "human" and the "interior" must be made to prevail over the scientific and the fixedly exterior if the vitality of literature is to be ever renewed instead of once and for all stifled. The results of such studies are brilliant, spectacular, even at times persuasively luminous —but not finally very transferable. They superciliously bypass the function of criticism as an educating process. Poems about poems, they impress the imagination more than the understanding.

A visionary critic like Harold Bloom has an even more open disdain for the discrete critique. Behind his treatment of the individual author (all of whose works constitute a single corpus) is an all-unifying, monolithic, transcendent vision that absorbs all works and their authors into itself. The breath of meaning, issuing from the organic life that moves these visions and makes them one, can be received only as we merge work with author (as creative imagination), merge authors into a "visionary company," and merge all with the sublime vision. Again the objective, as impersonal, as distanced, is rejected in the romantic denial of space, the romantic explosion of distinctions.

Ihab Hassan, we have seen, looks toward another sort of neoromantic apocalypse, an unmediated breakthrough to body from which the Word is finally excluded. The flesh, then touched in its immediacy, can dispense with the falsely metaphorical illusion that claims the Word-become-flesh. And, when the re-won bodily realities of our instincts can rush in, the middleman of art need not—nay, dare not—enter. The writers who celebrate this "dismemberment of Orpheus," Miller and Beckett and a host of younger novelists, create an anti-art, an anti-word, directed at the extinction of art, at total silence.[2]

To a great extent, then, the attack upon the poem as object and upon criticism as discrete analysis is an attack upon word-worship, upon the mediating function of language and our willingness to settle

[2] See Hassan's "The Dismemberment of Orpheus: Notes on Form and Antiform in Contemporary Literature," in *Learners and Discerners*, ed. Robert Scholes (Charlottesville, Va.: University Press of Virginia, 1964), pp. 135–65; "Beyond a Theory of Literature: Intimations of Apocalypse?" *Comparative Literature Studies* 1 (1964): 261–71; *The Literature of Silence: Henry Miller and Samuel Beckett* (New York: Alfred A. Knopf, 1967).

for the medium, for the empty carton with its generic label. It is also an attack upon form-worship and upon the entire post-Kantian mood of our criticism of the last century and a half. What mediates subjective experience for the more aesthetic of us is not so much mere words as the special forms created by words, the order-producing impositions that become fixed, static objects. In molding chaos, in taming outrage, in directing chance, in rendering the casual into the causal—in other words, by converting all the raw materials of a no-longer-mediated human subjectivity into the willed perfections of Aristotelian inevitability—humanity has allowed the formal impulse (licensed as an act of freedom by Kant, Schiller, and many who follow) to end by destroying human freedom. For it destroys the subjective freedom of the random, of the unstructured, of the indeterminate, in its service of the formal impulse that was to allow the person, as human, triumphantly to transform the subjective into the objective, thereby redeeming the irrational within himself. But, with its formative impulse, the human is seen as betrayer of its free person.

The formal and classic, then, must come to be seen as stasis, that which arrests the dynamics of temporality in the deadness of shape, of spatial thereness. The still classical *Stürm und Drang* antagonism to Lessing's *Laokoön*, for all its promise of freedom of mingling among the arts, ends by freezing literature into sculpture. Time's jagged unpredictabilities are rounded into place. This may have been enough for Kant and Goethe, Schiller and the post-Kantians—indeed it was their grandly humanistic dream—as they tried to replace the divine mediation by Christ with the human mediator, now granted divinely creative powers. But the modern, with a more radical sense of human freedom, negates them as Mann's Leverkühn negates Goethe's Faust and "takes back" the human hallelujah of Beethoven's *Ninth*. The very formative categories of Kant are rejected in the return to the unformed continuum of the raw "given."

Such a temperament views poetic form as the mediating element, as that totalitarian force that everywhere subdues the wayward to its overwhelming autotelic purposiveness, thus delivering death to our subjective freedom. For form, being contextual, ought to involve the rigorous marshaling of words, the systematic transformation of all that comes to it from without into the "new word" within, whose totality of definition is constituted by its every serving part. All indeterminacies are rendered determinate under an irresistible Hegelian functionalism. The all-unifying human imagination, our gift from Coleridge, and the Kantian and post-Kantian tradition behind him, has, like God, conquered chaos, has used its *fiat* to make it order.

But this sort of human god, imposed by Kant, Goethe, Schelling,

Coleridge, or even Nietzsche upon a world no longer mediated by the divine-human paradox authored by the true God, is for Hassan or the early Hartman an inflated phantom bent on depriving the fleshly creature of his newly won freedom from the word, that presumptuous surrogate for body. His body, which he knows in its instinctive immediacy from the inside, no longer need yield to an outside transubstantiating authority. If God, author of mediation, is dead, then the man-god should embrace the truly autonomous, unchartable freedom of the immediate rather than try to impose his own mediation, his own ersatz cosmos in the microcosm of the poem. For the entire notion of cosmos, of microcosm and macrocosm as mutual reflections, is seen as existentially obsolete, whether God-made or man-made. Thus Hassan, looking at the (to him) false mediations of an outmoded literature that seeks perfect speech instead of total silence, characterizes such language as a series of equations which his apocalyptic prophet must shun: language equals sublimation equals symbol equals mediation equals culture equals *object*ivity equals abstraction equals death. As point-by-point apocalyptic alternatives, silence (as the identity of nothingness and the indiscriminate, chaotic all) has as its equations (instead of sublimation) indulgence, (instead of symbolism) flesh, (instead of mediation) outrage, (instead of culture) anarchy, (instead of objectivity) subjectivity, (instead of abstraction) particularity, (instead of death) instinctual life. And the anti-poet, who writes his "anti-book" for the anti-critic with his anti-aesthetic, cultivates the accidental, the indeterminate, the "unstructured or even random element in literature," refusing to absorb it into the authority of form, insisting on its persisting on its own out there, radically autonomous in its caprice, as testimony of its and our own capricious freedom, nurtured in the gratuitous act. Hassan himself tells us that "Apollonian Form finally becomes Abstract Authority" (with the capital letters their emblem of Abstract Authority). From here we can see his Dionysian alternative lurking. True life, in its chaotic subjectivity, has regained its primacy over the trim lines of art. Indeed, art is to obliterate itself into the unmediated terrors of existence, into the rites and mysteries of the orphic act. Orpheus, then, is to aid in his own dismembering. "Imitative form," which is—as Yvor Winters taught us—no form at all but a dissolution into the formlessness of raw experience, yields up all aesthetic pretensions to wallow in the mimetic surrender to human darkness. The *Dunciad* has indeed become the *Inferno*.

I have given myself perhaps too expansively to dealing with Hassan, since I have granted that he is immeasurably more extreme than our more influential anti-mediators. I thought it worth doing because in him I found the neoromantic impulse against the formal or mediating principle in its purest form. It should be helpful with the less immodest claims of more subtle minds. As a matter of fact, Hassan himself, in his moments of retreat, of recognition of the not-altogether-abandoned poet, is such a more subtle mind. He can at times see the artist's need forever to turn on himself, finally to make even the random element somehow *his* random element, the anti-book somehow part of his total (and totally absorptive) book. Thus the act converts to intellectual gesture. Hassan himself can intellectualize even to this extent:

> Literature recoils from the withering authority of the new Apollo, but it does not surrender itself wholly to the frenzy of Dionysus. It only *feigns* to do so. It employs self-irony and self-parody, as in the novels of Mann and Camus; it develops, as in the works of Beckett or Genet, forms that are antiforms. . . . Literature, in short, pretends to a wordy wordlessness and participates in the Dionysian denial of language not with its own flesh, but with the irony of its divided intelligence.[3]

This is a long way from Hassan's more extreme justification of total silence as the last refuge of "the freedom of language to seek some purposeless and indeterminate antiform," or of a language that "becomes indiscriminate, random, fluent beyond words" in its dedication to its "outrageous vision."[4] His more balanced view that has the poet resist total identity with Dionysus in a turning upon himself allows for the poet's turning of the anti-book into *his* book. And, of course, this is a reintroduction of aesthetic mediation.

As such it would quite satisfy me as a critic dedicated to return at last to the poem as an object, though enriched by what those suspicious of the mediating nature of language have revealed about the death-threatening tendencies of the word. The would-be objective critic, who wants to defend his art against the skepticism of the anti-mediators by meeting it head-on, must begin by agreeing about the paralyzing consequences of mediation. He, too, must be suspicious of discourse as a mere medium, that which by definition precludes immediacy and which by its action freezes all flow. But, having shared the visionary critic's distrust of the medium, he must yet try to exempt poetry from its deadening powers. Having condemned mediation, he must yet save poetry. He can accomplish this only if he does not deny the poem as object, that is, only if he does not force an immediacy in the poem's relation to its creator by collapsing the poem into con-

---

3 "The Dismemberment of Orpheus," pp. 148–49.

4 Ibid., p. 162.

sciousness or vision. To make the poem a special object, one without
the object's deadly there-ness, its spatial "fix," he must be prepared to
ask, "When is a medium not just a medium? How can a medium be
free of its pre-destined curse of mediation?" And he must be prepared
to earn and to believe his answer: "When it can be the thing itself,
holding the dynamism of flux in its coils." For the poem as discourse
and thing is motion and is in motion. Yet it is motion in stillness, the
stillness that is at once still moving and forever still.[5]

All these are theoretical problems, steep and troublesome. As such
they demand something beyond the unquestioning, blithe pursuit of
discrete explication, the sort of explication that in its late days helped
create, and justified, the anti-objective reaction which now demands
that we take such theoretical troubles—or else abandon to the vi-
sionaries the maintenance of literature as a live art and act.

The theoretical task is easier when the opposition to recent criticism comes from those who would overmediate, those whose impatience with the tentative delicacies of analysis leads to crude
interposings. For the tentative delicacies of the critic are his responses
to the uniqueness of his objects, his efforts to fit his discourse to ever-
new systems that defy his common measures. And it is this uniqueness
—the critic's tribute to that unmediating medium, that space-eluding
object—which the stubborn overmediator cannot wait to pause over.
We have seen that, even if the critic must resist yielding to the anti-
mediator who bypasses all form for uninhibited subjectivity, he still
must try to preserve the special life of his object by fighting for its
immediacy, for the medium *malgré lui*. But the overmediator is finally
willing to freeze his object by spatializing its form, universalizing it by
absorbing it into common formulas—models—broader than the work
(or, in cases, broader than literature itself). This sense of the model is
what is placed between the work and our private response, shaping
both work and response to our awareness of that model. The deadening effect upon work and response is almost enough to send us, by way
of reaction, to the dynamic vitality of the anti-mediator, except that
we know of that danger too. But we know we must not surrender his
sense of life to paint a frozen model.

When we sweep aside the recently fashionable language of structuralism with its models, we find the very instinct for universalizing
the individual work which lay behind the pre–New-Critical attitudes,
whether socio-historical or biographico-psychological, the instinct

[5] I expand this idea in my essay "The Ekphrastic Principle and the Still Movement
of Poetry; or *Laokoön* Revisited," *The Play and Place of Criticism* (Baltimore: Johns
Hopkins Press, 1967), pp. 105–28.

which made the New Criticism necessary. The unregenerate over-mediator, who preferred to learn nothing from the contextualist revolution, sounds pretty much like those who preceded that revolution, as he tries to adapt the work to extramural commonplaces. For example, the social concerns of Walter Sutton, which move him to keep the lines between literature and culture at once, continually, and broadly open, are not markedly different from the pre–New-Critical concerns which led Ransom, Tate, Brooks, and others—by way of reaction—to make their defense of poetry several decades back.[6] Against such arguments as Sutton's, based as they are on the failure to grasp the organismic assumptions, the New-Critical defense is still valid, although there is now the need to deepen its theoretical basis and extend its theoretical consequences.

Other more subtle forms of overmediation also threaten to preclude the criticism of the poem as a unique language system. They all have their attractiveness to the extent that we cherish the encyclopedist's pretentious hope of unifying our knowledge and our languages. (Nor should we give up the encyclopedist's universal dream of a logocentric utopia, except grudgingly.) But the cost to literature as authentic discourse is high. The structuralist—a Lévi-Strauss or a Jakobson—runs the risk that the peculiarly literary will slip away when poetic structures, general linguistic structures, and anthropological structures come to be juxtaposed, not only as analogous, but even as homologous. Again, the methodological issues may not finally be very different from those that brought the New Criticism into existence. It is just this fear of the overuniversalizing, overmediating tendencies of such latitudinarian structuralism which moves sympathetic observer-participators like Michael Riffaterre and Geoffrey Hartman to their critiques and qualifications.[7] These latter suggest structuralist efforts that would preserve the uniqueness of the poetic structure and resist the adaptation to generic models; but they would appear to abandon the distinctively structuralist ambition and would pose no real opposition to contextualism.

Another variety of structuralism—René Girard's—combines it with something very like Poulet's method of bypassing mediation, as we see the extremes (of anti-mediation and overmediation) meet. In

6 See Sutton's "The Contextualist Dilemma—or Fallacy?" *JAAC* 17 (1958): 219–29, and "Contextualist Theory and Criticism as a Social Act," *JAAC* 19 (1961): 317–25. See my comments in "Contextualism Was Ambitious," *The Play and Place of Criticism*, pp. 153–64.

7 I refer to two important essays in the "Structuralism" double issue of *Yale French Studies*, no. 36–37 (1966): Michael Riffaterre, "Describing Poetic Structures: Two Approaches to Baudelaire's *les Chats*," pp. 200–242, and Geoffrey Hartman, "Structuralism: The Anglo-American Adventure," pp. 148–68.

his conclusion to *Deceit, Desire, and the Novel,* Girard finds that all novels end by becoming the same novel: he uncovers at last the "banal" structure hidden in the common conclusions of all novels.[8] But the structural uniformity is a uniformity in the discoveries of self-consciousness in that the single conclusion creates its conversion by having the protagonist at last turn upon his mediator, so that in the end all barriers, all mediation, between the vision of a character and his author (and, as Poulet would extend this, between the author and us) are destroyed. A single pattern creates an always similar break-through in which distinct entities merge into instantaneity and identity. Anti-mediation is found to be the single structural model for the novel. Perhaps Girard can serve to remind us that Poulet himself, for all his anti-formalism, for all his anti-mediation that suggests anti-structuralism, may strengthen the structuralist impulse by his methodological monism. His work always seems to lead to the glorious identity of consciousness shared by reader, poet, and work, to the collapsing of the distinct categories of time and space in the instantaneous union between every critic and author. The very overcoming of mediation becomes a universal principle of writers, each of whom moves toward becoming Mallarmé or Proust. Or, finally, there is Northrop Frye, who, like the structuralist, works from a model, though in his case it is restricted to a model literary universe; but the overpowering shadows cast by his many-faceted monolithic structure upon the little lonely work have by now often enough been lamented. The overmediation often shrieks its impositions, even as it excites us with the monolithic set of forms which structures the common human imagination and its common human dream.

Whatever the alternative critical attitudes that have followed upon the criticism which emphasized discrete analyses of poems as objects, these attitudes have been taken up in part as a reaction against that emphasis; but they have not removed the need for such a criticism and have not overcome the arguments in support of this need. Whether the anti-contextualist proceeds from the desire to destroy the poem as a mediating object by seeing through it to the poet's immediacy, or from the desire to destroy the poem's immediacy by burdening it with universalizing mediations, he has not precluded the need to preserve the object as at once object *and* immediate.

But we have noted also the extent to which these responses have been generated by failures within the New-Critical movement and by a flagging of its theoretical impulse to justify what it was doing. Its

---

[8] *Deceit, Desire, and the Novel: Self and Other in Literary Structure,* trans. Yvonne Freccero (Baltimore: Johns Hopkins Press, 1965), pp. 290–314.

evangelical mission to save poetry dwindled into the Sunday sermon, moving routinely from text to text. It is this explication for explication's (and ingenuity's) sake that late defenders of criticism must not resort to, must move beyond. If Frye's totally absorptive system is seen as too universal, causing total deprivation to the singular, the critic of the discrete must resist the mere compilation of isolated perceptions as part of an endless bill of particulars. This critic must at least move back to the world from his internalized systems: what has turned inward must at last, and in a special way, open outward; the mutually reflecting mirrors (to borrow a metaphor I have used elsewhere) must be transformed to windows that capture a newly visioned reality. The "new word" that is the poem, still fully released from what the old words had been, yet returns to our common language to enrich it by renewing its powers of reference. And the critic must help, not only in defining that new word, but—perhaps more crucially, if less easily—in tracing its return to its culture and language, illuminating as it goes. If the critic stops with mere explication of the system, if he does not return it to its subtle function in the world of reference, its redefinitions of language and of vision; then he may be sure that his own role will be usurped by the impatient non-contextualist, who will open the language of the poem outward at once and without taking pains, who will make it serve the world of reference in a vulgar way that deprives poetry of those special powers which the critic of the discrete poem should be dedicated to serve and preserve. And he will deserve to be replaced.

It may very well be that only by his taking the theoretical issues very seriously can the critic prevent himself from succumbing to the myopia which his endlessly attractive objects induce in him. He is obliged, at considerable pain, to convert a terminal experience of a self-sufficient object into an instrumental occasion: he must ask "why?" and "to what end?" even as he accounts for the "finality" that asks no more. Again we see it is his double need, the need to see the paradoxical poetic medium at once as immediate and as that which mediates the general meanings of the world beyond. At stake is the nature of language generally. The poet may subvert that language, words in their general naming function, but only to save and serve the possibilities of *his* language, a language created *pour l'occasion* out of its own general incapacities. This is the stuff of which the rarest of dreams, of visions, are made—the rarest since, in their ultimate immediacy, they are not transferable, can occur nowhere but here in this work. And this work at once denies the power of its words, and yet, by its very being, denies that denial.

Sir Philip Sidney, in his *Astrophel and Stella* (considerably more than in his *Apology for Poetry*, where he more properly might have done so), often confronted this very problem of the uses and limitations of language as the poet must find it and refine it. Perhaps nowhere does he manage this confrontation more explicitly and more brilliantly than in "Sonnet 35" ("What may words say, or what may words not say"), a poem which I have treated elsewhere in detail.[9] In conclusion here I should like to use it only as a sort of allegory of the argument of this paper. For the movement of the sonnet springs (as its first line tells us) from the poet's awareness of the absurdities of language in its normal uses: his explicit distrust of language-as-names yields a special sort of anti-nominal system.

The poem proceeds under the reasonable control that produces and sanctions a series of outrageously irrational compliments, all governed by the initial confession of the incapacity of words. The paradoxes that follow are made up of words colliding with themselves in a desperate flight from meaninglessness. With reason itself supervising the process, the operation of language has been undermined by the perfection of Stella which outdoes all reason. Yet the unique immediacy of her presence, having negated language, has become its own language—the language of *this* poem—which has transcended the emptiness of a language that functions only as mediation. Out of the mutual blockages of language, then, the poet has broken through to his own language, with meaning newly restored out of the accumulated verbal wreckage of conventional meanings. Further, such a language comes freighted with its rarities of vision, although I cannot pursue them here. Poems like these give us access to immediacies of consciousness as perhaps no other object does (and I say "object" pointedly now, seeing the object in its dynamic freedom).

Is our sense of language or of vision ever quite the same again? "What may words say, or what may words not say" indeed! By denying that words can say anything, these specially empowered words can say it all. My argument has been that it is clearly the role of criticism to listen closely to such words, hearing and overhearing all that they can affirm and deny, and neither to obliterate them in search of wordless vision nor to move through them to the stereotyped visions we had before this configuration of them, this poem, came along. And, while it listens this closely, what many things must it clearly become and continue to be the function of criticism to say? Dare one have the temerity to propose more precisely than these vague notions of mine

9 See the opening essay of this volume.

suggest? In the second part of this essay I shall try to dare. But you will rightly remember that most theorists have uttered such fond hopes before, so that you will not expect too much. And I fear I may give you no more than you expect.

II

Through diverse critical traditions, through many centuries in the history of criticism, the veil has appeared as a metaphorical equivalent of the aesthetic symbol (a variety, perhaps, of the garment figure, although it lends itself to far more ambiguous adaptations). The mediating character of art has thus been implicitly recognized as it has—through the veil—entered the very vocabulary and primary conceptions of the critical theorist. And the ambivalent attitude toward the role and value of the veil, in its relation to whatever reality was claimed to be behind it, is clue to the ambivalence of attitude toward art's mediation itself.

It is all part of the problem—as old as criticism—concerned with the opposition between particularity and universality in art. Or, to convert to more theological terms, it is the opposition between the sensible and the intelligible, the earthly and the transcendently spiritual. It is the problem of the sin, as well as the saving virtue, of art, Augustine's concern over Dido slain, the awesome question that asks whether art, as particular embodiment, is an avenue to heaven or an earthly drag that blocks our upward path. Is the symbol the incarnate thing (i.e., spirit) itself, a substitute needed by imperfect man in his need to find a sensuous equivalent, or is it a perverse substitute for which man in his lowliness lusts, as an obstacle he places in his own way? Is it a sacred effigy of the true God or a profane idolatry? And so the several Platonisms, neo-Platonisms, and anti-Platonisms have wrestled with one another through the centuries.

As orthodoxy and heterodoxy struggled through the Middle Ages and Renaissance to find a satisfactory formulation of the role of art, the fortunes of the veil (as synonym for art) fluctuated: now it was the false mediator, purveyor of illusion, of distortion, the obscuring element; now it was the indispensable threshold to the absolute—pure transparency itself. Thus it could be restricted to its frustrating function as replaceable surrogate in the thinness of allegory or it could be expanded to the rich double life of another sort of allegory offered by the typological *figura*: both the pointer and that to which it points, which it bears immanently within itself. But in neither case was there any question about the ultimate reality of that universal, transcendent realm, whether the veil is that which obscures it or is our sensuous access to it.[10]

It is not to be unexpected that, with the revolutionary inversions of the secular world in these last centuries, reality eventually is transformed into the irreducible particulars that are swept along in the flux of experience. This fluid reality is now seen to be veiled by the false, non-existent universals projected by our anti-existential need for mediation. So, as particulars and the universal exchange places, the concrete sensuous "given" that formerly functioned as veil now is in *its* turn veiled as the universal is revealed as a fraud invented for our comfort. After all, one cannot make an ontology out of the projection of universals by the Kantian categories without anthropomorphically blundering into things-in-themselves; and the universals can claim no further metaphysical authority, no matter how heroic an imposition they may be by man, who in his quest for sanity refuses to surrender to the chaos of sense data. Kierkegaard extends this Kantian notion— after Hegel's vainglorious attempt to restore the illusion of final reality for these universals—to the existentialist extreme of denying all ontology, affirming only subjectivity, only the particular as absolute. Thus the veil of false universals now becomes the veil of Maya, seen by Schopenhauer and Nietzsche as the agent of will which the Bergsonian T. E. Hulme calls upon poetry to strip away. Poetry, then, becomes the anti-mediator, destroying the mediating universal. Kierkegaard had denied this possibility—as his condescending distrust of the aesthetic kept art within the universal, refusing to allow it existential immediacy. For Kierkegaard insisted on the formal incommunicability of the unmediated, accepting it as being by definition incommunicable, as beyond language. He is only a little more denying than Georges Poulet was to be, Poulet who (as we saw in Part I, above) finally must get beyond the aesthetic even if he does not quite go beyond language—which is where we saw Ihab Hassan bring us.

A principal aim of the first part of my essay was, similarly, to establish that the universal, as the spatial, is the mediator, hence is the veil, but—in contrast to Poulet—to put the aesthetic symbol on the other side, as the correlative (hopefully objective) of unmediated particularity. Though it is itself a final object, yet it is to be intimately related to reality as existential and to be differentiated from the universal in experience and language even as the existential itself is.

Let me recapitulate: I granted that the phenomenological and

---

[10] The role of the veil in medieval and Renaissance theory is usefully and effectively traced in Katharine E. Gilbert and Helmut Kuhn, *A History of Esthetics* (New York: The Macmillan Co., 1939), pp. 149–72.

existentialist manners of constructing our world of experience in its immediacy require us to distinguish in our experience between the existential as unmediated and that selection from the existential (in accordance with some principle of order) which creates the universal as the mediated. I granted further that our anti-objective existential quest might lead us to transfer this dichotomy between the unmediated and the mediated—between consciousness and its objects—in our experience to a similar dichotomy in language. If we did, we could emerge with poetry as a language of "human time," of "interior distance," a subjective, anti-formalistic celebration of the instantaneous flight that bypasses all mediation, with the rest (the frozen world of fixed objects to be related to one another and speculated about) left to the non-poet. Thus the critic involved with unmediated self-consciousness can allow distinctions in experience to reflect themselves directly in language: there is either the language of objects (mediated) or the language of Cartesian pre-objective consciousness (unmediated), the latter seeming to be almost an abdication from language as well as an abdication from the formal obligations of poetic discourse. But can language do no more to bridge the gap, language released from its normal bondage? What could a total indulgence in language allow that a total abdication from it would not?

Given the distinction in experience between unmediated and mediated, can we rather distinguish in our language between the poetic (contextually conceived as unique systems) and any other (systematically propositional or ordinary), claiming that only the poetic has access to the existential, from which the latter has removed itself by its generic nature? But, it can be argued by the critic of unmediated self-consciousness, the poem also is a form and formula, a fixed object that in its frozen state incapacitates itself from capturing the immediate. It, too, occurs in a medium and, hence, it is mediate rather than immediate and thus is subject to the anti-mediator's rejection of it and flight from it. Such an argument can be answered, as I tried to answer it in part one, only by referring to the paradoxical nature of poetic discourse, which thus becomes at once the source and mouth of meaning, at once a fixed form and yet, through its dynamics of interrelations capturing stillness in movement, attaining objective immediacy. It thus converts into a medium that is at war with its role, language that subverts the normal behavior of language in order to attain the character of sacred communion which symbolism has lost in the secular world.

So at least the argument goes that would seek to recover the poem as object without having it forgo the existential immediacy that the contextualist, no less than the anti-mediator, must seek to keep within the poem's unique domain. The veiling function of poetic language, so long viewed ambivalently, is now seen as systematically ambiguous, if not downright miraculous. But the heart of the problem remains, since all we have been offered is a verbal mystique that cannot pretend to be a solution. In what follows I shall see if I can press these issues further.

The very formulation of the problems would seem to preclude our progress. Once we adopt enough of the existentialist stance to distinguish firmly between the immediate and the mediate in experience, how can we hope to capture or transmit the immediate in the mediate forms of language? Does not the very use of language carry with it the abandonment of the immediate to the extent that we commit ourselves to our symbolic systems? How can we justify our belief that our symbols can do better? There is, then, the "given" in experience in its immediacy, and there is the fixed object. How can the latter embody the former without losing the former's existential immediacy? That is to ask, how does the "given" in experience find its way into the vision of the whole work considered as an aesthetic form, a spatio-temporal moving finality?

I am aware that, at a time when "visionary" critics are in the ascendancy, I cannot use the word *vision* as my central term without trying to set off my sense of it from the sense it has commonly been earning—especially when I see the force of its common meaning as separating it from the work's totality even as I try to identify the two.[11] I must see the work not as a projection of a pre-existing vision, formed in the self behind it, but as a dialogistic entity that comes into being out of the dramatic conflict of forces and of language which constitutes its finished form. Thus it was that Leo Spitzer used "vision" as a pre-aesthetic category that characterized how the author saw rather than how the poem meant, reserving his aesthetic claims for what became of vision when the whole went to work on it by becoming a "work." Though in the spirit of Spitzer, I prefer to use "vision" for what comes out rather than for what goes in.[12]

But it is the construction upon the "given" which creates the forms of a vision that creates, and is created by, its form. So we, too, must begin once more with the "given." In my book *The Tragic Vision* I

11 Perhaps it is for this reason an error for me to employ the term *vision*, and indeed I might have searched for an alternative had I known when I began *The Tragic Vision* what the contemporary and subsequent use of "vision" was to do to it.

12 Leo Spitzer, "*Explication de texte* Applied to Three Great Middle English Poems," in *Essays on English and American Literature*, ed. Anna Hatcher (Princeton: Princeton University Press, 1962), pp. 193–247, esp. pp. 216–19.

began with the common assumption that our routine (which is to say pre-tragic) existence depends upon the universalizing veils (that word again) that our social and moral necessities force us to hold between ourselves and the brawling chaos—the jumble of unique instances—that is out there (and within us) ready to show its Manichaean face to any who dare thrust the veil aside to look. And it is that forced confrontation of extremity—the unpalliated series of ineluctable consequences which practicality normally persuades us to shun—that creates the tragic existent and sets his tragic course on its way.

If we assume, then, the existential immediacy of the Manichaean face of reality as irreducibly there for the stricken existent, we assume also the multidimensionality of the unique particularity of this experience, now viewed without the universalizing veils that comfort automatically imposed. In its particularity this experience is thus inaccessible to the reducing or abstracting habits of our usual linguistic apparatus, of our rational—or at least propositional—responses which we have so well and universally learned. In its uniqueness (instantaneous because it is not just an instance, but an instant) it resists all but its own unrepeatable, flowing, unadaptable self. It is surely utterly closed, shut off, because nothing else is like it; nothing else can explain it, its conjunction of impossible co-ordinate or simultaneous aspects. But—and here is the Bergsonian paradox—it is also and at the same instant utterly open, because, being instantaneous, it is not even an entity; rather, denying itself any discrete instance, it flows into all other instantaneous non instances and has them flow into it.

Well, then, inner experience is impervious to language, and we are trapped in the linguistic shadow world of the subjective critic of unmediated self-consciousness (really observer and voice-catcher more than critic), in the manner of Poulet, the commentator who tries to match his introspective, impressionistic language to the elusive structures of mental experience before him. We have more than once noted his necessary antipathy to form as the objectifying enemy.[13] Such a literary observer tends to see an unavoidable dichotomy in the options open to all literary observers, so that each must choose either the

---

13 I refer again to that most helpful and precise description of distinctions among critics of this sort in J. Hillis Miller, "The Geneva School," *Critical Quarterly* 8 (1966): 305–21. Miller carefully traces the differences in the ways they play off the counterattractions of consciousness and of literary forms. Perhaps, in both parts of my essay, I have made my task too easy by choosing as my representative of the Geneva school so extreme a critic as Poulet, whom Miller shows to be the most Cartesian (hence anti-phenomenological) and most anti-formalistic of the group. The less anti-formal, of course, are also less representative of the distinctive character of this critical mode.

subjective or objective aspect of the work.[14] For Poulet, the literary work is the representative of the author's thought if we but conceive this thought as physical place, a home for its constituted objects. Thus conceived, the work, like the thought, may seem to those of us not attuned to interior distances to be related most obviously to its objects, those things of the outside world which it presumably is *about*. Being most obvious, this relation gives rise to "objective" criticism as the most usual sort. But the work, again like the thought, with those entities which it houses so commodiously, is related more crucially, if less obviously, to the thinking subject, the self that has "redisposed" those objects, now newly created by mind. This "interior distance" between subject and his thought or work, thus conceived, and the redisposition of the objects in accordance with the housing demands in this inner space, is the less obvious but more urgent sort of criticism which must be practiced if the study of literature is truly to be humanized. It thus brings to light the hidden, dark side of the moon, the Cartesian *Cogito*.

But we cannot help but notice that, in his open anti-formalism, a literary observer like Poulet too easily disposes of all formal matters by ranging them on the side of the "objective" features of the work. This is to assume that formal features are of the same order as the external objects that thoughts or works presumably are *about*. But surely formal features, internally generated, cannot be reduced to external objects to which thoughts or works would seem to the naive critic to refer, objects which—to use the most naive notion—they would appear to "imitate." In his one-paragraph preface to *The Interior Distance*, Poulet blandly sees the "objective aspect" of literature as including "formal" elements (by which he seems to mean only generic elements, the "contours" leading us to "poems, maxims, and novels, plays") no less than what we have learned to call the referential elements, "accounts" or "descriptions" of "objects." And he promises to turn from both to the subjective side. It is a promise he keeps all too faithfully.

But if, in this reduction, he disposes of all formal matters by placing them indifferently with what we used to call objects of imitation as equally "objective" features, then perhaps he should be reminded to "redispose" his notion of form (as, after Mallarmé, he sees the mind in its "interior vacancy" redispose its world of objects) to

14 The most useful statement of the claims which follow occurs in the preface to Poulet's *The Interior Distance*, although I believe that, assumed rather than stated, similar claims underlie many writers in this "school." Again I refer the reader to Miller's essay "The Geneva School" for important differences among these critics which I am forced to blur here.

make it (as our best critics have made it) more than flat categories so dully externalized. Must we choose between the ineffably subjective and the naively objective? If so, are we not being too unsubtle? The external object does not stand in the same relation to the poem as that poem's form does, unless we are restricting ourselves to what has long been an obsolete eighteenth-century notion of form as universal generic mechanics. Clearly, as such it is too flattened out and externalized ever to have a vital existence, ever to do more than deaden through abstraction the particular living work to which it was to apply itself.

What else has literary criticism tried to do since Coleridge and before, except to work toward a notion of an organic form which would enable us to talk formally about a work without adapting it to stale generalities, but finding instead a form that is uniquely its own, expressive of its own unrepeatable characteristics? What else have these two essays of mine been about? This effort has led to examinations of the special properties of poetic discourse, its ways of meaning, which can permit it to open vistas of vision which normal discourse, by its very nature, seems determined to shut off. I have been pressing myself to show how the literary medium, though still only the words we all, like Hamlet, despise most of the time, manages to free the subjective, even while freezing it into a permanent form, to make the poem an *immediate* object rather than a mediate one. For, if the medium is at war with itself in literature, if language refuses to serve as it normally does, its struggle serves the higher fidelity to language that shows him who can master this extraordinary medium how thoroughly it can master the most inward folds of our experience. But still, though a medium rendered immediate, a poem's language works to make the poem an *object* and to that extent external and communicable—and in need of more than subjective observation. The dark side of the moon *is* what we are given, but the firm mastery gives it to us in a way we can hope to secure—for ourselves and others. It is a formal way, though of course "formal" here has so many other-than-formal elements in it if we restrict the term to the archaically formalistic meaning Poulet at times reserves for it.

All of which returns us, but I believe newly armed, to the matter of vision and the way it gets into literature. For I have meant to be claiming throughout that we need not see our inner experience as being, after all, impervious to all language once we remember the inward immediacies that our great poets can force their language to embody. Suppose we begin with the special sort of "given" which I saw the tragic vision assuming about moral experience, and suppose we can characterize that "given" in its extremity as unadaptably unique, at once an indissoluble lump among innumerable other equally autonomous but dissimilar lumps in the stream of chaos, yet at the same time the stream itself, always becoming but never having become, and thus never hardened to lump; then we have begun by seeming to put such a "given" and such experience beyond the generic, freezing powers of language. We can recall my remarks concerning Ihab Hassan's assault on the word, his fear that subjective "outrage" may be fatally compromised by culture's dedication to a mediating "object," with the consequence of abstraction, death. For him this is the necessary and only consequence of the word and its order of beauty, since he does not allow language to be tortured into an object that preserves immediacy and existential vitality, an object that for all its fixed eloquence can preserve a discursive silence. For him, as we saw in the first part of my essay, language must be either eloquent or silent: eloquent in its service of an object for culture (thus violating our "outrage"), or silent in its obedience to outrage (thus deserting all objects).[15]

But I must go further, in order to qualify our fears about the existential incapacities of language, by acknowledging that we have been speaking only of the "normal" powers of language, so that we may find a very abnormal series of possibilities in the history of our greatest literary works.

The subjective flow of the self's awareness of its experience must somehow be preserved, even while being preserved in a fixed object. The death-dealing immobility of the spatial impulse must yield to the dynamic, moving vitality of the temporal, while yet creating that which must persist in an unchanging form: I maintain this need despite those newest critics who claim—against all objectivity—that dynamism must be retained in the ever-changing vitalism of our responses to our inner experience. Despite all that contemporary personalism and existentialism have taught us about objectification (the making into things) as the murderer of the unique, I would want the critic to claim to have found in the abnormalities of poetic language the one way of having his object without surrendering the immediacy of its data.

There is in the work, as in the "given" of the experience, both the instance and the instant or even instantaneous, with the strange etymological and semantic coincidence of opposition and identity between these: the absolute and irreducible instance, which demands

---

15 I repeat what I said in the first part of my essay: that it is undoubtedly unjust to couple Hassan with the Geneva school and its followers, but the dialectic of my argument calls for them to be seen as united on this issue.

discreteness, a continual awareness of and pausing over the boundaries that constitute it as discrete, cutting it off from all that is not
itself; and the absolutely instant or instantaneous, which denies the
existence of bounds, of the entity-hood of the moment, in order to get
on with the movement, the flow of the moment becoming the next
without pausing to be marked. It is the role of poetic discourse to
undo the generic tendencies of discourse generally, and so to complicate its context with contingency as to create that language context as
its own unique body. Moving dynamically in time, the poem must yet
become transfixed into a spatial form.

Hence what I have elsewhere termed the ekphrastic principle becomes the poetic principle in that it invokes "still movement" (in
both the Keatsian and Eliotic senses of "still") as the special grace
with which poetry is to be endowed.[16] The critic's job is to locate (as
it is the poet's job to produce) the spatial orders within the temporal:
the circular principle within progression; the freezing principle
within the free flowing; the emblematic as the ekphrastic within that
which resists all spatial fixity; the multiple reflections of a mirrorized
world of internal relations within a seemingly semantic and syntactic
set of relations which, like all language, wants to open outward
toward all other language and its referents; the causal and yet—or
therefore—the casuistic within the casual; the logical within the
chronological; the still recurring within the still moving; the extremities of experience within the compromising muddles of the uncommitted middle. To the extent that our discourse seeks to follow its
nonpoetic, natural (which, paradoxically, is to say conventional) paths
—its "naturally" conventional paths, as it were—it seeks either to be
casual and free (in its unsystematic modes) *or* to be causal and frozen
(in its non-poetic systematic modes). The poet must have it as both at
once: he must create the language as *his* medium by fostering in it the
multiple capacities that transform the word into terminal entity,
body, effigy, emblem, even as it clearly seems to function in the semantic and syntactic ways that words have as their wont. So the "given" is
found in the work, preserved in its density and contingency and not
reduced to any conceptual formula, yet preserved and intact by being
an utterly formed object once and for all for one and all. It has a form
but is not a formula after all, is constitutive but not conceptual; that
is, it gives the forms for our reality but not concepts about it.

If the poem, then (as, alas, all too many poems do), should reduce
itself—as the straw-man formalist (attacked by Poulet) would have

[16] I refer once more to my essay "The Ekphrastic Principle and the Still Movement
of Poetry."

it—to fixity and only stand still, it would reduce itself to the frozen death of the spatialized discourse of non-poetic systems, losing the empirical dynamism of movement, the flowing vitality of experience in its subservience to universality, that Platonic archetype that levels particularity. But, if the poem should do the reverse, if—as a Poulet would have it—it should be still moving only in the sense of always moving, giving up the paradox of unmoving movement at the heart of the stillness of the Keatsian urn, then it would deny utterly its character as object in an unqualified yielding to the boundless, ceaseless flow of our experience; and we are no better off for art, an art that has given over all in worship of imitative form, form that decries form and cries for formlessness in imitating a formless welter of experiences.

My use of the term *vision* has been shown to be systematically distinct from that of our admittedly visionary critics who seek, in the literary work, signs (often related to signs found in other works) of the author's grasp of his reality as that constituted reality relates to the grasping self. For I seek no vision behind or before the work, though I do seek the vision that comes to be created in the work, *as* the work.[17] Perhaps, to borrow a tired notion from Eliot, it is that the visionary correlative I seek is objective, not subjective, although the fact that it is objective makes it no correlative but the thing itself. In its concern with vision my study is still within what I have called *thematics*, by which I have meant the formal study of an aesthetic complex which becomes more than formal because the complexities that it unifies, as unresolved tensions, reflect the tension of our pre-propositional and extra-propositional experience.[18]

If, unlike Poulet, I insist on the work—for all its elusive subjective churning—as an object, I nevertheless share his fear that the dead hand of objectification can destroy its unique voice by adapting it to alien structures or classes. But I believe I voiced my anti-structuralist, Crocean antagonism toward the *over*-mediators sufficiently in the first part of my essay.

If my argument has persuaded us to define vision only in terms of

[17] In Coleridgean terms, I seek in the work a direct reflection of the secondary imagination, which in its workings with language I must claim to be discontinuous with the primary imagination, "the prime agent of all human perception." Instead of merely being an "echo" of the primary, the secondary "dissolves, diffuses, dissipates" our reality as envisioned for us by our generally constitutive power, the primary. Coleridge uses both descriptions to make up an almost contradictory characterization of the secondary imagination. I choose to see only its character as creator, not that as echo.

[18] See *The Tragic Vision* (New York: Holt, Rinehart & Winston, 1960), pp. 242ff., for my original definition of *thematics*, together with a discussion of the consequences of that definition.

the unique work that constitutes it, we still must seek a more precise description of how that work achieves that unique vision, its objective formulation of all in the "given" that in its dynamics resists formulation. This is to ask, how does the infinitely variegated flow of experience achieve an aesthetically transcendent unity? In the midst of experiential chaos, endlessly divisive, we look, as desperately as Gerard Manley Hopkins did, for an aesthetic inscape that will satisfy our thematic craving.

> All things counter, original, spare, strange;
>> Whatever is fickle, freckled (who knows how?)
>> With swift, slow; sweet, sour; adazzle, dim;
> He fathers-forth whose beauty is past change . . .

Of course, as secular theorists we allow the miraculous metaphor of poetic incarnation to substitute for his theological Word made flesh. We resist Hassan's impulse to obliterate the word in order to embrace the flesh directly, unmediatedly. As I have argued elsewhere, figuratively (that is, in terms of the *figura*) the Trinitarian paradox is the very model of the poet's furthest claim for metaphor as transubstantiating miracle, with its union-in-duality of tenor and vehicle [19] So there is the aesthetic need and the thematic need to freeze experience in order most fully to feel its flow. With the subjectivity of experience behind and beyond, the work must be created formally as its emblem, a total object; and the work must be created existentially as its vision, the very word *vision* bestowing upon the work the spatial fixity of a thing seen.

How, then, is the poet to play the casual casuist? How is he to realize and master the muddled flow of the confused center of our experience through an aesthetic-thematic symbol? I speak of our experience in its subjective confusion as the "center of our experience" because it resists the purity of definition, the a fortiori clarity, of the polar extremes. Experience at its hard edges is no longer confused, though in its extremity it is not where we dare live it unless we are to become polar creatures, tragic existents, ourselves. For, as my examination of the tragic vision was to have demonstrated throughout, the existent cannot embrace at all costs either pole without having it transformed into its antagonist (as, for example, in the relation of puritanism to sensual debauchery in many works in this thematic

---

[19] My book *A Window to Criticism: Shakespeare's* Sonnets *and Modern Poetics* (Princeton: Princeton University Press, 1964) rests almost wholly on my attempt to demonstrate the contextually sustained metaphor as the secular substitute for a theologically sustained transubstantiation; see esp. pp. 200–204.

genre). Better the safe sanity, the ethical probity—if the visionary blindness—of the inconclusive, compromised middle.[20] But the poet dedicated to aesthetic resolution has to unmuddle the middle through a casuistic play that leads him to summon up and cultivate the extreme. However uncommitted existentially, however aesthetically committed to dialogue alone, he vicariously nourishes the extreme. His method of capturing the extreme (and, with it, all the impurities of the middle he has bypassed and yet, like the alchemist, distilled) is that of converting the endlessly variegated muddle into the terms of his extended metaphor for it. The critic's hypothesis of the work's form is his best guess about what this extended metaphor is, based on all in the work which feeds it.

The repetitive patterns of a work, which give stillness to the movement by freezing freedom, must be read by the critic into his hypothesis of the work's form, as he makes it a reductive metaphor—an emblem, a constitutive symbol—for all the moving life and liveliness of the work. The metaphor, while excluding so much of the middle in its reductive, extremist purity, is in its emblematic fullness at the same time all-inclusive. The hypothesis tests itself by its capacity to account for every aspect of the work, aesthetic and experiential, which is stuffed within it (if it is not being imposed by the over-anxious critic). At once puritan and catholic, the reductive metaphor must gather within itself the all of middle existence which it passes by in its pursuit of extremity, as it must gather within its holistic form the varied possibilities sloppily assembled in its tenor. Thus it becomes exclusively all-inclusive—at once existentially (or thematically) and aesthetically (or formally).

It may be helpful at this point for me to quote at length from my extended discussion of the reductive metaphor as both single and double, closed and open, in *A Window to Criticism: Shakespeare's Sonnets and Modern Poetics*.[21]

> The author plays the casuist, dedicated to extremity, by committing himself in the work absolutely to a reduction of one sort of experience to another, to a transfer of properties of one to those of another, a transfer to which every element in the work lends itself totally. Experience of a normal sort—messy, pre-poetic, of mixed and uncertain tendencies, veering in this direction and in that,

---

[20] This was the anti-tragic, anti-Dostoevskian, anti-Kierkegaardian plea which the late Philip Blair Rice saw Thomas Mann making, a plea for experience of the center rather than experience at the polar extremes. See Rice's "The Merging Parallels: Mann's *Doctor Faustus*," *Kenyon Review* 11 (1949): 199–217.

[21] *A Window to Criticism*, pp. 209–13.

impure in its continual compromise with the totality of definition—
is viewed under the aspect of an extremely delimited sort of experience that threatens, momentarily, within its context, to reduce
all experience to itself and to read life within its own awesome
terms as unbearable and—to a common-sense reason that needs life
as mixed—as irrational, even impossible.

Thus, in Mann's *Doctor Faustus*, for example, all forces lend
themselves to reveal the generally accepted world of artistic dedication and controlled artistic creativity exclusively under the
aspect of the world of disease, to reveal the world of decent austerity
and harsh asceticism exclusively under the aspect of the world of
license. But the total transfer of properties, the total reduction,
is deceptive. The terms I have used in my hasty oversimplification
of these worlds should indicate that even as the extremes are
poetically equated they remain polarized. In furnishing us a very
paradigm of the functioning of extremity, Mann allows no mediation between extremes, but forces one to support the other, even
to reflect the other, finally to become a mask for the other. Mann's
extreme necessarily bears its opposite within itself by the very
nature of its seemingly singleminded purity. The ill-defined, mixed
components of the life he deals with follow the path of their most
dangerous tendencies to extremes that are at once polar and reversible, opposed and identical. For the equation of the two worlds,
the reduction of one to the other, becomes a substantive metaphor.
As such it turns on itself, asserting for common sense the duality
of its terms, the distinctness of their properties, even as it works the
miracle of transubstantiation. Everything in the work—character,
incident, language, style—contributes to the collapsing of the broad
and mixed world to the narrow and pure one and thus to the
creation of the work as a total metaphor, except that, even as the
transfer becomes dramatically complete, the separateness of elements asserts itself to our rational, less totally committed selves.

I could go on from *Doctor Faustus* to discuss the reductive metaphors, at once transubstantiating and skeptically self-denying, in
others of the novels I treated as fully tensional bearers of the tragic
vision. For example, we can too briefly characterize Gide's *The Immoralist*, in which all forces lend themselves to transfer the drive to
assert the freedom of the self from the bonds of ethical restraint to its
appearance exclusively under the aspect of a total enslavement to the
senses. Or Malraux's *Man's Fate*, in which all forces lend themselves to
transfer the ethical drive to merge the self with social betterment to its
appearance exclusively under the aspect of the demoniac drive to the

violence of uninhibited self-expression. Or Melville's *Pierre*, in which all forces lend themselves to transfer the moral devotion to well-meaning self-sacrifice to its appearance exclusively under the aspect of a total perversion at the service of monstrous desires. Or Kafka's *The Trial*, in which all forces lend themselves to transfer the amoral routine of *quotidien* existence to its appearance exclusively under the aspect of blind and unmitigated, moment-by-moment guilt. Of course, the half-innocence in K.'s stumbling half-pursuit, his essential ignorance, proclaim the absurdity of this absolute transfer of properties even as they help us marvel at the nothing-left-out character of Kafka's contextual inclusiveness that allows him to "work" his metaphor. But so it is with all of these and other examples. Always the transfer is complete; the "aspect" under which we are forced to see *is* imposed exclusively. And yet, and yet . . . the polarities rebound; the muddled center reasserts itself; despite our utter captivation by the Word, our sensible selves skeptically reassert the recalcitrant world that resists all transfer and insists on doggedly, dully remaining itself. Still, the magic is never quite dispelled. We have it and we do not, we believe it and we do not, are hypnotically trapped and yet move freely in and out.

I now return to the passage from *A Window to Criticism*:

I see Mann's version of extremity as a paradigm that allows us to consider the poet's casuistry more broadly, so as to turn it into a generic literary strategy that can serve us with lyrics as well [indeed, even more easily, thanks to the obvious manipulation of devices of control in the lyric. Recall my comments on *Astrophel and Stella* 35, with the transfer of categories between the particular breathing lady and personified abstractions of universal virtues]. To use another obvious example . . . I can cite Donne's lovers in *The Canonization*, whose absorption by earthly love—which is shown in its normal state to be woefully mixed and incomplete in its nature— we are forced to view under the aspect of the total and unworldly dedication that earns sainthood. Everything in the poem, in the fullness of its contextual interrelations, works to bring off the equation, to complete the metaphor in its transfer of properties from tenor to vehicle (from earthly lovers to saints), even though the tenor and vehicle seem opposed to one another. Nevertheless this step-by-step extension of the metaphor carries along with it the covert guide of rationality that asserts the absurdity, even the speciousness, of this extension. It is not that the identity produced by the metaphor is being denied, since such a denial would lead us outside the context and its mutually dependent terms, but that the miracle can be asserted as miracle only by continually recognizing its impossibility, by continually acknowledging the intransigence of the materials and oppositions being mastered, though they are never destroyed.

Such a miracle of substantive identity should of course not be viewed as a propositional truth claim (*A* is *B*) any more than it is a dramatic demonstration of a propositional moral claim (*A* ought to be *B*). With its context totally working to create it, it is rather a total and totally committed incarnation, an effigy of mixed and intransigent experience which has been substantively transferred into, or rendered within, an extreme, unmitigated reduction of one pure and narrow aspect to whose sway all cooperates or conspires in order to make the transfer complete—even as the miracle asserts itself as such by urging an awareness of its denial. Like Shakespeare's Phoenix and Turtle, like my mirror and window, like the *in* and the *through* of contextualism, but perhaps most like Clarissa's scissors which the baron manipulates in *The Rape of the Lock*, the miraculous metaphor divides even while it joins. [That miraculous poem itself works, like the scissors, to divide as it joins, if we consider how thoroughly it creates its vision of the heavy prosaic world of flesh and blood under the aspect of the airiness of the pure world of absolute play.]

In its simultaneous performing of its dividing and joining functions, its opening-out and closing-in functions, the dual nature of the extremity that leads to miracle—but a special sort of miracle at once assertive and denying—can correct an unfortunate overemphasis that has for good reason bothered students of recent criticism. From Aristotle onward, critics, in insisting on the unity of the literary work, have insisted upon its convergent movement toward a unitary, sharply pointed conclusion and conclusive meaning. The *Poetics* traces, in the development of the literary work, the gradual, inevitable elimination of the multiple probabilities with which it began until, when the climax turns the complication into the dénouement, only the one way that—though hidden to us and to the protagonist—has been inescapably there all along is left and is pursued to its end. It has been hard to improve upon this classic formulation in its convergent simplicity. Thus it could not help seeming dangerously perverse to find recent critics [perhaps our best or most extreme example here would be William Empson] rather emphasizing almost exclusively the divergent meanings of literary works. While also insisting upon unity, they dwell upon the *organic* nature of that unity, upon the *variety* which is being unified. They celebrate the ambiguous instead of the unilinear, the unresolved tensions among centrifugal forces instead of the crowning assertion of the all-dominating centripetal force. At their more reckless moments they may seem to be claiming for the work no more narrowly unified a precision than that of a shotgun blast. And yet they have on the whole been persuasive about the many voices with which even an apparently simple poem may often speak. I am suggesting that literary extremity and its miracle, with the completeness of their absorption of alien, resistant, and incomplete materials together with the completeness of the unbridgeable separateness of these elements, can allow for the combined emphasis on the divergent and convergent natures of literary movement and meaning, the density and plenitude on the one side, the rarity and the order on the other. It can insist on the centrifugal thrust of a work only while placing its control within the pressing and uncompromising union of its finest and most centered point. The impossible combination of identity and polarity can make a total view of the object possible: the perspective is reduced to a single point even as, at the same time, the range of possibilities multiplies endlessly—thus the consequence of the object as both single substantive world and as bodiless reflection of multiple worlds beyond.

The reductive metaphor can in its closedness open an *im*mediate access to reality's figures, which is to say the way reality becomes "figured" for us, "figured" in the double sense of Auerbach: at once the concrete symbol of the single instance, instantaneous, and—while holding to this character—the *figura*, its ultimate human meaning for us, its allegorical representativeness that exceeds itself, but only by thoroughly being itself. Hence we come upon the vision, but not any vision that pre-existed the work in an individual psyche or in a culture's *"humanitas"* or in a normative structure held in potentiality for individual entities to fulfill; rather the vision that is attained figurally by cutting so fine a verbal figure *as* the work. Yet it *does* become the culture for the moment and for the minds that so constitute it metaphorically. The extremity of total transfer, of metaphor, becomes window to the reduced moment of vision which characterizes the reality created for a culture (created *as* the culture) by its most symbolically gifted seer-makers.[22]

22 See my discussion of Eliseo Vivas's terms, "subsistence," "insistence," and "existence" (from "The Object of the Poem," *Creation and Discovery* [New York: Noonday, 1955], pp. 129–43), as I try to relate the poetic context to the existential context in *A Window to Criticism* (pp. 59–63, 214–15). "For it is this metaphor, this total substitution, that allows us to see what an historical moment, in the privacy of hidden, personal inwardness has, in its most daring creations, in the

The hypothesis of the work's reductive metaphor thus becomes the formal opening to the work's existential vision. All of its directionless (because all-directional) experience, all of its "dappled," "pied" beauty, utterly ungraspable, is reduced to the emblematic unity that enables us to grasp its movements in a vicarious moment of vision. We are given this way (which neither precludes nor contradicts other ways) of seizing upon it as an entity we may perceive in its discrete entity-hood. It neither precludes nor contradicts other ways, because it gives us no propositional claim about the experience, a claim that, in its logic, would cheat that experience of its uniqueness and integrity by making it serve a universal law, reducing it to cipher, an enslaved particular that is therefore particular no longer. Instead, the metaphorical, visionary grasp gives us the particularity which the *poiesis* helps us to see as *one*, but as no more than one and as translatable to no others. Thus the metaphor, as the formal enabling cause of our vision, its source and its mouth, in the self-enclosure of its extremity, resists all propositional extrapolation, its persistent drama countering every would-be propositional claim with its antagonistic anti-claim.

The very reductive and yet all-embracing nature of the metaphor claimed by the critic's hypothesis must shout the rational denial of its absolute nature, the denial it bears within itself. It must force us to see nothing less than an identity between the muddle of its tenor and the pristine extremity of its vehicle. But the equation it proclaims as a self-enclosing metaphor it must proclaim in awareness of our skepticism. To be metaphor it must insist on the miracle by which things change their nature, become other than themselves, their substance dissolving into other things. It must, with the unrelenting tightness of a total aesthetic control exercised with equal pressure everywhere within its domain, create the vision that sees the messy center of our experience *becoming* its own purified reduction at the hard edge. For our vision it assumes a guise that alters the thing itself, thus proclaiming, however irrationally, the destruction of discrete entities, the blurring of the bounds, the limits, that create the property and propriety of entity-hood. Thus it achieves the fullness of capacity that (in the late Sigurd Burckhardt's terms) corporealizes itself and so attains the totality of definition of metaphor.

But, despite all such seeming magic, discourse—even poetic— remains only discourse, no matter how bent it may seem to be on subverting its own common nature as an open structure that leads us in and out, relating to other discourses and to the world that comes

---

total metaphors of its single, reduced moments of vision, dared to make of its world."

before and after all discourse (or so we assure ourselves in the naive realism that is our common sense of how things go with us). And we, as prosaic users of discourse (even as we are the victims of the subversive perfection of its involutions in poetry), stubbornly retain the openness of our relations to it and the world, persisting in an anti-Kantian confidence that sees us and our world as pre-existing our symbols. So there must be that in the poem which we find comforting to our anti-aesthetic resistances, our recalcitrance to the miracles of language fully, if too trickily, endowed. The poem's patterned turnings upon itself end by allowing a part of us to turn on *it*, or to turn it against its most contextual pretensions. Our more rational selves find hidden within the poem, for all that would make it a new word, the comforting assurances that our sense for distinction and for property —which is to say propriety—may yet be preserved. It is nothing less than the comforting assurance that it all has been but a verbal game; and we try to set at rest that apocalyptic challenge to make the word into the Word, which is to say the fleshly world.

But of course this challenge, so persuasively urged by the closing, all-reducing action of the all-inclusive metaphor, still remains to possess us. This is to say that the rational covert guide that threatens to undo the mask by revealing it as no more than mask undercuts the miracle of metaphor by proclaiming it not as equation but as miracle, with all the inspiration of awe—and of skepticism—which the notion of miracle engenders. It is no fact; it is no proposition; indeed, fact and proposition flatly deny it. It is but an *im*position upon our vision, sanctioned only by the daring leaps sponsored by the delicate play of language. As no more (but no less) than miracle, it can be held only in the teeth of all rational denials. For it goes without saying that, if we can believe in it as a rational possibility, it is no miracle. By definition its very existence for us as miracle depends upon that part of us which knows it cannot happen—except in a way that passes understanding, an understanding we cannot altogether yield up.

Thus it is that, even as the enclosing metaphor captures the motley variety of experience's soft center within the hard edge of its extremity, thereby reading all of life within its own closed visionary system, there is something else at work in the countermetaphorical motion: in the skeptical denial that restores distinction (that restores our sense of duality where there are two entities), there is an opening outward beyond the miracle (the metaphor, the work, and the world of its words) to the world we know and what that world refuses to permit. An ironic self-doubt arises from the state of dialogue in the work that comes to terms with itself and yet, on the sly, proclaims itself as play; this self-doubt finally can lead even beyond the still-limited visionary dialogue of the single work to the ultimate catholicity of vision that is the proper end of the contemplative life.

The expansion of consciousness I have been urging, the dual awareness, the dialogistic sense that returns with a furtive openness to what has been closed, sealed off, may seem to echo the claims for the anti-poem of neoromantic critics like Hassan. Let me remind you of this more moderate passage of his which I quoted in the first part of my essay:

> Literature recoils from the withering authority of the new Apollo, but it does not surrender itself wholly to the frenzy of Dionysus. It only *feigns* to do so. It employs self-irony and self-parody, as in the novels of Mann and Camus; it develops, as in the work of Beckett or Genet, forms that are antiforms. . . . Literature, in short, pretends to a wordy wordlessness and participates in the Dionysian denial of language not with its own flesh, but with the irony of its divided intelligence.[23]

If Hassan would concede more to what closed form can permit, this might seem a helpful way to indicate the Janus-faced character of the work. Its very closedness, its absolute commitment to its metaphorical reduction, its compression into its constitutive symbol, into its emblem—all are accompanied by its prompting our common-sense denial that dissolves its miracles and drags it to earth. All poems must covertly contain their anti-poems, must transcend themselves and their closed limits, transform themselves into *genera mixta*. I quoted earlier my claim that my argument must reconcile those traditions which characterize poetic form as convergent (as in Aristotelian unity) or as divergent (as in Empsonian ambiguity). The centripetal emphasis on an exclusive unity and the centrifugal emphasis on an inclusive variety, simultaneously asserted, are further reflections of the strange commingling of openness in the aesthetic closedness of the literary object. I mean to remind you here of my discussion of the paradoxical coexistence of openness and closedness in our discrete experience viewed at once as instant and instance.

I move on, in conclusion, to suggest some existential consequences of these claims. The extreme situation is that which, forgoing the ameliorations of the center, forces confrontation at the edge; but the existent who would confront is also the creator of the extreme situation. Buried in this circularity is the notion that the mess in the soft center of our experience is a mess that most of us have to create in order to muddle ourselves and preserve our sanity, to keep going as

---

[23] "The Dismemberment of Orpheus," pp. 148–49.

social animals who do not want to look too deeply into mirrors or into another's eyes. Our pursuit of endlessly diversified experience, veering in its infinitely various and self-aborting directions, our blunting the points we have sharply shaped, our lurching and starting and slowing and gliding and leaping, by turns, all are ways we hide from confrontation of what we dare not confront. As in Kafka's *The Trial* we must accept the ambiguous duality of K.'s having been seized for arrest gratuitously *and* K.'s having chosen the state of being arrested, so in this literature generally we must acknowledge both that extremity is there beckoning for him who would cast off all palliative veils to dare confront it and that extremity is a creation of those so willful as to choose the confrontation. The visionary courage—which is to say, the metaphorical courage—of those whose fear of blindness will not permit the diversion of their confronting impulse must be matched by the self-conscious insanity that forces them to wrestle—and to watch themselves wrestling—with casuistic phantoms instead of joining the rest of us in the center, going round and round in the dizzying dance of life. As we stop to look at them as our surrogates, if we observe closely enough, we find their struggle—combined with their consciousness of struggle—to have the purity and perfection of ballet. After such a vision, with what self-consciousness, with what new and corrective sense of our aimless heavy-footedness, do we return to make our motions?

17

Literary Analysis and Evaluation—
and the Ambidextrous Critic

I

EVER SINCE the critical revolutions we usually trace to T. S. Eliot and
I. A. Richards, theorists and practical critics—despite their self-
conscious methodological concerns—have often confounded problems
of description and problems of prescription, problems of fact and
problems of value. On the one hand there is the "reading" of the
literary work, the analysis or interpretation of it; on the other hand
there is the judgment we make of the aesthetic worth of that which we
have laid out. But this two-handedness, with its sensible division of
labor, has often been blurred into a confusing ambidexterity. Theoretical neatness may lead to an analytic separation of function; but
the limits have—and often profitably—been overrun in practice. Per-

This essay is an expanded version of a paper read to the General Topics I
(Poetics and Literary Theory) Group of the Modern Language Association in
December 1967. This session, concerned with the relation of literary value to
literary interpretation, consisted of position papers by Northrop Frye and me. I
have not here significantly altered the essay published in the volume which grew
out of that occasion. Although the central issues of theory have changed markedly,
the lines of the dialogue as they existed for Frye and me then seem to me still to be
worth pursuing.

303

haps only the rigorous apriorist, too dedicated to his trim lines of logical distinction that experience defies, need lament. But I must not allow my own judgment of these theoretical issues to intrude itself until later.

From the beginnings of that increasingly antique movement we have been calling New Criticism, the very definition of what we call poetry—as well as our attempt to define that single work before us— has been tinged by value considerations. Have our critics been asking, "What are these things one [anyone?] calls poems?" or rather have they not really been asking, "What had these things better be before we honor them with the title 'poem'?" On single works have they, like the scientist, been asking, "What is the nature of the workings of this entity before me?" or rather, like the prepossessed guardian of the heavenly empire, "What are its obligations to work in given ways for me if I am to allow it entrance?" As humanists, we should have to be pleased that such questions are not kept rigorously distinct, as we confess our inability to restrict ourselves to the first kind, the strictly descriptive.

Even someone as obsessed with the hegemony of scientism as was the early I. A. Richards could not allow his devotion to the supposed facts of neurology to overcome his greater obsession with the varying worth of poems, those supposed neutral stimuli of responses—stimuli, however, that turn out utterly value-ridden before he is done with them. We can recall his desperate attempt, in *Principles of Literary Criticism* (1925), to disdain any departure from the quantitative—his desperate attempt, that is, to reduce all poetic value to poetic response and to reduce all poetic response to response in general: to the num- ber of neurological impulses being aroused and satisfied, or at least sustained. How fervently Richards derided the most modest qualita- tive suggestion; how ascetically he remained faithful to his Ben- thamite calculation, refusing to proceed beyond his neutral (neural) quantitative analysis. But, alas, how self-deceptively he was at each crucial point seduced into happy inconsistency by his own critical powers as sensitive reader.

So, as he argued from the number of impulses (and of opposed impulses) organized in the reader to the stimuli in the provocative object, he enabled himself to distinguish between poems organized (as he put it) by inclusion and poems organized by exclusion, finally determining that those works controlled by irony had their inclusive- ness so expanded as to become poetry "of the highest order." And, contrary to his descriptive and psychological intentions, he was led to objective discriminations among the features *in* poems, features that are irreducibly aesthetic. How short a step it is from here to making the definition of true poetry an honorific one, to calling the poetry of exclusion, with its service of the will and its consequent failure of imagination, a mere pseudo-poetry or rhetoric in disguise, with the valued title of poetry reserved for the inclusive work, expressive of many-sided complexities. This is just the short step, occasionally suggested if not taken by Richards himself, which was taken, openly and firmly, by his followers—say, William Empson, Allen Tate, Cleanth Brooks. Their critical analysis is aimed at discovering whether its object deserves to be called a poem, whether it measures up to the high standard of their normative definition, so that with them the act of evaluation automatically, perhaps unconsciously, accompanies— nay, defines and becomes identical with—the act of analysis. These critics, with Richards, inherit their blurring procedure from their master, Coleridge, much of whose work seems singularly dedicated to discovering in the literature with which he deals the presence of "imagination," the alchemical faculty (or quality) that transmutes discourse into poetry and earns it that noble denomination.

Thus one can trace in recent criticism the "Platonic" methodological tradition which the late R. S. Crane and his fellow neo-Aristotelians disdainfully refer to as "critical monism," as they see it, for example, in the "irony" of Richards, the "ambiguity" of Empson, the "tension" of Tate, the "paradox" of Brooks. The neo-Aristotelians are complaining about the aprioristic establishment of a single poetic characteristic and the use of it not only to define a work as poetry but also, in the same act, automatically to judge it as a valuable example of that high literary mode. They lament the theoretical construction of the Procrustean bed, a practice from which a limited collection of most favored poems emerges, as all but those works responsive to this treatment come to be excluded from the canon of the very best or are admitted only after suffering major distortions. Nevertheless the neo-Aristotelians themselves, anxious to substitute pluralism for monism, many differentiated species for a monolithic poetry, end by falling prey to a similar confusion between the empirical and the a priori, between description and judgment. With a circularity that belies their announced inductive intention, they must end by judging the single work by its efficacy in fulfilling its final cause, the working-power of the peculiar pre-defined species which their analytic description has found it (or trimmed it, forced it) to fit.

This circularity seems universally indulged in by our analytically inclined critics, from so-called contextualists to neo-Aristotelians, whatever their other differences and their vain attempts to evade such circularity and to work toward what they would like to think of as inductive method. For the a priori categories are in control, constituting what they see by limiting how they see. The categories define their subject and erect value criteria for admission, so that for the work to attain the definition is for it to qualify as a valued individual in a valued class. The work comes to be discovered, defined, and valued as poetry only by way of a pre-existing generic characteristic which the critic began by adopting as his perspective glass to envision it.

Indeed, it should by now seem clear that these critics are doubly guilty of circularity. First, there is the evaluative circularity I have been pointing out, the judging of the work by its conformity to a generic trait or set of traits which are the very ones that have been used to define goodness in poetry, or really to define poetry or a kind of poetry as an honorific class. But, more extremely, there is circularity even in the value-free interpretation of works. Here we enter the "hermeneutic circle" which E. D. Hirsch, Jr., has so forcefully pressed us to understand and lament.[1] The critic can account for the meaning and function of the parts of a work only as they make up a whole; but the definition of the whole is required before the parts can be read in this way. This parts-and-whole curse is what, for the critic, dilutes the blessings of organic theory. We see only what our categories of vision permit us to see; and, having seen this way, we are reinforced in our prior vision by every detail, since each seems to support the theory of the whole that was required from the first for us to grasp the details as we have. In this manner, our every hypothesis about the total and partial meanings of a work is circularly self-enclosed. Thus insulated, the hypothesis is self-supporting—and utterly persuasive, even if sometimes its only victim is its creator.

Is this circularity of interpretive claims not really another guise for the circularity of value claims? Are the two not inevitably one at last? It is not farfetched to suggest that the perspective that determines what we would have the work be in order to make sense of its parts is in its turn determined by our prior notion, implicit or explicit, of what we will value in poetry—or value as poetry. My essay has begun, and it will have to end, with this suggestion, so that I must deal with problems of interpretation and evaluation almost indiscriminately. The overlapping, if not the identity, of these circles would seem to make somewhat futile Hirsch's attempt—for the sake of an objective, scientific hermeneutics—to cut off interpretation from criticism. This is an attempt, incidentally, in which, despite enormous differences between them, Hirsch resembles Northrop Frye.

[1] His most extended treatment of the problem and its consequences is his *Validity in Interpretation* (New Haven: Yale University Press, 1967), which includes, as an appendix, his influential essay, "Objective Interpretation," as it originally appeared in *PMLA* 75 (1960): 463–79.

II

We recall, from the opening of the manifesto to the critical revolution he sponsored, the "Polemical Introduction" of his *Anatomy of Criticism* (1957), that Frye pleaded—in the tradition of our most serious critics of all ages—that we distinguish "inductive" criticism from the mere expression of taste and, consequently, make the developing structure of criticism crucially different from the history of taste. We must, he urges, avoid turning criticism into the stock-market fluctuations of literary fashion. The critic must not permit the incestuous interrelations between poet-function and critic-function which can at once overvalue Donne in order to allow a necessary revolution in modern poetry and overvalue certain modern poetic tendencies that reinforce the dominance of the school of Donne in questions of evaluation. Or substitute Blake or Hopkins, as the spirit or necessities of the moment move him, and the problem pointed out by Frye is the same.

I have myself been conceding the practical impossibility of keeping criticism inductive, of keeping taste out of it, once we first concede—in post-Kantian manner—the constitutive role of our categories of perception in conditioning all we experience. This is what is guaranteed by the hermeneutic circle and the consequent evaluative circle. However great our obligation as critics to distinguish what we see and how we value it from what is potentially there to be seen and what its value is, there is little point in denying the limits of our access. Who indeed can look on beauty bare? This is as much as can be said in defense of the modern critical habit—as I have described it—of blurring the lines between analysis and evaluation and blurring both with an a priori definition, necessarily reductive, of what poetry is, or had better be. I have acknowledged elsewhere the obvious presence of an a priori theory, implicit or explicit, consistent or inconsistent, coming between us and our experiencing (and, consequently, our valuing) the work before us, conditioning all we see and how we like it.[2] In light of these confessional concessions about the critic's burdens and his limitations, we may wonder how wishful Frye's thinking must be as he seeks to divorce criticism, as an objective discipline moving toward becoming a science, from both our subjective experiencing and our valuing of the object, two actions which he sees as interrelated and equally beyond the hope of being tamed by objective or inductive criteria.

[2] In "The Disciplines of Literary Criticism," *The Play and Place of Criticism* (Baltimore: Johns Hopkins Press, 1967), esp. pp. 142–46.

Of course, Frye can save criticism from the subjectivity to which
experience and evaluation are condemned only because he defines
criticism as the systematic construct of a total hypothesis. For him it
deals, not with the individual work as an entity, but with its share-
holder's role in the total joint-stock enterprise which is all literature
as the projection of the total human imagination. So for him the task
of criticism is not the traditional one: it is to tell us, not what the
work in its distinct singleness is and how we are to value it, but what
its universalizing tentacles are that lead us outward to grasp other
works and, with them, the total dream of man. Because criticism
works only to establish this mythic *logos,* this system in its wholeness,
it can hope for the scientific objectivity of its hypothetical total structure, having abandoned to untutored subjectivity the discreteness of
our single aesthetic responses and their value. Those concerned with
the more traditional roles of interpretation and criticism, as applied
to single works, may wonder—once Frye's different use of the term
criticism has been taken into account—whether any escape from the
subjective has been achieved, indeed whether there has not been a
retreat from the little that criticism (as normally defined) has accomplished in mitigating the egocentricity of our predicament. It is such
terminological difficulties, perhaps, which have caused the endless disagreements about Frye's position on value.[3] Delicately poised as it is,
this position can be seen as resembling Hirsch's only if we define it
crudely and partially; it would take an essay as long as this one to
begin to place it accurately.

Nevertheless, this position, however distorted through crude formulation, can be used to bring us again to the more open—if not
totally dissimilar—proclamation by Hirsch of the desperate, long ig-
nored need to separate the internality of interpretation from the
externality of judgment. Unlike Frye, Hirsch has only the single literary work—or, as he prefers to call it, the single text—as his object to
be interpreted and valued. According to him, what we do with this
text is properly called interpretation if we limit ourselves to the
framework within which the author has willed or intended his creation. In this case we are concerned only with the text's "meaning." It
is called criticism if we measure the text's relevance to whatever
framework of our own we freely bring from the outside and choose to
impose. But now we are dealing, not with the text's "meaning," but

[3] See the essays and books referred to by John E. Grant in his "Checklist of Criticism
of Frye's Work," in *Northrop Frye in Modern Criticism: Selected Papers from the
English Institute,* ed. Murray Krieger (New York: Columbia University Press, 1966),
esp. pp. 176–80. See also pp. 81–84 of that volume, from W. K. Wimsatt's "Northrop
Frye: Criticism as Myth."

only with its "significance." This is but another way of saying that as critics we are dealing, no longer with the work itself, intrinsically, in its own terms, but with *our* conceptual terms to which a partial and distorted abstraction from the work is adapted. It is the particular version of "metaphysical pathos" carried by each of us that predetermines and limits our criticism, the "significance" it finds. Any claim of value which we make necessarily refers the work, outside its own limits, to an alien criterion that may have to do more with us than with the work. How honestly can any of us altogether deny these charges?

Hirsch treats the work itself as created in response to the demands of the mysterious entity he invents and terms its own "intrinsic genre" (not quite the work itself, since the work can be translated into it, yet as genre not broad enough to include any other work). It is this intrinsic genre that we as interpreters must find and use as our measure of the work. As soon as we have subjected the work to any other criterion, we impose upon it our own extrinsic genre and to this extent have violated the integrity of our (supposed) interpretive completeness, a completeness that should have been achieved by our establishing its intrinsic genre. We are to remember that this intrinsic genre has, for the author, been constitutive and not just heuristic. This is to say, it has become the formative principle in response to which the work has been created; it is not just our tentative invention of a helpful framework which never has been formulated as such or has functioned as an intrinsic control. For if this genre is merely heuristic, and not truly constitutive, then, no matter how close to the work itself it may be, the genre still is also an extrinsic genre only and enjoys no special privilege. Thus the intrinsic genre, as constitutive, has for Hirsch been a necessary theoretical invention to give interpretation a privileged, intrinsic status to which criticism can never be admitted. However, whether for the rest of us the intrinsic genre is more than a theoretical invention, whether any of us can see it as actually there—as not the work itself and yet so slightly broader that it comes tailored to suit only this work—all this is seriously questionable. The desire to free us from the contextualists' linguocentric trap, to allow a translation that still does not universalize, carries its own theoretical burdens of internal contradiction.

The invented entity, the intrinsic genre, may be as slightly useful, and as hazy, as that other invention used by Hirsch, the "intentional object." The "intentional object" is what the work phenomenologically becomes, out there beckoning to us in its singleness despite the chaos of our many varied "intentional acts." It remains out there where it has grown—a single, determinate entity—out of the author's intended or willed meaning. Such inventions—to which we may add that of a willed meaning—create what is for each or all of us inaccessible postulates as "mystical" as any of those in the recent critical tradition which Hirsch condescendingly rejects. We may suspect them of being a self-deceptive multiplication of merely verbal categories. And if we abandon the possibility of a constitutive intrinsic genre, with its strangely privileged status, then everything that we critics can make of the work or do to it is equally extrinsic and, finally, reducible to us and not it. We find no undistorted, neutral object to yield a neutral reading, no breathless object to precede our breathing upon it. Interpretation, then, must be thrown into the same pot as criticism, the one now seen to be as aprioristic as the other, as dependent upon the critic's projected categories. Once the author's constitutive genre is, reduced to the interpreter's heuristic invention to grasp the ungraspable, the interpreter's language is fated to be distinct from the author's precisely as the critic's language is. The post-Kantian epistemology absorbs interpretation and criticism alike and leads to the blurring of their functions. Still, the critic-interpreter (I now join the two) must wrestle with these limitations, so that Hirsch's directions for help do satisfy our objective yearnings and may serve as guidelines permitting us to judge how appropriate to the object is each of the endless variety of aprioristic answers which recent criticism has arrogantly supplied.

We began by briefly examining the tradition after Richards and Eliot that led critics like Empson, Tate, and Brooks (it would not be hard to add others) to interpret the poem, to define it as poetry, and to honor it as a favored example of the art by means of a priori, theoretically derived characteristics. And we lamented the severe costs to our inductive hopes of this multiplicity of perspectives, even as we lamented more the inevitability of this procedure. As we look at other schools of critics, however, we are struck by extra-literary impositions far less attentive to any claims of what Hirsch calls "objective interpretation." After all, the efforts of contextualist critics, like the neo-Aristotelians we might call the genre critics, were initiated in large part out of their desire to return to the object, their subservience to their own metaphysical pathos notwithstanding. The hermeneutic circle may overlap the contextual circle of the work to an infinite variety of degrees, but it remains the critic's own circle. Still, when we observe what—in contrast to the contextualist or the neo-Aristotelian—the social-political commentator sees as the work, or what the historian of ideas or the biographical-psychological commentator or his recent apocalyptic descendant, the "vision" critic, sees as the work, we can appreciate the pragmatic value of these differences of degree even if theoretically, methodologically, we cannot establish any difference in kind among those circles that rotate around that crucial one the critic cannot penetrate.

Indeed, even out of Frye's "inductive" objectives, the myth critic can end by looking for, and valuing most, the work he can most readily tailor to his specifications, thus joining the others in the parade of most favored hypotheses and the most favored poems read to order to support them. All are busy in their own ways creating their structural models to characterize and reduce the manifold workings of the human imagination. Every critic might appear his own structuralist, with that recent arrival, the self-proclaimed structuralist, himself the archetype of the critic, who necessarily adapts the work to a model he claims to find immanently within it and who ends by substituting the model for the work. Geoffrey Hartman has performed a valuable service by placing Frye within the larger (and mainly continental) structuralist movement as perhaps its most ambitious member.[4] Frye's continuing celebration of the creatures of imagination in their monumental configurations *is* a structuralist celebration. Like the structuralist, he must assume (as his a priori hypothesis of a total and coherent system) that structures in many sorts of discourse—literary and otherwise—are, in the end, open to similar analysis; are analogous, are through metaphorical transference related, and finally are potentially identical, as the analogous becomes the anagogic. Together as microcosm and macrocosm, they become the key to unlock the secret forming power of the human imagination. The critic thus projects a syntax—a generative grammar—of imagination upon the work which is made to match his structural model. Literature and other discourse are seen as the many versions of the Platonic Forms through which imagination, feeding itself and upon itself, grasps and creates its reality.

Though anti-formalist, Georges Poulet is finally not unrelated to this sort of structural monism. His phenomenological insistence always leads to the glorious identity of consciousness among reader, poet, work, the collapsing of the distinctnesses of time and space in the instantaneous union between every critic and poet-as-Mallarmé or Proust. And the most favored works, or the most favored readings which make most favored works, follow accordingly. In his structural probings in the novel, René Girard ends by at once destroying all barriers, all mediation, between the vision of a character and his

---

[4] In "Structuralism: The Anglo-American Adventure," *Yale French Studies* 36–37 (1966): 148–68.

author, and creating a single—however dynamic—structural pattern which permits such instantaneity and identity to occur.[5] He thus seems to combine Poulet's phenomenology and structuralist method. And with so uniform a reading, concluding in his universal claim that, structurally and phenomenologically, all novels become the same novel, we indeed see this kind of criticism as providing an archetypal confession of the apriorism that Hirsch, for all his method, cannot purge from criticism conceived as a humanistic exercise.

III

Having confessed this much, how can the critic perform if he is to accommodate the myopia which plagues him? Let him first confront the obvious: The major difficulty in assigning value, that seems to dictate the total separation of evaluation from interpretation, is the fact that value cannot be a secondary quality, to borrow a term from an old-fashioned epistemology. As a tertiary or axiological quality only, goodness in art cannot be described as can the perceptible characteristics of the object about which interpretations *can* argue. Thus, in a way that would seem to lend comfort to Hirsch as well as Frye, value can be assigned to the cluster of features in the object we have described only by the intervention of a subject *fiat*: "let that be termed valuable which. . . ." And then follows the formula which fits those works which have the features we want. "The work is what I have been showing you it is. Well, that is how works ought to be, although I can hardly show you this claim in the same way." Thus the antique axiological problem: the critic cannot reduce value to fact without sacrificing ought-ness. But if the critic is to function helpfully as a critic of value, he must still manage to "anchor" the axiological to the observable features of that object, preserving its ought-ness only by the intervention of the subjective *fiat*, although he must hope to cover as many fellow-subjects—other readers—with it as he can. Which is to say, his requirements must come as close as he can make them to the limits of the object, provided we can agree about those limits.

The claim to value might rest tentatively on a hypothetical procedure that is admittedly tautologous: what can we require of a poem if it is to function most effectively as what it is; if, that is, it is to persuade us to a peculiarly poetic response? At this point we could distinguish, analytically and heuristically, among kinds of response—

---

[5] See *Deceit, Desire, and the Novel: Self and Other in Literary Structure*, trans. Yvonne Freccero (Baltimore: Johns Hopkins Press, 1965), esp. pp. 293–310.

say, to use the usual Kantian triad, the cognitive, the moral, and the poetic (or, more generically, the aesthetic).[6] I call these distinctions analytic and heuristic because our purposes require us to define them, in advance of actual experiences, in their pure states even though the actual experience of the most pristine of us is very likely a messy composite of them. I am not interested in whether they occur as defined or in whether, if they did, that would be a good thing; I am interested only in what they would be like if they did, so that we can characterize what objects would be like that were constructed to lead us toward one or another of them.[7] It would not be difficult to find the distinguishing characteristic of aesthetic experience, in contrast to the others, to lie in its self-sufficiency, what Eliseo Vivas calls its "intransitive" quality. From the experience so defined, it would be even less difficult to move to describe the characteristics of an object that would be expressly constructed so as to facilitate that experience, to lead us toward it, provided we were willing to lay at rest our normal cognitive and moral propensities to go through objects rather than to be contained by them.

About several points let me make explicit the modesty of these claims. First, I am suggesting nothing about the value of the poetic or aesthetic experience. It is postulated only as a possible psychological datum, to be described as having certain characteristics, degrees of attentiveness, disinterestedness, and the like. Secondly, I am not suggesting that only certain kinds of works can produce this experience in us. As a psychological fact, it will occur when it occurs, and the control of it by the stimulating object cannot be predicted. Nor, thirdly, can I say the experience is better when it can be referred to and anchored in an object. But when it is, we can point to its cause and expect that it can be repeated with different subjects. So I can say, once we have agreed about the defining qualities of this experience as an a priori, analytic type, that certain objects can be seen and described as being so constructed as to produce it in us, provided we are willing, and knowledgeable enough, to submit. Every aspect of the work would contribute to keeping us enclosed within its symbolic world, preventing our escape to the world of reference and action

6 Here and in what follows I am clearly indebted to the analysis made in many places by Eliseo Vivas. See especially his "The Artistic Transaction," *The Artistic Transaction and Essays on Theory of Literature* (Columbus: Ohio State University Press, 1963), pp. 3–93. He would add the religious experience to those I have named, but since my interest here is to furnish a brief exposition rather than to argue whether there are three or four varieties, I stick with the more conventional distinctions of Kant.

7 Vivas, on the other hand, insists on the empirical basis of these definitions. See his complaint against my concessions, *The Artistic Transaction*, pp. 201–2n.

beyond, the world of external relations in which the cognitive and / or the moral tend to preclude the merely aesthetic. We can see how criteria like irony, ambiguity, paradox, tension are given value as means of preventing that escape. From this enclosure of internal relations, at once mutually inhibiting and mutually satisfying, can arise such a series of criteria according to which we can judge the work's efficacy as an *aesthetic* object, that is (to return to the tautology), one whose nature and purpose seem calculated to lead us toward the experience we have denominated aesthetic. But we predicate the nature of the experience only to get us toward certain kinds of characteristics in the object, characteristics that, by remaking language, transform its signs into weighty, substantive, corporeal symbols.

Is this an assertion of its value? Only if we return to the hypothetical statement with which we began. *If* we wish to consider the work only in terms of an aesthetic function (though there may be others, perhaps better ones), *if*, that is, we wish to have a work perform what literary discourse is uniquely able to perform, then we can speak about how successfully or unsuccessfully it performs such a function. Of course, this does not reduce tertiary to secondary qualities, value characteristics to descriptive ones. For we have really decided no value questions. It may, after all, be more valuable not to consider a work this way, so that what we have determined may very well be what Albert Hofstadter has termed aesthetic validity rather than aesthetic value.[8] Nevertheless, it is enough to let the critic proceed: his circular theoretical assumptions permit him to define what the poem *qua* poem, having a unique and indispensable function, must do insofar as he, as *literary* critic judging its literary (and thus aesthetic) quality, can speak authoritatively about the relative quality of its performance. What he sees and how he judges follow accordingly.

Obviously, this is how the contextualist critic has proceeded. We can define his methodological limitations and, from these, his own metaphysical pathos from which his vision, almost on its own, ensues. The predisposition about closed form dictates that all "literary openness" be automatically excluded from his realm of value (or validity). Whatever he relegates to allegory he excludes, as a crypto-rhetoric, from the honorific realm of poetry. Whatever he attributes to the intrusion of unformed experience, he charges with aesthetic illegitimacy in the service of that chaotic rebel, the anti-poem. For him either case leads away from the peculiar response that poetry alone

---

[8] "Validity versus Value: An Essay in Philosophical Aesthetics," *Journal of Philosophy* 59 (1962): 607–17. See Monroe C. Beardsley's response, "Beauty and Aesthetic Value," pp. 617–28.

can arouse. He would not detract from either of them, but, within the qualifications of that "if" clause, with which we saw him begin, the unenclosed work cannot be admitted into the domain of poetry. Similarly, we can see, in his predisposition toward the unique contextual system of meanings, in his distrust for normal language in its universal dimensions, an affinity for the unique dynamics, the existential immediacy of particularized experience, an experience that betrays contradictory elements beyond rational reconciliation. Even so formalistic a doctrine rests on thematic presuppositions, on what has been called metaphysical pathos. How, then, is this critic to deny the partiality of his vision and his judgment, the intrusion upon these of his role as twentieth-century man? But which of us can claim more or deny less, for all the barrage of objective procedures he lays down? The humanist is always embarrassed by his parochialism and restless within it, if too honest to deny it.

IV

So we grant that our hermeneutic methods are, as methods, pretty frustrating and, as a would-be science, not very promising. Nevertheless, we must not, through mistaken analogies, look for methods of establishing the meaning of texts as positive as those used to establish the texts themselves. For, as we have seen, texts and the meaning of texts do not at all have the same availability to us. We see with Hirsch the inevitability of the hermeneutic circle. From this the sad fact follows that the reader of criticism can only move from one argument-from-coherence to another, choosing among the several self-enclosed, self-justifying, self-convincing interpretations poised against each other but not speaking to each other, shut off in their several universes of discourse. Or is this too extreme? Can they really never speak? Can critical discourse really become as insulated as the fully functioning poetic system? But let us provisionally accept as much, reserving our qualifications until we have explored the consequences of so extreme a notion.

The only way to escape the hopeless movement among alternative interpretations as pictured by Hirsch is to search with him for the intrinsic genre, at once outside the work and encircling it. This search carries Hirsch outside the hermeneutic circles of so-called intrinsic meanings for the extrinsic evidence that can help us to narrow the range of probabilities within which our interpretation should occur. For we must move toward the author's intended or willed meaning and can use all the help we can find. We can, Hirsch suggests, move beyond alternative circles toward the more probable interpretation only if we continually narrow the genre that guides our vision of the work and defines how it is to take its meaning; but only by resorting to materials that can establish horizons, boundary limits, to all that our competing critical imaginations can claim to discover within the inner workings of the piece. The generic is the typical so that, as Hirsch demonstrates in his attempt to decide between Bateson and Brooks on Wordsworth's "A slumber did my spirit seal," the interpreter should invoke the "typical" Wordsworth to establish the bound or narrow the genre within which one reading is the more probable. With admirable candor Hirsch insists that he has given us a method to establish not correct readings, merely more probable ones. But, he persists, if interpretation is to grow as a rational procedure, then—as more exact sciences have learned—probability is as much as we can hope for.

But perhaps it is not in literary criticism as Aristotle says it is in tragic literature, that a probable impossibility is to be preferred to a possible improbability, although to acknowledge this much is to forgo our hopes for criticism as a progressive science. After these past decades of intensely pondering over the special intricacies of the syntax of poetic discourse, we have learned, perhaps more than anything else, that our greatest works achieve that status largely by their defiance— through transformation—of what we might predict as being typical or probable from all the extrinsic data we can summon. And the critic had better not surrender his rare chance to be correct in describing the work's miraculous movements just in order to be faithful to a notion of a "more probable" hypothesis. Is it better to support a "science" that would make so rare a chance non-existent? The great work, in its workings, its transformations, may very well demand the *less* probable, if not the least probable, hypothesis, if we were to judge from all that we could know before the work or outside the work. Hirsch continually maintains the Aristotelian truism that we must limit our methods by the capacities of our subject, that we must expect no more precision than the nature of our subject-matter permits. But since he does *not* see poetry as a specially empowering and empowered form of discourse, with systematic interrelations among its elements—language, character, scene—that allow its escape from the limited functions of other discourse, he need not yield up his general method for interpreting *all* texts (poetic and otherwise) by way of more probable rather than less probable hypotheses. For if poetry has as discourse no different ontological status, no other way of meaning, it can have no exemption claimed for it.

This, however, is to shut off an entire range of possibilities that recent criticism has tried to keep open. Hirsch can claim rightly that to deny in poetry the rights of the more probable hypothesis (the degree of probability depending on our ability to circumvent the circle by imposing evidence from the outside that can narrow the work's "intrinsic genre") is to deny any chance for positive knowledge in criticism, the knowledge of our probability of being right. But we must ask again whether, in poetry of the first rank, Hirsch's "intrinsic genre" is constitutive rather than merely heuristic. It may very well be so in non-poetry and in poetry not of the first rank, which must lean on (and open outward to) organizations of meaning beyond itself. But surely it is begging the question to begin by assuming that it is necessarily so in poetry of the first rank as well, so that this poetry is denied the power to create its meanings anew, out of its own system. Our empirical sense should warn us against this question-begging after all we have learned from recent criticism of these unpredictable powers of poetic discourse. The failures and excesses of this criticism need not lead us to insist that a science of criticism can be substituted for it, and its successes may rather lead us to believe that to assert the possibility of a science of criticism may indeed be to beg the question, so long as that would-be science depended upon a probability count determined by a constitutive intrinsic genre imposed from outside. Nevertheless, as the alternative from inside, we must grant Hirsch, only rival hypotheses, supported by data created by a vision each hypothesis allows, can throw the hard edges of their circles against one another.

What is the good, Hirsch laments, of limiting interpretations to what the text can adequately sustain, when—thanks to the hermeneutic circle—our ingenuity can force the text to sustain an unlimited number of *self*-sustaining, mutually incompatible interpretations? But has our experience not shown that the text does not, with equal adequacy, sustain all comers? that, in fact, the experienced reader can discriminate among all but a few through the failure of most of them to account for crucial features of the text? Hirsch would grant as much, being properly concerned by the rival claims of those few and our powerlessness to adjudicate with authority among them. We must all share this concern, although our anxiety to find a way to adjudicate must not lead us to adjudicate on the wrong grounds, to feel a security which our decision—and our way of reaching it—cannot support.[9]

The recalcitrant (or retrograde?) denials of Hirsch's claims may very well deny the interpreter his chance at *positive* knowledge, the

[9] We can, for example, share Hirsch's impatience with the mistaken student reading he cites of Donne's "A Valediction Forbidding Mourning": that it concerns an impending death rather than a more temporary separation of the lovers. Still

knowledge of our *probability* of being right. But what (we must answer by asking) if this very service to the rational probability of being correct often makes the interpretation in fact wrong? And what if the frequency of being wrong increases with the value of the work at hand? Would that not alter what is probable when it comes to that strange miracle, the fully functioning poem? The critic, then, if he must choose between the probability of being correct (via methods true of discourse generally) and actually being correct (though unable to know it or argue for it since it is an improbable correctness), must of course choose the latter or else desert his subject for another subject, one more conveniently dealt with. He would have to insist on a higher (and, on some grounds, an improbable) probability for poetry, though one attained by methods that are essentially non-transferable. At issue, of course, is whether or not the usual sort of probability tests, on which progress in textual interpretation normally depends, work' with the sort of discourse that our best works become. Nor can we, after invoking with Hirsch the Aristotelian injunction about matching methods and objectives to their subjects, begin by indiscriminately reducing all texts to the sort of text with which general probability-testing can deal. Hirsch so reduces them by making no distinctions among texts and thus conceding to the literary text no difference that would exempt it from the general method.

If verbal meaning were individual and not a type, it would not be knowable, Hirsch confesses in his final Appendix. Therefore, he argues, let us by all means always keep it a type. If, unlike other meanings, poetic meanings should turn out to be individual, as contextualists have insisted, then Hirsch would have to maintain that we must not confound meaning itself, which like the Kantian thing-in-itself would remain unknowable, with our hypotheses about meaning, which can be rationally debated and judged. His sensible claim is that we can make progress only by attending what can be rationally debated and judged (whence the imposition of types). My own notion is

---

he does spend disproportionate time on several occasions in *Validity in Interpretation* fearing the possible failure of internal evidence and invoking other sorts of evidence. Yet he admits the strength of our case, for the more modest reading can come from the poem before we turn for support to Donne's other valediction poems and to his general metaphorical habits. One metaphor after the other and the tone of the whole can be marshaled to demonstrate the temporary and even almost trivial separation rather than the deathbed separation seen by melodramatic students too romantically prepared—even if such students will not respond to the persuasiveness of such ample evidence. But, of course, no critic with critic friends wiser than himself can deny that there are cases far more difficult—if not impossible —to resolve.

that, confronted by the mysteries of a meaning that may not permit us to know it, we must choose either to bend our language and methods in order to grope after it, however imperfectly, catch as catch can, or to sit pristinely back, purifying our language and methods, in hopes that this purification is relevant and that this language and these methods may after all lead toward that elusive meaning. I clearly lean toward the sloppiness of the first of these alternatives, Hirsch toward the increased precision of the second. I allow the meaning to remain individual and hence even ultimately elusive; and I believe even Hirsch's evidence would lead in this direction, were he not so anxious not to preclude positive knowledge and its necessary methods. For me it is once more the old joke about the man who tried to find his precious lost object by looking for it, not where he lost it, but where he found the light to be brightest. The joke arises because he should have been looking for the object rather than for the light, however convenient the latter. I am suggesting that we stay in the murky area close to the meaning which is our object, that we avoid light for light's sake, the clear well-lighted methods and language that may after all be the wrong light, or light wrongly located, in view of what we must try—painfully, even perhaps futilely—to uncover.

On his side Hirsch could claim—and persuasively—that I am introducing an anti-rational mystification, that I am begging the question in my own way since I deny to his methodical procedure any access to our best works by declaring them out of bounds by *fiat*. It is so: my claim can break out of its own circle only by appealing to that common experience that assures us that the poetic system does work in ways that exempt it from our general classification of texts. With a method that disdains any scientific ambition, I can say no more than the special nature of the work's workings permits me to say: that the critic—trapped in the aesthetic object in its aesthetic function—does better to trap himself in his hermeneutic circle and, without resorting to those externally imposed boundary limits that may distort the work, to rely only on the clumsy give-and-take of the Socratic method to make his dubious progress toward satisfactory interpretation. He can do no more than throw his own self-enclosed circle against all comers in hopes of seeming more adequate to his data. On some rare occasions he may even change someone's mind or be persuaded to change his own. There will, as Hirsch would insist at once, be dismal impasses between mutually incompatible hypotheses, each persuasively self-enforced. But we must live with these, struggling—sometimes helplessly—between them, confident that it is not less necessary to do so here than in all other areas (most of them other-than-literary) of our profoundest verbal and substantive disagreements with our fellows. And we shall be truer to our data—our finest literary works—if we persist thus unprogressively in our retrograde circles rather than surrender their defiance of whatever external predictabilities and probabilities may be imposed in order to move toward the certainty that resolves contradictions. After all, this is the stubborn way our strongest criticism has always—and not altogether unsuccessfully—proceeded. It is questionable whether we can legislate a way of doing better.

Through this defense of intra-systematic, circular interpretation, my own (by now self-conscious) smuggling in of value notions has been hardly concealed. What else can I have been doing in my constant suggestion that the usefulness of Hirsch's method is inversely proportionate to the work's literary value—the better the work the less its nature permits it to succumb? The resistance to external appeals, the need to trace and retrace internal circularities—these become testimony to the work's aesthetic success. Convince us that external horizons *are* adequate as well as relevant, that the circle is *not* closed, and critics like me downgrade the work as poetry. Indeed we begin to withdraw that honored title, poetry, from the work and become ready to consider it as something else. For value remains embedded in our aprioristic definitions, as it has been shown to be for critics in this tradition from the start of this essay.

So criticism thus practiced is not to be a science, not even having enough method to separate matters of value from matters of fact. I follow this commonplace, that criticism is not a science, with the self-righteous assertion that it ought not to be, Hirsch (and, though less strenuously, Northrop Frye) to the contrary notwithstanding. Does not even Hirsch, who ends by looking in the poem by Wordsworth for evidence of that Wordsworthian typicality which he must assume before beginning, demonstrate that his broadening of method finally only broadens the range of his own circularity? Hence the further commonplace that criticism is but an art, a highly—and necessarily—imperfect art, a half-art. We must not, even theoretically, expect too much of it, though neither must we, out of our disappointments caused by its confusions with mere taste, surrender its intimate connections to the realm of value. Nor surrender the primacy of the critic's imaginative power, his constitutive power at once to project and perceive (or, more precisely, to perceive *by* projecting) interpretation and value. As critics we must always expect and hope for the perfection of the work of art. Perfection of the work itself, yes; but of criticism—especially as it includes judgment—never!

V

I have argued similarly in a recent book that criticism, though it may freely play, must remember its place. This was meant to be a humbling reminder of its unscientific and only half-artistic nature. Each critical performance, provided its object is a *proper poem* (defined in the questionable, aprioristic way I have outlined), is a struggle and compromise between the untranslatable symbolic structure that is the poem and the more commonplace symbols brought to it by the critic. These symbols define and limit the vision of each of us as critic. Thus it is that each of our critical performances is also a struggle and compromise between the new vision of the unique work and the old vision of its reader which seeks only to reinforce itself. There is the apparently paradoxical double activity which (1) permits us as self-conscious readers (really another term for critics) to grasp the work only by way of the categories of vision we bring to it—which is to say, only by reducing the work to what our prior selves will permit it to be—and yet (2) leads us to broaden what our vision has been in order to accommodate the newness in the work. In the latter case our limited view has become less limited, our old view renewed, literally reconstituted into something more comprehensive, freshened by immediacy into a reshaped definition. If we engage only in the first half of this double activity—if we only use the work for visionary reinforcement, accommodating it to our generic vision that pre-exists it—then of course we have denied literature and our traffic with it its proper function of making us more than—or different from—what we were, of educating us into *its* mode of vision. Why bother opening ourselves to the great imaginative works if we foreclose their impact? On the other hand, if the work as we perceive it is, in post-Kantian terms, defined by the visionary categories through which we constitute it, how *can* it reconstitute those categories? How can any element outside our categories, from the nakedly existing work itself, intervene to transform those categories, rendering their pre-existing versions obsolete?

Clearly the personal fact of what literary works do for us and the historical fact of what they have done for their cultures point to an inescapable phenomenological fact, of interest to Hirsch as well as to me: Though the work seems to exist for us only as our categories permit it to be defined, only as our commonplace, generic symbols reduce and distort its unique symbolic structure—still there must be something in the work as it must exist (or subsist?), on its own, outside our categorical structures and symbols. This something can force our structures and symbols to work radical transformations upon themselves, in response to their own commands, as it were, though prompted from beyond their autonomous realm. What more persuasive indication can we have that there is a something out there, beckoning us, soliciting our willful subjugation to its power to change our ways of seeing and of living? The control imposed by its objective, reconstituting force upon our subjective, constitutive powers challenges the limiting and distorting projections of our categories, finally breaking through the self-sufficient insulation of our visionary circles. What a Shakespeare or a Melville can do to the metaphysical and moral shapings of our imaginations, a Mallarmé or a Proust can do to our consciousness of space and time as he freezes our world or lets it flow.

Whatever our decision about the ontological status of the literary object, its existence, meaning, and value before we collide with it, we know that we can speak of it only out of the dust of that collision. We pick ourselves up, no longer quite the same selves, and try to speak with precision about what has struck us and the force of its impact. And we probably will give the usual one-sided version of what has transpired and what sort of antagonist we have encountered. Who is to correct us except others who have suffered similar encounters and whose descriptions will be as partial and as self-serving? None of us may deny the encounter, none deny how profoundly we have been changed by it; yet we each will have our own version, each levy our own assessment. Since each of us is changed, the alienating quality of the force and its forcefulness are beyond question. There should be a way of getting at the force itself by comparing versions and visions—a way of subtracting what we were from what we have become and finding some critical range among the differences. It is an inexact and inconclusive way, though perhaps the only way we have. For there is no way of getting at the force—despite radical disagreements about its nature—except through our radically diverse, autonomous experiences of it, even as our judgment of these experiences must be modified through dialogue. Our depositions attesting to the independent existence of the force, its neutral objectivity as *ding-an-sich*, are useless to us so long as we are not permitted to get at it in its independence and neutrality. Those of us whose impatience leads them to introduce systematically controlled, firmly generic criteria from the outside in order to eliminate the subjective angle of vision are deceiving themselves about the positive nature of the results they look for. The force which is the work itself lives only in those singular visions and in their mutual modifications by human beings honestly trying to look, and to move, beyond their own limitations, even as these limitations define who they are. Yet it is the force that helps define who they are to become.

Index of Names

Adams, Hazard, 201, 201 n. 9, 211, 215, 220–24, 228

Addison, Joseph, 41, 41 n. 2, 61 n. 9, 78, 83, 83 n. 10; *Cato*, 42, 61

Aesop, 5, 5 n. 2, 9, 37

Aquinas, Saint Thomas, 96

Aristotle, 5, 29, 31–39, 39–97, 41, 41 n. 3, 42, 62, 68, 78, 192, 265; *Ethics*, 35; *Poetics*, 35, 297; *Politics*, 35

Arnold, Matthew, xiii, 92–105, 105 n. 8, 106–7, 161, 173

Babbitt, Irving, 102

Barthes, Roland, 171–72, 216, 224

Beardsley, Monroe C., 314 n. 8

Bergson, Henri, 230, 251

Blake, William, 95, 103–4

Bloom, Harold, 113, 175 n. 4, 176 n. 7, 217–18, 274

Braybrooke, David, 238, 238 n. 1, 239–46

Brooks, Cleanth, 44–45, 51, 51 n. 16, 98, 108–9, 174, 174 n. 3, 175, 279, 305

Brown, Norman O., 272

Bulgarini, Belisario, 30

Bullough, Edward, 144, 144 n. 3

Burckhardt, Sigurd, 48, 48 n. 12, 49–51, 53, 193 n. 4

Burke, Edmund, 42, 61

Burke, Kenneth, 232

Calderwood, James, 52, 52 n. 17, 53

Camus, Albert, 226

Cassirer, Ernst, 127, 221

Castelvetro, Lodovico, 30, 66

Chaucer, Geoffrey, 40

Church, Joseph, 26 n. 12

Coleridge, Samuel Taylor, xiii, 32–33, 45 n. 8, 47, 96, 98, 122–23, 292 n. 17, 305; *Biographia Literaria*, 69; "Shakespeare's Judgment equal to His Genius," 43–44

Colie, Rosalie, xiii, 52, 52 n. 17, 53, 194, 194 n. 5

Conrad, Joseph: *Lord Jim*, 263; *Victory*, 256, 256 n. 8, 257

Crane, R. S., 305

Croce, Benedetto, 127

Dante, 6, 29–30, 95–96

de Man, Paul, xiii, 111, 113, 172–74, 174 n. 3, 182 n. 11, 221–22

Dembo, L. S., 212–13

Derrida, Jacques, 113, 149, 153 n. 7, 171–72, 201, 224, 229, 232

Dewey, John, 118, 243

Diderot, Denis, 233

Donne, John, 44–45, 174 n. 2; "The Canonization," 296

Donoghue, Denis, 199, 199 n. 4

Dostoevsky, Fyodor, *Notes from Underground*, 249, 249 n. 6
Dryden, John, 42, 50, 53, 63; "Alexander's Feast," 60; "An Essay of Dramatic Poesy," 40–41, 56

Eliot, T. S., 44, 92–95, 95 n. 1, 96, 96 n. 2, 97, 97 n. 3, 98, 98 n. 4, 103–7
Elliott, Robert C., 59 n. 3
Empson, William, 45, 48, 297, 305

Faulkner, William, *Light in August*, 257, 258 n. 9, 259
Fielding, Henry, *Tom Jones*, 147
Fish, Stanley, 17, 171, 176, 176 n. 6
Foucault, Michel, 6, 25–26, 171, 217–18, 224, 232
Freedman, Ralph, 211, 215, 233–36
Frye, Northrop, 6, 59, 92, 102 n. 6, 103–4, 104 n. 7, 105–7, 170, 189 n. 1, 232, 280–81, 306–8, 311

Garber, Marjorie B., 53 n. 19
Gide, André, *The Immoralist*, 295
Gilbert, Allan H., 29, 29 n. 1
Gilbert, Katharine E., 284 n. 10
Girard, René, 211, 215, 229–33, 279–80, 280 n. 8, 311–12, 312 n. 5
Goethe, Johann Wolfgang von, 103–5, 223, 275
Gombrich, E. H., xi, 8, 8 n. 4, 10, 142–43, 143 n. 2, 147, 167, 192, 192 n. 3, 207
Grant, John E., 308 n. 2
Gray, Thomas, 61 n. 8
Gudas, Fabian, 209, 209 n. 18

Hardison, O. B., 199, 199 n. 5, 201, 208, 208 n. 17
Hartman, Geoffrey, 113, 186, 187 n. 15, 271, 271 n. 1, 272, 276, 279, 279 n. 7, 311, 311 n. 4
Hassan, Ihab, 272, 274, 274 n. 2, 276–77, 277 n. 3, 277 n. 4, 290, 290 n. 15, 301, 301 n. 23
Hathaway, Baxter, 29, 29 n. 2
Hegel, Georg Wilhelm Friedrich, xiii, 248
Heidegger, Martin, 234–35

Heilman, Robert, 51, 51 n. 16
Herbert, George, 83 n. 10
Hirsch, E. D., 177 n. 8, 180, 306, 306 n. 1, 308–10, 312, 315–17, 317 n. 9, 318–21
Hofstadter, Albert, 314, 314 n. 8
Hopkins, Gerard Manley, 293
Horace, 36, 87
Hume, David, 56–57, 72
Huxley, Thomas Henry, 100–101

Ingarden, Roman, 142

Jakobson, Roman, xi, 184–85
James, Henry, 32, 96
Jenyns, Soame, 70–71, 71 n. 1, 73–74, 80–81
Johnson, Samuel, xiv n. 2, 41, 41 n. 2, 43 n. 6, 55–56, 56 nn. 1, 2, 57–71, 71 n. 1, 72–74, 74 n. 3, 75, 75, n. 5, 76, 76 n. 6, 77–82, 88–89, 96, 133; "Cowley," 69, 69 n. 14; "The Life of Pope," 60 n. 4, 73; "Milton," 60, 60 n. 6, 63, 73, 73 n. 2, 79; "On the Death of Mr. Robert Levet," 82 n. 7; "Preface to Shakespeare," 42, 56, 75, 77–79, 82 n. 7, 250, 250 n. 7; "Vanity of Human Wishes," 82, 82 n. 7
Jonson, Ben, 41–42, 174 n. 2

Kafka, Franz, *The Trial*, 296, 302
Kant, Immanuel, xiii, 89, 97, 103–4, 127, 144, 234, 275
Kierkegaard, Sören, 248, 248 nn. 2, 3, 249, 249 n. 5, 250, 253–54, 284
Kuhn, Helmut, 284 n. 10

Lacan, Jacques, 171
Lévi-Strauss, Claude, 229–31
Longinus, 41
Lucretius, 95

Malraux, André, *Man's Fate*, 295
Mann, Thomas, *Doctor Faustus*, 294 n. 20, 295–96
Marvell, Andrew, 98
Marx, Karl, 105 n. 8
Mazzoni, Jacopo, 5, 7, 28–38

Index

Melville, Herman: *Moby Dick*, 254–55; *Pierre*, 265, 296
Miers, Paul, 201, 201 n. 8, 202, 202 n. 12
Miller, J. Hillis, 108–11, 113–14, 273, 287 n. 13
Milton, John, 60
Mizener, Arthur, 45, 45 n. 9, 46–48, 50–51
Morris, Wesley, 202, 202 n. 11

Nietzsche, Friedrich, xiii, 105 n. 8, 172, 251

Peterfreund, Stuart, 166 n. 14
Plass, Margaret Webster, xv
Plato, 28–29, 33–36, 62, 79; *Sophist*, 31
Pope, Alexander, 41, 41 nn. 2, 3, 42, 74 n. 3, 84; "Arbuthnot," 85; *Dunciad*, 87 n. 12, 173; "Epistle to Augustus," 87; *Essay on Criticism*, 42 n. 4, 64, 69, 83; *Essay on Man*, 73, 80–83, 83 n. 10, 90–91; "Ode for St. Cecilia's Day," 60; "Preface to Shakespeare," 60 n. 7; *The Rape of the Lock*, 73–74, 85–86, 87 n. 12, 158–60
Pottle, Frederick A., 64 n. 11
Poulet, Georges, 170, 217, 232, 235, 273–74, 279–80, 284, 287, 287 n. 13, 288, 288 n. 14, 289, 292, 311

Raiffa, Howard, 246–47
Ransom, John Crowe, 44, 44 n. 7, 45, 45 n. 8, 46 47, 49 51, 108 9, 186, 186 n. 13, 279
Reynolds, Sir Joshua, 56
Rice, Philip Blair, 294 n. 20
Richards, I. A., 92–93, 98–99, 99 n. 5, 100–107, 109–10, 251–52, 304
Riddel, Joseph, 173
Riffaterre, Michael, 279, 279 n. 7

Said, Edward, 211, 215–20, 223–24, 237
Sainte-Beuve, Charles Augustin, 94
Santayana, George, 99
Sartre, Jean-Paul, 226
Saussure, Ferdinand de, 109–10, 149, 153 n. 7, 171–72
Scaliger, Julius Caesar, 4, 28, 37, 62
Scève, Maurice, 233–34

Schiller, Friedrich von, 99, 104, 275
Schlegel, August Wilhelm, 43
Scholes, Robert, 199, 199 n. 3, 201
Schopenhauer, Arthur, 251
Shakespeare, William, 39–69, 77–78; *Hamlet*, 93, 255; *1 Henry IV*, 51; *King Lear*, 52 n. 17; *Macbeth*, 51; *The Phoenix and Turtle*, 19–20, 51; *The Tempest*, 24; *Sonnets*, 13 n. 7, 18–19, 19 n. 9, 20–23, 23 n. 10, 24, 26–27, 46–48, 48 n. 11, 51, 148, 174 n. 2
Sidney, Sir Philip, 7, 10, 29, 37, 62, 66, 83 n. 10, 102, 174 n. 2; *An Apology for Poetry*, 4–5, 5 n. 2, 7–9, 23, 25, 28, 67; *Astrophel and Stella*, 12–14, 14 n. 8, 15–17, 23, 282, 296
Spenser, Edmund, *Amoretti*, 13 n. 7
Spitzer, Leo, 286, 286 n. 12
Steiner, George, 49, 49 n. 14, 53
Sterne, Laurence, *Tristram Shandy*, 89, 90 n. 15, 164–65, 165 n. 13, 166–68, 174 n. 2
Strozier, Robert M., 201, 201 n. 10
Sutton, Walter, 279, 279 n. 6
Swift, Jonathan, 74 n. 3, 82 n. 8, 87; *Gulliver's Travels*, 82; "The Lady's Dressing Room," 82

Taine, Hippolyte, 94
Tate, Allen, 44, 108–9, 279, 305
Tuve, Rosemund, 4, 4 n. 1, 5

Valéry, Paul, 233
Vendler, Helen, 110
Vico, Giambattista, 80, 183, 221
Virgil, 87
Vivas, Eliseo, 115–18, 118 n. 2, 119–21, 121 nn. 3, 4, 122, 122 nn. 5, 6, 7, 123–24, 124 nn. 8, 9, 125, 125 n. 10, 126–27, 127 n. 11, 128, 128 n. 12, 313 nn. 6, 7
Voltaire, 42

Watts, Harold M., 207, 207 n. 16
Weinsheimer, Joel, 199, 199 n. 1, 200, 200 nn. 6, 7, 201, 205, 207, 207 n. 15, 208
Wellek, René, 199, 199 n. 2

White, Hayden, 176, 176 n. 7, 182, 182 nn. 10, 11, 183–85, 211, 215, 224–29, 232

Wimsatt, W. K., 88, 88 n. 14, 199, 199 n. 2, 308 n. 3

Wind, Edgar, 243

Winters, Yvor, 174

Wordsworth, William, 60, 61 n. 8, 64, 64 n. 11, 69, 183 n. 12

Yeats, William Butler, 251

Young, Edward, 41, 41 n. 2

The Johns Hopkins University Press

This book was composed in Linotype Baskerville by the Maryland Linotype Composition Co., Inc., from a design by Charles West. It was printed on 50-lb. Eggshell Offset Cream Paper and bound by the Maple Press Company.

Library of Congress Cataloging in Publication Data

Krieger, Murray, 1923–
    Poetic presence and illusion.
    Includes index.
    1.   Criticism—Addresses, essays, lectures.
I.   Title.
PN85.K66   801′.951   79–14598
ISBN 0–8018–2199–1